BLACK CULTURE
& EXPERIENCE

BLACK STUDIES
& critical thinking

Rochelle Brock, Richard Greggory Johnson III,
and Cynthia Dillard
Executive Editors

Vol. 71

The Black Studies and Critical Thinking series
is part of the Peter Lang Education list.
Every volume is peer reviewed and meets
the highest quality standards for content and production.

PETER LANG
New York • Bern • Frankfurt • Berlin
Brussels • Vienna • Oxford • Warsaw

BLACK CULTURE & EXPERIENCE

CONTEMPORARY ISSUES

EDITED BY VENISE T. BERRY,
ANITA FLEMING-RIFE, & AYO DAYO

PETER LANG
New York • Bern • Frankfurt • Berlin
Brussels • Vienna • Oxford • Warsaw

Library of Congress Cataloging-in-Publication Data

Black culture and experience: contemporary issues /
edited by Venise T. Berry, Anita Fleming-Rife, ayo dayo.
pages cm. — (Black studies and critical thinking; vol. 71)
Includes bibliographical references.
1. African Americans—Social conditions. 2. African Americans—Race identity.
3. African Americans in mass media. I. Berry, Venise T., editor.
II. Rife, Anita, editor. III. dayo, ayo, editor.
E185.86.B5246   305.896'073—dc23   2015018543
ISBN 978-1-4331-2647-5 (hardcover)
ISBN 978-1-4331-2646-8 (paperback)
ISBN 978-1-4539-1638-4 (e-book)
ISSN 1947-5985

Bibliographic information published by **Die Deutsche Nationalbibliothek.**
Die Deutsche Nationalbibliothek lists this publication in the "Deutsche
Nationalbibliografie"; detailed bibliographic data are available
on the Internet at http://dnb.d-nb.de/.

Cover design and artwork by Jean Berry

The paper in this book meets the guidelines for permanence and durability
of the Committee on Production Guidelines for Book Longevity
of the Council of Library Resources.

© 2015 Peter Lang Publishing, Inc., New York
29 Broadway, 18th floor, New York, NY 10006
www.peterlang.com

Printed in the United States of America

Table of Contents

Acknowledgments

Venise T. Berry

I thank God for his continued love, guidance, and miraculous blessings.

I thank my co-editors for their knowledge and assistance.

I thank the contributors for sharing their research and wisdom.

I thank Dr. Rochelle Brock for believing in my project and accepting it into her Black Studies and Critical Thinking Book Series at Peter Lang.

Finally, I thank my family and friends for the valuable love and guidance I can always count on.

Anita Fleming-Rife

I am grateful to God who, without fail, gives me what I need.

I am grateful to my children, Donnyta Rife-Alexander, Donald and Charles Rife, and my grandchildren, Courtney, Charles, Christian, and Trey, for always believing in me. It drives me to keep trying to meet your expectations.

As my grandson Christian would say when he was given an unexpected gift, "For me? This is for me?" That's what I consider this opportunity to work with you, Dr. Venise Berry, a gift. What an honor it has been to work with you on what you have so fittingly referred to as our "labor of love."

ayo dayo

I want to thank my Lord and Savior, Jesus Christ, as well as my family and friends for their unyielding love and support.

Introduction: From Slavery to the Presidency

VENISE T. BERRY

From slavery to the presidency—adapting that popular Virginia Slims ad from the 1970s—We've come a long way baby! When Barack Obama became the first African American president of the United States on November 5, 2008, in many ways it was a milestone that marked an important turning point in American history. Some believed that it meant America had moved into a post-racial society (Schorr, 2008; Lum, 2009; Steele, 2008). Others argued that we were still in the middle of a crucial struggle for justice and equality, and a Black president simply widened the gap between us and them (C. Jones, 2015; Butler, 2013; Squires, 2014).

Unfortunately, it is impossible to claim true success as a culture based on individual achievement. There is no denying that African Americans have a lot to be proud of in the 21st century: prominent celebrities and athletes live million dollar lifestyles (Pomerantz, 2014; Rhoden, 2007); the number of Black politicians is increasing (Swarns, 2008); glass ceilings are being broken by Black vice presidents and CEOs in top White companies such as McDonald's, FedEx, and General Mills (Kirkwood, 2013); and successful Black businesses are expanding into areas like public relations, banking, private equity, and information technology (Hazelwood, 2014).

At the same time, Black men, today, are six times as likely as White men to be incarcerated in federal, state, and local jails (Gao, 2014); Black college students are graduating at a rate of 42% as compared to White college students at 62% ("Black Student College Graduation Rates Remain Low," 2015); Black students in fourth grade reading and eighth grade math are two and a half times more likely than their White counterparts to lack the basic skills they need in those areas (Education Trust, 2014); according to Al Sharpton, stop and frisk and stand your ground laws have taken us back to the same battles Dr. King fought (Stand Your Ground, Stop and Frisk," 2013); the Black unemployment rate is consistently twice that of Whites across the country (Desilver, 2013); Black on Black crime is increasing at unprecedented rates (Harrell, 2007); negative racial stereotypes are still prominent in the media (Adams-Bass, Stevenson, and Kotzin, 2014); and, the political back-pedaling concerning voting rights (Sais, 2014) and a woman's right to control her own body (S. Jones, 2013) is ongoing.

Social change advocate Andrew Grant Thomas (2008) suggests that the problem is that too many Americans see the world in black and white.

> The post-racialism claim builds on the reductive either-or dualism to which most Americans subscribe on race matters. So, for example, either President Bush's tepid response to Hurricane Katrina revealed him to be a "racist," or his selection of several nonwhites to prominent cabinet posts prove that he is "not a racist." No matter how often someone like Tiger Woods, or Obama himself, stresses his diverse racial heritage, he is almost always identified as African American: in the United States, a person is either black or not-black. Either people of color face insuperable obstacles to prosperity or none at all. Either the President-Elect's unprecedented achievement affirms what the *Wall Street Journal* calls the "myth of racism" or it is completely anomalous. When it comes to race, we are often blind to the shades of gray. (2008)

This anthology addresses those "shades of gray." While African Americans can point to wonderful success individually and in a few cultural arenas, it is the shades of gray that we must continue to improve. Each chapter addresses specific issues related to African American culture. The goal is to help readers understand where we are and where we still need to go, what is working and what we still need to work on, what's right and what is still wrong.

The bottom line: in the 21st century we can't afford to focus on just black and white and ignore the shades of gray. The shades of gray offer specific narratives that are tied to ideological beliefs about race, culture, poverty, gender, and difference. Broad assumptions too often take over and the simple definition becomes the easy way out. Specific narratives are accepted while others disappear within societal discourse, which means certain images and messages remain problematic. In other words, an African American family in the White House doesn't mean the end. Instead, it marks a new beginning. It is here that we need to start over by questioning, educating, and transforming society into Dr. King's dream, a place where the "promises of Democracy" are made real (King, 1963).

Part 1 of this anthology explores institutional, societal, and political issues. Tabbye M. Chavous, Seanna Leath, and Bridget L. Richardson in the first chapter,

Black Racial Identity: Promoting Academic Achievement and Excellence, Resisting Stereotypes, and the Myth of Acting White," discuss crucial issues related to education and Black youth. They argue that strong racial connectedness and racial pride can lead to a positive identity and that positive identity can build Black students' motivation and encourage achievement in educational environments.

John A. Fortunato and Jerome D. Williams explain in chapter 2, "The NFL's Rooney Rule: A Theoretical Analysis of its Societal Influence," how important it is to create opportunities for African American coaches at the professional-sports level. They analyze the impact that the Rooney Rule has had on White preferential treatment in sports hiring.

In chapter 3, "In God's Favor: Prosperity Theology in the 21st Century," Kayla Renée Wheeler explores the positive side of primetime religion. Wheeler argues that not all popular preachers are focused on materialism and individualism; some are also involved in significant community-building efforts. She demonstrates how two specific preachers, Creflo Dollar and T. D. Jakes, uplift their communities and the diaspora, making prosperity gospel a source of hope and empowerment.

Stephana Colbert, in chapter 4, covers important concerns in "Race and Racism: Inequities in the Criminal Justice System." She helps us understand the depth of the African American experience when it comes to issues of racial profiling, sentencing disparities, stand your ground laws, community policing, and Black on Black crime. She also takes a close look at the Black Lives Matter phenomenon as it has evolved.

LaToya T. Brackett investigates the relationship between African Americans and the American dream. In chapter 5, Attaining Wealth: The African American Struggle for the "American Dream", she discusses the current racial disparities between Blacks and Whites concerning the accumulation of wealth. Her analysis covers such problems as discrimination in employment, lending practices, educational achievement, and equal pay.

Chapter 6, by De Anna Reese and Malik Simba, is "Learning from History: Contemporary Issues in Black and Africana Studies." Reese and Simba offer a valuable perspective as we consider the future of Black and Africana Studies in higher education. They suggest that the reach of this academic field of study over more than fifty years has enabled many diverse students to appreciate and respect the African American experience and may have also aided in the election of the first African American president.

In "To Form a More Perfect Union: Frames of Double Consciousness in Presidential Candidate Barack Obama's Race Speech", chapter 7, Anita Fleming-Rife examines the dynamics of identity. Fleming-Rife's goal is to explore the nuances of the speech based on W. E. B. Du Bois' construct of double consciousness. She suggests this speech was an important answer to America's race problem from the first Black man running for the highest office in the United States.

Part 2 covers social, cultural & community issues. In chapter 8, Staja Q Booker and Tamara A. Baker take on the Affordable Care Act. "Pain, Chronic Disease, and the ACA: Implications for Better Healthcare in the Black Community," involves a discussion of pain disparities and inequities at all levels of care in the Black community. Booker and Baker explain how the Affordable Care Act might change the situation through pain care legislation, insuring the previously uninsured, public/private initiatives, and Medicare expansion.

E-K. Daufin argues in chapter 9 that the definition of obesity in our society today is problematic. Her chapter, "Big, Black, and Beautiful Women: Health at Every Size Offers a New Paradigm," explains how the "war on obesity" has negatively impacted the Black community, specifically African American women. She offers a debate on the effectiveness of diets and exercise with weight loss as the goal and advocates instead for the more comprehensive health at every size project.

"Birds of a Feather? Black Men's Experiences and Behavior in Marriage and Romantic Relationships," by Armon R. Perry, Derrick R. Brooms, and Siobhan E. Smith, gives us a bird's eye view of Black men's relationships. Chapter 10 explores the attitudes that Black men form concerning relationships and how those attitudes are sometimes influenced by their peers. These authors focus on how the beliefs and behaviors of Black men can change when it comes to the support from peers as they consider marital status.

In chapter 11, "Fifty Shades of Brown: Understanding the Social, Sensual, and Sexual Lives of African American Women," Asher Pimpleton and Nikita Murry provide insight on the sexual decision-making process of African American women, particularly as it is influenced by a woman's self-efficacy and her eternalized locus of control.

Danielle M. Wallace and Sonja Peterson-Lewis, in chapter 12, explore the strong preference that Black women have for Black partners. "Interracial Relationships: Attitudes among Heterosexual College-Educated African American Women" studies various elements such as stage in life, age, past experience, and perceptions of Black men to reveal Black women's receptiveness to interracial liaisons.

William Oliver takes a close look at Black on Black crime and other misunderstandings in African American culture. Chapter 13, "Cultural Racism and Violence in African American Communities," explores the social and psychological implications of cultural racism in American institutions like education, mass media, and religion. Oliver argues that the glorification of European characteristics and achievement adversely impacts violent crime and victimization in African American communities.

Part 3 examines media, pop culture and technology issues. Kristina Graaff and Vanessa Irvin, in chapter 14 titled "The Rise of Urban Fiction," explain the growth of this genre as it relates to the naturalist movement, the Harlem renaissance, and the Black Power Literary Arts phenomenon. They also show how urban fiction has produced positive outcomes including business opportunities, increased reading for youth, and self-rehabilitation among inmates in prison.

In chapter 15, "An Affair to Remember: Hip Hop and the Feminist Perspective," Donnetrice C. Allison offers a realistic take on today's changing Hip Hop culture. Allison describes her problem with Hip Hop—a music she once loved—after the birth of her daughter. Looking through the lens of feminist and womanist philosophies, she mourns the negative changes and questions the music's potential control over young Black girls and boys.

Ernest L. Wiggins and Kenneth Campbell surveyed twenty-five years of images and messages in Super Bowl commercials. Their findings in chapter 16, "(Un)Comfortable Contact? Viewing Race and Interaction in 25 Years of Super Bowl Commercials through the Lens of Social Distance," suggest that Blacks and Whites exist in separate worlds in many of these ads, and they have limited cross-cultural exchanges or interactions.

Ilia Rodríguez clarifies in chapter 17 the need for African American newspapers to balance the voices of immigrants. Her chapter, "The Construction of Black Diasporic Identities in News Discourse on Immigration in the U.S. Black Press," investigates the way immigrants and American minorities are pitted against each other in African American newspapers and shows how the antagonism and marginalization, ultimately, can impact immigration matters.

Omotayo O. Banjo presents an interesting notion in chapter 18 about the inclusion of White characters in predominantly Black films. In "Now You See Me: The Visibility of Whiteness in Black Context Films," Banjo explains why the social construction of whiteness in Black-oriented films is tied to controversies surrounding the dominant culture. She suggests that the stereotypes of Whites in Black films, such as the authority figure, the savior, and the wannabe, are just as problematic and stigmatizing as Black stereotypes.

"Black Masculinity and Representation in Popular Culture: A Case Study of Quentin Tarantino's Film *Django Unchained*" looks at a popular 21st-century film character based on the real-life character of Bass Reeves. Tammie Jenkins, in chapter 19, demonstrates how the fictionalized character of Django is rooted in cultural aesthetics. She examines the oral texts and patterns of behavior that are attributed to Black masculinity and representation in the film.

Finally, chapter 20, written by George L. Daniels, Theadoris Morris, and Ellisa Bray, offers an interesting look at the cultural significance found in the development of Black Twitter. Since Twitter is considered a viable means of cultural conversation, "Bridging the Digital Divide: The Case of Black Twitter as a 21st-Century Platform for Cultural Expression" demonstrates how social media are fast becoming a societal collective for the Black community.

As this anthology documents, it is the shades of gray that African Americans must concern themselves with in the 21st century. For example, in a June 2013 Atlantic/Aspen Institute Values Survey, when participants were asked who is the most divisive figure in America, President Obama held the top spot at 33%; yet in that same survey participants were also asked who is the most unifying figure today, and President Obama came out on top again with 21%. It is in the shades of gray where the 44th president of the United States, the first African American leader of America, represents both a negative and a positive image in our society. We've come a long way, but we still have a long way to go!

REFERENCES

Adams-Bass, V., Stevenson, H., & Kotzin, D. S. (2014, April 25). Measuring the meaning of Black Media stereotypes and their relationship to the racial identity, Black history knowledge and racial socialization of African American youth. *Journal of Black Studies, 5*(5), 367–395.

Black student college graduation rates remain low, but modest progress beings to show. (2015, February 27). *Journal of Blacks in Higher Education*. Retrieved from http://www.jbhe.com/features/50_blackstudent_gradrates.html

Butler, A. (2013, September 13). Post-racial? No: With a Black president all issues are racialized. *MSNBC*. Retrieved from http://www.msnbc.com/msnbc/post-racial

Cohn, B. (2013, June 28). The divided states of America, in 25 charts. *The Atlantic*. Retrieved from States-of-america-in-25-charts/277303 http://www.theatlantic.com/national/archive/2013/06/the-divided-states-of-america-in-25-charts/277303/

Desilver, D. (2013, August 21). Black unemployment rate is consistently twice that of Whites. *Fact Tank*. Pew Research Center. http://www.pewresearch.org/facttank/2013/08/21/through-good-times-and-bad-black-unemployment-is-consistently-double-that-of-whites/

Education Trust. (2014, June). *The State of Education for African American Students*, Washington, DC. http://edtrust.org/wp-content/uploads/2013/10/TheStateofEducationforAfricanAmerican Students_EdTrust_June2014.pdf

Gao, G. (2014, July 18). Chart of the week: The Black-White gap in incarceration rates. *Fact Tank*. Pew Research Center. Retrieved from http://www.pewresearch.org/facttank/2014/07/18/chart-of-the-week-the-black-white-gap-in-incarceration-rates/

Harrell, E. (2007, August). *Black victims of violent crime*. U.S. Department of Justice Statistics Special Report, Office of Justice Programs, NCJ 214258, Washington, DC.

Hazelwood, J. (2014, July 2). BE 100s: Nations most successful Black-owned businesses. *Black Enterprise*. Retrieved from http://www.blackenterprise.com/small-business/be-100s-nations-most-successful-black-owned-businesses/

Jones, C. (2015, February 4). Black History Month: From slavery to Obama and beyond. *The Huffington Post*. Retrieved from http://www.huffingtonpost.com/news/post-racial-america/

Jones, S. (2013, September 16). Taking away "right to choose" may consign women to a "life of poverty." CNSNews.com. Retrieved from http://cnsnews.com/news/article/susan-jones/taking-away-right-choose-may-consign-women-life-poverty

King, Dr. M. L., Jr. (1963, August 28). I Have a Dream Speech. Lincoln Memorial, Washington, DC.

Kirkwood, L. (2013, August 19). 10 of the nation's successful Black-owned businesses. *USA Today*. Retrieved from http://www.usatoday.com/story/news/nation/2013/08/19/march-on-washington-black-owned-businesses/2646703/

Lum, L. (2009, February 5). The Obama era: A post-racial society? *Diverse Issues in Higher Education*. Retrieved from http://diverseeducation.com/article/12238/

Pomerantz, D. (2014, June 30). Beyoncé Knowles tops the FORBES Celebrity 100 list. Forbes Business. http://www.forbes.com/sites/dorothypomerantz/2014/06/30/beyonce-knowles-tops-the-forbes-celebrity-100-list/

Rhoden, W. (2007). *Forty million dollar slaves: The rise, fall and redemption of the Black athlete*. New York: Broadway.

Sais, S. (2014, April 9). New voting laws roll back U.S. civil rights strides of the 1960s: Bill Clinton. *Reuters*. Retrieved from http://www.reuters.com/article/2014/04/10/us-usa-clinton-rights-idUSBREA3905W20140410

Schorr, D. (2008, January 28). A new "post-racial" political era in America [Transcript]. NPR Special Series. Retrieved from http://www.npr.org/templates/story/story.php?storyId=18489466

Squires, C. (2014, April 4). *The post-racial mystique: Media and race in the twenty-first century*. New York: New York University Press.

Stand your ground, stop and frisk, "21st century version of what Dr. King fought," says Sharpton. (2013, October 2). *News Nation*. Retrieved from http://www.msnbc.com/news-nation/stand-your-ground-stop-and-frisk-21st-cent

Steele, S. (2008, November 5). Obama's post-racial promise. *The Los Angeles Times*. Retrieved February 22, 2015, from http://www.latimes.com/opinion/opinion-la/la-oe-steele5-2008nov05-story.html#page=1

Swarns, R. (2008, October 13). Quiet political shifts as more Blacks are elected. *The New York Times*. Retrieved from http://www.nytimes.com/2008/10/14/us/politics/14race.html?pagewanted=all

Thomas, A. G. (2008, December 5). Does Barack Obama's victory herald a post-racial America? *Colorlines*. Retrieved from http://colorlines.com/archives/2008/12/does_barack_obamas_victory_her_1.html

Part 1:
Institutional, Societal, and Political Issues

Black Racial Identity: Promoting Academic Achievement and Excellence, Resisting Stereotypes, and the Myth of Acting White

TABBYE M. CHAVOUS, SEANNA LEATH, AND BRIDGET L. RICHARDSON

Researchers and educators have offered various explanations for Black achievement and underachievement. Many implicate the role of racial identity beliefs, or youths' self-constructed views concerning the importance of and meanings associated with their racial group membership (Sellers, Smith, Shelton, Rowley, & Chavous, 1998). Black youth in the United States often face structural and social risks as a function of their racial group, including racial barriers, discrimination, and negative stereotype-based treatment; and these risk factors have been linked to negative educational outcomes. Therefore, a popular perspective within social science literatures and in educational and popular discourse is that a stronger Black identity places youth at risk for decreased academic engagement and achievement. However, there is more historical, theoretical, and empirical evidence that a strong connection to racial identity, including racial pride and an awareness and understanding of racial bias, can promote Black youths' achievement and help them maintain academic motivation and engagement, especially in the face of racial barriers or negative stereotypes.

In this chapter, we address these perspectives by providing an overview of social science frameworks positioning Black racial identity as detrimental to or promotive of Black youths' achievement. Based on our review, we posit that the continued positioning of Black identity as incompatible with pro-education values and achievement—despite strong evidence to the contrary—reflects historical and contemporary deficit framing of African Americans. Our review also suggests important next steps for scholarship and practice. For example, one implication is that parents, schools, and communities can play important roles in supporting youths' positive racial and personal identity development. A second implication is the need to move away from "colorblind" or "post-racial" approaches and, instead, recognize Black youths' racial identities as cultural assets that can help schools and educators create inclusive settings to better serve youth.

RACIAL IDENTITY: SIGNIFICANCE DURING ADOLESCENCE

Considering the links between racial identity and academic outcomes is particularly relevant during adolescence and young adulthood. During adolescence, youth begin to construct a more internalized sense of their personal identity, or their personal definitions of who they are, what is important to them, and appropriate ways to think and behave. Given the salience of race in the United States, a sense of racial identity becomes important for many Black adolescents. Racial identity scholars note that individuals' constructions of their racial identities are varied, complex, and multidimensional (Sellers, Smith et al., 1998, Phinney, 1990, 1992; Vandiver, Fhagen-Smith, Cokley, Cross, & Worrell, 2001). For instance, the Multidimensional Model of Racial Identity (MMRI) (Sellers, Smith et al., 1998) is a conceptual framework that defines African American racial identity as the significance and qualitative meaning that individuals attribute to their membership within the Black racial group. A distinguishing characteristic of this framework is its distinction between the significance of race to an individual's self-concept and the affective and evaluative feelings that the individual holds for his or her racial-ethnic group. As such, adolescents may vary in views of the importance of being Black to their overall identities and in the meanings they attach to being Black. This includes their own affective feelings of racial pride and their thinking about how society regards their racial group. Understanding their racial identity can influence their actions and behaviors within domains in which that identity is salient. As race is often salient in educational contexts, Black adolescents' racial identities may be particularly relevant in shaping how they think about themselves in relation to school and how they interpret and respond to race-related experiences in their social and classroom contexts at school.

In addition, the importance of an individual's racial group and the meanings attached to it can change, shift, and evolve over time, especially during the developmental period of adolescence. Compared to younger children, adolescents have developed social-cognitive abilities around understanding themselves and their experiences in more complex, abstract ways, including heightened awareness of how they are viewed by others. Subsequently, Black adolescents often become more cognizant of the relevance of race in society—including social and economic opportunities and constraints for themselves, their families, and communities—and have a higher likelihood of interpreting their experiences in terms of race (Brown & Bigler, 2005; Spencer, Dupree, & Hartmann, 1997; Thornton, Taylor, & Tran, 1997).

Along with individual differences in social cognition, interactions in their primary social contexts influence how they develop understandings of themselves in relation to the social groups to which they belong (Harter, 1990; Spencer, Dupree, & Hartmann, 1997). Adolescents' racial identity beliefs derive in large part through their understanding and internalization of socialization messages they receive from families and communities about their group's history and values (Bennett, 2006; Neblett, Smalls, Ford, Nguyen, & Sellers, 2009). For example, Neblett and colleagues (2009) link parents' earlier racial socialization messages (e.g., around group pride, racial barriers, self-worth) with adolescents' later racial identity such that adolescents who experienced more frequent, positive parental racial socialization messages came to feel that race was more central to their self-concept, were more likely to emphasize the uniqueness of their Black identity, and less likely to emphasize American assimilation views.

Finally, adolescents' increased exposure to personal and societal racism influences their racial identity development (DuBois, Burk-Braxton, Swenson, Tevendale, & Hardesty, 2002; Garcia Coll, Crnic, Lamberty, Waski, Jenkins et al., 1996; Greene, Way, & Pahl, 2006; Hughes & Chen, 1999). Unfortunately, many of these experiences occur within the school context (Fisher, Wallace, & Fenton, 2000; McGee, 2013; Rosenbloom & Way, 2004; Wright, 2011), and school contexts often involve social structures (e.g., tracking) that emphasize racial group differences in negative ways, including stereotypes. Secondary teachers and class structures emphasize social comparison more than in earlier educational stages, resulting in heightened attention to group differences in achievement and performance (Seidman, Allen, Aber, Mitchell, & Feinman, 1994). Additionally, Black adolescents are most likely to have White teachers from middle-class backgrounds, even in urban schools; and teachers in general are unlikely to have received extensive, quality training in multicultural education (Banks, Cochran-Smith, Moll, et al., 2005; Ford & Harris, 1996).

Black youth routinely report discriminatory treatment in school as common occurrences like perceiving that they received poor grades or evaluations from teachers and other adults at school or harsher discipline due to race, and social exclusion or harassment from peers due to race (Fisher et al., 2000; Cogburn, Neblett, Philip, & Sellers, 2006) and at higher rates than do other groups of youth (Green et al., 2006). Thus, Black youths' educational settings can influence their racial identity development, including the extent that they perceive their Black identity as consistent or inconsistent with achievement.

RACIAL IDENTITY AND ACADEMIC ACHIEVEMENT:
RISK OR PROMOTIVE FACTOR?

To explore the "debate" there are a number of questions that must be answered: Is an emphasis on Black identity compatible with a pro-academic identity? Does having a strong connection to their racial heritage and identity promote Black youths' academic achievement? Or, does strong Black identification relate to academic disengagement and underachievement and viewing academic achievement as "acting White?"

Over the past several decades, education scholars and practitioners have been concerned with these questions, leading to the exploration of whether a connection to racial identity leads to adaptive or maladaptive academic outcomes for Black youth. Two prevalent perspectives for explaining links between Black identity and academic achievement are the "racial identity as risk" perspective and "racial identity as promotive" perspective (Smalls, White, Chavous, & Sellers, 2007).

In the racial identity as risk perspective, scholarly and popular discourse often emphasizes—implicitly or explicitly—that a Black identity is incompatible with a pro-achievement orientation. For instance, an immensely popular notion is that Black youth come from a culture that views educational attainment as "acting White" (Fordham & Ogbu, 1986). Several well-known theories posit that a strong connection to their Black racial identity places adolescents at risk for decreased academic engagement due to youths' heightened awareness of the negative societal status of their racial group (Aronson, 2002; Fordham, 1988; Mickelson, 1990; Steinberg, Dornbusch, & Brown, 1992). The cultural-ecological framework offered by Fordham and Ogbu (1986), for instance, asserts that because African American populations immigrated to the United States under conditions of oppression and opportunity constraint, they developed a collective group racial identity that rejects institutions that are dominated by the oppressive mainstream culture, including the American educational system. As a consequence, youth's identification with Black identity came to entail a rejection of pro-achievement orientation, including attitudes and behaviors associated with being successful in school. Fordham (1988) expands on this framework, positing that school success for high-achieving Black students necessitates minimizing connectedness to their racial identity in exchange for mainstream values better aligned with an academic identity, a process termed as becoming "raceless."

A similar theme in education research is the notion that a "colorblind" perspective is the best way to ameliorate racial differences in achievement. The vast majority of public school teachers are White and from backgrounds that differ from their students of color. A common ideology among teachers entering their profession and classrooms is that it is best to simply not see race or racial group differences at all but view students only as individuals (Markus, Steele, & Steele, 2002; Rousseau & Tate, 2003). However, the underlying presumption is that racial minority youth must de-emphasize their racial-cultural backgrounds in order to develop a positive academic identity. They must emphasize thinking and acting in ways more consistent with White middle-class norms (Delpit, 1995; Ladson-Billings, 1995; McAllister & Irvine, 2000).

Other theoretical perspectives viewing Black identity as a risk factor have focused on the stigma associated with identifying with a minority group in the United States. This work posits that Black youth "dis-identify" or disconnect their personal identity and values from school and academics because the academic domain is one in which their racial group is regarded negatively (Crocker & Major, 1989; Osborne, 1997; Wolfe, Schmader, Major, Spencer, & Crocker, 1998). While this coping strategy is theorized to protect individuals' self-concept from the negative impact of perceiving racial devaluation, it can inhibit the motivation necessary for good school performance. Similarly, stereotype threat theory (Steele & Aronson, 1995) posits that Black students' academic underperformance results from apprehensions around supporting negative racial stereotypes related to Blacks' intellectual ability. And over time, these racial threat experiences lead to dis-identification with academics and disengagement in the learning process (Aronson & Inzlicht, 2004; Steele, 1997). Implicit across these perspectives is that Black students who perceive societal discrimination or stigmatization for their racial group may disengage with the educational process, and those who emphasize their racial identity are particularly vulnerable.

BLACK RACIAL IDENTITY AS RISK AND BLACK IDENTITY AS PROMOTIVE

The Black-identity-as-risk view has become the dominant story, or "master narrative," in discussions of Black culture and schooling, despite the fact that there is little empirical evidence in support of the approach. For instance, in the widely cited ethnographic study of urban African American high school students (Fordham & Ogbu, 1986), although lower-achieving students' perceived particular behaviors associated with school success—such as spending time in the library studying, reading and writing poetry, being on time—as inconsistent with their personal identities, students were not asked about their racial identities nor did the youth mention race when discussing their academic identities (e.g., youth connected pro-achievement behaviors to being a nerd or "brainiac," not necessarily as being inconsistent with a Black identity). Other evidence used in support of the risk approach includes studies showing smaller associations between

Black adolescents' self-concept and academic grade performance relative to other racial groups (Demo & Parker, 1987; Oyserman, Gant, & Ager, 1995) and lower academic task performance for Black college students for whom racial stereotypes were made salient (Croizet & Claire, 1998). None of these studies, however, directly assessed students' racial identity beliefs and thus were unable to demonstrate the presumed links between Black identity and academic engagement. In sum, while Fordham's and Ogbu's framework and subsequent literature on stigma effects acknowledge the negative consequences of historical and contemporary racism on Black youth, the frameworks have tended to be oversimplified and/or misinterpreted in ways that are ahistorical and at odds with empirical evidence (Lundy, 2003). Unfortunately, the wide and continued acceptance of the Black-identity-as-risk perspective derives from a broader tendency in our society (and in social science) to view and study Black populations from a deviance perspective, framing the group as "damaged" and emphasizing risks and deficits relative to a White, middle-class norm (Milner, 2010).

The "racial identity as promotive" perspective is a growing alternative to the "identity as risk" approach. Scholars of ethnic minority psychology have traditionally conceptualized racial identity as an important psychologically protective set of beliefs that individuals develop and use to buffer the impact of racial discrimination and stigmatized status (Sellers, Smith et al., 1998; Neblett, Rivas-Drake, & Umana-Taylor, 2012). As such, researchers have begun to conceptualize racial identity as an important source of resilience in the normative development of Black youth (Cross, Strauss, & Fhagen-Smith, 1999; Spencer, Cunningham, & Swanson, 1995; Sellers et al., 2003). This view, while recognizing significant challenges that confront many Black youth, also acknowledges that these youth can be resilient in the face of those challenges. An approach that views a strong, positive sense of racial identity as promoting achievement is consistent with a historical view of Black communities in the United States. This view recognizes that because Black people were denied opportunities for social advancement (during and after slavery) or came to the United States in search of opportunities for mobility (other Black immigrant groups), they placed an especially strong emphasis on the importance of learning and education as a primary route to social and economic achievement (Chavous, Bernat, Schmeelk-Cone, Caldwell, Kohn-Wood, & Zimmerman, 2003; Perry, 1993; Perry, Steele, & Hilliard, 2003). Through dire circumstances of slavery, oppression, and deliberate disenfranchisement, African Americans have historically been resilient, and valuing education has been a key part of this resilience. For example, despite the rampant illiteracy of ex-slaves, virtually every account by historians stresses the demand by ex-slaves for and efforts to attain universal schooling (Anderson, 1988). This historical record in fact contradicts the notion that stronger ties to a Black community, culture, or identity are inconsistent with achievement (Perry, 2004).

Also, unlike the risk approach that often assumes uniformity in how youth define being Black, a promotive approach explicitly acknowledges individual differences in racial identity attitudes. Individual differences in academic outcomes are considered because of the focus on racial identity as a source of resilience. That is, racial identity can support a meaning-making process that affords members of historically oppressed groups an opportunity to define their own group membership in such a way that academic success is seen as valuable despite individual and structural barriers to that success (Smalls et al., 2007; White & Worrell, 2012; Way, Hernandez, Rogers, & Hughes, 2013). In fact, like historical accounts, contemporary social science research indicates that a strong and positive connection to their racial group and community serves as a significant cultural asset and resource to many Black youth, promoting their motivation to succeed in educational domains.

Below, we highlight key findings from contemporary research supporting the promotive perspective. Included are examples from our work in the Center for the Study of Black Youth in Context (CSBYC) at the University of Michigan (https://sites.lsa.umich.edu/csbyc/). The CSBYC focuses on research and action in relation to the social, psychological, and educational development of Black youth from a strengths-based approach. It documents ways communities, schools, cultural, racial, and family contexts influence the positive development of Black children and adolescents. This chapter highlights some of the unique risks many Black youth normatively experience as a function of their race and offers evidence of ways that an emphasis on a strong and positive Black identity enhances youths' academic and social adjustment.

The risks, barriers, and constraints extant in Black youths' lives as members of their racial group can influence their academic attitudes and behaviors as well as psychological and behavioral outcomes related to achievement. Studies increasingly show the prevalence of racially stigmatizing experiences in the daily lives of Black youth, including racial discrimination, stereotype-based treatment, low expectations, peer harassment and exclusion, and resulting negative effects (Chavous, Harris, Rivas, Helaire, & Green, 2004; Sellers, Linder, Martin, & Lewis, 2006). For example, Richardson and colleagues (2015) note deleterious impacts of racial discrimination from teachers and peers at school on youths' racial connectedness, racial pride, and view of Blacks as stigmatized in society. Other studies link school-based racial discrimination to lower academic self-concept, values, and achievement (Chavous, Rivas-Drake, Smalls et al., 2008) and to more engagement in peer groups with problem behaviors (Wong, Eccles, & Sameroff, 2003).

Given the prevalence of racial stigma in Black youths' daily lives, researchers began to examine linkages between racial identity and achievement, providing empirical tests of the risk and promotive perspectives. This line of work is demonstrating that Black youth with strong and positive connections to their Black identity and more awareness of societal racial bias have more positive school engagement, academic motivation, and achievement outcomes (Baber, 2012; Butler-Barnes, Williams, & Chavous, 2012; Butler-Barnes, Chavous, Hurd, & Varner, 2013; Chavous, Bernat et al., 2003). For example, Butler-Barnes and colleagues (2013) examined Black adolescents' racial pride, self-efficacy, and self-acceptance as "cultural and personal assets" and found that youth higher in all three assets showed the most academic persistence. The authors suggested that youth's racial pride enhanced their feelings of self-efficacy and self-acceptance and functioned together to promote academic engagement, whereas youth with less racial pride were likely to show lower self-efficacy and self-acceptance. Similarly, Hope, Chavous, Jagers, and Sellers (2013) report that Black college students with stronger racial connectedness and racial pride showed stronger psychological well-being and achievement, relative to students with weaker, negative racial identity connections. In fact, studies with diverse Black youth samples—in terms of age, family and community background, education level—indicate that youth with a strong, positive sense of racial identity show more positive adjustment along a number of educationally relevant outcomes, including academic motivation, self-concept, and persistence, career commitment and aspirations, and pro-social behaviors and community involvement (Ani, 2013; Lindsey & Mabie, 2012; White-Johnson, 2012). Similarly, these identity beliefs have been linked to positive psychological adjustment, including lower depression, anxiety, and fewer antisocial-delinquent behaviors (Neblett, Cooper, Banks, & Smalls-Glover, 2013). Furthermore, despite the assertion in the risk perspective that Black youth peer culture devalues educational achievement, high-achieving Black students are often well liked by their peers (Madyun, Lee, & Jumale, 2010) and view their own achievement as consistent with their Black racial identity rather than in opposition or as "acting White" (Stinson, 2011; Wildhagen, 2011).

Finally, along with promoting positive adjustment, a strong, positive sense of racial identity and awareness of societal racism can serve to buffer, or protect youth from internalizing racism experiences (such as discrimination, stereotype-based treatment, racial exclusion, or harassment) known to decrease academic engagement (Chavous, Rivas-Drake et al., 2008; Wong, Eccles, & Sameroff, 2003) and psychological well-being (Sellers, Linder et al., 2006). For example, Chavous and colleagues (2008) found that among adolescents with a stronger connection to their Black identity, school-based discrimination affected their later motivation and grade performance less negatively than for youth whose Black identity was less important. The noted literature reflects a growing body of empirical research that does not support the idea that a Black identity entails resisting or devaluing academics and educational achievement. Instead, many youth draw on their Black identities to resist educational structures and individuals within these structures that devalue and stereotype them.

Considerations of racial identity processes among Black youth also raise important questions related to gender. Black boys and girls experience variations in expectations, treatments, and social roles concerning their proximal and distal contexts, based on unique societal racial stereotypes and images of African American males and females (e.g., Black males as violent and threatening, Black females as sexualized and loud) (Chavous, Rivas-Drake et al., 2008; DuBois, et al., 2002; Hill, 2002; Swanson, Cunningham, & Spencer, 2003). Consequently, the experience of racial identity among Black youth might be examined as a gendered phenomenon. Scholars highlight the unique roles of racial identity for Black boys and girls. While a fuller review on gender and Black identity is beyond the scope of this chapter, our studies, for example, indicate that Black adolescent boys report significantly more school-based racial discrimination from teachers and peers than do girls (Richardson et al., 2015, Chavous, Rivas-Drake et al., 2008). Among boys, a strong connection to their racial group was more closely associated with achievement and sustained motivation than for girls, especially for those experiencing teacher and peer discrimination (Chavous, Rivas-Drake et al., 2008). This work indicates that boys may benefit academically from a strong, secure sense of racial identity. It also considers the unique forms of discrimination Black girls and boys may face as a function of gendered racial stereotypes, and the different ways that boys and girls may experience family socialization and draw on their cultural and racial identities to counter racial discrimination and stereotype-based treatment (Chavous & Cogburn, 2007; Richardson et al., 2015).

CONCLUSIONS AND IMPLICATIONS

In sum, a growing body of contemporary research demonstrates the benefits of a strong, positive sense of racial identity for Black youths' academic achievement and overall well-being. The noted scholarship has important implications. It does not support the increasing emphasis and popularity of the idea of society as colorblind or post-racial. Instead, the literature demonstrates that Black youth continue to experience daily challenges to a healthy identity in schools and communities through discrimination, low expectations, and stereotype-based treatment. Our CSBYC research and that of other scholars highlight the strengths of Black youth and the ways they draw on their racial identities to persist and achieve. It argues for the importance of acknowledging and affirming the identities that students value rather than de-emphasizing them.

This chapter suggests that there are important roles tied to the socialization of Black youth around their racial identity in family and community contexts. Black parents must make strategic choices about how to prepare their children concerning race issues based on the opportunities, barriers, and social dynamics they perceive in their neighborhoods, communities, and society. Thus, there is no one "right" type of racial identity, nor is there one "right" way for parents to engage with their children around race. That said, the research does suggest that when the complements between Black people's heritage and societal achievement are emphasized and valued, Black youth tend to view their own racial identity and academic achievement as connected. Similarly, an awareness of and sense of connectedness to Blacks' collective struggles and achievements also allows youth to connect positive characteristics (i.e., hard-working, intelligent, etc.) with their racial group and provides models for them to draw on as they develop into young adults. This helps to counter the negative effects of discrimination or stereotypes. Thus, socialization messages in the home and community that affirm positive racial identities and support youth in making sense of negative race-related experiences can prevent them from internalizing such experiences in ways that lead to negative adjustment (Richardson et al., 2015). In addition to parents, studies such as those by Hurd and colleagues (2012, 2013) argue that adult mentors and positive role models are important outside of the family in supporting positive identity development and adjustment. These functions are critical, given noted evidence that Black youth across age and grade/education levels continue to experience racial discrimination, devaluation, and/or low expectations in their daily interactions in schools and communities and in prevalent societal and media messages (McGee, 2013; Way et al., 2013).

Although racial identity is influenced by cultural values and experiences in the home and community, schools play a significant role too. One area of this work considers how the organization and practices of schools and classrooms and young people's interactions with adults and peers at school convey messages to those young people about the meaning of race in ways that can support or inhibit achievement and adjustment. Studies by Byrd and Chavous with middle school, high school, and college youth show that school climates involving negative messages about Blacks (from teachers/instructors/peers/curriculum) or in which discussions of race and racism are minimized or avoided can be similarly detrimental to youths' academic motivation and psychological well-being (Byrd & Chavous, 2011, 2012; Chavous, 2005). Furthermore, youth are less likely to feel a sense of belonging in school settings in which they experience incongruence between their racial identity beliefs about connectedness and pride and those values conveyed by the setting. Over time, this lack of belonging can lead to decreased motivation in school. Thus, youth who enter their school settings with a strong sense of Black identity and high achievement motivation may experience marginalization through various experiences like stereotype-based treatment from teachers and peers or the colorblind ideology embedded in school cultures that guide teachers' interactions with students.

Unfortunately, teacher training continues to insufficiently equip teachers to work with diverse youth (Delpit, 1995; Ladson-Billings, 1995; Milner, 2003). Teachers often enter the profession or are trained in a colorblind or assimilation ideology, or a view that teachers' interactions with students should be the same regardless of the student's race (Rousseau & Tate, 2003; McAllister & Irvine, 2000). There is growing evidence that such a perspective does not relate to positive academic outcomes for minority youth (Choi, 2008; Delpit, 1995; Lewis, Chesler, & Forman, 2000), and this will continue to be a problem as U.S. racial minority populations increase. Similarly, research showing positive influences of a strong, positive racial identity on youth achievement suggests the colorblind approach hinders teachers from seeing the real needs of their Black students and acknowledging them in ways that facilitate achievement. Further, while teachers may not be formally trained in theory and research on multicultural education, many enter their classrooms more familiar with prevalent perspectives on race in education. That is, they are most likely to be familiar with the Black-identity-as-risk view—that Black youth and families devalue academics and define their racial identity as inconsistent with achievement (or "acting White")—while youth and families from other racial groups are framed as having cultural values that include embracing education (Brown, 2010). Ironically, Black parents and youth consistently report strong educational values—even relative to other racial groups (Neblett, Smalls et al., 2009).

In order to better support Black children and youth in reaching their achievement potential, school systems and practitioners must receive training around diverse youth and families that not only acknowledges unique risks experienced by Black youth but also considers how students' racial identities can serve as cultural assets in relation to achievement. Without such training, it is likely that teaching approaches and practices will be based on popular "common sense" views and ahistorical cultural deficiency discourses not supported by empirical research. Recent education reform approaches provide evidence that Black families and communities are demanding that education systems better acknowledge and serve their children. Examples of strengths-based approaches to reform include Oakland Unified School District's efforts (www.ousd.k12.ca.us/), and charter schools such as Chicago's Urban Prep Academy (http://www.urbanprep.org/about) and Detroit Edison Public School Academy (http://www.detroitedisonpsa.org/). While specific pedagogical approaches of these school systems vary significantly, a common thread is an assumption of compatibility between youths' Black identity and academic excellence—an emphasis on youths' assets and strengths, a culture of high expectations, and a sense of responsibility by teachers and administrators to cultivate students' strengths. These efforts are promising, but all youth do not have equal access to these types of educational experiences. Grounding educational practice in rigorous scholarship around the social and cultural characteristics of diverse Black students—including strengths and resilience associated with Black identity—is an important step in equalizing all Black students' opportunities for high-quality education and successful achievement outcomes.

BIBLIOGRAPHY

Anderson, J. D. (1988). *The education of Blacks in the South, 1860–1935.* Chapel Hill, NC: University of North Carolina Press.

Ani, A. (2013). In spite of racism, inequality, and school failure: Defining hope with achieving Black children. *The Journal of Negro Education, 82*(4), 408–421.

Aronson, J. (2002). Stereotype threat: Contending and coping with unnerving expectations. In J. Aronson (Ed.), *Improving academic achievement: Impact of psychological factors on education* (pp. 279–301). San Diego, CA: Academic.

Aronson, J., & Inzlicht, M. (2004). The ups and downs of attributional ambiguity: Stereotype vulnerability and academic self-knowledge of African American college students. *Psychological Science, 15*(2), 829–836.

Baber, L. (2012). A qualitative inquiry on the multidimensional racial development among first-year African American college students attending a predominantly White institution. *The Journal of Negro Education, 81*(1), 67–81.

Banks, J. A., Cochran-Smith, M., Moll, L., et al. (2005). Teaching diverse learners. In L. Darling-Hammond & J. Bransford (Eds.), *Preparing teachers for a changing world: What teachers should be able to do* (pp. 232–274). San Francisco: Jossey-Bass.

Bennett, M. D. (2006). Culture and context: A study of neighborhood effects on racial socialization and ethnic identity content in a sample of African American adolescents. *Journal of Black Psychology, 32*(4), 479–500.

Brown, C., & Bigler, R. (2005). Children's perceptions of discrimination: A developmental model. *Child Development, 76*(3), 533–553.

Brown, K. (2010). Is this what we want them to say? Examining the tensions in what preservice teachers say about risk and academic achievement. *Teaching and Teacher Education, 24*(4), 1077–1087.

Butler-Barnes, S., Chavous, T., Hurd, N., & Varner, F. (2013). African American adolescents' academic persistence: A strengths-based approach. *Journal of Youth and Adolescence, 42*, 1443–1458.

Butler-Barnes, S. T., Williams, T. T., & Chavous, T. M. (2012). Racial pride and religiosity among African American boys: Implications for academic motivation and achievement. *Journal of Youth and Adolescence, 41*(4), 486–498.

Byrd, C. M., & Chavous, T. (2011). Racial identity, school racial climate, and school intrinsic motivation among African American youth: The importance of person-context congruence. *Journal of Research on Adolescence, 21*(4), 849–860.

Byrd, C. M., & Chavous, T. M. (2012). The congruence between African American students' racial identity beliefs and their academic climates: Implications for academic motivation and achievement. In J. M. Sullivan & A. M. Esmail (Eds.), *African American identity: Racial and cultural dimensions of the Black experience* (pp. 345–369). Lanham, MD: Lexington.

Chavous, T. M. (2005). An intergroup contact-theory framework for evaluating the psychological impact of racial climate on predominantly White college campuses. *American Journal of Community Psychology, 36*(3/4), 239–257.

Chavous, T. M., Bernat, D., Schmeelk-Cone, K., Caldwell, C., Kohn-Wood, L., & Zimmerman, M. (2003). Racial identity and academic attainment among African American adolescents. *Child Development, 74*(4), 1076–1090.

Chavous, T. M., & Cogburn, C. D. (2007). The superinvisible woman: The study of Black women in education. *Black Women, Gender, & Families, 1*(2), 24–51.

Chavous, T. M., Harris, A., Rivas, D., Helaire, L., & Green, L. (2004). Racial stereotypes and gender in context: An examination of African American college adjustment. *Sex Roles, 51*, 1–16.

Chavous, T. M., Rivas-Drake, D., Smalls, C., et al. (2008). Gender matters, too: The influences of school racial discrimination and racial identity on academic engagement outcomes among African American adolescents. *Developmental Psychology, 44*(3), 637–654.

Choi, J. (2008). Unlearning colorblind ideologies in education class. *The Journal of Educational Foundations, 22*(3), 53–71.

Cogburn, C., Neblett, E., Philip, C., & Sellers, R. (2006). African American adolescents' discrimination experiences and academic achievement: Racial socialization as a cultural compensatory and protective factor. *Journal of Black Psychology, 32*(2), 199–218.

Crocker, J., & Major, B. (1989). Social stigma and self-esteem: The self-protective properties of stigma. *Psychological Review, 96*(4), 608–630.

Croizet, J., & Claire, T. (1998). Extending the concept of stereotype threat to social class: The intellectual underperformance of students from low socioeconomic backgrounds. *Personality and Social Psychology Bulletin, 24*(6), 588–594.

Cross, W., Strauss, L., & Fhagen-Smith, P. (1999). African American identity development across the lifespan: Educational implications. In R. Sheets (Ed.), *Racial and ethnic identity in school practices: Aspects of human development* (pp. 29–47). Mahwah, NJ: Erlbaum.

Delpit, L. (1995). *Other people's children.* New York: New Press.

Demo, D., & Parker, K. (1987). Academic achievement and self-esteem among African American and White college students. *Journal of Social Psychology, 127*, 345–355.

DuBois, D., Burk-Braxton, C., Swenson, L., Tevendale, H., & Hardesty, J. (2002). Race and gender influences on adjustment in early adolescence: Investigation of an integrative model. *Child Development, 73*(5), 1573–1592.

Fisher, C., Wallace, S., & Fenton, R. (2000). Discrimination distress during adolescence. *Journal of Youth and Adolescence, 29*, 679–695.

Ford, D., & Harris, J. (1996). Perceptions and attitudes of Black students toward school, achievement, and other educational variables. *Child Development, 67*(3), 1141–1152.

Fordham, S. (1988). Racelessness as a factor in Black students' school success: Pragmatic strategy or Pyrrhic victory? *Harvard Educational Review, 58*(1), 54–84.

Fordham, S., & Ogbu, J. (1986). Black students' school success: Coping with the "burden of acting White." *Urban Review, 18*, 176–206.

Garcia Coll, C., Crnic, K., Lamberty, G., Waski, B. H., Jenkins, R., et al. (1996). An integrative model for the study of developmental competencies in minority children. *Child Development, 67*(5), 1891–1914.

Greene, M., Way, N., & Pahl, K. (2006). Trajectories of perceived adult and peer discrimination among Black, Latino, and Asian American adolescents: Patterns and psychological correlates. *Developmental Psychology, 42*(2), 218–238.

Harter, S. (1990). Issues in the assessment of the self-concept of children and adolescence. In A. M. LaGreca (Ed.), *Through the eyes of the child: Obtaining self-reports from children and adolescents* (pp. 292–395). Boston: Allyn & Bacon.

Hill, S. A., (2002). Teaching and doing gender in African American families. *Sex Roles, 47*(11–12), 493–506.

Hope, E., Chavous, T., Jagers, R., & Sellers, R. (2013). Connecting self-esteem and achievement: Diversity in academic identification and dis-identification among Black college students. *American Educational Research Journal, 50*(5), 1122–1151.

Hughes, D., & Chen, L. (1999). The nature of parents' race-related communications to children: A developmental perspective. In L. Bater & C. S. Tamis-LeMonda (Eds.), *Child psychology: A handbook of contemporary issues* (pp. 467–490). Philadelphia: Taylor & Francis.

Hurd, N. M., & Sellers, R. M. (2013). Black adolescent's relationships with natural mentors: Associations with academic engagement via social and emotional development. *Cultural Diversity & Ethnic Minority Psychology, 19*(1), 76–85.

Hurd, N. M., Varner, F., & Rowley, S. J. (2012). Involved-vigilant parenting and socio-emotional well-being among Black youth: The moderating influence of natural mentoring relationships. *Journal of Youth and Adolescence, 20*, pp. 789–809.

Ladson-Billings, G. (1995). Toward a theory of culturally relevant pedagogy. *American Educational Research Journal, 32*(3), 465–491.

Lewis, A., Chesler, M., & Forman, T. (2000). The impact of "colorblind" ideologies on students of color: Intergroup relations at a predominantly White university. *The Journal of Negro Education, 69*(1), 74–91.

Lindsey, T., & Mabie, B. (2012). Life skills yield stronger academic performance: A course for freshman boys teaches them about the Black experience and each other—and leads to improved self-concepts and academic performance. *Phi Delta Kappan, 93*(5), 33–36.

Lundy, G. (2003). The myths of oppositional culture. *Journal of Black Studies, 33*(4), 450–467.

Madyun, N., Lee, M., & Jumale, M. (2010). A social network analysis of acting White. *Procedia Social and Behavioral Sciences, 2*, 3231–3235.

Markus, H., Steele, C. M., & Steele, D. M. (2002). Color blindness as a barrier to inclusion: Assimilation and nonimmigrant minorities. In R. A. Shweder, M. Minow, & H. Markus (Eds.), *Engaging cultural differences: The multicultural challenge in liberal democracies* (pp. 453–472). New York: Russell Sage.

Mazama, A., & Lundy, G. (2013). African American homeschooling and the question of curricular cultural relevance. *The Journal of Negro Education, 82*(2), 123–138.

McAllister, G., & Irvine, J. (2000). Cross-cultural competency and multicultural teacher education. *Review of Educational Research, 70*(1), 3–24.

McGee, E. (2013). Threatened and placed at risk: High achieving African American males in urban high schools. *Urban Revolution, 45*, 448–471. doi: 10.1007/S11256-013-0265-2

Mickelson, R. (1990). The attitude-achievement paradox among Black adolescents. *Sociology of Education, 63*, 44–61.

Milner, R. (2003). Reflection, racial competence, and critical pedagogy: How do we prepare preservice teachers to pose tough questions? *Race, Ethnicity, and Education, 6*(2), 193–208.

Milner, R. (2010). What does teacher education have to do with teaching? Implications for diversity studies. *Journal of Teacher Education, 61*(1-2), 118–131.

Neblett, E., Cooper, S., Banks, K., & Smalls-Glover, C. (2013). Racial identity mediates the association between ethnic-racial socialization and depressive symptoms. *Cultural Diversity and Ethnic Minority Psychology, 19*(2), 200–207.

Neblett, E. W., Philip, C., Cogburn, C., & Sellers, R. M. (2006). African American adolescents' discrimination experiences and academic achievement: Racial socialization as a cultural compensatory and protective factor. *Journal of Black Psychology, 32*(2), 199–218.

Neblett, E., Rivas-Drake, D., & Umana-Taylor, A. (2012). The promise of racial and ethnic protective factors in promoting ethnic minority youth development. *Child Development Perspectives, 6*(3), 295–303.

Neblett, E. W., Smalls, C. P., Ford, K. R., Nguyen, H. X., & Sellers, R. M. (2009). Racial socialization and racial identity: African American parents' messages about race as precursors to identity. *Journal of Youth and Adolescence, 38,* 189–203.

Osborne, J. W. (1997). Race and academic disidentification. *Journal of Ed Psychology, 89,* 728–735.

Oyserman, D., Gant, L., & Ager, J. (1995). A socially contextualized model of African American identity: Possible selves and school persistence. *Journal of Personality & Social Psychology, 69,* 1216–1232.

Perry, T. (1993). *Toward a theory of African American school achievement* (Report No. 16). Baltimore: Center on Families, Communities, Schools and Children's Learning.

Perry, T. (2004). *Young, gifted, and Black: Promoting high achievement among African-American students.* Boston: Beacon.

Perry, T., Steele, C., & Hilliard, A. (2003). *Young, gifted, and Black: Promoting high academic achievement among African American students.* Boston: Beacon.

Phinney, J. S. (1990). Ethnic identity in adolescence and adulthood: A review and integration. *Psychological Bulletin, 108,* 499–514.

Phinney, J. S. (1992). The Multigroup Ethnic Identity Measure: A new scale for use with diverse groups. *Journal of Adolescent Research, 7,* 156–172.

Richardson, B. L., Macon, T. A., Mustafaa, F. N., Bogan, E. D., Cole-Lewis, Y., & Chavous, T. M. (2015). Associations of racial discrimination and parental discrimination coping messages with African American adolescent racial identity. *Journal of Youth and Adolescence, 44*(6), 1301–1317.

Rosenbloom, S. R., & Way, N. (2004). Experiences of discrimination among African American, Asian American, and Latino adolescents in an urban high school. *Youth & Society, 35*(4), 420–451.

Rousseau, C., & Tate, W. (2003). No time like the present: Reflecting on equity in school mathematics. *Theory into Practice, 42*(3), 210–216.

Seidman, E., Allen, L., Aber, J. L., Mitchell, C., & Feinman, J. (1994). The impact of school transitions in early adolescence on the self-system and perceived social context of poor urban youth. *Child Development, 65*(2), 507–522.

Sellers, R. M., Caldwell, C. H., Schmeelk-Cone, K., & Zimmerman, M. A. (2003). Racial identity, racial discrimination, perceived stress, and psychological distress among African American young adults. *Journal of Health and Social Behavior 44*(3), 302-317.

Sellers, R., Linder, N., Martin, P., & Lewis, R. (2006). Racial identity matters: The relationship between racial discrimination and psychological functioning in African American adolescents. *Journal of Research on Adolescence, 16*(2), 187–216.

Sellers, R. M., Rowley, S. A., Chavous, T. M., Shelton, J. N., & Smith, M. A. (1997). Multidimensional Inventory of Black Identity: A preliminary investigation of reliability and construct validity. *Journal of Personality and Social Psychology, 73*(4), 805–815.

Sellers, R., Smith, M., Shelton, J., Rowley, S., & Chavous, T. (1998). Multidimensional model of racial identity: A reconceptualization of African American racial identity. *Personality and Social Psychology Review, 2*(1), 18–39.

Smalls, C., White, R., Chavous, T., & Sellers, R. (2007). Racial ideological beliefs and racial discrimination experiences as predictors of academic engagement among African American adolescents. *Journal of Black Psychology, 33,* 299–330.

Spencer, M., Cunningham, M., & Swanson, D. (1995). Identity as coping: Adolescent African American males' adaptive responses to high-risk environment. In H. W. Harris (Ed.), *Racial and ethnic identity: Psychological development and creative expression* (pp. 31–52). Florence, KY: Taylor & Francis/Routledge.

Spencer, M., Dupree, D., & Hartmann, T. (1997). A phenomenological variant of ecological systems theory (PVEST): A self-organization perspective in context. *Development and Psychopathology, 9*(4), 817–833.

Steele, C. (1997). A threat in the air: How stereotypes shape intellectual identity and performance. *American Psychologist, 52,* 613–629.

Steele, C., & Aronson, J. (1995). Stereotype threat and the intellectual test performance of African Americans. *Journal of Personality and Social Psychology, 69,* 797–811.

Steinberg, L., Dornbusch, S., & Brown, B. (1992). Ethnic differences in adolescent achievement: An ecological perspective. *American Psychologist, 47*(6), 723–729.

Stinson, D. (2011). When the "burden of acting White" is not a burden: School success and African American male students. *Urban Revolution, 43,* 43–65.

Swanson, D., Cunningham, M., & Spencer, M.B. (2003). Black males' structural conditions, achievement patterns, normative needs, and "opportunities." *Urban Education,* 3(5), 608-633.

Thornton, M., Taylor, R., & Tran, T. (1997). Multiple dimensions of racial group identification among adult Black Americans. *Journal of Black Psychology, 23*(3), 293–309.

Vandiver, B. J., Fhagen-Smith, P. E., Cokley, K. O., Cross, W. E., Jr., & Worrell, F. C. (2001). Cross's Nigrescence model: From theory to scale to theory. *Journal of Multicultural Counseling and Development, 29,* 174–200.

Way, N., Hernandez, M., Rogers, L., & Hughes, D. (2013). "I'm not going to become no rapper": Stereotypes as a context of ethnic and racial identity development. *Journal of Adolescent Research, 28,* 407–431.

White, L., & Worrell, F. (2012). Intersections of race, identity, and academic achievement. *Human Development, 55*(2), 97–106.

White-Johnson, R. (2012). Prosocial involvement among African American young adults: Considering racial discrimination and racial identity. *Journal of Black Psychology, 38*(3), 313–341.

Wildhagen, T. (2011). Testing the "acting white" hypothesis: An explanation runs out of empirical steam. *Journal of Negro Education, 80*(4), 445–463.

Wolfe, C., Schmader, T., Major, B., Spencer, S., & Crocker, J. (1998). Coping with negative stereotypes about intellectual performance: The role of psychological disengagement. *Personality and Social Psychology Bulletin, 24*(1), 34–50.

Wong, C. A., Eccles, J. S., & Sameroff, A. (2003). The influence of ethnic discrimination and ethnic identification on African American adolescents' school and socioemotional adjustment. *Journal of Personality, 71*(6), 1197–1123.

Wright, B. (2011). I know who I am, do you?: Identity and academic achievement of successful African American male adolescents in an urban pilot high school in the United States. *Urban Education, 46*(4), 611–638.

CHAPTER TWO

The NFL's Rooney Rule: A Theoretical Analysis of Its Societal Influence

JOHN A. FORTUNATO AND JEROME D. WILLIAMS

INTRODUCTION

February 4, 2007, was a monumental day in professional sports as the Super Bowl featured two teams with African American head coaches, Tony Dungy for the Indianapolis Colts and Lovie Smith for the Chicago Bears. This achievement for African American head coaches in the National Football League (NFL) is a direct result of the NFL's Rooney Rule. Historically, on October 3, 1989, Art Shell became the first African American head coach in the NFL since Fritz Pollard in 1921. In 2002, there were only two African American head coaches in the NFL. More recently, at the conclusion of the 2012 regular season, no African American candidates were chosen for any of the eight head-coaching vacancies or seven general manager openings. At the conclusion of the 2014 regular season, only one African American was hired for the seven head-coaching vacancies. At the start of the 2015 season there are five African American head coaches and seven general managers for the 32 NFL teams.

In an attempt to counter this historical inequity in African American hiring, the NFL instituted the Rooney Rule in 2003. The Rooney Rule requires that a minority candidate be interviewed when a team is hiring a head coach. In 2009, the Rooney Rule was expanded to include interviewing practices for all senior NFL positions. While there is evidence that the Rooney Rule has expanded opportunities for minorities in the NFL, the necessity and importance of the policy needs to be understood through the potential of its larger societal influence. This chapter will document the history of the Rooney Rule and offer an analysis of its societal influence focusing on (1) the importance of opportunities in the NFL because of the league's media exposure, (2) social identity theory, and (3) discriminatory hiring practices in some circumstances driven by unconscious bias.

The importance of creating opportunities in professional sports is that these leagues receive considerable media exposure. Theories such as cultivation and agenda setting demonstrate that media exposure can influence how people think about certain issues. What people are actually witnessing through the media therefore becomes important. If African Americans are given opportunities in the very popular NFL, their success will be widely publicized. It is the exposure of witnessing success at the highest level of the sport that can precipitate positive societal change, such as facilitating head-coaching opportunities at all levels of football. This concept is explained through social identity theory, which posits that people value group membership of a social category and view positively groups with which they can identify. Media exposure can produce positive social identity and create a belief for people that they too can achieve at that level. However, the benefits of media exposure in the NFL only occur if opportunities are provided.

In terms of discrimination in sports, certainly there is ample evidence of overt racism and prejudice throughout the history of professional and collegiate athletic programs. There is evidence that the public's witnessing of sporting events that confronted prejudicial beliefs did help change the sports landscape. Notable examples include the 1966 NCAA Championship basketball game in which Texas Western started five African American players in defeating the University of Kentucky (see Frank Fitzpatrick's book *And the Walls Came Tumbling Down: The Basketball Game that Changed American Sports*), and the 1970 football game when the integrated University of Southern California team traveled to Birmingham and beat the all-White University of Alabama team (see Steven Travers' *One Night, Two Teams: Alabama vs. USC and the Game that Changed a Nation*). Prejudicial beliefs about the quarterback position have also been studied in the context of race (Buffington, 2005; Byrd & Utsler, 2007).

The ultimate problem of negative racial portrayals in the media is that people form erroneous beliefs and these beliefs manifest themselves in decision making, notably hiring decisions. In terms of hiring practices discrimination does not have to be intentional. Researchers have found that racial inequality is sustained more by Whites' preferential treatment of members of their own social networks, particularly through unconscious associations that prescribe meaning to other races rather than through overt racism (Collins, 2007; DiTomaso, 2013; Feagin, 2014;

Greenwald & Krieger, 2006; Lawrence, 1986/1987). Collins explains that because "unconscious bias is unintentional and not easily recognizable, it will not disappear unless specifically addressed" (p. 912).

Thus, because of factors such as unconscious bias there are occasions when policy is needed to create the opportunity that is otherwise not being provided. Collins (2007) contends that "since many forms of prejudice are often unconsciously maintained, in certain instances someone or something outside of the establishment must propose innovative policies that promote exposure-based methods in order to dismantle deeply-rooted ideological beliefs" (p. 873). In other words, the understanding of unconscious bias along with the potential positive influence of media provides the necessity of the Rooney Rule.

MEDIA EXPOSURE AND PORTRAYAL THEORY

The discussion of sport's societal influence is advanced through an understanding of media theories. Cultivation theory examines the influence of media exposure over long periods of time (Gerbner, Gross, Morgan, Signorielli, & Shanahan, 2002; Signorielli & Morgan, 2009). The difference in the amount of media exposure, either light or heavy, will be the determination of the cultivation effect with heavy media users more likely to take on the reality as expressed by the media.

Similar to cultivation theory, the agenda-setting theoretical model explains the influential role of media with exposure also as the key influential variable. The core concept of agenda-setting studies is that the media select certain issues for exposure and emphasize certain issue attributes to the exclusion of others. It is these issues and attributes that are emphasized in the media coverage that the audience will deem important (McCombs, 2005; McCombs, Shaw, & Weaver, 2014). It is important to note that both cultivation theory and agenda setting recognize that the audience's experiences and interpretive abilities are a mitigating factor in any ultimate effect that a media message might have.

In light of the influential role of media exposure, studies that focus on racial portrayals within the media are also necessary to examine. The media portrayal of race in sport is of particular interest to many scholars (Andrews, 2013; Armstrong, 2011; Byrd & Utsler, 2007; Cunningham & Bopp, 2010; Eagleman, 2011; Eagleman & Martin, 2013; Van Sterkenburg, Knoppers, & De Leeuw, 2010). Eagleman and Martin (2013) claim, "The way in which race in sport is portrayed by the media can have profound impacts on our own perceptions and interpretations of race" (p. 369). Bruce (2004) simply argues that "most Americans understand race through media representations" (p. 863).

In a content analysis of *Sports Illustrated* and *ESPN The Magazine*, Eagleman (2011) found that White baseball players were more often depicted as hard working while Black players were often portrayed as having overcome obstacles. It is when media portrayals of race such as these are negative that the influential claims of cultivation theory and agenda setting become problematic. A constant negative media portrayal sets up a narrative that people come to believe and perpetuate. For example, Woodward (2004) documents how certain races tend to dominate certain positions in professional football. He reported that even scouts often saw White athletes as hard working and described in terms of their mental capabilities while Black athletes were seen in terms of their athletic abilities. In a study specifically focused on the portrayal of coaches, Cunningham and Bopp (2010) examine 191 press releases issued by universities to announce the hiring of a new assistant football coach. They found that Whites were often praised for their coaching abilities and experience while African American coaches were highlighted for helping with recruiting and monitoring athletes on the team.

Conversely, if the public is witnessing positive portrayals through the media, such as professional success, according to media theories societal influence may be positive. The benefits of positive media exposure can be explained through an examination of social identity theory, which posits that people want to have some form of group association and value group membership of a social category (Mael & Ashforth, 2001; Tajfel, 1982). Researchers document that sports play a significant role in creating social identities (Hartmann, 2000; Ogden & Hilt, 2003). Sherif (2001) provides an important variable to consider in this group association dynamic, pointing out that people tend to view positively groups with which they can identify. To build this social identification people need to witness success either through personal experience or the media. However, the benefits of media exposure creating a positive social identity only occur if opportunities are provided. Fortunato and Williams (2014) point out that it is the responsibility of the sports league to develop the strategies that build this social identity with an audience. They add that a positive social identity on the part of the audience can, ultimately, lead to positive market outcomes for the league.

Tajfel and Turner (1986), however, caution that social identity theory can have a negative outcome. They use social identity theory as an explanation for "in-group" bias, explaining that some might find their racial identification leading to "in-group" favoritism. This social identity characteristic can manifest itself negatively in hiring decisions by preventing "out-group" opportunities. Often the social identity associations driving decision making are not at the forefront of people's thought process. In fact, it can be an unconscious or implicit attitude (Collins, 2007; DiTomaso, 2013; Feagin, 2014; Greenwald & Krieger, 2006; Lawrence, 1986/1987).

UNCONSCIOUS BIAS

Negative media exposure and portrayal can contribute to what is referred to as unconscious bias. Lawrence (1986/1987) explains the culture context as the totality of an individual's family, friends, authority figures, as well as the media, conveys beliefs and perceptions. These beliefs and perceptions are not explicitly taught, but do become part of an individual's view of the world. According to Lawrence the individual is unaware that the continuous presence of cultural stereotypes has influenced his or her beliefs and perceptions. Unconscious beliefs and perceptions can factor into an individual's behavior and decisions. Lawrence suggests the "injury of racial inequality exists irrespective of the decision-makers' motives" (p. 319). He contends,

> Traditional notions of intent do not reflect the fact that decisions about racial matters are influenced in large part by factors that can be characterized as neither intentional—in the sense that certain outcomes are self-consciously sought—nor unintentional—in the sense that the outcomes are random, fortuitous, and uninfluenced by the decision-maker's beliefs, desires, and wishes. (p. 322)

In his research, Collins (2007) argues that unconscious bias is one reason for the low percentage of minority coaches in the NFL. He claims unconscious bias influences hiring decisions through the internalization of African American stereotypes as intellectually inferior and the establishment and maintenance of old-boy networks. DiTomaso (2013) finds that special privileges from family, friends, and acquaintances due to race usually continue throughout one's career. Rather than describing racial inequality as overt discrimination, her research suggests it should be viewed through a lens of White privilege. DiTomaso explains that Whites do not need to do bad things to minorities to secure and maintain privileged positions, such as head-coaching positions; they need only engage in helping each other through what she labels as the mechanism of "opportunity hoarding." In other words, racial inequality in NFL head-coaching ranks, DiTomaso might argue, could be produced as much through the favoritism of Whites toward each other as through active discrimination of Whites toward minorities. Feagin (2014) similarly suggests that systemic racism is not only about the construction of racial definitions, attitudes, and identities; it is also about the maintenance of White privilege.

The concern over unconscious bias and implicit racial attitudes perpetuated in the NFL is amplified when considering it is not only having owners and general managers selecting White head coaches that creates the problem but that these White head coaches might not select African Americans as their assistant coaches—particularly since assistant coaches comprise a substantial portion of future head-coaching prospects.

When there are few minority head coaches, having proper mentorship for aspiring minority head coaches is a concern. Advancement in many fields, including coaching, is largely dependent on getting proper mentorship. The need to have same race mentorship for effective mentoring is open for debate. There are those, however, who feel that mentors matched on racial and ethnic background are better equipped to understand the social and psychological challenges of their mentees and tend to engender greater levels of trust. As a matter of fact, research on mentorship in the field of business suggests that minority protégés should be mentored very differently than their White counterparts (Thomas, 2001). In the education field, one recent study argues that professors are less likely to want to mentor minority students, especially in fields that lead to the most lucrative careers (Milkman, Akinola, & Chugh, 2014). The lack of mentorship may be a similar impediment in the NFL. This means a policy change had to be inserted at some point to break the old-boy network, confront unconscious bias, provide proper mentorship, and eradicate erroneous racial stigmas held in society.

THE ROONEY RULE

In September 2002, with only two African American head coaches in the NFL, attorneys Cyrus Mehri and Jonnie Cochran issued a report detailing the scope of the problem. Their report demonstrated that when given the opportunity African American coaches were often more successful than White head coaches (see Maravent, 2006, for a comprehensive review of the Mehri and Cochran report). Mehri and Cochran threatened legal action against the NFL. They also formed the Fritz Pollard Alliance, which advocates for diversity and equal opportunity for NFL hiring of coaches, front office, and scouting staffs.

In response to a possible lawsuit as well as the public relations scrutiny coming from the Mehri and Cochran report, the NFL formed the Committee on Workplace Diversity, consisting of owners and front office personnel. The committee was chaired by Pittsburgh Steelers owner Dan Rooney (Duru, 2011, provides a detailed explanation of the evolution of the Rooney Rule and the personalities behind the movement). On December 20, 2002, the committee issued its recommendations to promote diversity. The main recommendation was that any team hiring a head coach would have to interview at least one minority candidate. This recommendation became referred to simply as the Rooney Rule.

To further assist diversity hiring the Committee on Workplace Diversity compiled a career information book of minority assistant coaches and coordinators of prospective head coaches. Also, expanded interview training programs for minority candidates were created (NFL press release, December 20, 2002). The final recommendation was to eliminate the rule where assistant coaches were not available to interview for head-coaching positions until their team was eliminated from the playoffs. With a team's desire to hire its head coach without waiting, this change allowed qualified coaches to avoid missing out on an important opportunity.

Marvin Lewis became the first African American head coach to be hired after the Rooney Rule when he was named head coach of the Cincinnati Bengals prior to the 2003 season. Lewis was not only the first African American head coach in the history of the Bengals, he was also the first African American the Bengals had ever interviewed for that position (Briggs, 2003). Lewis was the defensive coordinator of the 2000 Super Bowl Champion Baltimore Ravens, considered one of the best defensive teams in the history of the NFL. After that win it was widely speculated that Lewis would soon receive a head-coaching position. However, because of the rule that did not allow assistant coaches whose teams were still in the playoffs to interview, Lewis missed out on interview opportunities for openings with the Houston Texans, Washington Redskins, and the New York Jets. In a statement at the time Lewis acknowledged the familiarity aspect in hiring. He stated, "The person we know best, not just as a friend, but as a colleague and a professional, that's the person you're going to be most comfortable with because you have an idea how he'll react in a stressful situation" (Willis, 2001).

Lewis returned to Baltimore as defensive coordinator for the 2001 season and then interviewed in 2002 for the head-coaching position with the Tampa Bay Buccaneers. Citing a desire to hire an offensive coach after six seasons with defensive-minded head coach Tony Dungy, the Buccaneers hired Jon Gruden. Lewis took the defensive coordinator position with Washington for 2002, becoming the highest paid assistant coach in the NFL (Maske & Shapiro, 2002), before getting the Cincinnati job in 2003. In 2015, Lewis remains the head coach of the Bengals.

Failure by a team to comply with the Rooney Rule results in a substantial fine. The Detroit Lions were fined $200,000 in 2003 when they hired former San Francisco 49ers head coach Steve Mariucci without interviewing a minority candidate. In this situation when it appeared that the Lions had targeted Mariucci, the minority coaches who were contacted by the Lions turned down the interview requests (Briggs, 2003). Sometimes a team would previously identify the person they wanted for head coach then conduct sham interviews with minority coaches only to satisfy the Rooney Rule (Maravent, 2006; Willis, 2010). Several examples of what appear to be interviews by teams of minority candidates only to satisfy the Rooney Rule can be found. When Washington hired two-time Super Bowl–winning head coach Mike Shanahan it was being reported that the private plane of team owner Daniel Snyder was on its way to get Shanahan as the front office was interviewing secondary coach Jerry Gray. When the Seattle Seahawks hired Pete Carroll, who had won two national championships at USC, it was reported that he had already reached an agreement with the team as Seattle was interviewing Vikings defensive coordinator Leslie Frazier (Willis, 2010).

In 2011, the NFL reached its high of eight minority head coaches. But in 2013, there were six African American general managers and three African American head coaches. This statistic is stark when considering that the percentage of players in the NFL in 2013 was disproportionately African American, 66.3% (University of Central Florida's Institute for Diversity and Ethics in Sports, www. tidesport.org). The issue of minority hiring came to the forefront in 2013 when none of the eight head coaching or seven general manager openings went to a minority. NFL commissioner Roger Goodell called it unacceptable (Fenno, 2013). Cyrus Mehri, co-author of the critical report of African American hiring a decade earlier, commented, "This hiring cycle is a wake-up call for how tenacious the good ol' boy network is and why we need to work so hard to level the playing field so there's fair competition" (Bell, 2013, p. C4).

Prior to the 2014 season two of the seven NFL head-coaching vacancies were filled by African Americans. Lovie Smith was hired by the Tampa Bay Buccaneers and Jim Caldwell by the Detroit Lions, bringing the total number to four. In response to Smith and Caldwell being hired, John Wooten, chairman of the Fritz Pollard Alliance, stressed it is more about the process than the numbers of head coaches hired. He stated, "We believe so strongly in the process, that it's the right way to do it. We want the owners to only interview a candidate if it's someone they would really be willing to hire. We don't want it to just be compliance with the rule. We want there to be true interest" (Maske, 2014, p. D3).

A THEORETICAL UNDERSTANDING OF THE ROONEY RULE

The necessity and importance of the Rooney Rule can be understood through various theoretical frameworks. Some of the reasons why African American coaches have been overlooked might not have been because of malicious racist intent. Theoretical concepts such as social identity and unconscious bias offer reasons why many African Americans were not provided opportunities. The requirement to interview an African American candidate helps address the negative consequences of social identity by Tajfel and Turner (1986) and the concept of unconscious bias by Lawrence (1986/1987) and Collins (2007).

Collins (2007) also suggests that the Rooney Rule counters unconscious bias. He contends the effectiveness of the Rooney Rule "lies in its potential to deconstruct the hidden biases inherent in NFL social networks" (p. 904). Collins argues that "the NFL's longstanding hiring practices and networking systems have consistently allowed front-office decision-makers to avoid interacting with qualified African American candidates. Without any substantive exposure to such candidates, decision-makers commonly—and often unconsciously—rely on racial stereotypes depicting African Americans as natural born, instinctive athletes whose success is attributable to their innate physical gifts rather than their hard work and intellect" (p. 872). He adds that although the Rooney Rule is not a perfect cure, at a bare minimum it forces these decision-makers to "to actively confront their own unconscious bias by mandating face-to-face contact and social interaction with African-American candidates" (p. 912).

To further demonstrate the crucial impact of the Rooney Rule, more than an opportunity for any one person, the hiring of an African American for a head-coaching position in the NFL has a far-reaching influence. To begin with, having an African American head coach eliminates unconscious bias in selecting assistant coaches. The African American head coach will be more sensitive to offering other African American coaches opportunities and taking on the responsibility to properly mentor these coaches. Having African American assistant coaches is obviously important because these men help comprise the pool of future head coach candidates.

To illustrate this point, the 2015 Coaching Mobility Report documents how Tony Dungy, as head coach of the Tampa Bay Buccaneers, in 1996 hired Herman Edwards as his assistant head coach and Lovie Smith to his first NFL coaching position as the linebacker's coach. Edwards would become the head coach of the New York Jets and later the Kansas City Chiefs. Smith would become the head coach of the Chicago Bears. In Chicago, Smith hired Ron Rivera, a Mexican American, to his first defensive coordinator position. In 2014, Smith was named head coach of the Tampa Bay Buccaneers. Smith hired Leslie Frazier as his defensive coordinator. Frazier became the head coach of the Minnesota Vikings before being terminated after the 2013 season. Frazier got his first defensive coordinator position from Marvin Lewis when Lewis was named head coach of the Cincinnati Bengals in 2003. Frazier was also a member of Tony Dungy's coaching staff along with Jim Caldwell when the Colts won the Super Bowl. Caldwell took over as head coach of the Colts when Dungy retired. He lost the position in 2011, moved to the Baltimore Ravens as quarterbacks coach during their 2013 Super Bowl win, and later was named the head coach of the Detroit Lions.

The media exposure that the NFL receives is also important in providing opportunities for African American head coaches at other levels of coaching. Seeing an African American head coach succeed at the highest level of the sport can foster the positive aspect of social identity theory for an individual athlete and the belief that he too could succeed as a coach. For example, the hiring of African American coaches in college football continues to be slow with only 13 out of the 120 major college football-playing universities in 2013 having African American head coaches. Speculation has thus occurred about instituting a Rooney Rule at the collegiate level. Nichols (2008) even claims that if a Rooney Rule is not enacted for college football coaches, litigation under Title VII of the Civil Rights Act of 1964 that bans discrimination in federally assisted programs on the basis of race, color, religion, sex, or national origin might be a strategy worth pursuing. He does point out that because of the "multitude of factors" that are involved in the interviewing and hiring of a college football coach "it appears possible—but not probable—that a Title VII lawsuit could succeed" (p. 172).

For the 2014 season there were, however, two prominent examples of progress in college football when Penn State and the University of Texas hired African American head coaches for the first time in either program's history. James Franklin was named as the head coach at Penn State after reviving Vanderbilt. Charlie Strong was named the head coach at Texas after a successful tenure at Louisville, which included a Sugar Bowl victory after the 2012 season. Head coaches at major football universities are also positioned well for NFL head coaching jobs. Similar to the NFL, these African American collegiate head coaches are cognizant of providing opportunities when comprising their staffs. Strong has named six African Americans as assistant coaches to his staff at Texas, including the defensive coordinator, recruiting coordinator, and strength and conditioning coach. Franklin has four African American assistant coaches at Penn State.

CONCLUSION

The Rooney Rule requires that a minority candidate be interviewed when a team is hiring a head coach. The Rooney Rule is designed to provide opportunities that might not have been available if the policy was not put into place. In this instance of the NFL a policy change had to be inserted to confront the old-boy network, unconscious bias, provide proper mentorship, and eradicate an erroneous stigma held in society.

The positive impact of the Rooney Rule reaches far beyond the NFL and the men who benefited from this policy. Similar to the Title IX law passed in 1972 that addressed gender inequities in sports, more than opportunity for the participants alone, the ability to see people succeed in these roles can have a positive societal influence. There is a level of societal acceptance and acknowledgment that comes from the media exposure of seeing Mia Hamm or Cheryl Miller play her respective sport or Tony Dungy or Mike Tomlin lead his team to a Super Bowl victory.

While not everyone will have the ability to play collegiate sports or coach in the NFL, African American athletes can believe that they too will achieve or that, at least, their participation in those activities is not going to be questioned or ridiculed. Policies such as the Rooney Rule provide the opportunity, the talents of the athletes and coaches allow them to take full advantage of that opportunity, and the media exposure as witness to their success motivates others to achieve completing an important transition to what is considered the norm.

BIBLIOGRAPHY

Andrews, D. L. (2013). Reflections on communication and sport: On celebrity and race. *Communication & Sport, 1*(1–2), 151–163.

Armstrong, K. L. (2011). Lifting the veils and illuminating the shadows: Furthering the explorations of race and ethnicity in sport management. *Journal of Sport Management, 25,* 95–106.

Bell, J. (2013, January 22). Playing field still not level. *USA Today,* p. C4.

Briggs, B. (2003, September 7). Minority report: The hiring of Marvin Lewis is hailed as progress, but the NFL still is lacking for Black head coaches. *Denver Post,* p. J1.

Bruce, T. (2004). Marking the boundaries of the "normal" in televised sports: The play-by-play of race. *Media, Culture, and Society, 26*(8), 861–879.

Buffington, D. (2005). Contesting race on Sundays: Making meaning out of the rise in the number of Black quarterbacks. *Sociology of Sport Journal, 21,* 19–37.

Byrd, J., & Utsler, M. (2007). Is stereotypical coverage of African-American athletes as "dead as disco?" An analysis of NFL quarterbacks in the pages of *Sports Illustrated. Journal of Sports Media, 2*(1), 1–28.

Collins, B. W. (2007). Tackling unconscious bias in hiring practices: The plight of the Rooney Rule. *New York University Law Review, 82*(3), 870–912.

Cunningham, G. B., & Bopp, T. (2010). Race ideology perpetuated: Media representations of newly hired football coaches. *Journal of Sport Media, 5*(1), 1–19.

DiTomaso, N. (2013). *The American non-dilemma: Racial inequality without racism.* New York: Russell Sage.

Duru, N. J. (2011). *Advancing the ball: Race, reformation, and the quest for equal coaching opportunity in the NFL.* New York: Oxford University Press.

Eagleman, A. N. (2011). Stereotypes of race and nationality: A qualitative analysis of sport magazine coverage of MLB players. *Journal of Sport Management, 25,* 156–168.

Eagleman, A. N., & Martin, T. G. (2013). Race portrayals in sport communication. In P. M. Pedersen (Ed.), *Routledge handbook of communication* (pp. 369–377). New York: Routledge.

Feagin, J. R. (2014). *Racist America: Roots, current realities, and future reparations.* New York: Routledge.

Fenno, N. (2013, February 7). Minority candidates need more from NFL. *Washington Times,* p. 1.

Fitzpatrick, F. (2000). *And the walls came tumbling down: The basketball game that changed American sports.* Lincoln: University of Nebraska Press.

Fortunato, J. A., & Williams, J. D. (2014). Using marketing theory to increase African-American participation with Major League Baseball. In L. L. Martin (Ed.), *Out of bounds: Racism and the Black athlete* (pp. 55–80). Santa Barbara, CA: Praeger.

Gerbner, G., Gross, L., Morgan, M., Signorielli, N., & Shanahan, J. (2002). Growing up with television: Cultivation processes. In J. Bryant & D. Zillmann (Ed.), *Media effects: Advances in theory and research* (2nd ed., pp. 43–67). Mahwah, NJ: Lawrence Erlbaum.

Greenwald, A. G., & Krieger, L. H. (2006). Implicit bias: Scientific foundations. *California Law Review, 94*(4), 945–967.

Harrison, C. K., & Bukstein, S. (2014). *NFL Occupational Mobility Patterns (Vol III), A Report for NFL Diversity and Inclusion.* Good Business Series. Retrieved from coachingmobilityreport.com

Hartmann, D. (2000). Rethinking the relationship between sport and race in American culture: Golden ghettos and contested terrain. *Sociology of Sport Journal, 17*(3), 229–253.

Lawrence, C. R. III. (1986/1987). The id, the ego, and equal protection: Reckoning with unconscious racism. *Stanford Law Review, 39*, 317–388.

Mael, F. A., & Ashforth, B. E. (2001). Identification in work, war, sports, and religion: Contrasting the benefits and risks. *Journal for the Theory of Social Behavior, 31*(2), 197–222.

Maravent, B. (2006). Is the Rooney Rule affirmative action? Analyzing the NFL's mandate to its clubs regarding coaching and front office hires. *Sports Lawyers Journal, 13*, 233–273.

Maske, M. (2014, January 16). Diversity is praised in recent NFL hires. *Washington Post*, p. D3.

Maske, M., & Shapiro, L. (2002, February 11). Turnabout: Lewis signs on to run Redskins defense. *Washington Post*, p. D1.

McCombs, M. E. (2005). A look at agenda-setting: Past, present and future. *Journalism Studies, 6*(4), 543–547.

McCombs, M. E., Shaw, D. L., & Weaver, D. (2014). New directions in agenda-setting theory and research. *Mass Communication and Society, 17*(6), 781–802.

Milkman, K. L, Akinola, M., & Chugh, D. (2014). *What happens before? A field experiment exploring how pay and representation differentially shape bias on the pathway into organizations.* Retrieved from http://ssrn.com/abstract=2063742

Nichols, M. J. (2008). Time for a Hail Mary? With bleak prospects of being aided by a college version of the NFL's Rooney Rule, should minority college football coaches turn their attention to Title VII litigation? *Virginia Sports and Entertainment Law Journal, 8*(1), 147–172.

Ogden, D. C., & Hilt, M. L. (2003). Collective identity and basketball: An explanation for the decreasing number of African-Americans on America's baseball diamonds. *Journal of Leisure Research, 35*(2), 213–227.

Sherif, M. (2001). Superordinate goals in the reduction on intergroup conflict. In M. A. Hogg & D. Abrams (Eds.), *Intergroup relations: Essential readings. Key readings in social psychology* (pp. 64–70). New York: Psychology.

Signorielli, N., & Morgan, M. (2009). Cultivation analysis: Research and practice. In D. W. Stacks & M. B. Salwen (Eds.), *An integrated approach to communication theory and research* (pp. 106–121). New York: Routledge.

Tajfel, H. (1982). *Social identity and intergroup relations.* Cambridge: Cambridge University Press.

Tajfel, H., & Turner, J. (1986). The social identity of intergroup behavior. In S. Worchel & W. V. Austin (Eds.), *Psychology of intergroup relations* (pp. 276–293). Chicago: Nelson Hall.

Thomas, D. A. (2001). The truth about mentoring minorities: Race matters. *Harvard Business Review* (April), 98–107.

Travers, S. (2007). *One night, two teams: Alabama vs. USC and the game that changed a nation.* Lanham, MD: Taylor Trade.

Van Sterkenburg, J., Knoppers, A., & De Leeuw, S. (2010). Race, ethnicity, and content analysis of the sports media: A critical reflection. *Media, Culture, and Society, 32*(5), 819–839.

Willis, G. (2001, January 24). A sign of the times: Lewis set to be NFL's next Black head coach. *New York Post*, p. 77.

Willis, G. (2010, January 12). The "rule" is broken; Rooney statute has outlived its purpose. *New York Post*, p. 58.

Woodward, J. R. (2004). Professional football scouts: An investigation of racial stacking. *Sociology of Sport Journal, 21*, 356–375.

CHAPTER THREE

In God's Favor: Prosperity Gospel in the 21st Century

KAYLA RENÉE WHEELER

INTRODUCTION

While many scholars have pointed out the importance of tithes and offerings in prosperity gospel as a means of investing in God to secure future rewards, far less has been written on how some current ministries are being used for community-building efforts (Jones & Woodbridge, 2010). Recognizing their limited power to change a system that has left Black Americans and impoverished people in subjugated positions, today many Black prosperity churches have turned inward to help uplift their communities and the diaspora, mirroring the efforts of early 20th century Black religious leaders, such as Daddy Grace and Father Divine. Following in line with scholar Marla Frederick, this chapter explores how prosperity gospel is becoming a source of hope and empowerment for Black Americans.

The chapter begins by providing a brief history of prosperity gospel's evolution, which can be traced back to the New Thought Movement of the mid-1800s. Then it will explain how prosperity gospel preachers have used media to expose new people to their message and increase their impact. Finally, the chapter will finish with a focus, specifically, on the developing ministries of Creflo Dollar and T. D. Jakes. Both have been included in the label of prosperity preachers in the United States with broad appeal that includes people of all races and socioeconomic classes, including celebrities such as Deion Sanders and Tyler Perry. While it is easy to point to their flashy cars and loud suits as examples of exploitation, this chapter will examine the service to their community that is central in both of their ministries. In today's new expression of prosperity gospel, we will see how God can reward faithful people in order to help uplift others, both within the local community and the diaspora.

HISTORY OF PROSPERITY GOSPEL

Modern prosperity gospel can trace its roots back to the New Thought Movement in the 1840s. The movement was based on the belief that a person could harness the ability to control their reality through proper use of the mind, mainly focusing on bodily and mental healing. Phineas Quimby was central to the movement's early success. Quimby believed that he had been healed of his tuberculosis through harnessing his mental powers (Bowler, 2013, p. 13). Hoping to spread the good news to others, Quimby created a philosophy that involved reinterpretations of the Bible, mesmerism, and talk therapy (Bowler, p. 13). He believed that people could will themselves out of any negative situation. His ideas quickly shifted to include the belief that one could use their mind not only to heal themselves but also to gain financial success. The movement was especially popular among White women who sought physical and economic independence from their husbands (Hladky, 2012, p. 85). For instance, one of Quimby's most successful students, Mary Baker Eddy, would go on to found the Christian Science organization (Mitchem, 2007, p. 52). As theologian Stephanie Y. Mitchem points out, Black churches were not drawn to the movement during the 19th century because such views could already be found in "African-derived faith consciousness" infused in Black Christianity (p. 54). In other words, for many Black Christians, the central tenet to the New Thought Movement that one can speak things into reality was nothing new.

During the Great Depression in the 1920s and 1930s, Black Americans, who were already economically oppressed, faced even more hardships. Hoping to find more social and economic opportunities, many Black Americans moved out of rural areas and into large southern and northern cities such as Chicago, Detroit, Birmingham, Cleveland, Atlanta, and New York City. Known as the Great Migration, the massive exodus of Black people into big cities allowed for an explosion of religious and cultural creativity (Hladky, 2012, p. 87). While the New Thought Movement was dwindling within the White middle class, it found new life among Black people. During this period two popular and sometimes competing figures emerged, Daddy Grace and Father Divine. In her book, *Daddy Grace*, religious studies scholar Marie W. Dallam (2009) points out that many scholars writing on Black new religious movements often talk about Grace and Divine together, flattening differences and, in some cases, even confusing the two (p. 13). It is clear that they both played a major role in introducing the New Thought Movement to Black Americans and that their legacies continue with current prosperity preachers such as Creflo Dollar and T. D. Jakes. A number of the 21st-century prosperity ministries are committed to more than a popular preacher. They are determined to also uplift people who suffer personally, professionally, and economically. This chapter will discuss several Black prosperity preachers, past and present, who have taken the original philosophy a step further to create within their own communities a process to harness enough economic power to affect change.

Daddy Grace was born Marcelino Manuel da Graca in Cape Verde off the coast of northwest Africa around 1881 (Dallam, 2009, p. 4). He was raised in the Catholic Church and maintained that he was Catholic even after founding his own church. After immigrating to the United States as an adult, Grace began experimenting with other forms of Christianity (Dallam, p. 4). He founded the United House of Prayer for all People in 1919 in West Wareham, Massachusetts, and combined Holiness, Pentecostal, and Nazarene theology (Dallam, p. 43). Like many prosperity preachers, Daddy Grace was a charismatic leader who lived a lavish lifestyle that included wearing kimonos, shoulder-length hair, and two-inch long nails that were often painted red, white, and blue, as well as owning multiple cars and houses. Although he had followers from all socioeconomic backgrounds, Grace mainly attracted poor Black people with his promise that they would live a better life by placing their faith and money in his hands (Harrison, 2005, p. 133). He used offerings to buy the House of Prayer and gave his followers an actual stake in the church (Mitchem, 2007, p. 58). Members created a closed community, as Grace discouraged them from associating with outsiders (Dallam, p. 44). The excess money was used to start a number of businesses that helped put money back into the church, including restaurants that fed the needy in the community and housing for senior citizens (Adams, 2002).

Little is known about Father Divine's early life. Scholars suggest his name might have been George Baker Jr. or Frederick Edwards and he was born in North Carolina, Maryland, or Georgia (Mitchem, 2007, p. 57). The mystery surrounding his early life only added to Divine's mystique as a popular preacher. What is known for certain is that Father Divine founded the International Peace Mission Movement in Long Island, New York. A staunch antiracist, Divine toured the country preaching to integrated audiences about the need for racial and social justice. Divine reached some level of success on this end, as nearly half of his followers were White, including upper-class people, as far as England (Griffith, 2001, p. 119). Additionally, he encouraged women to shake themselves of their traditional roles that left them in the private sphere (Mitchem, p. 58). Members lived in communal enclaves, laboring for the good of the community. Instead of lobbying the U.S. government to correct the country's racist structures, like other religious leaders, such as Martin Luther King Jr. and Jesse Jackson, Divine encouraged his members to pursue entrepreneurial ventures that would provide them with a sense of autonomy (Mitchem, p. 59). The Peace Mission owned several restaurants, grocery stores, and barber shops, allowing the community to be largely self-sufficient.

While these preachers were important to the early development of prosperity gospel, the doctrine came to center stage through Kenneth Hagin and the Word of Faith movement in the 1960s. Not all people who support prosperity gospel are members of the Word of Faith movement, however their influence is undeniable. After having spent much of his childhood bedridden and receiving several visions from God, Hagin started his preaching career as an Assemblies of God pastor in Texas in 1949. He converted to Pentecostalism and went on the road as a missionary soon after (Hladky, 2012, p. 89). While Hagin is credited with starting the Word of Faith movement, he is indebted to E. W. Kenyon. Many of Hagin's sermons are inspired by or directly taken from Kenyon's writings, synthesizing New Thought, Unity Church ideas, and Pentecostalism into one theology (Hladky, 2012, p. 90; Souders, 2011, p. 29). In 1974, Hagin opened up the Rhema Bible Training Center in order to train an "army" of prosperity gospel ministers (Souders, p. 43). One of his earliest students to emerge from Rhema was Kenneth Copeland who would go on to become Hagin's spiritual successor (Souders, p. 43). Copeland, along with Frederick K. Price would bring prosperity gospel to television for the first time in the late 1970s, ushering in a decade dominated by White televangelists such as Jim and Tammy Faye Bakker, Jimmy Swaggart, and Benny Hinn.

Following a series of fraud and adultery scandals involving prosperity preachers, many of whom were associated with the Faith movement, the 1990s saw the rise of what some call "soft prosperity." Preachers began to tie mental fitness to financial success (Bowler, 2013, p. 125). This philosophy suggested that people had to get in the "right state of mind" before they could truly prosper. Soft prosperity gospel is therapeutic and has a self-help message that even non-Christians can get behind (Bowler, p. 125). Notable soft prosperity preachers include two of the preachers this chapter will focus on, T. D. Jakes and Creflo Dollar.

One of the most important elements of prosperity gospel involves reinterpreting Jesus's role. Through Jesus's death and resurrection, faithful Christians were given a total victory, ensuring physical and financial prosperity (Lee, 2005, p. 99). Conversely, poverty within prosperity gospel is characterized as a curse from the devil, which comes from lack of faith and trust in God. One central element included from the World of Faith movement is the belief that God provides physical and financial prosperity to all faithful followers. Members can claim their divine right to individual prosperity through positive confession, offerings, and persistent faith (Hladky, 2012, p. 83). Through positive confession, adherents are literally able to will reality through proper faith in God. Perhaps the most well-known element of prosperity gospel is "seed faith giving." Believers sow a seed of faith by providing an offering to the church in the hopes of reaping the reward of faithfulness in the future.

This soft prosperity gospel represents a significant change in the movement. It has become popular around the world because it allows people to measure their faith, and then figure out where their shortcomings lie and make improvements (Bowler, 2013, p. 77). Believers are not passive participants in their faith, just handing over their money; they are told in order to prosper they must open themselves up to hear, speak, and do God's word (Bowler, p. 65).

THE IMPACT OF MEDIA ON PROSPERITY GOSPEL

Like many Americans, on Sundays when she cannot make it to her own church, my grandmother will tune into her favorite televangelist. In her case, it is Joel Osteen. With the proliferation of media, many people have access to the Word of God as interpreted by televised prosperity ministers 24/7 through television, the Internet, and various publications. Media have been important for prosperity preachers in gaining and maintaining followers, as well as increased fundraising. Black Protestants have used new media technologies to recruit members and fundraise for their churches since the early 1920s (Walton, 2011, p. 175). The popularization of prosperity gospel and the founding of the Word of Faith movement enabled Black ministers to play an important role in disseminating information through the use of technology. In fact, one of the first prosperity gospel ministers to preach on national television was Frederick K. Price, a Black minister who founded the Crenshaw Christian Center, based in California (Souders, 2011, p. 43).

Offering nonstop Christian programming, the Trinity Broadcasting Network (TBN), owned by Paul and Jan Crouch, and the Christian Broadcasting Network (CBN), founded by Pat Robertson, are two of the largest Christian-centered televangelism channels in the United States. Via satellite television, TBN and CBN can be found in the Caribbean, Western Europe, and parts of South America. Sermons from T. D. Jakes and Creflo Dollar can be heard on both channels, as well as on their websites. Owning a cable network or being able to buy airtime on a station is an opportunity for such preachers to display their success and ultimately prove that their message of prosperity is true. It also helps to increase the church's wealth though a broad base of giving.

On several occasions, I have watched live streams of Creflo Dollar's Sunday service on my laptop from the comfort of my bedroom instead of getting dressed in my "Sunday best" and joining fellow members of my community to hear a minister preach in person. Some might argue that televangelism undermines the commitment of Black churches to community building and group empowerment. In her book *Between Sundays*, anthropologist Marla Frederick (2003) confirms such suspicions by pointing out that televangelists have been successful because of their individualistic framing (p. 145). However, she argues that tuning into televangelists can provide means for individual empowerment because of a "make things better" approach (2003, p. 134). Viewers have access to sermons covering specific topics like marital, financial, and health problems, as well as personal issues that might affect them throughout the entire week.

In reality the use of media does not allow for much community building, especially when that community extends across several states and, in some cases, across continents. However, social media has been helpful in providing a broader mental sense of community among participants, as well as a quasi-connection with their leader. Facebook, Twitter, and Instagram allow followers to get up-to-date information about mission trips, services, or other activities in their preacher's life. For instance, T. D. Jakes has 1.5 million Twitter followers. He uses the platform to promote his books and conferences, as well as to help promote other preachers. Jakes often posts pictures of the large, diverse crowds that attend his services, conveying to the audience both his popularity and commitment to racial integration.

UNDERSTANDING TODAY'S PROSPERITY PREACHERS

The evolution of Creflo Dollar and T. D. Jakes must be put in proper context to understand how their ministries fit within the historical development of Black religion in the United States. Both grew up in the South and started their ministries after the height of the Civil Rights Movement. Following this period, communities became more integrated and Black people had more economic opportunities, yet this did not mean that Black people's lives were without struggle. People needed a theology to explain how, despite the advancements made since the mid-1960s, some Black people continued to live in abject poverty while others seemed to succeed in all aspects of their lives. The prior message that had once been directed toward the poor and disenfranchised seemed to fit better with the middle class and upwardly mobile. However, as the great recession of the 21st century, characterized by the loss of home mortgages and high rates of unemployment hit, Blacks and the already poor are disproportionately affected.

It is not my intention to breeze over the controversies that surround prosperity gospel, but rather to provide a more balanced view. The lavish lifestyle that many prosperity preachers live while some members of their flock live in poverty has drawn criticism from outsiders and in 2007 resulted in a Senate investigation headed by Sen. Chuck Grassley of Iowa (Bowler, 2013, p. 196). However, as Walton (2009) points out, painting all prosperity preachers as dishonest showmen and their parishioners as hapless victims robs the millions of people who attend or tune in to services every week of their agency (p. 168). These preachers are selling something that people already believe in and in many cases parishioners actually encourage their leaders to live a comfortable lifestyle. I would argue that not only are prosperity church members active participants in the creation and transmission of the message, but the rhetoric and actions of current Black prosperity preachers offer a tradition of Black religious movements that focus on social uplift. And while the attention to individualism might be a new and somewhat problematic addition, it might be necessary to maintain followers in a postmodern world.

Central to Jakes' and Dollar's ministries, as with many others, is the emphasis on members providing money to the organizations through tithing. Generally speaking, tithing is considered to be an obligation and involves giving one's church 10% of earnings. One might see tithing as another burden for people, especially when so many struggle to pay their household bills. However, as Frederick (2003) points out, tithing gives members a stake in the institution, which can be an empowering act (p. 171). Additionally, when those funds are used to support the charitable wing of these churches, tithers are helping to build and maintain their communities. When examining the ministries of T. D. Jakes and Creflo Dollar, it is clear that most Black prosperity churches are in fact promoting a form of social uplift for their parishioners. With the use of technology connecting people across states, countries, and continents, the community can no longer be defined by geographical proximity. Instead, it should be reimagined as people connected by shared interests and beliefs.

PRESTIGE MINISTRIES

Today the spiritual son of Kenneth Copeland, Creflo Dollar is one of the most popular Black preachers in the Word of Faith movement. Born in 1962 in College Park, Georgia, Creflo Dollar's early life was fairly average, missing the dramatic upbringing that is common among many charismatic preachers. He was raised in a two-parent household during which his hometown was slowly integrating. Dollar did not become particularly religious until his freshman year of college when he accepted Christ (Mumford, 2011, p. 219). Originally, he had entered college with the hopes of becoming a professional football player. However, after an injury ended his career plans, Dollar turned his attention to studying the Bible with his roommate (Mumford, p. 219). He became an ordained Baptist minister and began the World Changers Church with the help of his wife Taffi in his former high school cafeteria. Within three years, his ministry outgrew the cafeteria. Eventually Dollar moved his church to Atlanta, and grew his church's membership to more than 30,000 people with satellite churches in locations such as Boston, Cleveland, and Australia.

The basic component of World Changers is the same. A person who attends church meetings, donates monthly, and helps recruit others to donate can become a partner. This partnership with the Creflo Dollar Ministries, the charitable wing of Dollar's church, involves a "mutual exchange of faithfulness" (CDM Partnership, n.d.). In other words, for providing a financial commitment, the Dollars promise to pray for all of their partners and the community. They believe through their prayers it is possible for partners to prosper financially, mentally, and spiritually. In essence, partners are sowing seeds twice: once for themselves and another for the community. In addition to the partners' motives, the financial contribution is also used to fund a number of significant services including providing meals to the homeless, care for the elderly, drug rehab, and guidance on how to start a business.

Perhaps the most noteworthy service offered by Creflo Dollar Global Missions is the charitable branch of World Changers Church International, Prestige Ministry. This ministry is focused on reaching out to women involved in sex work and adult entertainment. It is broken into two parts: diversion and outreach. Through the diversion aspect, which has a partnership with the Atlanta court system, those that want to get out of that life have access to GED and job-training classes, credit counseling, drug recovery, and housing assistance. Taffi Dollar and her volunteers also engage in outreach by going to strip clubs and areas where sex workers congregate. They hand out care packages that include food and towels, as well as information on the ministry. While Creflo Dollar might be the head of World Changers Church, the Prestige Ministry was founded and is run by his wife, Taffi, who is a co-pastor in the church. Prestige Ministry focuses on a group of people who are often ignored in traditional Black churches and addresses a problem that has plagued the Black community for some time. Like Jakes, Dollar got his start by appealing to women, who continue to make up the majority of his membership.

THE POTTER'S HOUSE

Born in Charleston, West Virginia, in 1957, T. D. Jakes' childhood was marred with struggles. He cared for his father who suffered from terminal kidney disease and he watched his parents get divorced (Walton, 2009, p. 104). Jakes began preaching in an apostolic church on the Ohio-West Virginia border at the age of nineteen. He quickly climbed the ranks within the church and became a bishop by the age of thirty-one (Walton, 2009, p. 105). With the help of his wife Serita Jakes founded his own church in 1979 and worked tirelessly for ten years to build his membership base. He finally struck gold with his Sunday school class, Woman Thou Art Loosed, which helped women spiritually and psychologically recover from sexual abuse and domestic violence (Walton, 2009, p. 105). The class became so popular that Jakes adapted it for an annual conference presentation, a book, a play, and eventually a movie starring Hollywood heavy hitters Kimberly Elise and Loretta Devine. In 1996, he had enough money and followers to move his ministry, which he named the Potter's Church, to Dallas, Texas.

Many scholars, including social ethicist Jonathan L. Walton (2009), have challenged whether T. D. Jakes is a prosperity gospel preacher (p. 109). Jakes has been very critical of prosperity gospel and the excess of some prosperity preachers. On November 17, 2009, during an interview with Larry King, Jakes explained, "I don't consider myself a prosperity preacher." He went on to deny that any of the tithes and offerings of the church go to him, declaring that his money comes from his books, productions, and investments (King, 2009). Still, others, like sociologist Shayne Lee (2005), who has written extensively on Jakes and his ministries, place Jakes squarely within the prosperity gospel movement, pointing to his ostentatious lifestyle, fundraising efforts to help expand his empire, and his connection to other Word of Faith ministers (p. 104).

This chapter argues that despite the label, Jakes has done much to broaden what it means to preach and live prosperously. While financial success might be a sign of God's blessings, for T. D. Jakes and his followers, it is also a call to give back to one's community, both local and global. This can be attributed to Jakes' Pentecostal roots. Increasingly, upwardly mobile Black Pentecostals are changing their views of the world and materialism. As Marla Frederick (2012) writes, they are no longer trying to escape from the world; rather they are investing in fixing it up (p. 388). Jakes challenges his followers to move beyond spreading the "good news" to non-Christians in distant lands, arguing that Christians must help build other's religiosity, but more important their economy. Unlike Dollar's mission, much of the work done by Jakes' followers is not done in the hopes of receiving future blessings from God; rather it is a sacrifice made by those who are in the privileged position to give. This is what Frederick calls an emphasis on care (2012, p. 384).

One example is Jakes' community service ministry Megacare. In 2008 when Jakes held the MegaFest, an annual two-day festival, in Soweto, South Africa, hundreds of parishioners from the United States, the Caribbean, and the United Kingdom made the journey for fellowship and to provide aid. Those who could not make the expensive trip were able to watch the conference online and were encouraged to donate to sustain the aid. The trip to Soweto, which featured tours of shantytowns and meeting with locals, was meant to give American parishioners an image of true poverty, for, as Jakes argues, impoverished people in the United States would be considered wealthy by South African standards (Frederick, 2012, p. 391).

Overseas, MegaCare offers free health exams, including HIV/AIDS screening and builds wells to provide clean water. It is telling that Jakes chose South Africa as the site for his first MegaFest International. There are areas of the world in as much need and even closer to home than South Africa, such as Central

America or even Appalachia. Yet, it does not hold the same emotional or socio-cultural connection for Jakes and his Black followers, who account for his largest membership base. For them, South Africa represents an imagined homeland and Jakes' Black followers are successful children returning to help their siblings in Christ rebuild. By going to Soweto, instead of simply sending money there, Jakes was making an important stand. For Jakes, boosting a region's economy by renting hotel rooms, hiring workers to build structures, and purchasing handmade goods can make a bigger impact than donating money. His goal is to lend a helping hand and empower others rather than giving a handout.

A NEW FORM OF PROSPERITY GOSPEL

In both of these examples, we see that although the two churches are not focused on structural changes to ease the suffering of Black people both in the United States and the diaspora, they are trying to provide help for greater access to wealth and health with the potential to affect change. For the most part, the emphasis is on finances rather than race relations. We cannot ignore that both ministries choose issues that largely affect Black people around the world, such as HIV/AIDS and domestic violence. Which means, while these ministries might hope to be postracial and aim for individualist interpretations, they are not ignorant to the reality.

It has not been my goal to compare Creflo Dollar and T. D. Jakes. My examination of the two preachers was designed to articulate how prosperity gospel is expanding among Black Christians. Jakes' ministries seem to be committed to services for others based on community good, while Dollar's ministries may have a somewhat more inward approach, helping others while helping oneself.

Furthermore, Jakes' ministries seem to have more room for critiques of racism and systematic oppression because he is not restricted by the same institutional norms as Dollar. The Word of Faith movement was founded and remains under the control of White preachers, who espouse a postracial ideology. While they recognize that this country has been plagued by institutional racism, these leaders argue that that time has passed. They suggest that any individual prejudice can be alleviated through integration and reconciliation. Dollar's own rise to prominence was partly due to a dispute with Frederick K. Price, the leading Black minister in the Faith movement, and the Hagin family. Price heard a sermon by Kenneth Hagin Jr. in which he denounced interracial marriages (Walton, 2009, p. 148). Angered by this racism, Price turned to the elder Hagin in hopes of gaining his support. Instead, Hagin Sr. sided with his son, causing Rev. Price to begin a campaign against racism within the Word of Faith movement and Christianity in general (Walton, 2009, p. 148). His rejection of the postracial ideology that fuels the movement led to Price's marginalization within the Faith community. He was given less airtime on major Christian networks and many of his White ministerial allies distanced themselves from him. Dollar was aware of this incident, which means he may only push his ministry so far. As an independent preacher with a large membership base and stable finances, T. D. Jakes is in a better position to develop and pursue a broader prosperity message.

As sociologist Milmon Harrison (2005) points out, Black American religious institutions have never been solely dedicated to matters of the spiritual realm. The political, social, and material needs of their followers have always been a priority (p. 133). This commitment to provide for the needs of Black people was embodied in the missions of early Black New Thought proponents such as Father Divine and Daddy Grace although not to the same extent. While Dollar and Jakes might have borrowed language and ideas from White prosperity preachers, they have continued to further a distinctively Black version of prosperity gospel that seeks to improve the lives of those who strive for success.

BIBLIOGRAPHY

Adams, F. (2002, August 16). *Oral History Interview R-0168*. Southern Oral History Program Collection (#4007). Wilson Library, University of North Carolina at Chapel Hill.

Bowler, K. (2013). *Blessed: A history of the American prosperity gospel*. Oxford & New York: Oxford University Press.

CDM Partnership. (n.d.). Retrieved from http://www.creflodollarministries.org/About/Partnership.aspx

Dallam, M. W. (2009). *Daddy Grace: A celebrity preacher and his house of prayer*. New York: New York University Press.

Frederick, M. (2003). *Between Sundays: Black women and everyday struggles of faith*. Berkeley & Los Angeles: University of California Press.

Frederick, M. (2012). Neo-Pentecostalism and globalization. In R. A. Orsi (Ed.), *Cambridge companion to religious studies* (pp. 380–402). New York: Cambridge University Press.

Griffith, R. M. (2001). Body salvation: New thought, Father Divine, and the feast of material pleasures. *Religion and American Culture: A Journal of Interpretation, 11*(2), 119–153.

Harrison, M. F. (2005). *Righteous riches: The Word of Faith movement in contemporary African American religion*. Oxford & New York: Oxford University Press.

Hladky, K. (2012). I double-dog dare you in Jesus' name! Claiming Christian wealth and the American prosperity gospel. *Religion Compass, 6*(1), 82–96.

Jones, D., & Woodbridge, R. (2010). *Health, wealth and happiness: Has the prosperity gospel overshadowed the Gospel of Christ?* Grand Rapids, MI: Kregel.

King, L. (Host). (2009, November 17). T. D. Jakes interview. *Larry King Show*. Los Angeles: CNN.

Lee, S. (2005). *T. D. Jakes: America's new preacher*. New York: New York University.

Mitchem, S. Y. (2007). *Name it and claim it? Prosperity preaching in the Black church*. Cleveland, OH: Pilgrim.

Mumford, D. J. (2011). Rich and equal in the eyes of almighty God! Creflo Dollar and the gospel of racial reconciliation. *Pneuma, 33*, 218–236.

Souders, M. C. (2011). *A god of wealth: Religion, modernity, and the rhetoric of the Christian prosperity gospel.* Unpublished doctoral dissertation, University of Kansas, Lawrence.

Van Biema, D. (2007, October). Oral Roberts to the rescue? *Time.* Retrieved from http://content. time.com/time/nation/article/0,8599,1677098,00.html

Walton, J. L. (2009). *Watch this! The ethics and aesthetics of Black televangelism.* New York & London: New York University Press.

Walton. J. L. (2011). Introduction: Will the revolution be televised? Preachers, profits and the "post-racial" prophetic! *Pneuma, 33*, 175–179.

CHAPTER FOUR

Race and Racism: Inequalities in the Criminal Justice System

STEPHANA COLBERT

INTRODUCTION

Whether recalling the ordeal of the wrongly convicted Scottsboro Boys (Linder, 2013) or the indiscriminate imposition of the death penalty against Black defendants[1] whose crimes were often fabricated,[2] or the failure of law enforcement to protect Emmett Till[3] and the scores of African Americans lynched or on whom dogs and high pressure water hoses were turned by sheriffs and other law enforcement during civil rights demonstrations (Hailey, 1963), there is ample historical evidence of great racial inequity in the U.S. criminal justice system for African Americans.

Today, there are a number of critical areas in the criminal justice system where African Americans have been negatively impacted—including racial profiling, police brutality, the relatively new stand your ground laws, sentencing disparities, and issues affecting African American juveniles in the criminal justice system. Despite recent efforts to address racial disparities and inequities in the criminal justice system the success of those efforts has been minimal (Sherman, 2001).

In discussing African Americans and the criminal justice system, it also seems important to address African Americans as victims of crimes (Harrell, 2007) where the perpetrators of those crimes are also African American. While African Americans are still the overwhelming majority of victims of hate crimes (Elliot,

2014), African Americans are also often (nearly 78% of the time) the victims of fatal and nonfatal violent crimes where their victimizers are also Black (Weatherspoon, 2004).

RACIAL PROFILING, STOP AND FRISK LAWS, AND POLICE BRUTALITY

The historic tendency toward racial profiling of African Americans in this country when combined with what some consider the unfettered discretion given police by stop and frisk laws[4] and a lack of proper police training and/or restraint[5] leads to both incidents of police brutality and a disproportionate number of African Americans thrust into the criminal justice system. Once in the "system" African Americans are subjected to different—disparate—treatment than their White counterparts, from overcharging by police and prosecutors (Floyd & Sinclair, 2008), to bail hearings where judges consider race rather than risk of flight (Wright, 1987) to convictions based on tainted evidence as well as mandatory sentencing prescribed by laws that focus more on considerations of race than the particulars of a given crime.[6]

Racial profiling, often called "driving while Black [or Brown]" or "DWB" has been defined as

> the discriminatory practice by law enforcement [which includes police officers, security guards at department stores, and airport security] of targeting individuals for suspicion of a crime based on the individual's race, ethnicity, religion, or national original. Criminal profiling, generally, as practiced by police, is the reliance on a group of characteristics they believe to be associated with crimes.[7]

Racial profiling of African American men is considered pervasive (Weatherspoon, 2004).

In 1996, the U.S. Court of Appeals for the 9th Circuit held in *Washington v. Lambert* that

> In this nation, all people have a right to be free from the terrifying and humiliating experience of being pulled from their cars at gunpoint, handcuffed, or made to lie face down on the pavement when insufficient reason for such intrusive police conduct exists.... [I]in balancing the interests in freedom from arbitrary government intrusion and the legitimate needs of law enforcement officers, we cannot help but be aware that the burden of aggressive and intrusive police action falls disproportionately on African-American, and sometimes Latino, males...as a practical matter neither society nor our enforcement of the laws is yet color-blind...Cases, newspaper reports, books, and scholarly writings all make clear that the experience of being stopped by the police is a much more common one for Black men than it is for White men.[8]

In 1999, President Bill Clinton called racial profiling a "morally indefensible, deeply corrosive practice...[and] is in fact the opposite of good police work, where actions are based on hard facts, not stereotypes. It is wrong, it is destructive, and it must stop."[9] In 2001, then-president George W. Bush directed that racial profiling be formally banned, stating that racial profiling "is wrong and we will end it in America."[10] Also in 2001, the Community Oriented Policing Services (COPS) Office of the U.S. Justice Department funded the Reducing Racial Profiling initiative designed to "develop best practices and technical assistance guides to help police agencies reduce racial profiling while helping these agencies create and strengthen local efforts at building trust between the police and their communities."[11]

President Barack H. Obama, the 43rd president of the United States and the first African American to hold the office, sponsored a bill as an Illinois legislator seeking to record and analyze statistics of police stops in Illinois to determine whether racial profiling played a role in the stops (Seelye, 2009). After the acquittal of George Zimmerman, the Neighborhood Watch volunteer who shot and killed an unarmed 17-year-old African American, Trayvon Martin, while he was walking home from a convenience store, President Obama said, "Trayvon Martin could have been me 35 years ago" (Cohen, 2013). He was referencing racial profiling experiences of his and other African American men, as well as this country's "history of racial disparities in the application of our criminal laws." With Zimmerman's acquittal, will racial profiling now then also extend to others who ascribe to stereotypes that cause them to judge African Americans as suspicious or a threat—or even to those who dislike some aspect of African American culture (Alcindor, 2012)—with the same tragic consequences?

At the federal level, the U.S. Department of Justice has policies with respect to racial profiling, specifically "prohibit[ing] federal agents from using race as a factor in their investigations unless there is specific, credible information that makes race relevant to a case" (Apuzzo, 2014). At the state level, racial profiling is restricted against motorists and pedestrians in 16 states,[12] while 6 states have laws against racial profiling for motorists only.[13] Other states have no racial profiling ban in place at all.[14] As a result of a civil suit, New York City's practice of racial profiling mostly African American and Latino men through stop and frisk has been ruled unconstitutional.[15]

Law enforcement officials say they need the discretion to stop individuals who they believe have committed or are committing crimes (Weatherspoon, 2004). The U.S. Supreme Court has said that except on a highway, where a traffic violation is reason enough to stop an individual, law enforcement officials must have a "reasonable suspicion" that a person is armed and dangerous, even if there otherwise would not be probable cause to arrest (*Terry v. Ohio*). The key question here is where does reasonable suspicion become racial profiling and harassment?

As noted by the examples below, the consequences of racially profiling innocent African Americans have been historic, distressing, and tragic.

In 1989 the Central Park Five were five innocent African American and Latino boys, ages 14 to 16, who were rounded up, convicted, and sent to prison for 7–13 years for the brutal beating and rape of a Central Park jogger, all based on racial profiling. The actual perpetrator of the crime confessed several years after the convictions.[16] In 1995, Jonny Gammage, an African American male, was stopped while driving his cousin's Jaguar and subsequently choked to death by several New Jersey police officers (Jenkins, 1995). Amadou Diallo was shot 41 times while standing in front of his apartment building in 1999 by four New York police officers who said he fit the general description of a serial rapist—who ironically had already been caught.[17]

In Connecticut, a new law requires police departments to keep records of traffic and other stops so that after an analysis of the records, determinations can be made about whether racial profiling is continuing to occur (Merrigan, 2014). Curtailing and eradicating racial profiling may be much farther down the line.

Under the law of *Terry v. Ohio* in 1968, the U.S. Supreme Court affirmed the idea that police can briefly stop a person if law enforcement has a reasonable suspicion that the detainee was involved in a crime—even though that suspicion does not amount to probable cause to arrest.[18] If the officer also has a reasonable belief that the individual has a weapon in his or her possession that poses a danger to the officer or others, the individual may be subjected to a limited search, sufficient to determine if a weapon exists. This brief detention and search was characterized by the Court in *Terry* as "stop and frisk."

African Americans argue that the stop and frisk laws have been abused, amounting to illegal racial profiling, with the impact falling most heavily in the African American and Hispanic communities (Tunde 2012).While African Americans are not the largest group of illegal drug users, for instance, "[they] are most often stopped, questioned, searched and arrested by law enforcement."[19] New York City's stop and frisk practice perpetuated racial profiling and was ruled unconstitutional in 2013 (Gardiner, 2013). The city appealed the ruling under previous NYC mayor Michael Bloomberg even though New York City's stop and frisk law overwhelmingly (85%) targeted African American and Latino men.[20] In 2011, for instance, Black men were stopped and frisked 168,126 times. Yet, only 158,406 Black men lived in NYC at that time. That means that there were more stop and frisks of Black men in NYC that year than actual Black men living in the city (Mathias, 2012). New York City's new mayor, William de Blasio, has sought to reform New York City's stop and frisk policies by withdrawing the city's appeal in the two class-action lawsuits challenging the NYPD's stop and frisk practices (Hurtato, 2014) and by establishing a monitoring program (Iyengar & DeWast, 2014) much like Connecticut's racial profiling law.[21]

Finally, police brutality is the use of excessive physical force by law enforcement officials in the stop, arrest, or any other contact with members of the general public (Holmes, 2000). Despite the negative publicity endured by the Los Angeles and NYC police departments after the videotaped beating of Rodney King by LAPD in March 1991 and the sodomizing and brutalization of Abner Louima by NYC policemen after his arrest in 1999 (Fried, 1999), allegations of police brutality in the United States persist—and with deadly consequences (Packman, 2011). Recent cases in Oakland, New York City, Denver, Oklahoma City, and other cities throughout the country suggest that the issue of police brutality remains.[22]

After the Rodney King beating in 1991, the Violent Crime Control and Law Enforcement Act of 1994 was enacted, giving the Justice Department the authority to file a civil suit against law enforcement agencies that engage in a pattern or practice of misconduct.[23] In fact, in President Barack Obama's first term, the Justice Department launched 15 investigations of police departments (Goode, 2013). Several of those—including Seattle, Detroit, New Orleans, and Albuquerque—are under the supervision of the Justice Department as a result of brutality allegations (Wing, 2014). After an investigation of allegations of police brutality and excessive force, in May 2015, newly confirmed Attorney General Janet Lynch announced that the Justice Department had reached an enforceable agreement with City of Cleveland to reform the Cleveland Division of Police after finding a pattern or practice of excessive force.[24] Determining whether the Justice Department's investigation and subsequent oversight of and agreements with local police departments is a deterrent to incidents of police brutality remains to be seen.

Perhaps acknowledging the lack of minority representation among rank-and-file police officers and in police administration within the communities served by the police department may be a start. In New York, for instance, police officers are not required to reside in the boroughs they patrol—or in New York City for that matter (Robinson, 2006). Therefore, understanding and relating to the people and the issues inherent in the neighborhoods for which they are responsible may be difficult. An increase in minority representation on all police forces can cause police departments to be more accountable to the communities and less inclined to physical force, that is, police brutality (Smith & Holmes, 2003).

Swift and severe punishment for proven acts of police brutality may be a second step. While one police officer was charged, convicted, and jailed in the Abner Louima case, it took years to convict another individual of participating in the attack and two others who lied about it were eventually prosecuted. Initially, none of the officers in the precinct where the brutal assault occurred reported the abuse (Feuer, 2000). In the Oklahoma City case, the punishment for the officer applying a chokehold to a paramedic attempting to get his patient to a hospital was a five-day suspension (Martinez, 2009). Until a clear pattern of punishment and accountability is established for proven acts of police brutality, African American communities can have little confidence that such practices will end.

DISPARITIES IN SENTENCING OF AFRICAN AMERICANS

African Americans who are on the receiving end of racial profiling, stop and frisk policies, and police brutality often end up arrested, charged, and convicted of crimes. Despite the fact that the majority of crimes are not committed by minorities, minority defendants are charged with crimes requiring a mandatory minimum prison sentence more often than their White counterparts. African Americans comprise approximately 13% of the population of the United States; however, according to the Bureau of Justice Statistics, one in three Black men—33%—can expect to go to prison in their lifetime (Carson & Sabol, 2012).

Moreover, we now know that many African Americans will go to prison for crimes they did not commit. The discovery of innocence in several high-profile cases may result in some reparation or recompense for the wrongful convictions; however, such innocent defendants often serve significant time in prison with low odds in most cases of proving their innocence (Grimsley, 2013).

The statistics for Black youth and Black women are equally bleak. Black and Hispanic students experience more student-related arrests and referrals to law enforcement and are more often incarcerated in such instances and sent to adult prisons than their White peers. Although Black juveniles comprise only 16% of the youth population, 58% of their cases are moved to criminal court and 58% are sent to adult prisons. Similarly, African American women are three times more likely to be jailed than White women (Kerby, 2012).

When the disproportionate numbers of African American men, women, and youth are arrested, tried, and convicted, research shows that the sentences imposed are longer than those of their White counterparts for the same crimes. Black men are six times more likely to be incarcerated than White men, a third are under the supervision of the criminal justice system, and 12% of Black men in their 20s and 30s are incarcerated. These high incarceration rates are not due to growing crime rates but to greater use of incarceration for lesser offenses and drug offenses (Taibbi, 2014; Oliver, 2012).

Despite this grim picture, since 2005 there are some positive signs that some of the effects of historical sentencing disparities are being ameliorated if not eradicated. Examples include the passage of the Fair Sentencing Act, a recent vote by the U.S. Sentencing Commission, and two relatively recent U.S. Supreme Court cases involving juveniles, at least on the federal level. The federal Fair Sentencing Act (FSA) of 2010 reduced the crack/cocaine sentencing quantity disparity triggering mandatory minimum penalties from 100:1 to 18:1 (Grindler, 2010) and eliminated the five-year mandatory minimum sentence for simple possession of crack cocaine. California is currently attempting to pass a Fair Sentencing Act of its own, designed to have much the same effect as the federal FSA.[25]

At the insistence of then U.S. Attorney General Eric Holder on behalf of the Obama administration, in April 2014, the U.S. Sentencing Commission unanimously voted to lower penalties across drug types, resulting in a sentence reduction of about 11 months for eligible prisoners (Gotsch, 2011). In July 2014, the Commission unanimously voted to make the changes agreed upon in April retroactive. As a result, thousands of prisoners incarcerated for federal drug offenses hope to gain early release beginning in 2015.[26]

Two relatively recent court rulings affecting juveniles are important to note. First, in *Roper v. Simmons*, by a vote of 5–4, the U.S. Supreme Court, on March 1, 2005, held that the 8th and 14th Amendments forbid the execution of offenders who were under the age of 18 when their crimes were committed (Lane, 2005). The decision canceled the death sentences of 72 others for crimes they committed while younger than age 18. Prior to the *Roper* decision, there were 22 executions of juveniles since 1976, 13 of them in Texas (Lane).

More recently, on June 25, 2012, in *Miller v. Alabama*, the U.S. Supreme Court ruled that juveniles cannot be sentenced to life without the possibility of parole.[27] However, this latest ruling is not applicable—as yet—to all juveniles. The question of whether the ruling is retroactive, that is, will it apply to any juvenile who has previously been sentenced to life without parole, has also yet to be fully determined (Egan & Baldas, 2014).

STAND YOUR GROUND LAWS AND SELF-DEFENSE

In addition to changes to the sentencing laws and guidelines on the federal level that seem likely to benefit incarcerated African Americans, there has been a proliferation of the stand your ground laws in several states that may pose problems for both African Americans and other victims of abuse.

Florida (the first) and more than 25 other states have passed stand your ground laws or approved the castle doctrine, designed to eliminate the duty of an individual to retreat before using deadly force in self-defense (Chaney, 2014; Voloka, 2014; Li, 2014). Previously, deadly force was only legally permissible in defending one's home or family against burglars and trespassers (Lithwick, 2014). While that is still the case in some states the stand your ground law such as that adopted in Florida permits use of force, including deadly force, if you are anywhere you think you have a right to be and reasonably believe you need to use force to defend yourself or deadly force to prevent death or serious bodily harm (Mahoney, 2014a). Two recent incidents involving the stand your ground law in Florida had different, and seemingly disparate, results, one resulting in death, the other in no injury to any person.

As mentioned earlier, 17-year-old Trayvon Martin was on his way home from a trip to a convenience store armed with Skittles and juice. He was wearing a hooded sweatshirt ("hoodie") and to George Zimmerman, an armed neighborhood watch volunteer, he looked suspicious. Zimmerman called the police; they told him to stay in the car and they would investigate. Instead, he got out of his car, followed, confronted, and shot Martin dead. Zimmerman was not arrested until two months after the shooting (Robles, 2012). The police said they did not arrest him because under the stand your ground law they had to have specific evidence disproving self-defense—which they say they did not have in this case (Robles). While they did not call it stand your ground, the jury's instructions were based on that law. Zimmerman claimed self-defense and was acquitted (Spradley, 2013).

Marissa Alexander, the mother of twins and a nine-day-old infant, with no prior criminal record, fired what she described as "warning shots" into the wall of her home when confronted by her estranged, allegedly abusive husband. Alexander was lawfully in possession of the weapon; and there were no injuries. She was immediately arrested and charged with aggravated assault with a deadly weapon (Horwitz, 2012). The judge in Alexander's trial denied her motion for immunity from prosecution under Florida's stand your ground law, holding that her actions were "inconsistent with a person who is in genuine fear for his or her life" (Nelson, 2014). Although she still asserted self-defense at trial, Alexander was quickly convicted and sentenced to a mandatory 20 years in prison. The judge chose the 20-year term mandatory as Alexander discharged a weapon in the commission of a crime, which is considered aggravated assault (Nelson).

Alexander was granted a new trial in 2013 based on faulty jury instruction, and in June 2014, Florida's governor signed an amendment to the stand your ground law extending coverage to those firing a warning shot. Nonetheless, and vowing to retry Alexander—this time seeking a 60-year sentence—the state's attorney argued that the law was not retroactive and did not apply to Alexander (Maxwell, 2015). A plea deal was reached forcing Alexander to plead guilty to three counts and serve three years in prison. With credit for time served and the proviso that she serve the remainder of her time on house arrest Ms. Alexander was released from jail on January 27, 2015 (Hannan, 2014; Crockett, 2015).

CRIME IN THE AFRICAN AMERICAN COMMUNITY: BLACK VICTIMS, BLACK OFFENDERS

Chicago has John H. Johnson Enterprises (*Ebony* and *Jet*). It has Oprah. And it produced the first African American president—Barack Obama. In 2014, however, the news out of Chicago was mostly about violence—much of it involving Black victims and Black offenders (Mahoney, 2014b). And it is not just Chicago. It seems every weekend dozens of shootings and other violent activity in major cities result in serious injury or deaths of innocent people—innocent African Americans. The offenders are often young Black men and the victims are usually Black people—particularly Black children and teens for whom gun violence is the leading cause of death (Frost).

The problem received national attention after Barack Obama's second inauguration when 15-year-old Hadiya Pendleton, a participant with her Chicago-area high school band in Mr. Obama's inauguration celebration, was shot and killed a week later while gathered with her friends in a Chicago park. Two young African American men—one 18, the other 20—were arrested for her murder (Gray, 2013). According to police her murder was a case of mistaken identity by gang members who thought they were protecting their turf (Babwin, 2013).

In Chicago and elsewhere there are many more—too many—similar stories.[28] According to CNN reporter Don Lemon, "Shooting violence is up 10 percent, so much so that some residents, who celebrated when the city's controversial stop-and-frisk policy was scaled back, are now wondering if it should make a return" (Lemon, 2014). Solutions to the problem of violence within the African American community are elusive. Certainly a single solution, or any solution, may be unrealistic until we understand the causes of this level of violence, explore potential solutions, and commit to developing greater concern for each other—and most especially our children.[29] However, to stop the violence, the African American community has to be involved.

BLACK LIVES MATTER

Hands up. I can't breathe. Black Lives Matter. Justice for Tamar Rice and John Crawford. T-shirt slogans? Yes. Protest chants? Yes. Perhaps more important, these slogans appear to be a rallying cry for many Americans weary of the brutalization and unnecessary use of lethal force against African American men, women, and children. In July 2014, 43-year-old African American husband and father Eric Garner was killed by a police officer who literally choked the life out of him by continually applying an illegal choke hold, despite the fact that Mr. Garner could be heard on a video repeatedly saying, "I can't breathe" (Berman, 2014). Garner's death was precipitated by concern over his selling unlicensed cigarettes in Staten Island, New York.

In August 2014, 18-year-old unarmed Mike Brown was shot and killed by a Ferguson, Missouri, police officer while several witnesses reported his hands were up, attempting to submit to police authority. His lifeless, uncovered body was left in the street for more than four hours (Bosman & Goldstein, 2014). Despite evidence of possible wrongdoing on the part of the officers, grand juries impaneled in both cases refused to indict the police officers responsible for the deaths of Brown and Garner. The indictments would not have been guilty verdicts, but rather would have required the officers to stand trial for their actions (Goodman & Baker, 2014).

In November 2014, seconds after pulling up to 12-year-old African American Tamir Rice, who was playing with a BB gun in a park, two Cleveland police officers, apparently without issuing warnings, opened fire, killing him. The officers claimed they were not aware that the calls made about Rice indicated he was likely a child playing with what was probably a fake gun (Fitzsimmons, 2014). Of note, the police officer firing the fatal shots had been deemed unfit for duty in 2012 while employed by the Independence, Ohio, police department. He resigned before he was fired (Mai-Duc, 2014). On January 1, 2015, it was announced that Cleveland police were conducting a search for an outside agency to investigate the killing; however, the failures to indict in the Brown and Garner killings has left much skepticism about justice in the Rice killing—with some suggesting it is unrealistic to expect justice when the police are responsible for policing themselves.

In addition to Black men, Black women also suffer injustice and brutality. In August 2014, a California Highway Patrol officer was caught on camera mercilessly beating a homeless woman, Melissa Barclay, on the side of the highway. He says he was trying to help her; the video suggests otherwise (Demarinis, 2014).[30] In January 2015, Daniel Holtzclaw, a police officer in Oklahoma City, was charged with 36 felonies, including 13 counts of rape and sexual misconduct. His alleged victims were primarily African American women whom he stopped while acting in his capacity as an on-duty police officer. Despite the number and gravity of the charges, he was given bail—which was extended even after he violated the conditions of that bail (Holloway, 2014). The Holtzclaw charges perhaps most clearly demonstrate the issues addressed by Professor Kali Nicole Gross in her article "Demands for Justice Are Failing Black Women and Girls" (2015). The rallies and protests of the killings of African American boys and men have yet to shed significant light on the brutalization and killings of African American women—in other words, the cries for justice for men of color must also apply to women of color. Black lives—both male and female—matter.

One of the most prominent examples occurred on July 10, 2015 in Waller County, Texas. Sandra Bland, a 28-year-old African American woman while en route to a new job at her alma mater, Prairie View A&M University in Texas, was pulled over by state trooper Brian Encinia for failing to signal a lane change—a minor traffic infraction. The stop escalated into her being thrown on the ground, handcuffed and arrested for allegedly assaulting the state trooper. On July 13, 2015, Ms. Bland was found dead in her Waller County jail cell, allegedly having hanged herself. Despite an autopsy by a Texas County medical examiner, which ruled Ms. Bland's death a suicide, on July 16, Texas authorities and the FBI announced a joint investigation into Bland's death and the Waller County district attorney's office said that Ms. Bland's death would be investigated as a possible murder (Crockett, 2015).

We are a broken society with respect to race relations and racism. A large component of that reality is the endemic brokenness of our criminal justice system—from law enforcement to prosecutors to grand juries, to judges to legislators who sit on their hands as injustice reigns. These are facts that in light of events unfolding in recent months are hardly in dispute. Is there any hope? Perhaps.

These most recent killings of African Americans at the hands of law enforcement have made news and sparked protests across the country—violent and peaceful. The protests have been joined by concerned citizens of all races, creeds, and colors—including a surprising number of high-profile athletes and celebrities.[31] As despair turns into activism the challenge is to determine how these demonstrations can lead to meaningful change. Will the crowds dwindle, the voices become muted and then silent—signaling a return to the status quo? Or will this time be different? There is precedent for change—the Civil Rights Movement of the 1950s and 1960s, where Black folk stopped sitting in the back of the bus and started on the road to equality.

Ava DuVernay, the African American woman who directed *Selma* (2014), said she was concerned that the movie, which focused on civil rights leader Martin Luther King and the marches and protests he led in Selma, Alabama, and elsewhere in the 20th century, demanding an end to the second-class citizenship of African Americans, would not be currently relevant in the 21st century. Then Michael Brown was killed and she added, "We were here talking about the marches of Selma and I could hear people marching outside…(referencing the tens of thousands of demonstrators marching in New York City and around the nation in 2014). For this piece of art to meet this cultural moment is something that was never designed…and, to me, it's a jaw dropper" (Serjeant, 2014).

CONCLUSION

This is admittedly a bleak picture, but there are glimmers of hope: new sentencing laws and policies; Justice Department oversight of failing police departments where excessive force is the norm; efforts like those in NYC to ameliorate the inequities of its stop and frisk laws; laws regarding the death penalty and life sentences that give juveniles a second chance; protests that bring much needed attention to the discrepancies in the criminal justice system; and efforts within the African American community to curb the violence and care for our children—from preventing the influx of guns into our communities[32] to actions like President Obama's My Brother's Keeper Initiative,[33] focusing on mentoring and education.[34]

Finally, there is hope for an end to the racial disparities that have been discussed here. Whether these glimmers of hope turn into bursts of change or a return to clouds of despair is a conscious choice that we as individuals and as the collective citizens of these United States must make—and live with.

NOTES

1. U.S. Department of Justice (death penalty statistics indicate that of the 682 defendants sentenced to death between 1995 and 2000 48% were African American, 29% Hispanic, and 20% White). See also Baldus, D. C., Pulaski, C. A., & Woodworth, G. (1990). *Equal justice and the death penalty: A legal and empirical analysis.* Boston: Northeastern University Press.

2. Cf. Black Entertainment Television series, *Vindicated*, produced in association with the Innocence Project (series highlights cases of African American defendants falsely accused). See also *An Epidemic of Prosecutorial Misconduct*, White Paper Center for Prosecutor Integrity, 2013, pp. 1–2. To date, more than 1,200 persons have been exonerated.

3. Emmett Till was a 14-year-old boy from Chicago brutally murdered while visiting relatives in Mississippi in 1955 after he was accused of flirting with a White woman. His mother insisted upon an open casket. Emmett Louis Till. (2014). http://www.biography.com/people/emmett-till-507515

4. *Terry v. Ohio*, 392 U.S. 1, 88 S. Ct. 1868, 20 L. Ed. 2d 889 (1968). (U.S. Supreme Court establishes "stop and frisk" guidelines.) See also *U.S. v. Watson*, 423 U.S. 411 (1976).

5. Cf. *African American Quality of Life Initiative*, 2007, Austin, TX (designed to improve cultural awareness within the Austin Police Department with better training and accountability). See two-year report retrieved from http://www.ci.austin.tx.us/edims/document.cfm?id=125797

6. See Innocence Project (convictions overturned where based on DNA, evidence tampering, including failure to release exculpatory evidence is demonstrated). Retrieved from www.innocenceproject.org; http://www.sentencingproject.org/crackreform/

7. Racial Profiling: Definition, ACLU (2005, November 23). Retrieved from https://www.aclu.org/racial-justice/racial-profiling-definition; see also Weatherspoon, F. D. (2004, Winter). Racial profiling of African-American males: Stopped, searched, and stripped of constitutional protection race. *Racism & the Law, 439.*

8. *Washington v. Lambert*, 98 F.3d 1181 (1996). Retrieved from http://caselaw.findlaw.com/us-9th-circuit/1228870.html

9. Attorney General's Conference on Strengthening Police-Community Relationships, Report on the Proceedings. Washington, DC, U.S. Department of Justice, June 9–10, 1999, at 22–23.

10. February 27, 2001. Address to a Joint Session of Congress; see also U.S. Department of Justice. Retrieved from http://www.justice.gov/opa/pr/2003/June/racial_profiling_fact_sheet.pdf

11. http://www.cops.usdoj.gov/default.asp?Item=463

12. Washington, California, Montana, Utah, Colorado, Nebraska, Kansas, Oklahoma, Texas, Arkansas, Illinois, Kentucky, Maine, New Jersey, and Florida.

13. Nevada, Alaska, Minnesota, Missouri, West Virginia, and Maryland.

14. Racial Profiling Laws, CivilRightsLawFirms.com. Retrieved from http://www.civilrightslawfir ms.com/civil-rights-basics/racial-profiling-discrimination-help.htm

15. *Floyd et al. v. City of New York, et al.*, 08 Civ. 1034 (AT), (2013).

16. A settlement in the Central Park jogger case. (2014, June 20). *New York Times*, editorial page. Retrieved from http://www.nytimes.com/2014/06/21/opinion/a-settlement-in-the-central-park-jogger-case.html

17. Amadou Diallo. Retrieved from http://topics.nytimes.com/top/reference/timestopics/people/d/amadou_diallo/index.html

18. *Terry v. Ohio*, 392 U.S. 1, 88 S. Ct. 1868, 20 L. Ed. 2d 889 (1968).

19. Desmond-Harris, J. (2014) Why Are Black People Nearly 4 Times as Likely to Be Arrested for Weed? *The Root, courtesy ACLU.*

20. Stop-and-Frisk Data, Racial Justice, NYCLU. Retrieved from http://www.nyclu.org/content/stop-and-frisk-data. See also *Floyd et al. v. City of New York et al.*, 08 Civ. 1034 (AT) (2013). (Out of the 2.3 million frisks between 2004 and 2012, almost 99% of the frisks failed to yield a single weapon.)

21. January 30, 2014. City of New York and Center for Constitutional Rights Announce Agreement in Landmark Stop and Frisk Case, Center For Constitutional Rights. Retrieved from press@ ccrjustice.org

22. See Hunnicutt, T., & Risling, G. (2010, November 6). Mehserle sentenced to 2 years for BART shooting. *Huffington Post*. Plocienniczak, M. (2010, July 27). New York City settles Sean Bell lawsuit. CNN. See also Bloom, D. B., & Imam, J. (2014, July 21). New York man dies after chokehold by police. CNN. Alexander Landau police beating: Denver settles lawsuit for $795,000. (2011, May, 2). Westword.

23. The Violent Crime Control and Law Enforcement Act of 1994, 42 U.S.C. § 14141.

24. Justice Department Reaches Agreement with City of Cleveland to Reform Cleveland Division of Police Following the Finding of a Pattern or Practice of Excessive Force; Retrieved from http://www.justice.gov/opa/pr/justice-department-reaches-agreement-city-cleveland-reform-cleveland-division-police

25. California's Fair Sentencing Act (SB1010). Retrieved from http://www.sentencingproject.org/detail/publication.cfm?publication_id=555&id=106

26. New rule permits early release for thousands of drug offenders. (2014, July 18). *New York Times.*

27. *Miller v. Alabama*, 132 S. Ct. 2455 (2012). See also *Graham v. Florida*, 130 S. Ct. 2011 (2010) (retroactive ruling banning life without parole for juveniles not convicted of murder).

28. Williams, C. (2014, July 30.) Detroit police: Sleeping boy, 8, shot and killed by stray bullet. Associated Press. Parker, R. (2014, July 28.). Philadelphia carjacking suspects charged with murder in death of 3 kids. *Los Angeles Times*. Community mourns 3-year-old killed by stray bullet. (2014, August 2). Associated Press. Destefano, A. M. (2014, April 15.). Gun violence in NYC on rise. *New York Newsday*. See also Pastor: Slain Chicago teen Hadiya Pendleton the face of "epidemic of violence." (2013, February 9). Associated Press; Lutz, B. J., & Petty, L. (2014, May 30) Chicago teacher killed in gang crossfire. NBC 5 Chicago.

29. Harrell, E. (2007, August). *Bureau of Justice statistics special report, Black victims of violent crimes* supra. Hardiman, T. (2012, August 28). Understanding the root cause of violence in Chicago's African-American community. *Huffington Post* Chicago Blog. See also and *The Guide to Preventing Youth Violence.* Chicago Activism. Retrieved from http://www.chicagoactivism.org/archives/10546

30. In September 2014 the CHP announced that the officer involved, Daniel Andrew, was stepping down and that the agency agreed to pay $1.5 million to settle a civil rights lawsuit brought by the victim, 51-year-old Marlene Pinnock. See *Woman beaten by CHP officer settles, but activists*

'want him in prison.' Retrieved from http://www.latimes.com/local/lanow/la-me-ln-chp-settles-woman-punched-by-officer-activists-want-charges-20140925-story.html30

31. Including Samuel Jackson; members of St. Louis Rams; Lebron James; Derrick Rose; Reggie Bush; Chris Baker; Kyrie Irving of the Cavaliers and four Nets—Kevin Garnett, Deron Williams, Jarrett Jack, and Alan Anderson; Usher, Kobe Bryant; Beyonce; Jay-Z; Macklemore; Chris Brown; Wale; and Dave Chappell. See also More Pro Athletes Joining Protests Against Police Killings in New York, Ferguson. (2014, December 9). CNN Wire; Heigl, A. (2014, December 15). Samuel L. Jackson urges celebrities to join in protesting racist police. *People Magazine.* Retrieved from http://www.people.com/article/samuel-l-jackson-video-song-eric-garner-protests

32. Cf, Peterson, I. (2014, March 20.). Race matters in efforts to curb gun violence. MSR Online. Retrieved from http://spokesman-recorder.com/?s=Race+Matters+in+Efforts+to+Curb+Gun+Violence&search+submit=GO. See also the *Guide to Preventing Youth Violence*, n28.

33. The My Brother's Keeper Initiative was designed to "break down barriers and find and develop opportunities for young African American men." Retrieved from http://www.whitehouse.gov/my-brothers-keeper

34. Black Youth Project, University of Chicago, Center for the Study of Race Politics and Culture, Chicago. Retrieved from http://research.blackyouthproject.com/; National Cares Mentoring Movement, founded in 2005 by Susan L. Taylor, New York. Retrieved from http://www.caresmentoring.org/national_cares/about_us/aboutus.aspx; Council of the Greater City Schools. (2014, October.) *A Call for Change: Providing Solutions for Black Male Achievement, Executive Report.* Retrieved from http://www.cgcs.org/cms/lib/DC00001581/Centricity/Domain/87/Black%20Male--Blueprint%20for%20Action%20Final%20Draft.pdf

REFERENCES

Alcindor, Y. (2012, April 19). Trayvon Martin's father says he warned son about stereotypes. *USA Today.* Retrieved from http://usatoday30.usatoday.com/news/nation/story/2012-04-14/african-american-parents-talk-to-sons-about-race/54258448/1

Allen, F. (2012, August 5). Gun violence leading cause of death of Black children and teens. BlackVoiceNews.com.

Apuzzo, M. (2014, January 15). U.S. to expand rules limiting use of profiling by federal agents. *New York Times.*

At least 40 shot in weekend Chicago violence. (2014, July 21). *NBC Chicago.* Retrieved from http://www.nbcchicago.com/news/local/At-Least-40-Shot-in-Weekend-Chicago-Violence-267847961.html

Babwin, D. (2012, February 12). Michael Ward and Kenneth Williams, Hadiya Pendleton's alleged killers, ordered held without bail. *Huffington Post.*

Berman, M. (2014, July 21) Investigations, outrage follow police chokehold and Eric Garner's death. *The Washington Post.* Retrieved from http://www.washingtonpost.com/news/post-nation/wp/2014/07/21/investig

Bosman, J., & Goldstein, J. (2014, August 24). Timeline for a body: 4 hours in the middle of a Ferguson street. *New York Times, p. A1.*

Carson, E. A., & Sabol, W. J. (2012). U.S. Bureau of Justice Statistics: Prisoners in 2011, Table 8. Retrieved from http://www.bjs.gov/content/pub/pdf/p11.pdf

Chaney, R. (2014, April 29). Missoula teen's death could test "castle doctrine." *Missoulian.* Retrieved from http://missoulian.com/news/local/missoula-teen-s-killing-could-test-castle-doctrine/article_4732de74-cf01-11e3-981a-0019bb2963f4.html

Cohen, T. (2013, July 19). Obama: "Trayvon Martin could have been me." CNN Politics.

Crockett, S (2015, January 28). Marissa Alexander Released From Prison. *The Root.* Retrieved from http://www.theroot.com/articles/news/2015/01/marissa_alexander_released_from_prison.html

Crockett, S. (2016, July 16). Sandra Bland Drove to Texas to Start a New Job, so How Did She End Up Dead in Jail? *The Root.* Retrieved from http://www.theroot.com/articles/news/2015/07/sandra_bland_drove_to_texas_to_start_a_new_job_so_how_did_she_end_up_dead.html?wpisrc=newsletter_jcr%3Acontent%26

Demarinis, O. (2014, July 5). California Highway Patrol officer caught on tape punching woman on freeway. LatinPost.com. Retrieved from http://www.latinpost.com/articles/16491/20140705/highway-patrolman-caught-tape-punching-woman-freeway.htm

Desmond-Harris, J. (2014, March 22). Why are Black people nearly 4 times as likely to be arrested for weed? The Root. http://www.theroot.com/articles/culture/2014/03/racial_disparities_in_marijuana_arrests_aclu_launches_advocacy_tool.html

Egan, P., & Baldas, T. (2014, July 9). Court: Mich. juvenile lifers might not get re-sentenced. *Detroit Free Press.*

Elliot, J., Jr. (2014, July 18). Hate crime investigation grows in Mississippi. *The Dispatch.* Retrieved from http://www.cdispatch.com/news/article.asp?aid=34901

Feuer, A. (2000, June 28). Ex-officers are sentenced for roles in Louima torture. *New York Times.* Retrieved from http://www.nytimes.com/2000/06/28/nyregion/3-ex-officers-are-sentenced-for-roles-in-louima-torture.html

Fitzsimmons, E. (2014, November 26). Video shows Cleveland officer shot boy in 2 seconds. *New York Times.* Retrieved from http://www.nytimes.com/2014/11/27/us/video-shows-cleveland-officer-shot-tamir-rice-2-seconds-after-pulling-up-next-to-him.html

Floyd, J., & Sinclair, B. (2008). Prosecutorial overcharging. Retrieved from http://www.johntfloyd.com/blog/prosecutorial-overcharging

Foster, H. (1963, May 4). Dogs and hoses repulse Negroes at Birmingham. *New York Times.* Retrieved from http://partners.nytimes.com/library/national/race/050463race-ra.html

Fried, J. P. (1999, May 20). In surprise, witness says officer bragged about Louima torture. *New York Times.* Retrieved from http://www.nytimes.com/1999/05/20/nyregion/in-surprise-witness-says-officer-bragged-about-louima-torture.html

Frost, F. (2013, August 14). Gun Violence Leading Cause of Death of Black Children and Teens, (citing *Children's Defense Fund Report, Protect Children, Not Guns*).

Gardiner, S. (2013, August 12). Judge rules NYPD stop and frisk practice violates rights. *The Wall Street Journal.* http://www.wsj.com/articles/SB10001424127887324085304579008510786797006

Goode, E. (2013, July 27). Some chiefs chafing as Justice Department keeps closer eye on policing. *New York Times.* Retrieved from http://www.nytimes.com/2013/07/28/us/some-chiefs-chafing-as-justice-department-keeps-closer-eye-on-policing.html?_r=0

Goodman, D. and Baker, A. (2014, December 3) Wave of Protests After Grand Jury Doesn't Indict Officer in Eric Garner Chokehold Case. *New York Times.* Retrieved from http://www.nytimes.com/2014/12/04/nyregion/grand-jury-said-to-bring-no-charges-in-staten-island-chokehold-death-of-eric-garner.html?_r=0

Gotsch, K. (2011). *Breakthrough in U.S. Drug Sentencing Reform.* The Sentencing Project.

Gray, M. (2013, January 30). Chicago girl who performed at Obama's inauguration killed in shooting. *Time.* Retrieved from http://nation.time.com/2013/01/30/chicago-girl-who-performed-at-obamas-inauguration-killed-in-shooting/

Grimsley, E. (2013, March 29). African American wrongful convictions today. Innocence Project. Retrieved from http://www.innocenceproject.org/news-events-exonerations/african-american-wrongful-convictions-today

Grindler, G. (2010, August 5). Memorandum for all Federal Prosecutors: Fair Sentencing Act of 2010. U.S. Department of Justice. Retrieved from http://www.justice.gov/sites/default/files/oip/legacy/2014/07/23/fair-sentencing-act-memo.pdf

Gross, K. N. (2015, February 21). Demands for justice are failing Black women and girls. *HuffPost* [Black Voices Blog].

Hannon, L. (2014, November 24). Alexander takes deal in criminal case; Out of jail January 27. *The Florida Times Union,* Jacksonville.com. Retrieved from http://jacksonville.com/news/crime/2014-11-24/story/alexander-takes-deal-criminal-case-out-jail-jan-27

Harrell, E. (2007, August). *Bureau of Justice Statistics Special Report, Black Victims of Violent Crimes.* U.S. Department of Justice. Retrieved from http://www.bjs.gov/content/pub/pdf/bvvc.pdf

Holloway, L. (2014, August 23). Okla. cop accused of sexually assaulting Black women. The Root. com. Retrieved from http://www.theroot.com/articles/culture/2014/08/oklahoma_city_police_officer_daniel_holtzclaw_arrested_on_sexual_assault.html

Holmes, Malcolm D. (2000). Minority threat and police brutality: Determinants of civil rights criminal complaints in U.S. municipalities. *Criminology 38* (2): 343–368.

Horwitz, J. (2012, May 29). Protecting Marissa at the expense of the next Trayvon. *Huffington Post.* Retrieved from http://www.huffingtonpost.com/josh-horwitz/protecting-marissa-at-the_b_15 51998.html

Hurtato, P. (2014, August 6). NYC withdraws challenge to U.S. stop-and-frisk police suits. Bloomberg News. Retrieved from http://www.bloomberg.com/news/articles/2014-08-06/nyc-withdraws-challenge-to-u-s-stop-and-frisk-police-suits

Iyengar, R., & DeWast, L. (2014, February 3). How will the NYPD stop-and-frisk court monitor work? *New York World.* Retrieved from http://www.thenewyorkworld.com/2014/02/03/nypd-stop-and-frisk-court-monitor/

Jenkins, B. (1995, November 27). Three White police officers charged in death of Black man. CNN News. Retrieved from http://www.cnn.com/US/9511/gammage/

Kerby, S. (2012, March 13, 2012). *Top 10 Most Startling Facts about People of Color and Criminal Justice in the United States.* Center for American Progress. Retrieved from https://www.americanprogress.org/issues/race/news/2012/03/13/11351/the-top-10-most-startling-facts-about-people-of-color-and-criminal-justice-in-the-united-states/

Lane, C. (2005, March 2). 5–4 Supreme Court abolishes juvenile executions. *Washington Post,* p. A01.

Lemon, D. (2014, July 10). Don Lemon on why stop and frisk could make a comeback, like it or not. Retrieved from http://blackamericaweb.com/2014/07/10/don-lemon-on-why-the-very-people-who-denounced-stop-and-frisk-want-it-back-fast/

Lever, A. (2009, January 1) *Ethical issues in racial profiling.* London School of Economics and Political Science.

Li, V. (2014, August 8). States with stand-your-ground laws have seen an increase in homicides, reports task force. *ABA Journal*. Retrieved from http://www.abajournal.com/news/article/states_with_stand_your_ground_laws_have_more_homicides

Linder, D. (2013, February). The "Scottsboro Boys" trials. Retrieved from http://law2.umkc.edu/faculty/projects/FTrials/scottsboro/scottsb.htm

Lithwick, D. (2014, February 25). "Stand your ground" nation. Slate.com. Retrieved from http://www.slate.com/articles/news_and_politics/jurisprudence/2014/02/_stand_your_ground_nation_from_trayvon_martin_to_jordan_davis_how_our_understanding.html

Mahoney, G. (2014a, June). Florida extends "stand your ground" to include warning shots. ABC News. Retrieved from http://abcnews.go.com/US/florida-extends-stand-ground-include-warning-shots/story?id=24244906

Mahoney, G. (2014b, July 7). More than 60 shot, 9 dead in Chicago's bloody holiday weekend July 7, 2014. ABC News. Retrieved from http://abcnews.go.com/US/violence-mars-chicago-holiday-weekend-50-reportedly-injured/story?id=24446308

Mai-Duc, C. (2014, December 3). Cleveland officer who killed Tamar Rice had been deemed unfit for duty. *Los Angeles Times*. Retrieved from http://touch.latimes.com/#section/-1/article/p2p82176167/

Martinez, E. (2009, July 23). Trouper who choked medic suspended. CBS News. Retrieved from http://www.cbsnews.com/news/trooper-who-choked-medic-suspended/

Mathias, C. (2012, May 15). NYPD stop and frisks: 15 shocking facts about a controversial program. *Huffington Post*. http://www.huffingtonpost.com/2012/05/13/nypd-stop-and-frisks-15-shocking-facts_n_1513362.html

Maxwell, Z. (2015, January 29). How stand your ground laws failed Marissa Alexander. *Essence Magazine*. Retrieved from http://www.essence.com/2015/01/29/how-stand-your-ground-laws-failed-marissa-alexander/

Merrigan, M. (2014, April 10). Connecticut makes "significant" progress on tracking racial profiling. *New Haven Register*. Retrieved from http://www.nhregister.com/general-news/20140410/connecticut-makes-significant-progress-on-tracking-racial-profiling

Nelson, S. (2014, March 3). Marissa Alexander now faces 60 years for 'warning shot' at abusive husband. *US NEWS*. Retrieved from http://www.usnews.com/news/articles/2014/03/03/marissa-alexander-now-faces-60-years-for-warning-shot-at-abusive-husband

Oliver, P. (2012). *Racial Disparities in Criminal Justice*. University of Wisconsin, Institute for Research on Poverty and the National Science Foundation. Retrieved from http://www.ssc.wisc.edu/~oliver/RACIAL/RacialDisparities.htm#WisconsinDisparitiesProject

Packman, D. (2011, April 5). *2010 National Police Misconduct Reporting Project*. Cato Institute. Retrieved from http://www.policemisconduct.net/statistics/

Robinson, G. (2006, April 17). Residency requirements. *Gotham Gazette*. Retrieved from http://www.gothamgazette.com/index.php/topics/3218-residency-requirements

Robles, F. (2012, March 27). Sanford cops sought warrant to arrest George Zimmerman in Trayvon Martin shooting. *Tampa Bay Times*. Retrieved from http://www.tampabay.com/news/publicsafety/crime/sanford-cops-sought-warrant-to-arrest-george-zimmerman-in-trayvon-martin/1222259

Seelye, K. (2009, July 23). Obama wades into a volatile racial issue. *New York Times*. Retrieved from http://www.nytimes.com/2009/07/23/us/23race.html

Serjeant, J. (2014, December 18). U.S. racial justice quest comes full circle in film "Selma." *Reuters*. Retrieved from http://www.reuters.com/article/2014/12/18/us-film-selma-idUSKBN0JW29E2 0141218

Sherman, L. (2001, July). *Trust and Confidence in the Criminal Justice System*. Fels Center of Government, University of Pennsylvania, Philadelphia.

Smith, B., & Holmes, M. (2003). Community accountability, minority threat and police brutality: An examination of civil rights criminal complaints. *Criminology, 41*, 1035–1037.

Spradley, J. (2013, July 13). George Zimmerman not guilty: Jury lets Trayvon Martin killer go. *Huffington Post*. Retrieved from http://www.huffingtonpost.com/news/george-zimmerman-not-guilty/

Taibbi, M. (2014). *The divide: American injustice in the age of the wealth gap*. New York: Spiegel & Grau.

Tunde. (2012, June 19). Stop & frisk: Racial profiling or keeping us safe? Single Black Male. http://www.singleblackmale.org/2012/06/19/stop-frisk-racial-profiling-or-keeping-us-safe/

Volokh, E. (2014, June 27). What "stand your ground" laws actually mean. *Washington Post*. Retrieved from http://www.washingtonpost.com/news/volokh-conspiracy/wp/2014/06/27/what-stand-your-ground-laws-actually-mean/

Weatherspoon, F. D. (2004). Racial profiling of African American males: Stopped, searched, stripped of constitutional protection race, racism & the law. *John Marshall Law Review, 38*(2).

Wing, N. (2014, December 5). What the Justice Department finds when it investigates city police is truly disturbing. *Huffington Post*. Retrieved from http://www.huffingtonpost.com/2014/12/05/justice-department-police-review_n_6271660.html

Wright, B. (1987). *Black robes, White justice*. Secaucus, NJ: L. Stuart.

CHAPTER FIVE

Attaining Wealth: The African American Struggle for the "American Dream"

LATOYA T. BRACKETT

INTRODUCTION

African Americans have been working since emancipation in hopes of attaining the "American dream", and some free Black men even before then. They have been trying to accomplish this goal using the accepted path: get an education, get a job, get married, buy a house, have a family, work until retirement age, retire and live off of savings and accomplished wealth. This is the order that most American people believe that the "American dream" will manifest (Rank, 2014). However, many African Americans cannot follow this route due to the systematic discrimination that occurs during, among other things, secondary education. Higher education success can impact job discrimination in hiring practices and income discrepancies, in mortgage lending practices, and fewer opportunities of inheritance. These are not the only concerns African Americans have to deal with on the road to accumulating wealth but are some of the hardest hitting. In 2013, Thomas Shapiro, Tatjana Meschede, and Sam Osoro published their 25-year study *The Roots of the Widening Racial Wealth Gap: Explaining the Black–White Economic Divide*. Their research showed the discrepancies between these two groups. This study found that the wealth gap between Whites and African Americans grew by $152,000 over the 25-year span, with Whites attaining the most wealth. The study concluded that such disparities in wealth occurred because of the following discriminatory practices in order from most influential to least: homeownership, household income, unemployment, college education, and financial support or inheritance.

This chapter will discuss what wealth is and provide further documentation about the racial disparities between Whites and African Americans. It will discuss the meritocracy myth of education and success and how education may make wealth that much more difficult for low-income individuals to attain. In addition, an exploration of the difficulties of obtaining and maintaining employment and equal pay across racial and gender lines will be included. The process of buying a home and how lending practices and home location hinder wealth growth for African Americans who do have the opportunity to purchase a home is examined. Last, this chapter will discuss how financially supporting family members deters from growing wealth and how, despite minimal opportunities of inheritance, African Americans cannot grow their wealth at the same rate as Whites. What will be examined throughout this chapter is how, despite all attempts to attain wealth, African Americans continually face discriminatory setbacks that disallow obtaining that rags-to-riches-dream—that "American dream."

WEALTH AND ITS RACIAL DIVIDE

When one thinks of the word "wealth," it is mostly spoken in terms of owning expensive homes and cars, a lucrative business, and having financial advisors to ensure that they remain wealthy. Most Americans strive for something less extravagant than this; they strive to be financially stable with room for vacations, education for their children and a comfortable retirement. In order to have that extra money to make this a reality, one must obtain a positive wealth status. For example, the U.S. Census defines wealth or one's net worth as "the sum of the market value of assets owned by every member of the household minus liabilities owed by household members" (Gottschalck, Vornovytskyy, & Smith, 2011). To put it in basic terms it is one's assets minus one's liabilities, and there is such a thing as a negative net worth. Assets range from stocks, home ownership, vehicles, and checking accounts. Liabilities range from mortgages, vehicle loans, credit card debt, educational loans, and medical debt. It is almost impossible for the majority of Americans to obtain assets without liabilities. Most African Americans have more liabilities than assets in comparison to their White counterparts, which creates a major wealth gap between the two groups. There are five major reasons as to why this gap exists in the first place, why it continues to exist, and why it is growing (Shapiro, Meschede, & Osoro, 2013).

In 2011 the U.S. Census Bureau reported that the net worth of non-Hispanic Whites was $110,500 while the African American net worth was $6,314. This amounts to a gap in excess of $100,000. The research conducted by the IASP was based on data collected from the Panel Study of Income Dynamics beginning in 1968. The data that Shapiro and colleagues (2013) analyzed was specifically from 1984 through 2009. They evaluated 1,700 households of working-age persons and the gap they found is even more staggering than the 2011 Census data. In 1984 the net worth difference between Whites and African Americans was approximately $80,000. Twenty-five years later the gap grew to be more than $235,000 separating the two groups. According to the date analyzed by Shapiro, Meschede, and Osoro (2013), the White household net worth, in the IASP study, grew from $90,851 in 1984 to $265,000 in 2009, while the African American net worth grew from $5,781 to only $28,500 over the same span of time (p. 2). Testing various possibilities for this gap increase and the small wealth growth among African American households, they found the primary predictors of the wealth growth were: (1) the number of years of homeownership, (2) household income, (3) the occurrences and lengths of unemployment, (4) college education and financial support/inheritance, and (5) the number of years of home ownership. These five reasons will be used to determine how the wealth gap can be diminished in the 21st century.

GET AN EDUCATION

What most Americans believe, and want to believe, is that getting an education is the equality tool in this society. This concept, meritocracy, is the idea that people move up in the world based on their abilities and not other subjective characteristics. When one looks at the history of African American schooling, throughout history education has not been equal, thus the development of African American students' abilities has also not been equal (Harris, 2010). According to the IASP report, "Neighborhoods have grown more segregated, leaving lower-income students—especially students of color—isolated and concentrated in lower-quality schools, leaving them less academically prepared to enter and complete college" (Shapiro, Meschede, & Osoro, 2013, p. 5). Nevertheless African Americans have made strides in education in the past and continue to do so. In 1940 the rate of African Americans who obtained college degrees was 1% for males and 2% for females. By 2000 those rates had grown; 10% of males have degrees and 15% of females (Kroll, 2012, p. 3). African Americans are entering higher education at the highest rates in history: however their rate of completion is lower than their White counterparts. This stems from the lack of equal high-quality education prior to college and other circumstances that can hinder persons of color despite their merit (Shapiro, Meschede, & Osoro, p. 6).

According to Jared Bernstein (2007) all students are more likely to attend college if their parents attended college; in fact "researchers have found that about 40 percent of the extent of a person's educational attainment is determined by that of their parents" (pp. 26–27). Putting this together with the very small percentage of African Americans in 2000 with degrees only reinforces the gap in educational attainment between Whites and African Americans. It is not only college attendance by a parent that directly corresponds to college achievement. Shapiro and colleagues and Bernstein found that the income level of students' parents held a stronger relationship to the students' college completion than merit alone. Research conducted in 2005 on the correlation between eighth grade math test scores, parent income status, and college completion suggested that in all levels of scores having a higher income status meant a higher college completion rate (Bernstein, p. 26). For example, students with low scores and low income graduated college at a rate of 3% while students with those same low scores but high income graduated at a rate of 30%. Low-income students with high scores graduated at a rate of 29%, while high-income and high-scoring students graduated at a rate of 74% (p. 28).

Merit was not the essential determinant in the high-score case, which in a meritocracy would be the defining quality. In 2009 the median income for Black households was $32,584, while it was $51,861 for Whites (U.S. Bureau of Labor Statistics, 2012). Since 1990 there has been a consistent gap of approximately $20,000 between these racial groups according to the 2012 U.S. Census. It can, therefore, be concluded that, on average, African Americans are more likely to fall in the lower-income bracket, which in turn reduces their chances of obtaining a college degree. These situations establish evidence of a system that is not meritocratic. It seems that the "work hard, get an education and you will succeed" mantra is a myth, on some levels at least. Despite being just as smart as a higher-income student based on tests and other assessments, a lower-income student is much less likely to graduate from college.

Of course there are a number of low-income African Americans who do complete college despite various circumstances, but the question remains, how economically leveling is obtaining a college degree when it comes to African Americans? According to the IASP study, over the 25-year span, Whites gained more wealth from education than African Americans did. The data suggests that education held a 5% contribution to the wealth gap between the races, and that "highly educated households correlate strongly with larger wealth portfolios, so similar college degrees produce more wealth for Whites" than for African Americans (Shapiro, Meschede, & Osoro, p. 2). Recall that wealth is equal to assets minus liabilities. A major liability that African Americans obtain is debt from attending college; and they obtain this at a higher rate than their White counterparts because of lower family incomes (Shapiro, Meschede, & Osoro, p. 5; Prudential Report, 2013, p. 13). The IASP study found that 80% of Blacks and only 64% of Whites graduate college with debt (Shapiro, Meschede, & Osoro, p. 5). This does not account for all of the African Americans who did not complete school but still accumulated debt. African Americans are more likely to leave higher education because of financial concerns as well (p. 5). Due to the lack of wealth within the African American community, this group receives more loan assistance for schooling, and it, in turn, increases their liabilities, which reduces their amount of wealth. It could definitely create a perpetual cycle of not having wealth and needing college loans, thus creating less wealth because of this debt for each generation.

What is most alarming is the unemployment and underemployment rates for African Americans with college degrees. In 2013, the unemployment rate of Black college graduates, ages 22 to 27, was 12.4% compared to 5.6% of all college graduates in the same age range (Ross, 2014). African American college graduates are also underemployed by 56% in comparison to 45% for all recent college graduates (Ross). The goal of obtaining an education does not always benefit African Americans equally. It can harm those who do not finish and also those who do because of debt and employment difficulty. Jobs are not plentiful for any college graduate, but even when African Americans obtain jobs, what is the cost?

OBTAINING AND MAINTAINING EMPLOYMENT AND EQUAL PAY

As mentioned earlier, employment for college graduates is problematic and it is even more difficult for African Americans without a degree to obtain employment. Just as the education system holds barriers to this racial group so, too, does the workforce. To reiterate, 6% of college-educated African Americans have a higher unemployment rate while Whites with college degrees have an unemployment rate of 3.5% (Ross, 2014). But it must not be overlooked that the overall unemployment rate, regardless of education, for African Americans was 16.7% in 2012 compared to White unemployment at 8% (Kroll, 2012, p. 51). African Americans have been unemployed at twice the rate of Whites for more than 50 years (Ross). Some of the causes of such a staggering divide include the stereotypical perception of African Americans and the power of employers to make decisions based on those perceptions that many times go unnoticed. It is the hidden racism engrained in American society that is hard to prosecute against even when its occurrence is realized.

The disparity in the unemployment rate was analyzed by Duke University public policy expert Kroll in 2012. He argues that Blacks are "the last to be hired in a good economy, and when there's a downturn, they're the first to be released" (p. 51). In other words, it is not a question of if it is happening, but why it is happening. Simply getting an interview for a job based on qualifications is often more difficult for many African Americans. One obvious example is the negative perception of African American applicants where racial identity is influenced by a name. Between 2001 and 2002, the University of Chicago, in collaboration with the Massachusetts Institute of Technology, conducted a study on the likelihood of receiving a call back from a potential employer based on the perception of an applicant's name. Investigating the perception that there are "White-sounding" and "Black-sounding" names, the results of this study document how discrimination in hiring practices connects to higher unemployment rates. "Black-sounding" names such as Lakisha and Jamal were 50% less likely to be called by a potential employer than applicants with "White-sounding" names such as Emily and Greg (Bertrand & Mullainathan, 2002).

Another stereotypical perception that can decrease the hiring of African American men, specifically, is the notion that African American men are more dangerous. In a recent issue of the *National Journal* a series of studies found "that when trained sets of Black and White testers with identical resumes are sent on interviews, White men with recent criminal histories are far more likely to receive calls back than Black men with no criminal record at all" (Ross, 2014). This discrepancy alludes to the perception of most Black men as criminals; it doesn't matter if they are criminals or not, they are more likely to be seen as one. Or, explained differently, White men, despite a criminal record, are still seen as the better choice over a Black man without a criminal record and the exact same credentials. These examples of negative stereotypical perceptions concerning a racial group are steeped in the history of a systematically racist society. Such perceptions continually suppress the African American community from economic advancement. They push college-educated African Americans into jobs they are overqualified for, and lock non-college-educated African Americans into low-skill, low-benefits, and low-pay occupations.

It is not just unemployment that is hindering African Americans from climbing the wealth ladder. Underemployment is also harmful, especially for those who are college educated. As a matter of fact, African Americans are more likely to be underemployed than all others, which means that many work in jobs that do not require the educational credentials they have (Ross; Broman, 2001, p. 836). In general African Americans, including those less educated, "are overrepresented in unskilled occupations, with low wages, poor working conditions, and job instability" (Broman, p. 836). The types of jobs most fitting this description are service jobs, such as working in retail stores and restaurants. African American women are more likely to hold service jobs than African American men, but African Americans as a whole are more likely to work in a service occupation than Whites or Asians (U.S. Bureau of Labor Statistics, 2012). Twenty-eight percent of African American women and 22% of African American men work in service occupations, compared to 14% for White men and 20% for White women (U.S. Bureau of Labor Statistics, 2012). Most White men occupied professional and management occupations. Other than service, Black men were highly represented in production, transportation, and material-moving occupations. The number of African American and White women when compared were almost identical in sales and office occupations, but African American women were more represented in service jobs. It is important to remember that underemployment explains just a portion of the injustice in pay between Whites and African Americans as salary disparities are prevalent as well.

Building wealth can only occur with gaining income and investing monies that are not needed for required living expenses such as residual income. There is something hidden within the structure of the American system that creates wage discrepancies not only along racial lines but also along gender lines. According to the U.S. Bureau of Labor Statistics the highest paid racial group is Asians, followed by Whites. In 2012, White women earned 92% of what Asian women earned while Black women earned 78% of what Asian women earned (U.S. Bureau of Labor Statistics, 2013). White men earned 83% of what Asian men earned, and Black men earned 63% of what Asian men earned (U.S. Bureau of Labor Statistics, 2013). Within the Black racial group, Black women earned 90% of what Black men earned, a higher percentage than women in other racial groups in regards to their respective male counterparts. Because Asians serve as the baseline for earnings, future discussion may alter in regard to the situation of economic and employment competition for African Americans and also Latinos, who earned the least on the dollar. Nevertheless, there is a 14-point difference between female groups and a 20-point difference between males. The prevalence of a gap in earnings is not the only major concern in regards to income, as wealth accumulates differently for each racial group.

According to Shapiro et al. household income accounted for 20% of the widening wealth gap between Whites and African Americans. A major reason for wealth growth is increasing income, yet a White and Black family could have the same increase in income but the accumulation of wealth associated with the increase may not be the same for both groups. The IASP data shows that "income gains for Whites and African-Americans have a very different impact on wealth. At the respective wealth medians, every dollar increase in average income over the 25-year study period added $5.19 wealth for White households, while the same income gain only added 69 cents of wealth for African American households" (Shapiro, Meschede, & Osoro, p. 4). This is a major finding in that African Americans are already earning less on the dollar in comparison to Whites but even with an earnings increase, African Americans are only building 13% of the wealth that Whites are building. At this rate is it possible for this wealth gap to decrease in a significant way, or decrease at all?

Overall, African Americans are at a severe disadvantage with earnings and wealth accumulation based on income. Discriminatory employment practices in hiring and other problematic practices in pay and benefits account for the divide between White and Black wealth opportunities. Despite working hard, most of a family's wealth would have to come from saving and investing. In general, since African Americans have less residual income, when they do have extra income they use it to first pay down debt rather than to save or invest. The growth of wealth for this racial group based on residual income is difficult because of the lower amount available, their understanding of investments, their lack of significant inheritance, and the correlation to wealth growth that money brings. Adding to the difficulty of productively using residual income, African Americans give more monetary assistance to others (e.g., family, friends) than Whites do (Ruggles, 1994). These situations are significant in hindering wealth growth for this group.

BUILDING WEALTH THROUGH INHERITANCE AND INVESTMENT

Assumptions have been made that African Americans do not save well and that is why they are behind in gaining wealth. The reason for a lack of wealth development based on savings is not because African Americans do not want to save; in fact between 1998 and 2009 African Americans desire to save rose from 46% to 53% (Leigh & Wheatley, 2010, p. 2). These respondents said they wanted to save but could not.

The highest financial priority for African Americans is to reduce debt, which is essential considering that 94% of this racial group experienced some sort of debt in 2011 (Carrns, 2013). According to a survey by Prudential Insurance Company, out of the remaining racial groups 82% of this population is in debt; therefore, African Americans' debt amounts to 50% more than the remaining population (2013, p. 13). Considering the grave number of people with debt and paying down debt being seen as a priority, there is little room for saving and investment based on the little residual money remaining. However, African Americans often must assist family members financially at almost double the rate of the general population (p. 4). Six out of ten African Americans provide financial support to someone else, helping one's family and community. This impacts the building of a wealth portfolio for the individual household. Specifically, African Americans are 16% more likely to support their parents than their White counterparts (p. 7).

It should not be overlooked that this group also makes strong and consistent investments in life insurance. According to Gutter and Hatcher, African Americans are more likely to obtain life insurance policies because they view it as security—you pay in and you will receive what was earned or promised (2008, p. 683). Today the premium rates at which African Americans purchase life insurance are comparable to those of Whites. In the past African Americans were considered more of a risk so their premiums were higher, or they were denied the insurance all together (LIMRA, 2010). Despite investing in life insurance, African Americans also make the mistake of insuring less human capital in their households than Whites do. The amount invested in the policy determines the payout. In other words, being less informed and having less to spend African Americans also experience a racial gap with insurance as well, and life insurance is part of inheritance.

In the IASP study financial support/inheritance accounted for 5%, one of the least amounts in the growth of the wealth gap between African Americans and Whites. The data illustrated that over the 25-year span, Whites were five times more likely to have an inheritance than African Americans. Shapiro and colleagues found that "inheritances converted to wealth more readily for White than Black families: each inherited dollar contributed to 91 cents of wealth for White families compared with 20 cents for African-American families" (p. 5). The authors state that Whites are more likely to have this larger-scale wealth growth because their economic portfolio is considerably larger to begin with. In other words, there is smaller income for African Americans, higher unemployment, and larger school debt and general debt, which cancels out residual income. So inheritance is less likely because saving and investing is not possible because the focus is more toward reducing liabilities that subtract from assets, which in turn reduces the net worth.

HOMEOWNERSHIP

One key component to the "American dream" is to own a house. Historically African Americans have had problems buying homes, from saving money for the down payments, to acquiring low-interest mortgage loans, to having access to good neighborhoods. Circumstances related to overt racist laws and more subtle discriminatory practices today serve to exacerbate this problem in the African American community. Despite the difficulties, African Americans view homeownership as the most beneficial investment because it is seen as less risky than any other investment (Prudential, p. 4; Gutter & Hatcher, p. 679). Most of African Americans' wealth is composed of homeownership (Hamilton, 2009). "Homeownership is an even greater part of wealth composition for Black families, amounting to 53 percent of wealth for Blacks and 39 percent for Whites" (Shapiro, Meschede, & Osoro, p. 3). Despite homeownership being a great portion of their wealth, African Americans own fewer homes than Whites by 28.4% (p. 3). Considering the gap in actual homeownership, and the difference in wealth importance of homeownership between the two racial groups, it is no wonder that the number of years of homeownership accounts for more than 25% of the wealth gap.

When the recession hit in 2007, African Americans lost wealth due to the decline in the housing market. Twenty-one percent of African American households compared to 12% of White households lost wealth due to the recession (Shapiro, Meschede, & Osoro, p. 4). "Overall, half the collective wealth of African-American families was stripped away during the Great Recession due to the dominant role of home equity in their wealth portfolios and the prevalence of predatory high-risk loans in communities of color" (p. 4). Predatory lending is one way in which African Americans continue to suffer injustice in the fight to obtain wealth through the "American dream" of owning a home.

Within the 2007 major foreclosure event, amounting to 10.9 million homes going into foreclosure, people of color were not the majority of those who lost their homes but they were twice as likely to lose their homes as Whites (Shapiro, Meschede, & Osoro, p. 4). "These higher foreclosure rates reflect a disturbing reality: borrowers of color were consistently more likely to encounter predatory lending and receive high-interest risky loan products, even after accounting for income and credit scores" (p. 4). According to Darrick Hamilton, in some areas of the country African Americans are twice as likely to be denied a home loan even if their income amounts to three times that of a White applicant. If African Americans are actually approved for a loan they are three times more likely to have a subprime loan (Hamilton, 2009; Shapiro, Meschede, & Osoro).

When African Americans secure the subprime loan they are systematically pushed into neighborhoods that are segregated because of historical situations that created the division in the first place. In these segregated neighborhoods home equity hits a ceiling, which limits home appreciation and the ability to grow wealth (Shapiro, Meschede, & Osoro, p. 3). Another aspect to lack of homeownership involves African Americans having less access to down payment money than Whites. This goes back to residual income and being able to save and also the smaller amount of inheritance for African Americans. Because Whites have more access to these things "they buy homes and start acquiring equity an average eight years earlier than Black families" (p. 3). When one is able to pay more up front, the interest rate and lending costs may be reduced (Shapiro Meschede, & Osoro, 2013, p. 3).

In other words, per the IASP 2013 report, homeownership is the largest determining factor for the wealth gap between Whites and Blacks over a 25-year span. It is difficult for African Americans to attain homeownership, maintain it, and gain wealth from it. Having less access to down payment monies and respectable loans, and being more likely to lose their homes during hard times, means gaining wealth is less likely to occur through homeownership. But one must remember that most African American wealth resides in their homes. Even though African Americans have grown their wealth as a result of homeownership over the decades, it is also homeownership that increases the divide between wealth attainment of African Americans and Whites. Despite all the work to gain wealth, even something that seems like a sure win is not for the African American community.

CONCLUSION

This chapter brings to light the wealth gap between Whites and African Americans, based on the findings of a 25-year study, particularly the $236,500 gap due to disparate education, employment, income, financial support, and homeownership experiences. African Americans are suffering from less educational attainment, the perpetual cycle of debt, and the myth of a meritocracy. African Americans have higher rates of unemployment and underemployment. Income of African Americans is smaller and the accumulation of wealth is much less than Whites even as income increases. African Americans are less likely to receive inheritance and that inheritance accumulates into little wealth for them. Most African American wealth comes from homeownership, but Blacks are more likely to have less access to owning a home and are more likely to lose their wealth in their homes. Homeownership accounts for 25% of the wealth gap between the two groups, yet all five factors—homeownership, household income, unemployment, college education, and financial support/inheritance—have detrimental effects on African Americans more so than Whites. Although many African Americans are taking America's idealized steps to gain wealth, it just doesn't seem to work the way it is supposed to work.

This is not to say that wealth cannot be attained by African Americans, but it is to suggest that the traditional steps may not be appropriate based on historically discriminated and marginalized community opportunities. In addition to dismantling systematic racism in an attempt to create a more equal standing, African Americans could benefit from financial literacy and other supportive programs to help with homeownership, education, and employment. It is clear that based on the American system, the racial wealth divide will not easily be bridged, and the "American dream" is not easily accessible to all.

REFERENCES

Bernstein, J. (2007). You can take it with you: Income and wealth across generations. In B. D. Smedley & A. Jenkins (Eds.), *All things being equal: Instigating opportunity in an inequitable time* (pp. 19–38). New York: New Press.

Bertrand, M., & Mullainathan, S. (2002). *Are Emily and Brendan more employable than Lakisha and Jamal? A field experiment on labor market discrimination.* University of Chicago Graduate School of Business.

Broman, C. L. (2001). Work stress in the family life of African Americans. *Journal of Black Studies, 31*(6), 835–846.

Carrns, A. (2013, May 21). African Americans see debt reduction as top priority. *The New York Times.* Retrieved from http://bucks.blogs.nytimes.com/2013/05/21/african-americans-see-debt-reduction-as-top-priority/

Gottschalck, A., Vornovittsky, M., & Smith, A. (2011). *Household wealth in the U.S.: 2000 to 2011.* U.S. Census Bureau. Retrieved from http://www.census.gov/people/wealth/files/Wealth%20Highlights%202011.pdf

Gutter, M. S., & Hatcher, C. B. (2008). Racial differences in the demand for life insurance. *Journal of Risk and Insurance, 5*(3), 677–689.

Hamilton, D. (2009, August 14). *Race, wealth, and intergenerational poverty. The American Prospect.* Retrieved from http://prospect.org/article/race-wealth-and-intergenerational-poverty

Harris, A. (2010). The economical and educational state of Black Americans in the 21st century: Should we be optimistic or concerned? *Review of Black Political Economy, 37*(3–4), 241–252. doi 10.1007/s12114-010-9065-z

Kroll, A. (2012). What we don't talk about when we talk about jobs: The continuing scandal of African-American joblessness. *New Labor Forum, 21*(1), 49–55.

Leigh, W. A., & Wheatley, A. L. (2010). *Retirement savings behavior and expectations of African Americans: 1998–2009.* Joint Center for Political and Economic Studies.

LIMRA. (2010, June 16). LIMRA study finds African Americans value life insurance protection more than general population. Retrieved from http://www.limra.com/Posts/PR/News_Releases/LIMRA_Study_Finds_African_Americans_Place_More_Value_on_Life_Insurance_Protection_Compared_to_Total_Population.aspx?LangType=1033

Prudential Report. (2013). African Americans making financial progress but still facing financial challenges. Prudential Research Study. http://www.prudential.com/media/managed/aa/aafacingthechallenge.shtml

Rank, M. R. (2014). *Chasing the American dream: Understanding what shapes our fortunes.* New York: Oxford University Press.

Ross, J. (2014, May 27). African-Americans with college degrees are twice as likely to be unemployed as other graduates. *National Journal.* Retrieved from http://www.nationaljournal.com/next-america/education/african-americans-with-college-degrees-are-twice-as-likely-to-be-unemployed-as-other-graduates-20140527

Ruggles, S. (1994). The origins of African American family structure. *American Sociological Review, 59,* 136–151.

Shapiro, T., Meschede, T., & Osoro, S. (2013, February). *The roots of the widening racial wealth gap: Explaining the Black-White economic divide.* Institute on Assets and Social Policy. Research and Policy Brief.

U.S. Bureau of Labor Statistics. (2012). *Occupational employment by race and ethnicity, 2011.* Washington, DC: Author.

U.S. Bureau of Labor Statistics. (2013). *Highlights of women's earnings in 2012.* Washington, DC: Author.

CHAPTER SIX

Learning from History: Contemporary Issues in Black and Africana Studies

DE ANNA REESE AND MALIK SIMBA

After five decades of hammering the insensate walls of the "White Ivory Tower," Black Studies has enabled a whole new generation of Americans to develop a neoconsciousness, making them less false and less racist than their parents and grandparents. One could argue that Black Studies generates a new type of antiracist thinking and that thinking aided in the election of President Barack Obama. Yes, we believe this has been a goal achieved indirectly, but with good fortune for the nation. Over the decades, Black Studies programs and departments have matriculated thousands of White students who understand, in the words of one such "White" Fresno State student, "the more we know, the less we fear" (Webb, 2014). There are a significant number of diverse students who matriculate through courses in Africana, African American, and Black Studies and their thinking often moves from fear to acceptance. President Obama needed this type of enlightened thinking to reach a turning point percentage in the electorate and attain the White House. In other words, the matriculation of tens of thousands of American students via required courses in either explicitly Black Studies or multiculturalism (MI GE req.) has led to a less racist America and reduced the fear of the "black planet."[1]

Recently, the *New York Times* published an essay with pictures about First Lady Michelle Obama's slave ancestry that also became a book. The *Time*'s essay and the book were both written by Rachel Swarns (2013). It is interesting to note that the First Lady and her biographer are both connected to America's slave past and both received their baccalaureate degrees in Africana Studies (Fikes, 2009). We note this academic connection because so many contemporary public figures have verified the importance of Africana Studies in their lives as Africana Studies matriculates. Such individuals include Mae Jemison, NASA astronaut; Aaron McGruder, award-winning political journalist; James Forman, SNCC activist; Gloria Naylor, novelist; Angela Bassett, actress; Sanaa Lathan, actress; Bill Whitaker, CBS news correspondent; and many more. Swarns's book is titled *American Tapestry: The Story of the Black, White, and Multiracial Ancestry of Michelle Obama.*

However, most Africana Studies graduates, unbeknown to themselves, selected their major consistent with Countee Cullen's poem "Heritage." A few lines of this poem reflect the origins, growth, and future of Black Studies. Cullen asks:

> What is Africa to me?...Strong bronze men, or regal black Women from whose loins I sprang when the birds of Eden sang? One three centuries removed from the scenes his fathers loved...What is Africa to me? (Jackson, 2013)

Africana Studies matriculates tend to be inquiring minds. They want to understand how the past, in numerous ways, dictates the present. Confronting the past in the present was a fundamental dynamic for those participating in the movements of the 1960s. It was during the decade of the 1960s that an insurgent intellectual and cultural movement—Black Studies—emerged to challenge the White Ivory Tower of higher education and its curriculum. (Robinson, Foster, & Ogilvie, 1969). This academic challenge has its twin in the better known Civil Rights Movement that challenged White America; both movements used similar tactics to achieve similar goals.

The decade of decision for this academic and political change had its prelude in the late 1940s Cold War political realignment. The progressive wing of the Democratic Party issued the declaration of war on Jim Crow with the 1948 document "To Secure These Rights" (Dudziak, 2011). To win the hearts and minds of people of color in the Third World, Democrats understood they needed to win the hearts and minds of America's people of color, with Black Americans being first and foremost. President Harry S. Truman supported securing these rights by first desegregating the armed forces.

The regressive wing of the Democrats became Dixiecrats under Strom Thurmond's leadership. Civil rights victories, beginning with the 1954 Supreme Court case of *Brown v. Board of Education*, prompted a virulent racist reaction. White males retreated into the "Dixiecratic Party" and later produced the 1955 document "Southern Manifesto,"[2] which foreshadowed George Wallace's clarion "Segregation now, segregation tomorrow, segregation forever."[3] This was the beginning of the retreat of White males into independent politics that moved from Thurmond, to George Wallace's White supremacist presidential campaign to today's

Tea Party, and, ultimately, the heavily saturated White masculine GOP (Dudziak, 2011). The history of the past tends to contour the conditions for the present. This history of reaction is the basis for the current attacks on both the progressive policies of President Obama and the growth of Black Studies. In other words, the actions of conservative leaders in mainstream politics today has a continuity with leaders of the past.

Conservative Whites today are grating against progressive calls for diversity, multiculturalism, and enhanced Black Studies The cultural wars over National Endowment for the Humanities funding is the tip of the proverbial iceberg (Panas, 2013). As we begin to investigate the contemporary issues in Africana Studies, we must keep in mind George Santayana's twin observations that "those who cannot remember the past are condemned to repeat it," and "only the dead have seen the end of war" (1905). Since the political victories of President Barack Obama, there has been an explosion of literature about a possible postracial America. The paradox of this explosion is a concurrent explosion, via the Internet, of virulent racist images of President Obama's African origins. One of the most infamous is the image morphing the first family as "apes." This image is consistent with an alleged GOP satirical comment characterizing President Obama's inauguration as a scene from the film *Planet of the Apes.*

Sadly, for many White and some Black American educators, social scientists, and parents of matriculating Black students who have embraced postracialism, this America translates as "Black no more." No more need for federal or governmental policies that foster inclusion and eliminate the residual effects of Jim Crow in new forms, or as Michelle Alexander characterizes it, "The New Jim Crow" (2010).

One of the major challenges of Africana Studies today is to be an intellectual and scholarly watchdog against the revolution sliding backward. This backward slide includes a culture war where race appears marginal and those raised by the families of slave descendants presumably lack the values and skills important to secure future success. When singer-songwriter Pharrell Williams referred to himself as part of "The New Black," he spoke to the sentiment, now common among a growing number of successful African Americans who view Blackness as not blaming other races for our issues but instead seeing color as a mentality—that will either work for or against you (Elan, 2014). This "New Black" is a far cry from the race pride and consciousness articulated by the "New Negro" during the Harlem Renaissance of the 1920s. Although its major proponents were also members of a privileged class of poets, novelists, and artists, their purpose involved a belief in their own power and capacity to change the world by uncovering the richness and beauty of their African past (Meier & Rudwick, 1986), an important past sure to elude future generations if not for the role played by Black Studies.

Among the challenges facing Black Studies programs is the changing demographic composition of our student body and with it the meaning of race and ethnicity. The centrality of race is fundamental to understanding America, especially the festering levels of inequality that limit the life choices of many ethnic minorities. And yet, race has been diluted under the guise of "diversity" and "multiculturalism," commanding less attention and relevance, especially for those who choose to deemphasize their African heritage in favor of other parts of their ethnic identity. Black Studies prepares all students to critically understand the experiences of people of African descent, but it must also find ways to tell and transmit this history to students who increasingly view themselves as distinct, if not separate, from the realities associated with race and Blackness.

Historically, Americans have been taught to think of themselves in singular race terms. As early as the 17th century, the mixed children of slave mothers were considered Black by law and shortly thereafter, slaveholders developed anti-miscegenation laws that went into effect even before the United States became a nation. For 300 years, both law and norm affirmed the notion that having Black ancestry was a social liability (Chinema, 2011). Today, many biracial persons by choice or appearance call themselves "Black" regardless of their mixed parentage.[4] With the election of President Obama, who is racially mixed, racial identity has been a source of both frustration and inspiration, especially among millennials, persons ages 18 to 30. Many now choose to publicly identify with more than one part of their ethnic background, even if historically considered Black.

In 2010, those who identified with more than one race increased by more than 50%, leading to what is now the largest group of mixed-race people ever to come of age in the United States (U.S. Census Bureau, 2010; Ojalvo, 2011). The nonprofit organization Race Forward: The Center for Racial Justice Innovation also reports that multiethnic or mixed race persons now make up the largest, most racially and ethnically diverse generation the United States has ever known (Millennials, Activism, and Race, 2012). This accelerated trend toward claiming more than one ethnic identity stands in contrast with the legal choices confronting mixed race Black people only a generation ago. Subject to the hypo-descent rule in which a drop of Black blood made one "Black," Susie Guillory Phipps unsuccessfully sued the Louisiana Bureau of Vital Records to change her racial classification from Black to White in 1982. She was labeled "Black" on her birth certificate in accordance with a state law that declared anyone with one 32nd "Negro blood" to be Black, so Phipps' racial identity was upheld by the state court, legally validating the assignment of individuals to a specific racial group (Omi & Winant, 2015).

In the 21st century, these changing definitions of race and ethnicity shape how Black Studies must approach the teaching of Black culture and history to a growing number of multiethnic and immigrant students from across the diaspora who grapple with where they "fit," in a larger narrative that often emphasizes the struggle and contributions of African people whose ancestors endured slavery in North America. While millennials believe that race is still a significant factor in

American life, their understanding of the extent and continued significance of race and racism in areas such as education, employment, the criminal justice system, and immigration varies depending on their exposure and education (Millennials, Activism, and Race). In turn, changing demographics affect how younger students perceive and relate to Black Studies as a discipline. Not only are Black students with an immigrant or non-Black parent changing definitions of "Blackness," they are also raising questions within the academy and beyond on whether they "deserve" the same preferred treatment given to Black American students (typically within educational settings) who can trace several generations of relatives born in the United States.

The growth of ethnic Black students across college campuses also follows the quadrupling of African and Caribbean immigrants and their upward mobility over the last half-century. In 2009, the U.S. African community numbered 1.5 million compared to only 35,000 in 1970, nearly 4% of the entire immigrant population (Dinnerstein & Reimers, 2009). This migration developed in response to more welcoming U.S. immigration policies during the 1960s and the chilly reception adopted by former colonial nations. As part of a new wave of immigration, African and Caribbean immigrants arrived on student visas, earned advanced degrees, and chose to settle in America rather than returning home (Dinnerstein & Reimers). Among the best educated of any post-1945 immigrant group, recent studies show that the children of African immigrants now make up a quarter of all Black students admitted to elite U.S. colleges (John, 2014). The admission of more students of African heritage to colleges and universities has many asking why African American students have not performed as well—questions that are best addressed through the examination of how history and culture are taught in Black Studies courses.

New terms such as "regular Black" or "just Black" (JB) have become part of the shorthand at some colleges for distinguishing Black students whose parents were born and raised in the United States. According to Diana Eromosele (2014) such students find their domestic roots are less conversation worthy than the international roots of their peers. Being African "American" simply wasn't sexy enough for the Black population at one student's school. At parties and cultural events, "ethnic black" students, described as those with at least one parent who migrated to the United States from Africa or the Caribbean, proudly displayed elements of their national heritage, including flags, food, dances, and music. They were also much more likely to speak with a unique English accent, visit relatives in London, Barbados, West Africa, and Canada, and believed to have a strong sense of nationalism and cultural pride. They were different from "regular Blacks," believed to lack the same level of cultural and intellectual grounding, and, thus their consciousness is seen as Black no more (Eromosele). Despite the social chasm generated by digital posts on social media sites, interest in one's culture is a typical part of the college experience, where students learn more about themselves and their peers. However, some students have found that even while spoken in jest, these terms often infer underlying assumptions about class and culture. In one case, a "regular Black" student mentioned comparisons made between the culture of her ethnic Black peers and her own, the latter of which was presumed to be inferior and less sophisticated (Sharp, 2014).

Recent headlines have also inflated the distinctions made between regular versus ethnic Blacks, such as Kwasi Enin, the suburban New York high school student who was accepted into eight Ivy League schools. Having chosen to attend Yale, Enin's achievement is directly attributed to his parents, who emigrated from Ghana in the 1980s, and steadily encouraged the academic success of both their children (Eltman, 2014). While raised in America, some argue that Enin's academic prowess is the result of his upbringing, namely his first-generation status and the cultural values instilled in him by his family, including hard work and perseverance—qualities many "regular Black" students allegedly do not have. In their book, *The Triple Package*, Jed Rubenfeld and Amy Chua examine the provocative role of culture and ethnicity in determining success for six ethnic groups. Among these groups are Nigerian Americans whose attendance at elite U.S. universities is ten times their population percentage. College degrees have also placed Nigerian Americans at the top of the economic ladder with nearly 25% of households making more than $100,000 compared to less than 11% of Black households as a whole (Garvin, 2014).

With more "ethnic" Black than "regular" Black students represented at elite and Ivy League schools, questions abound on whether the former is entitled to the fruits of mobility earned by the ancestors of the latter who faced slavery and Jim Crow. Various sources offer numerous reasons why some ethnic Black students fare better than American Black students, but the main differences are culture and environment. Student visas have allowed the parents of many ethnic Black students entry into the professional classes along with an exposure to Black majority cultures where crucial traditions have been allowed to exist and thrive. In contrast, American Black students confront varying degrees of stigma, stereotypes, and institutional racism over the course of their lives, which, when left unchecked, can severely impact their motivation and self-esteem. Either way, such explanations divisively suggest that the success of ethnic Blacks can only occur at the expense of Black Americans and vice versa (John, 2014; Eromosele, 2014). By engaging students in a meaningful dialogue on issues like this one, Black Studies has both an opportunity and an obligation to raise awareness on our collective struggle, and the external forces that continue to shape our perceptions of Black progress and identity.

Moreover, Black Studies offers a bridge to help students engage the issues that unite our pasts and connect us to the global society in which we now live. Like the students of the 1960s who used Black Studies to develop a curriculum born of their self-determination, Black Studies faculty must play a key role in teaching students, be they Black American, ethnic Black, biracial, multiethnic, or other, the intersections and commonalities that bind together the history of Black people across the world. There is much to learn and value within the distinctive cultures that make up the diaspora, and the interdisciplinary nature of Black Studies offers students the best opportunity for exposure, collaboration, and dialogue with histories and cultures not only essential to understanding the richness and diversity of African peoples but of all humanity.

Recent events reveal how the contemporary issues in Black Studies are rooted in the transformative historic struggles of the Civil Rights Movement. This includes conservative reaction to not only that movement, but also more specifically, how that movement transitioned to Black Power with its emphasis on liberation, the huge step beyond mere freedom. The recent attack on the Voting Rights Act of 1965 and the bipartisan federal budget negotiated by the GOP Congressman Paul Ryan both seek to eliminate the last remaining vestige of the War on Poverty. For the GOP no one is dead and the war continues. In the 1960s, most clear thinkers understood there is a dialectical relationship between powerlessness and poverty. The emergence of Black Studies during this transformative period was to help students and the broader Black community to, in part, understand this dialectic as rooted in American history and culture. In understanding this dialectic we must reflect upon Herbert Aptheker's observance that "history potency is mighty. The oppressed need it for identity and inspiration, while the oppressor needs it for justification, rationalization, and legitimacy. Nothing illustrates this more clearly than the history writing on the American Negro people" (1968, p. 1). Black Studies is rooted in southern civil rights history and, thus, these southern origins of Black Studies took contemporary form when the late and noted Black theological historian Dr. Vincent Harding helped co-found the Institute of the Black World[5] in Atlanta in corroboration with the Martin Luther King Library. As one can see, Black Studies became the academic extension of the civil rights struggle into the White Ivory Towers of American education. The curriculum would be desegregated.

Like the Student Nonviolent Coordinating Committee (SNCC) kids' use of direct action via sit-ins, wade-ins, and pray-ins, Black students in predominately White universities and colleges also used direct action to desegregate the White supremacist curriculum in the White Ivory Tower. Students in a wide variety of institutions demanded the hiring of Black faculty and the teaching of pedagogically relevant Black experience courses. At times the militancy of the Civil Rights Movement mirrored student takeovers of university buildings, deans' offices, and some chairs' offices. The irony of collegiate desegregation was that a number of SNCC student leaders were recruited to these White Ivory Towers. Anne Moody, in her autobiography, *Coming of Age in Mississippi* (2004), recalls how her first boyfriend and student leader, David Jones, was recruited north while in the midst of voter registration. As civil rights laws successfully desegregated the broader American society, college and university administrators' integration of their student bodies led to a dramatic shift in the number of Black students attending White universities and abandoning historical Black colleges and universities. David Jones became just one of thousands. By the early 1970s, close to 1 million Black students were following in Jones's footsteps (Marable, 2000). This critical mass of students jammed administrative buildings and offices demanding Black Studies (Robinson, Foster, & Ogilvie, 1969). Unbeknown to these student activists, the works they fought for were waiting in the dusty stacks of academe's libraries scholarship and were rarely used in the classroom. They were extant but not perceived by White scholars as germane to Black hegemony.

Black Studies then and now became rooted in these sequestered scholarly works, such as Carter G. Woodson's *The Mis-Education of the Negro* (1933), Gunnar Myrdal's *An American Dilemma: The Negro Problem and Modern Democracy* (1944), E. Franklin Frazier's *Black Bourgeois* (1957), and John Hope Franklin's *From Slavery to Freedom: A History of African Americans* (1947). Also hidden in broad daylight was the highly respected autobiographies and scholarship of W. E. B. Du Bois, including *Philadelphia Negro*; the inspirational research of slave revolts by Herbert Aptheker; Oliver Cromwell Cox's penetrating critical analysis of America's political economy; the playwritings of Lorraine Hansberry; and prominent Black authors such as Zora Neale Hurston, Richard Wright, J. Saunders Redding, Alain Locke, Langston Hughes, Joel Augustus Rogers, and other Harlem Renaissance writers.

Black Studies, much like the 1960 lunch-counter sit-ins in Greensboro, North Carolina, was sparked by a few students in 1968 at San Francisco State, and spread nationally like the proverbial prairie fire. This "fire" spread spontaneously and explosively appearing on large and small campuses. The demand for Black Studies became an insurgent curriculum movement that led to White administrators either acquiescing to demands outright or moderating them in dialogs of compromise. Even though the initial scholarly sources used in this new insurgent curricula were consistent with the scholarly sources cited above, conservative reaction led to a philosophical debate on the subject matter of Black Studies and the people studied.

The ambivalence of White reaction can clearly be seen in 1968 when noted American historian Thomas Bailey, taking his cue from the earlier writings of Woodson and Rogers, gave his presidential address at the Organization of American Historians. Professor Bailey said, "False historical beliefs are so essential to our culture.... How different our national history would be if countless millions of our citizens had not been brought up to believe in the manifest destined superiority...

of the White race "(1968, p. 15). However, Bailey continued with a philosophical point of contention that has been the driving dynamic used by conservatives then and now to prohibit, limit, or retrench Black Studies. Bailey continued by ringing the "fire-bell in the night alarm" by asserting that "newly formed hyphenated groups...are now understandably clamoring for historical recognition...insisting on visibility, if not over-visibility, in the textbooks" (p. 15).

Professor Bailey's very perceptive analysis references the White conservative reaction to the rise of Black Studies. White Americans became quite comfortable embracing these essentially false historical beliefs that drove the racist behavior confronted by the clarion for an insurgent curriculum. Such false essentialisms are captured by John W. Burgess of Harvard University who observes, "Black skin means membership in a race of men which has never of itself succeeded in subjecting passion to reason and therefore [has] never created any civilization of any kind" (Reese & Simba, 2011, p. 14). Such false historical observations were replicated in popular culture; for example, with the 1915 D. W. Griffith–produced film *Birth of a Nation* and Victor Fleming's 1939 *Gone with the Wind*. When big screen false images are combined with those on radio and television, White Americans then, and sometimes now, only see Black Americans as "toms, mammies, mulattos, coons, and bucks" (Bogle, 2001).

The challenge of Black Studies in its original thrust, in its maturation phase, and in its future was and is to tirelessly help America's citizens of all social races understand the need to de-falsify this way of thinking. Therefore, Black Studies also serves as an intellectual watchdog. Defining the discipline had its origins in 1968, with an academic symposium organized by Yale University students' Black Student Alliance. Armstead L. Robinson, a student leader, eventually co-edited the symposium for the book *Black Studies in the University: A Symposium* (1969). The symposium's discussion touched on a variety of hot-button topics such as: Was there intellectual validity of studying the Black experience? What should be the role of Black Studies in undergraduate education? Is the road to the top through a more general higher education, rather than Black Studies? What is the impact of teaching Black history in the college curriculum and the teaching of African American literature?

As these debates and forums continued over the next two decades, hundreds of academic units of Black Studies were established throughout the nation. Essentially, these units took one of three forms. The first is the unit that has department status, the so-called Harvard Model, with joint appointments and tenure-track lines within the home department as a traditional academic unit (Blassingame, 1971). A second form is the program model with both joint appointments and tenure-track lines within the program. We have such a model at Fresno State. A third model is the Temple University model with only tenure-track appointments and department status. Each model creates ancillary units or research centers and institutes to continue to do the primary groundwork, advocated years before by Carter Goodwin Woodson. One of the best surveys conducted on the demand for Black Studies in reference to an ideal model was completed by the late and noted African American historian John W. Blassingame. He mailed out a survey to 77 scholars of whom 31 replied with insightful suggestions. A number of intriguing responses came from southern scholars at historically Black colleges and universities (HBCUs) who said what was needed in any such model was "a greater emphasis on the Black students need for pride, for improving his self-image" (pp. 229–230).

Unfortunately, each of the models for a Black Studies department or program face similar issues and problems; some externally in origins and purpose, while others are internal or philosophical due to the various administrative personalities and their visions for the discipline, or, as some argue, its interdisciplinary nature.

We think the list below includes key issues facing the present and future of Black Studies that will need to be addressed in the 21st century:

1. Changing demographics: How Black identity has changed—Regular versus ethnic Black identity—in the diaspora and how Black Studies must address this change.

2. The digital age: How Africana Studies will benefit from using technology and social media to better connect with a new generation of students. We see the website, Blackpast.org or the "Google of Africana" experience as a fine example of keeping in step with the digital age.

3. Service learning or giving back to the community: Most Africana Studies require some form of paying it forward with community fieldwork.

4. Archeological scholarship: To further solidify the image of "traditional" scholarly development within higher education, Africana Studies must have "archeological scholarship" that "digs," locates, and places new evidence in the public discourse of both the ancient and contemporary contributions made by people of African ancestry.

5. Discussion on the elimination of Affirmative Action, specifically its impact on the numbers of Black faculty and staff in higher education: This dovetails into the number of Black students recruited to college campuses as well. This development is consistent with the reaction from conservative America in both political and academic arenas.

6. Finally, diversity issues: How can Africana Studies assist in regaining and reclaiming the concept of race as the central importance for American education embracing the idea of inclusion? This centrality is rooted in the fact that there has been only one time in American history that the system completely broke down and became dysfunctional. That one

time occurred over the issue of race and the place of Black Americans in American society. The occurrence was the American Civil War. President Abraham Lincoln's Gettysburg Address is the ideological tool that Black Studies must use to reclaim its centrality when diversity is discussed today.

Some California politicians and educators are leaning toward eliminating Black Studies and replacing it with ethnic studies or multiculturalism. For example, Kitaro Webb, who teaches Advance Placement English at Santa Monica High School in California, has defined this new pedagogy with this explanation of the evolving concept of ethnic studies, which, he says, is "about civic engagement, responsibility, and fighting for what you believe in" (Caesar, 2014). At present, State Assemblyman Luis Alejo has sponsored a new bill to require a standardized ethnic studies curriculum throughout the state of California. As one young White progressive scholar observes, "Understanding race and ethnicity isn't a luxury, it's a necessity" (Remnick, 2014).

As new issues of standardization, ethnic studies, multiculturalism, and so forth become accepted as curriculum, Africana Studies must be an advocate for the concept of race as the litmus test for anyone successfully matriculating in either secondary school level or the collegiate level. Our challenge is to be a part of the dialog on the essential meaning of such terms as "diversity," "multiculturalism," and "ethnic studies" to ensure that race will remain central to the pedagogy of these evolving twists and turns. Our list of key essentials to Black Studies is not all-inclusive, but we feel that it is a broad outline directing those who are professionals within Africana Studies to a path that will help preserve the future of the discipline.

A number of years ago, the noted journalist Lerone Bennett (1972) wrote about the challenge of Blackness, and professionals who work within Africana Studies have accepted that challenge. The future of Africana Studies is driven by the need to chronicle the history and cultural contributions of Black Americans to the American saga. Achieving this will elevate their national status so, in the words of Dr. Martin Luther King, "When the history books are written in the future generations, the historians will have to pause and say, there lived a great people—a Black people who injected new meaning into the veins of civilization" (1958).

NOTES

1. Fresno State, unlike most of the 23 California State University (CSU) campuses, has a GE requirement for a multicultural/international (MI) course. The MI requirement can be fulfilled by many different courses from Africana Studies, anthropology, philosophy, sociology, women's studies, and other disciplines. Most of the courses fall under the College of Social Sciences. The

requirement means that Fresno State students have three more GE unit requirements than CSU Executive Order 1033 mandates. Dr. Meta Schettler, associate professor in Africana Studies, believes MI is important because it is interdisciplinary. She said the diverse makeup of Fresno State makes it essential. Students come back to her, even after many years, and tell her of the transformative power of MI courses. Schettler said that those sorts of courses led her to where she is today. For more information see Miller, T. (2009, December 9). Campus may cut multicultural GE requirements. *The Collegian* at (Fresno State).

2. "Southern Manifesto" was a document issued in 1956 by Southern congressmen declaring their opposition to the Brown case decision.
3. Infamous slogan given in the inaugural speech of Alabama governor George Wallace in 1963. Dudziak, M. (2011), p. 86.
4. The term "biracial" is commonly used to refer to persons with parents from two different ethnic backgrounds. The term's most popular usage refers to persons with one Black and one White parent.
5. See Institute of Black World. http://ibw21.org/

REFERENCES

Alexander, M. (2010). *The new Jim Crow: Mass incarceration in the age of colorblindness*. New York: New Press.

Aptheker, H. (1968). Foreword. In J. H. Clarke (Ed.), *Ten Black writers response to William Styron's Confessions of Nat Turner* (p. 1). Boston: Beacon.

Aptheker, H. (1993). *Anti-racism in American history: The first two hundred years*. Westport, CT: Praeger.

Bailey, Thomas A. (1968). "The Mythmakers of American History," *Journal of American History*, 55, (1).

Bennett, L. (1972). *The challenge of Blackness*. Chicago: Johnson.

Blassingame, J. (1971). *New perspectives on Black Studies*. Urbana: University of Illinois Press.

Bogle, D. (2001). *Toms, mammies, mulattoes, coons, and bucks: An interpretive history of Blacks in American films* (4th ed.). New York: Bloomsbury Academic.

Ceasar, S. (2014, June 3). Diversity push: A bid to standardize ethnic studies. *Los Angeles Times*, p. AA5.

Chinhema, B. (Director). (2011). *Multiracial identity* [DVD]. United States: Bullfrog Films.

Crowder, R. L. (2006). The historical context and political significance of Harlem's street scholar community. *Afro-Americans in New York Life and History, 30*(12).

Dinnerstein, L., & Reimers, D. (2009). *Ethnic Americans: Immigration and American society* (5th ed.). New York: Columbia University Press.

Dudziak, M. (2011). *Cold War civil rights: Race and the image of American democracy*. Princeton, NJ: Princeton University Press.

Elan, P. (2014, April 22). Why Pharrell Williams believes in "The New Black" [Blog]. *The Guardian*. Retrieved from http://www.theguardian.com/music/shortcuts/2014/apr/22/trouble-with-pharrell-williams-new-black-theory

Eltman, F. (2014, April 30). Suburban NY student picks Yale among all 8 Ivies. *Huffington Post*. Retrieved from http://www.huffingtonpost.com/2014/04/30/kwasi-eninyale_n_5242602.html?page_version=legacy&view=print&comm_ref=false

Eromosele, D. (2014, April 8). Among college students, parsing "regular Black" and "ethnic Black." *The Root*. Retrieved from http://www.theroot.com/articles/culture/2014/04/_regular_black_and_ethnic_black_experiences_at_elite_universities.html

Fikes, R. (2009). *What can you do with a Black Studies Major?* [Pamphlet]. San Diego: San Diego State University.

Garvin, G. (2014, February 16). Tiger mom Amy Chua roars with new controversial book about "America's elite." *Miami Herald*. Retrieved from http://www.miamiherald.com/2014/02/15/3937463/authors-some-groups-are-pre-wired.html

Jackson, M. (Ed.). (2013). *Countee Cullen: Collected poems*. New York: Literary Classics.

John, A. (2014, April 1). Why the all-Ivy League story stirs up tensions between African immigrants and Black Americans. *The Wire*. Retrieved from http://www.thewire.com/politics/2014/04/why-the-all-ivy-league-story-stirs-up-tensions-between-african-immigrants-and-black-americans/359978/

King, M. L. (1958). *Stride toward freedom*. New York: Harper & Row.

Marable, M. (2000). Black Studies and the racial mountain. *Souls, 2*(3), 17–36.

Meier, A., & Rudwick, E. (1986). *Black history and the historical profession, 1915–1980*. Urbana: University of Illinois Press.

Millennials, activism, and race...don't call them 'post-racial.' Race Forward: The Center for Racial Justice Innovation Research. Retrieved from https://www.raceforward.org/research/reports/millennials-activism-and-race-dont-call-them-post-racial

Moody, A. (2004) *Coming of age in Mississippi*. New York: Bantam Dell.

Ojalvo, H. (2011, February 1). What is your racial and ethnic identity? [Blog]. *New York Times*. Retrieved from http://learning.blogs.nytimes.com/2011/02/01/what-is-your-racial-and-ethnic-identity/comment-page-7/

Omi, M., & Winant, H. (2015). *Racial formations in the United States: From the 1960s to the 1980s* (3rd ed.). New York: Routledge.

Panas, R. (2013, March 11). Arizona's law banning Mexican-American studies curriculum is constitutional, judge rules. *Huffington Post*. Retrieved from http://www.huffingtonpost.com/2010/03/11/arizona-mexican-american-studies-curriculum-constitutional_n_2851034.html

Reese, D., & Simba, M. (2011, March). Historiography against history: The propaganda of history and the struggle for the hearts and minds of Black folk. *Socialism and Democracy, 25*(1), 13–43.

Remnick, N. (2014, July 3). Why ethnic studies in California, especially, understanding race and ethnicity isn't a luxury, it's a necessity. *Los Angeles Times*, p. A19.

Robinson, A. L., Foster, C., & Ogilvie, D. (1969). *Black Studies in the university*. New Haven, CT: Yale University Press.

Rojas, F. (2007). *From Black power to Black Studies: How a radial social movement became an academic discipline*. Baltimore: Johns Hopkins University Press.

Santayana, G. (1910). *Reason in common sense, the life of reason; or; the phases of human progress*. London: Constable.

Sharp, D. (2014, April 14). "Regular Black" vs. "ethnic Black": Why the divide? *The Root*. Retrieved from http://www.theroot.com/articles/culture/2014/04/regular_black_vs_ethnic_black_why_the_divide.html

Simba, M. (2006). Joel Augustus Rogers: Negro historians in history, time, and space. *Afro-Americans in New York Life and History, 30*(12).

Simba, M. (2013). "Trayvon stood his ground," philosophy of the Black experience. *The American Philosophical Association Newsletter, 13* (1).

Swarns, R. (2013). *American tapestry: The story of the Black, White, and multiracial ancestry of Michelle Obama*. New York: Amistad.

U.S. Census Bureau. (2010). *Census shows multiple-race population grew faster than single-race population*. https://www.census.gov/newsroom/releases/archives/race/cb12-182.html

Webb, T. (2014, February 14). The less you understand the more you fear. *Fresno Bee*. Valley Voices.

Wolfenstein, E. V. (1981). *The Victims of Democracy*: Malcolm X and the Black Revolution. Berkeley: University of California Press.

CHAPTER SEVEN

To Form a More Perfect Union: Frames of Double Consciousness in Presidential Candidate Barack Obama's Race Speech

ANITA FLEMING-RIFE

At the turn of the century, I think it is safe to say that in the United States, if not the world, people never imagined that the country would elect its first Black president, but the 21st century ushered in winds of epic change on a number of fronts that made anything possible—even the unthinkable. The rejoinder to the unthinkable was "yes, we can," and this mantra helped fuel the most exciting and engaging presidential campaign of my lifetime. Ever since the dust settled, I have reflected on the campaign and on the rhetorical messaging that had many of us swept up in fervor on one side or the other. Even before the election of the first African American president of the United States, the *New York Times Sunday Magazine* (Bai, 2008) asked, "Is Obama the End of Black Politics?" The implied question and explicit examination in the article is: have we now entered into a postracial society?

The *Times* question is a reminder of W. E. B. Du Bois's ambivalence about this issue in one of his early novels, *Dark Princess*, in which his protagonist, Manuel Mansart dies immediately following the 1954 U.S. Supreme Court decision in *Brown* (Stewart, 2004). Du Bois writes:

> If for another country, we Negroes taught our children—in our own bettering schools, with our own trained teachers—we would never be Americans but another nation with a new culture. But if beginning now, gradually, all American children, Black and White, European, Slavic and Asiatic are increasingly taught as one—in one tradition and one

ideal—there will be one race, one nation, one world...(He then ponders and asks the question), Am I glad? I should be, but I am not. I dreamed too long of a great American Negro race. Now, I can only see a great Human Race. It may be best, I should indeed rejoice (p. 106).

Mansart then dies—never to realize that more than 60 years since the Supreme Court ruled in *Brown v. Board of Education*, a postracial society has failed to materialize. So this chapter will consider the *NYT*'s query by examining the frames of double consciousness in one of now second-term President Barack Obama's most lauded speeches: We the People in Order to Form a More Perfect Union (2008).

What prompted that speech was the enduring controversy over remarks—that some considered "racist" and "incendiary"—made by his pastor, Dr. Jeremiah Wright, a proponent of Black liberation theology. The basic premise of this theology is that Christianity must be rooted in the African American experience of oppression. This view was also held and expressed long ago by Du Bois who said that the Black Church should be a vehicle for enhancing activities designed to produce freedom and dignity (Stewart, 2004). While Black liberation theology has been a part of mainstream seminary curriculum for nearly four decades, many from the majority community were not aware of it and expressed outrage over what they considered an extremely racist view of Christianity.

The outrage was directed at one of Wright's sermons undergirded in Black liberation theology. The snippets of that September 16, 2001, sermon were played and looped continuously on media channels. It is important to note that efforts were not made to provide needed context to convey the more complex and intended message. There were, of course, exceptions—one was the *Chicago Tribune* (Brachear, 2008), but the larger audience was bombarded with 16-second sound bites void of context, therefore, misconstruing the message.

While acknowledging that Obama confronted a very tough challenge of trying "to explain the racial and religious context of how these assertions materialized" in the first place, Cohen (2008) asserts that Obama "confronted some very unpleasant truths about race in America...and he has done so in a nuanced manner that is pretty much unprecedented for campaign rhetoric." What Obama's speech responded to was a race "problem" encountered as a Black man running for the highest office in the land. The "problem?" His pastor—not Obama—called the United States racist and imperialistic. However, Obama had to respond to this "problem" out of political necessity (Harlow, 2009). According to Du Bois, this is an occurrence experienced by all Black people at one time or another—the question posed by Du Bois in "Of Our Spiritual Strivings" (Du Bois, 2007, p. 7) is: "How does it feel to be a problem?"

This chapter will examine the nuances of Obama's 2008 race speech. These nuances can be characterized as a result of the dynamics of identity—the most famous of which is Du Bois' construct of psychic duality or double consciousness (Stewart, 2004). In Du Bois' *The Souls of Black Folk* (1999), double consciousness is defined as follows:

> It is a peculiar sensation, this double-consciousness, this sense of always looking at one's self through the eyes of others, of measuring one's soul by the tape of a world that looks on in amused contempt and pity. One ever feels his twoness—an American, a Negro; two souls, two thoughts; two un-reconciled strivings; two warring ideals in one dark body, whose dogged strength alone keeps it from being torn asunder (p. 3).

Zuckerman's (Du Bois, 2004) interpretation of double consciousness is not only that identity is often "fractured by numerous social identities and social roles within one being but also that these social identities and roles can sometimes be at odds with one another" (p. 8). Lewis (1993) suggests that double consciousness is a revolutionary conception because implicit in Du Bois' notion is that African Americans possess the gift of "second-sight in this American world." In fact, Du Bois (1999) theorizes that this "world yields him (the African American) no true self-consciousness, but only lets him see himself through the revelation of the other world" (p. 3).

Clearly, as has been noted by Stewart (2004), the dynamics of identity development among peoples of African descent is complex—particularly for scholars, but I also add individuals and the media because of their efforts to distinguish Obama from the multitude of African Americans who have an enslaved past. Of course this is not a new phenomenon. Stewart submits that "exploitation by Europeans organized around a collective perception of a distinctive racial identity has continuously distorted the socialization of peoples of African descent and set in motion a continuing cycle of inter-group conflict" (p. 90).

Not only have media made such racial distinctions because he is biracial, born of a White mother and reared by her parents, but what has further obfuscated Obama's identity is his Kenyan-born father. To some extent, it is his upbringing and public media–driven racial identity that makes his messages ideally suited for examination of frames of double consciousness. But despite these factors, I submit that he was, from the very beginning, reared as a Black American and regarded as such by himself, his immediate family, and by others, because of this country's rules and laws of hypo descent." Obama is a Black American. He did not discover his Blackness on the South Side of Chicago in his early 20s but in the living room of his home from his immediate family.

In the preface of *Dreams from My Father* (2004) a 12- or 13-year-old Barry— what Obama was called as a young boy—said that people had to discover his racial background because he refused to acknowledge his mother's race because doing so might suggest that he was ingratiating himself to Whites. At six years old, he noted that his father did not look like anyone else in his household—his father was pitch black and his mother milk white (p. 10). His family shared stories of his African father being called "Nigger" when he studied in Hawaii. From a young age, there were stories shared about relationships with Blacks in Kansas and in Hawaii—with Blacks always depicted as subordinate.

Moreover, his mother—young, from Kansas, and living in Hawaii—had the wherewithal to teach her son who he was in such a way that he was proud of his African American heritage. Obama said that his mother's "message came to embrace Black people generally" (p. 50). For example, he said, his mother would come home with books on the Civil Rights Movement, the recordings of Mahalia Jackson, and the speeches of Dr. Martin Luther King Jr. She also told him stories of schoolchildren in the South who were forced to read books handed down from White schools, but despite these disparities and indignities they went on to become doctors, lawyers, and scientists. From his mother, he learned that "every Black man was Thurgood Marshall and every Black woman Fannie Lou Hamer. To be Black was to be the beneficiary of a great inheritance, a special destiny, glorious burdens that only we were strong enough to bear" (p. 51). Moreover, his Kenyan father, who came to visit him when he was ten, taught him about the parallels between Black Kenyans' struggle to attain freedom and the struggle of African Americans and how many Kenyans had been enslaved because of the color of their skin just as had African Americans.

A final example came from his grandfather who thought it was important that young Barry know the Black community in Hawaii, so he would take him along to visit the Black men that he knew and with whom he played cards. According to Du Bois if an Afro-centric appreciation of racial differences occurs early rather than later in an individual's life, balance in double-consciousness is more sustainable (Stewart, 2004). Clearly, Barry—from a young age—was raised to appreciate his blackness, to be a Black American, and to understand the struggles of being such in America.

One final thought on double consciousness, according to Du Bois (1999), "The African American...possessed the gift of second sight in this American World, an intuitive faculty...enabling him/her to see and say things about American society that possessed heightened moral validity" (p. 281). Du Bois contended that this was possible because "the African American dwelt equally in the mind and heart of his oppressor as in his own beset psyche" (Lewis, 1993, p. 281). One might not have to look far to find that moral validity in Obama's race speech—it is implicit in its title: We the people, in order to form a more perfect union—as he calls on us to remember the charge of the Framers of the Constitution.

FRAMING AND OBAMA'S RACE SPEECH

Goffman (1974) defines frames as "schemata of interpretation" that enables individuals "to locate, perceive, identify, and label" occurrences or life experiences (p. 21). Pan and Kosicki (2001) suggest implicit in Goffman's definition is the idea that framing is concerned with how various social actors act and interact "to yield organized ways of understanding the world" (Reese, Gandy, Jr., & Grant, 2001, p. 38). A case in point is the backdrop against which Obama's race speech was delivered. As the political actor, he organized the way he wanted the audience to understand his message. He did so using both a historical and a patriotic frame. In this way, he provided a straightforward schemata of interpretation for his audience. First, "We the People...in order to form a more perfect union" comes from the Preamble to the Constitution. Second, with regard to physical proximity, his address was presented from Philadelphia's historic National Constitution Center, across the street from Independence Hall where the founding fathers signed this supreme document into law. Third, standing tall, not as a Black candidate (his staffers had—as much as possible—played down race and ethnicity in the campaign) but framed as the man who stood for democratic and civic values—the likes of which had not been seen since FDR (Marable & Clarke, 2009). Wearing a dark suit and a blue tie that almost matched the blue backdrop, Obama stood draped on both sides by the United States flag. This visual organization/framing aided the public in interpreting the content of this message as unquestionably American.

Framing, according to Reese, Gandy, Jr., and Grant, organizes in a number of ways. One way is cultural framing, which is relevant to this study. "Cultural" frames invite the audience "to marshal a cultural understanding and keep on doing so beyond the immediate information" (2001, p. 13). That is exactly what the aforementioned physical setting of the speech did for the audience. A cultural understanding speaks to the broader dominant culture and/or to minority cultural groups within the larger society. However, Du Bois would argue that because of the gift of double consciousness, only African Americans have the ability to read and understand texts designed for the larger community while at the same time recognizing texts designed for them alone. The majority community, according to Du Bois, does not have this gift. Among those who disagree is Carl Jung (Gates, 2003), a Swiss psychiatrist and founder of analytical psychology, who visited the United States during the heyday of the separate but equal doctrine. He said the shocking thing wasn't that Black culture was not equal; the shocking thing was that it was not separate. "The naïve European thinks of America as a White nation. It is not wholly white...it is partly colored. Since the Negro lives within your cities and even within your houses, he also lives within your skin, subconsciously"

(Gates, p. 31). Whether this is the case or not, Reese suggests that frames vary at any given time in the number of people who may find them useful and share them.

Schudson (1989) explicates the functionality of frames. He notes that frames are the vehicle by which activists and reformers shape meanings and convey their claims, grievances, and proposals. They use cultural resources, beliefs, ideologies, values, and myths to make their goals persuasive. Furthermore, activists and reformers strive to make their proposals resonate among a certain audience by connecting them to popular beliefs, whether by amplifying previously muted themes or re-expressing old ideas in new idioms. Again, this, too, was evident in the setting of the Philadelphia race speech. This study will organize around Entman's (1993) four framing functions to reveal frames of double consciousness in the Obama race speech. They are defining problems, diagnosing causes, making moral judgments, and suggesting remedies.

To date, much of the framing research has focused on media messages, specifically on journalists in terms of how they frame their stories, but this chapter examines the message crafted by presidential candidate Barack Obama to determine:

1. Are there frames of double consciousness in Obama's speech?
2. If so, how are these frames manifested in the message?
3. What are the functions of the framing devices used in Obama's race speech?

For this preliminary examination, using the double-consciousness concept, I have examined the content of the To Form a More Perfect Union speech for the framing devices inherent in psychic duality as described by Du Bois (1999, 2004), Stewart (2004), Lewis (1993), and others. Additionally, I have used Entman's articulations of the four functions of frames to determine if and how they apply to the frames conceptualized by Du Bois. I will examine the frames that speak from the majority voice to the majority culture (second sight) and those from the African American voice (African American psyche) to the African American culture, and finally, from psychic duality (African American and majority voice).

Definitions

Majority voice: This means being aware of self, but, at the same time, being aware of how the majority group perceives you, your message, and your values. An example is the very purpose of this speech—to address what Du Bois calls "a problem,"—Obama's relationship with Rev. Wright, concerns about his background, his values, and validation of his Americanism. What Obama recognizes is the power of White stereotypes on Black life and he willingly uses them when he speaks from the majority voice, so he allows himself to be forced into a context of misrepresentation of his own people while also having the knowledge of reflexive truth.

African American voice: The awareness of how the majority perceive African Americans, so speaking to all of the stereotypical and/or negative ideas that one perceives the majority group to hold of African Americans.

Psychic duality: Speaking from dual consciousness such as his mixed heritage—and/or simultaneously embracing two different cultures and his "voice" reflects that. His voice (message) reflects two-ness: being a Negro and being an American at the same time.

Additionally, I will explain how each of these frames function—defining the problem, diagnosing the causes, making moral judgments, and suggesting remedies.

Findings

The majority of the frames used in Obama's race speech spoke through his majority voice to the majority population, from the patriotic framing of the backdrop to the content of his speech. This is not surprising because it was necessary for then-candidate Obama to reach the majority audience because of his need to explain the "problem," his relationship to the Reverend Dr. Wright. Harlow (2009) says this speech was made of political necessity to a group whose support he needed. Moreover, Harlow makes the argument that Obama's race message to the majority group served the framing function of defining the "problem" of race at the individual level of thinking on race. He did this by evoking the dominant frame of a post-racial society in which systemic racism no longer existed and every individual was equally responsible for and suffering from racial pain. He effectively assuages the majority of fear that he might be aligned with or shared the same values or beliefs as Wright.

An example comes from his explanation as to why Wright's speech was wrong and derisive. It was, according to Obama, a racially charged speech that should not have been made at a time when we, as a country, needed unity. Obama addressed Wright's remarks as "perceived injustice," a "profoundly distorted view of this country—a view that sees white racism as endemic, and that elevates what is wrong with America above all that we know is right with America." As Harlow points out, contrary to this notion, racism is a "structural phenomenon—not…an individual level occurrence of the past" (2009, p. 167).

Using the duality psychic voice, he diagnoses the causes of the problem in the first sentence: The document signed by the framers of the Constitution was "stained by this nation's original sin of slavery." But he immediately speaks from his majority consciousness to suggest that it is a "Constitution that had at its very core the ideal of equal citizenship under the law; a Constitution that promised its people liberty, and justice, and a union that could be and should be perfected over time." Without assigning a structural cause for and perpetuation of slavery and injustice, Obama assigns individual responsibility for freedom. "What would be needed were Americans in successive generations who were willing to do their part—through protests and struggle."

Only one paragraph of that speech spoke from his African American voice to an African American audience. "We still haven't fixed segregated schools, fifty years after Brown." The function of the Black voice frame is revealed when Obama makes the moral judgment that it is responsible for its ills: "It means taking full responsibility for our own lives—by demanding more from our fathers and spending more time with our children, and reading to them, and teaching them that they may face challenges and discrimination in their own lives...; they must always believe they can write their own destiny."

Again, Obama used the psychic duality voice when he acknowledges that he is the son of a Black man from Kenya and a White woman from Kansas...raised by a White grandfather—who survived the Depression and served in Patton's Army during World War II—and by a White grandmother. Through this framing, he aligns himself solely with the majority community, but uses the psychic duality voice to acknowledge that his wife, a "Black American...carries within her the blood of slaves and slave owners." According to Walters, this framing is important in that it effects legitimate interest representation. He is saying here, I am more like you.

Finally, the majority race frame is used to function as a remedy for this "race problem." He tells the story of Ashley, "a young, twenty-three-year old White woman," who organized for him in South Carolina. The backdrop to the Ashley story is a lone "old" Black man who says it is because of Ashley that he is supporting the campaign. This was a familiar media frame—perpetuated by Obama—that young Whites made his win possible.

DISCUSSION

The census data (Monday, July 20, 2009) reported that by age, voters ages 18 to 24 were the only group to show a statistically significant increase in turnout, with 49% casting ballots, compared with 47% in 2004. But Blacks had the highest turnout rate among this age group—55%, or an 8-percentage point jump from 2004. In contrast, turnout for Whites ages 18 to 24 was basically flat at 49%. Asians and Hispanics in that age group increased to 41% and 39% respectively.

Frey (2009), a demographer for Brookings Institution, says, "While the significance of minority votes for Obama is clearly key, it cannot be overlooked that reduced white support for a Republican candidate allowed minorities to tip the balance in many slow-growing 'purple' states" (http://www.today.com/id/32012618/ns/today-today_news/t/voting-rate-dips-older-whites-stay-home/#.VX8x8zdgI20) referring to key battleground states that don't notably tilt Democrat or Republican.

According to census data, "66 percent of Whites voted in November, 2008, down one percentage point from 2004. Blacks increased their turnout by 5 percentage points to 65 percent, nearly matching Whites. Hispanics improved turnout by 3 percentage points, and Asians by 3.5 percentage points, each reaching a turnout of nearly 50 percent. In all, minorities made up nearly 1 in 4 voters in 2008, the most diverse electorate ever" (http://www.today.com/id/32012618/ns/today-today_news/t/voting-rate-dips-older-whites-stay-home/#.VX8x8zdgI20).

While this research and others (Harlow, 2009; Moraga, 2011) have shown that Obama's race speech was delivered to a majority White audience, it shows also that there are varying reasons for his focus on the White audience. Moraga argues that "the speech was a noble and compassionate attempt to educate Whites about African Americans' justified anger" (p. 2). Harlow suggests otherwise. She asserts that during the Obama campaign, he did "nothing to address the structure of inequality in this country" and only cared about getting the White vote (p. 164). I believe that the unconscious nature of psychic duality is the foundation for the articulation of the To Form a More Perfect Union speech that may account for the opposite views from both Moraga and Harlow. It is clear from this examination that Obama's most prominent voice was that of majority to the majority. Unfortunately, when he did speak to the African American audience, it was to assign blame by using the well-known stereotypes of irresponsible fathers, Black communities depending on others for their destiny, Black parents not reading to their children.

To respond to the *New York Time*'s query, "Is this the end of Black politics?" the answer is glaring, just read Obama's Philadelphia race speech.

REFERENCES

Bai, M. (2008). Is Obama the end of Black politics? *New York Times Sunday Magazine*, p. 1.

Brachear, B. A. (2008). Wright's sermons fueled by complex mix of culture, religion. *Chicago Tribune*. https://www.census.gov/newsroom/releases/archives/voting/cb09-110.html

Cohen, M. Obama's Race Speech. http://www.democracyarsenal.org/2008/03/obamas-race-spe.html

Du Bois, W. E. B. (1957). *The Black flame: A trilogy. Vol. 1. The ordeal of Mansart*. New York: Mainstream.

Du Bois, W. E. B. (1959). *The Black flame: A trilogy. Vol. 2. Mansart builds a school*. New York: Mainstream.

Du Bois, W. E. B. (1961). *The Black flame: A trilogy. Vol. 3. Worlds of color*. New York: Mainstream.

Du Bois, W. E. B. (1999). *The souls of Black folk*. New York: Norton.

Du Bois, W. E. B. (2004). *The social theory of W. E. B. Du Bois* (P. Zuckerman, Ed.). Thousand Oaks, CA: Sage.

Entman, R. M. (1993). Framing: Toward clarification of a fractured paradigm. *Journal of Communication, 43*(4), 51–58.

Gates, H. L. (2003). The close reader: Both sides now. *International New York Times.*

Goffman, E. (1974). *Frame analysis: An essay on the organization of experience.* Boston: Northeastern University.

Harlow, R. (2009). Barack Obama and the significance of his presidential campaign. *Journal of African American Studies, 13,* 164–175.

Lewis, D. L. (1993). *W. E. B. Du Bois biography of a race, 1868–1919.* New York: Henry Holt.

Marable, M., & Clarke, K. (2009). *Barack Obama and African-American empowerment: The rise of Black America's new leadership.* New York: Palgrave Macmillan.

Moraga, C. L. (2011). *A Xicana codex of changing consciousness: Writings, 2000–2010.* Durham, NC: Duke University Press.

Obama, B. (2004). *Dreams from my father: A story of race and inheritance.* New York: Random House.

Pan, Z., & Kosicki, G. M. (2001). Framing as a strategic action in public deliberation. In Reese Gandy, Jr., & Grant (Eds.). *Framing public life: Perspectives on media and our understanding of the social world* (pp. 35-65). New York: Taylor & Francis.

Reese, S. D., Gandy, O. H., Jr., & Grant, A. E. (2001). *Framing public life: Perspectives on media and our understanding of the social world.* New York: Taylor & Francis.

Schudson, M. (1989). How culture works: Perspectives from media studies on the efficiency of symbols. *Theory and Society, 18,* 153–180.

Stewart, J. B. (2004). *Flight in search of vision.* Trenton, NJ: Africa World. http://www.today.com/id/32012618/ns/today-today_news/t/voting-rate-dips-older-whites-stay-home/#.VX38uDdgI20

Part 2:
Social, Cultural, and Community Issues

Pain, Chronic Disease, and the ACA: Implications for Better Healthcare in the Black Community

STAJA Q. BOOKER AND TAMARA A. BAKER

I've discovered that the greatest friends any of us have are knowledge and information.
—HARRY BELAFONTE (HEWLETT, 1999, NO PAGE)

INTRODUCTION

Although Black Americans account for only 13% of the total U.S. population (U.S. Census Bureau, 2012), they are reported to have a higher prevalence of being diagnosed with multiple chronic and debilitating health conditions (Centers for Disease Control & Prevention [CDC], 2012). Chronic diseases such as diabetes, cardiovascular disease, arthritis, HIV and AIDS, asthma, sickle cell disease, lupus, renal disease, and obesity are much more problematic for many Black Americans than their White counterparts despite being equitable in socioeconomic status. While factors defining these differences remain enigmatic, the resulting physical (chronic pain, disability) and mental health outcomes (anxiety, posttraumatic stress disorder [PTSD], chronic stress, depression, and suicide) are equally inexplicable among Black Americans. But why should we be concerned about chronic disease and outcomes such as chronic pain?

INTERSECTION OF PAIN AND CHRONIC DISEASE IN THE BLACK COMMUNITY

Chronic pain, in particular, is one such outcome that is associated with many chronic diseases (see table 8.1) that proves disparate across race, age, and socio-economic groups. Management depends on accurate and timely diagnosis of the underlying chronic disease and resulting pain condition, but Black Americans' reports of pain are often masked by various disease processes, leading to misdiagnosis and undertreatment (Baker & Green, 2005). This is all the more important in defining the impact chronic disease and pain have on the health and well-being of Black Americans because it is often forgotten that the wealth of a community is intricately related to the health of the community.

Table 8.1. Black Americans' Linguistic Descriptions of Chronic Disease & Pain Symptoms.

Chronic Disease (Mortality rate in Blacks)	Black Americans' Linguistic Descriptions of Chronic Disease	Pain Symptom(s) in Chronic Disease	Black Americans' Linguistic Descriptions of Pain
Chronic Diseases	Black folk diseases, Black diseases	Chronic pain	misery or miseries
Diabetes (4)	sugar, sugar diabetes	Neuropathy; pain from slow healing wounds	nerve pain
Cardiovascular Disease (1)			
Hypertension	[high] blood pressure, pressure, silent killer	Headache	headache, head hurt
Stroke (3)		Neuropathy, Complex Regional Pain Syndrome	nerve pain
Arthritic Conditions	arthritis, ole itis	Joint pain	joint pain, bones hurt
Sickle Cell Disease	Negatively referred to by some health-care professionals as "sick blood"	Widespread pain, vascular pain	crisis pain

Chronic Disease (Mortality rate in Blacks)	Black Americans' Linguistic Descriptions of Chronic Disease	Pain Symptom(s) in Chronic Disease	Black Americans' Linguistic Descriptions of Pain
HIV and AIDS	the virus, the AIDS	Myalgias, neuropathy, abdominal pain	
Lupus		Joint pain	joint pain
Respiratory Diseases (7)			
Asthma		Painful shortness of breath, bronchoconstriction	chest pain
Renal Disease (6)	kidney disease, kidney failure	Bone pain, headaches, muscle cramps, lower back pain	
Cancers (2)		Widespread pain, bone pain	
Obesity	overweight, healthy, big-boned, thick	Arthritis in weight-bearing joints (hips, knees, ankles)	Same as arthritic conditions

Copyright 2014. Staja Booker, MS, RN, & Tamara A. Baker, PhD. "Black Americans' Linguistic Descriptions of Chronic Diseases and Pain Symptoms."

Research shows that Black patients prefer the healthcare provider to treat the underlying chronic condition rather than the pain (Rhee, Kim, & Kim, 2012). Unhealthy perceptions such as this, in addition to negative cultural and social stigma associated with chronic pain and certain chronic disease diagnoses, illustrate the critical need to go beyond describing the amalgam of issues contributing to the inequitable treatment of chronic disease outcomes. Rather, the goal is to remedy perceptions and find solutions to reduce these disparities. Yet, while the impact of the disease-pain relationship (see figure 8.1) has received overwhelming attention, evidence assessing this association among Black Americans has received less attention. Recognizing this deficiency, this chapter examines: (1) the profound impact chronic disease and pain have in the Black community, and (2) ACA initiatives being implemented to remedy health disparities, while acknowledging the complexity in addressing this health dilemma among Black Americans.

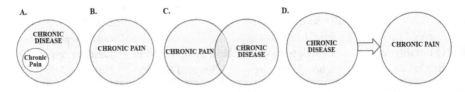

Figure 8.1. Disease-Pain Dyads.

A. depicts chronic pain as a symptom of a specific chronic disease, B. chronic pain as a chronic disease, C. the overlap of chronic pain and chronic disease as separate disease entities, and D. the development of chronic pain as a health outcome of chronic disease. Copyright 2014. Staja Booker, MS, RN, & Tamara A. Baker, PhD. "Disease-Pain Dyads."

CHRONIC DISEASE AND BLACK AMERICANS

Whether through personal experience or in knowing someone (friend, family, co-worker), Black Americans are excessively burdened with the onset and deleterious outcomes of various chronic diseases (Underwood et al., 2005). Even after accounting for social and demographic factors, Black adults have a higher incidence of at least two (or more) chronic conditions (CDC, 2012). The generational pervasiveness of chronic illnesses in the Black community gives a different metaphorical meaning to the term "The Black Plague," a bacterial disease that became a health pandemic that killed more than 100 million Europeans during the 14th century. Today chronic disease diagnosis and mortality are in epidemic proportions within the Black community. While some health outcomes have improved for Blacks, for example, incidence of end-stage renal disease, hospital admissions for uncontrolled diabetes (Agency for Healthcare Research and Quality [AHRQ], 2014), an important question remains: Why do Black Americans, despite many medical advances, continue to be diagnosed with and are more debilitated from chronic diseases?

When a patient is diagnosed with a health condition, health providers only "see" the person in his or her present state, thereby negating the (historical) circumstances of that individual. However, it must be fully understood that circumstances attributing to disease onset begins in early life, specifically the consequential additive effects of social determinants such as environment, age, genetic makeup, socioeconomic status, geographic location, and lifestyle behaviors have on impact (Non et al., 2014). A paradigm shift, known as the life course perspective, has begun to account for the total person, thereby embodying a holistic perspective in how patients define health and manage disease. Life course perspectives include everyday decision-making, and who individuals entrust to manage their health. In determining the meaning and cause(s) of this difference in diagnosis(es), health initiatives also include the multitude of factors involved in defining chronic conditions.

For example, what is characteristically similar across disciplines in how chronic disease is defined is the duration of the disease, the need for (immediate) medical attention, the impact that the diagnosis has on daily functioning, and the time and resulting limitations (Goodman, Posner, Huang, Parekh, & Koh, 2013). Despite these characteristics, there remain a number of barriers to diagnosis, treatment, and management, particularly when addressing the needs of those diagnosed with multiple chronic conditions. Barriers include low literacy, inadequate self-management, denial of chronic disease, chronic life stress, inadequate health coverage/financial support, limited access to and poor quality of care, use of spirituality (Levin, Chatters, & Taylor, 2005), and corporatization of medicine (Meghani, 2011). These conditions further amplify the susceptibility of being diagnosed with a chronic disease, how the disease is defined by the patient, how (and which) symptoms are reported, adherence to a plan of care, and from whom the patients seeks medical treatment.

Access to care is a longstanding issue and of rising concern for Black Americans given that access-related health indicators did not improve in 2013 for Black Americans (AHRQ, 2014). One area recognized in contributing to the access to and quality of care is the relationship between the patient and healthcare provider. It is well documented that the patient-provider relationship can affect access to and satisfaction with care, where satisfaction is defined by the efficaciousness of that relationship (Dawson et al., 2002; Chan & Azman, 2012; Hirsh et al., 2005; Peck, 2011). The extent to which the importance of treatment goals are expressed by the healthcare provider is often contingent on the patient's trust and confidence in issues surrounding how effective that information is communicated and the level of comfort the patient has in presenting his or her concerns (Baker, O'Connor, Roker, & Krok, 2013; Coelho & Galan, 2012; Janssen & Lagro-Janssen, 2012; Peek, Wagner, Tang, Baker, & Chin, 2011). Numerous studies have identified facilitators and barriers (e.g., prejudice, discrimination, access to services) in maintaining these relationships (Williams, Yan, Jackson, & Anderson, 1997), where the priority (on behalf of the patient and provider) must involve equity, cultural sensitivity, patient-centeredness, and patient safety. Yet, despite this recognition, Black Americans are still less likely to receive equitable primary and tertiary care (Institute of Medicine [IOM], 2003, 2011), with chronic pain presenting as one of the main outcomes contributing to these reported disparities.

CHRONIC PAIN AND BLACK AMERICANS

PAIN—Pain in African Americans Impacts the Nation! In 2008, pain-related costs in the United States reached an estimated $600 billion, with costs surpassing the combined medical expenditures of diabetes, cardiovascular disease, and cancer (Gaskin & Richard, 2012; IOM, 2011). Provisions within the ACA (as a task of the IOM) were to increase awareness of and recognize pain as a major public health problem. The report documents that chronic pain (1) affects more than 120 million Americans, (2) is dismissed as a chronic condition in itself, (3) results in exponential personal and economic costs, and (4) is a health outcome where Black Americans are less likely to receive adequate assessment, diagnosis, treatment, education, and follow-up evaluation.

As bell hooks put it, "Black people have been traumatized and physically wounded. This is something we cannot discuss enough at this historical moment" (Hewlett, 1999, no page). Historically, Blacks have been presumed to be insensitive to pain (Drwecki, Moore, Ward, & Prkachin, 2011; Forgiarini, Gallucci, & Maravita, 2011; Kaseweter, Drwecki, & Prkachin, 2012; Kenny, 2007; Sartin, 2004; Trawalter, Hoffman, & Waytz, 2013; Wandner, Scipio, & Hirsh, Torres, & Robinson, 2012). This assumption is often perpetuated at multiple levels (patient, provider, and policy) and has led to serious misconceptions impacting the diagnosis and treatment of pain among Black Americans (see table 8.2). Results from a recent survey show that a little more than one-third of healthcare providers agreed that undertreatment of pain is more common among racial and ethnic minorities and those socially and economically disadvantaged. Hence, more than half of the providers are unaware of existing pain inequities and disparities (Bekanich et al., 2014). Data further show that "only" one in five healthcare professionals who completed the survey reported biases in treating racial or ethnic minority patients who reported chronic pain (Bekanich et al., 2014). The term "only" undermines the significance of the problem, particularly among the Black community, with evidence suggesting discrimination, prejudice, and stereotyping as sources of mis- and under-treatment of pain (IOM, 2011).

A number of studies have shown perceived discrimination is associated with higher levels of pain in Blacks (Burgess et al., 2009; Burgess et al., 2013; Edwards, 2008; Goodin et al., 2013). For example, a recent study on cancer pain treatment revealed that older Blacks perceived discrimination due to their race, whereas older Whites perceived discrimination based on age (Baker, O'Connor, Roker, & Krok, 2013). It is, therefore, important to recognize the multitude of factors contributing to the assessment and treatment of pain. Clearly, there is an intersection of race, education, income, and geographic location in determining why differences among diverse minority race populations continue to permeate the social structure in the United States.

Table 8.2. Five Misconceptions and Facts about Pain in Black Americans.

Misconception	Fact
1. Black Americans are less sensitive to pain.	1. Black Americans are more sensitive to pain and report higher pain intensities. In fact, Blacks are also more sensitive to sensing others' pain (Mathur, Richeson, Paice, Muzyka, Chiao, 2014).
2. Black Americans are emotionally and physically strong and do not feel pain.	2. While Black Americans exhibit great emotional strength and perseverance, they have poorer physical health and report greater amounts of pain.
3. Black Americans are likely to misuse and abuse opioid medications.	3. Black Americans are less likely to misuse or abuse opioid medications.
4. Black Americans are opposed to taking medications to manage pain.	4. Black Americans are reluctant to take strong pain medications and are cautious of the amount and side effects associated with medications. Black Americans express concerns about addiction, but often addiction is confused with tolerance (when the body becomes used to the medication and requires higher doses to adequately control pain).
5. Black Americans receive equal pain care.	5. Black Americans experience unequal and lower quality pain care.

Black Americans face innumerable barriers to healthcare including access to that care. Access to care not only refers to access to a healthcare provider, but also access to and availability of prescription medications and financial resources to cover medical expenses. Even with health insurance, Black Americans and other racial minorities encounter more difficulty in paying for healthcare and pain treatments, which may prohibit access to and utilization of adequate services (Edwards, Moric, Husfeldt, Buvanendran, & Ivankovich, 2005; Nguyen, Ugarte, Fuller, Haas, & Portenoy, 2005; Riley, Gilbert, & Heft, 2005). Additionally, un- and underemployment, salary inequities, high co-payments and deductibles, limited benefits, and financial debt hinder many Black Americans from receiving treatment from a pain specialist (Green, Baker, Smith, & Sato, 2003; Burgess, van Ryn, Crowley-Matoka, & Malat, 2006).

Other areas to consider in the management and treatment of pain are the institutional and system-level domains. What is often assumed is that simply providing care to patients is sufficient. While true, this is only part of the equation. It is important to recognize that the quality of care received is just as significant. Reports show that some Black Americans believe that their healthcare provider lacks cultural sensitivity and does not take the time to address their pain (health) complaints and other related issues. In a recent study by Henry and Eggly, ethnic minority patients spoke with their healthcare provider about their pain an average of six minutes (2012). Considering the complexities associated with the pain experience and medical illness, patients felt that six minutes provided too little time to address the major concerns surrounding their diagnosis. This results in difficulty in managing pain and lack of knowledge and resources further confound the issue (Booker, 2014; Mingo, McIlvane, Jefferson, Edwards, & Haley, 2013; Parker et al., 2012).

Carmen Green argues, "We have learned that pain complaints of racial ethnic minorities and women and also the elderly receive less attention than others" (Field, 2004, no page). Beyond access and quality, disparities in prescription medication treatment and use are also problematic. Mounting data show that Blacks are less likely to be urgently triaged (for pain) in an emergency situation (Shapiro & Howard, 2011), and they are also more likely to be underprescribed pain medications (Burgess, Nelson, et al., 2014; Green & Hart-Johnson, 2010; Johnson et al., 2013; Joynt et al., 2013; Meghani, Byun, & Gallagher, 2012; Young, Hern, Alter, Barger, & Vahidnia, 2013) and have more difficulty accessing pain medications (opioids) at neighborhood pharmacies (Green, Ndao-Brumblay, West, & Washington, 2005; Morrison, Wallenstein, Natale, Senzel, & Huang, 2000). For example, Black military service members have the highest incidence for acute low back pain (Knox, Orchowski, & Owens, 2012), yet Black veterans under the age of 65 are prescribed analgesic medications less often than White veterans (Burgess, Nelson, et al., 2014).

For those who have access to or are prescribed opioids, they are more likely to be subjected to random drug testing in clinics and/or have restricted refills because of biased assumptions that Black patients have a higher risk for abusing opioid medications (Becker, Starrels, et al., 2011; Hausmann, Gao, Lee, & Kwoh, 2013). Yet, contrary to this assumption, research has shown that Black American patients are less likely to abuse opioid medications compared to White patients (Becker, Sullivan, Tetrault, Desai, & Fiellin, 2008). This shows that the multiplicity and complexity in adequately managing pain, from the patient to the medical institution, can significantly contribute to and perpetuate the cycle of pain disparities and health inequities within the Black community.

THE ACA: THE PROMISE, PARADOX, AND PUZZLE

The financial costs of managing chronic disease and chronic pain can be exorbitant, and without adequate financial support to obtain medical care, many live with the results of having their disease underdiagnosed and inadequately managed. The inception of the ACA is positioned to improve healthcare costs, access, quality, equity, sustainability, safety, and outcomes (Meghani, Polomano, et al., 2012). However, its novelty precludes definitive conclusions on its intended impact to ensure equal access and better quality of care for all people, regardless of race, nationality, economic status, gender, or age.

As of 2011, approximately 7 million Black Americans were uninsured. An initiative of the ACA is that it will provide greater availability of affordable and accessible healthcare for all Americans. While highly debated, the ACA has provided healthcare to more than 7 million Americans, with a significant number of those newly insured being racial and ethnic minorities (U.S. Department of Health & Human Services, 2014). With more insured Black Americans seeking medical services, the incidence of new chronic disease cases will likely increase. This massive expansion calls for a restructuring of healthcare that meets the needs of the Black community. Therefore, to deal with this emerging problem, there must be improved efforts at the national, regional, state, and local levels to attend to a much wider and diverse patient population.

Restructuring healthcare systems necessitates development of culturally congruent models of care for Black Americans that attend to the intrinsic realms of Black Americans' daily lives, including their religion, residential and work environment, psychosocial status, media usage, and language. Also within this model, services are needed to reduce chronic disease and pain disparities among Black Americans such as affordable health coverage, linguistically appropriate health services, preventative and wellness screenings, disease self-management education and support, and a strategic pipeline to increase the number of Black healthcare professionals.

While questions remain on the future of healthcare, particularly as the stratums of the ACA unfold (see table 8.3), we must remain proactive to ensure that all Americans have access to equitable and quality care for longer, healthier lives. One proactive approach is to increase grassroots advocacy work to develop partnerships between public and private corporations expanding collaborative healthcare services and coordination according to ACA standards. Moreover, communities must rally together to develop a community-level plan for prevention, management, and education of chronic disease and pain. This plan must include community-prioritized goals, specific actions, realistic time frames, and accessible resources.

Table 8.3. Relevant Affordable Care Act Provisions for Chronic Disease and Pain.

ACA Provision	Recommendations for Better Healthcare in Black Community
Title IV: Prevention of Chronic Disease and Improving Public Health	
Section 4004. Education and Outreach Campaign Regarding Preventive Benefits	• Increase awareness and knowledge of chronic disease, preventive and prenatal services, healthy lifestyle choices through media and community outreach • Engage lay health workers to assist in educating and providing basic services to community members • Provide funding to faith-based institutions to bring health services and wellness programs to community residents; healthier community transformation grants (Section 4201) • Offer free community-based chronic disease self-management programs through community partnerships
Section 4104. Removal of Barriers to Preventive Services in Medicare; Section 4106. Improving Access to Preventive Services for Eligible Adults in Medicaid	• Waive co-payments and deductibles for preventive screenings and lower monthly premiums • Ensure Prescription Drug Programs are readily accessible • Offer incentives for utilization of annual wellness visits • Allow dual enrollment in Medicare and Medicaid
Section 4305a. Convene IOM Pain Conference	• Increase pain disparities research in Black Americans • Reduce barriers to access to care: ensure reliable transportation, remove financial limitations (accepting delayed co-payments and developing financing programs), provide affordable resources, ensure pharmacies are stocked with pain medications • Improve quality of care: assess pain at every type of healthcare visit, tailor treatment to cultural values, provide care coordination and navigation

ACA Provision	Recommendations for Better Healthcare in Black Community
Section 4305b (PHSA Section 409J). Expand Pain Research through the Pain Consortium of National Institutes of Health	• Engage the Black community in pain research through ethical partnership, recruitment, and retention • Develop and encourage Black researchers to study pain in Black Americans • Develop pain research priorities from the perspective of Black Americans
Section 4305c (Section 759d). Develop and Implement Pain Care Education and Training	• Educate health professionals and students on health disparities, culture, misconceptions, appropriate prescribing and use of controlled substances and national standards for cultural and linguistic appropriate services and • Ensure interdisciplinary care ("It takes a village...")

CONCLUSION

This chapter has attempted to address some of the more critical social and environmental issues that contribute to differences and disadvantages in chronic disease and pain diagnoses, treatment, and management. Although the areas of concern are many, efforts to augment our knowledge of the disease-pain dyad among Black Americans are in the forefront. When we ask, is race relevant as we examine these health differences? The answer is, of course. However, emphasis should not only be on race, which is a descriptor of physical characteristics, but also on the intersection between race and social and economic factors. Emphasis on precursors such as racial inequities, environmental risk factors, lifestyle behaviors, and genetic predisposition is needed to fully understand the onset, diagnosis, treatment, and management of the many chronic illnesses that trouble the lives of many Black Americans.

With initiatives such as the ACA being implemented at the policy level, efforts are now aimed at improving access to and the receipt of quality and equitable care for all Americans. As U.S. demographics change along with healthcare delivery systems, it is essential that such cultural diversity at the individual, system, and policy levels be addressed if we intend to wage—and win—the war on health disparities. Lavin and Park suggest that "policy makers...identify flexible strategies that take into account the various values and norms of diverse older racial [and] ethnic groups to optimize access to pain treatment and to ensure that medical care is sensitive to their needs and cultural diversity" (2014, p. 286). This quote embodies the collective nature of Blacks in the United States, and how culture has and continues to play a significant role in their daily experiences.

Despite the many odds, there is a sense of resiliency, strength, and foresight among the Black American community that is dictated from generations past. The allegiance to do more, strive higher, and be the best has patterned actions of many Black Americans for success. So, despite what had been socially dictated as it pertains to the health and well-being of Black Americans, there is a sense of perseverance, where health equality and equity will be afforded to all, and that someday "We shall overcome!"

REFERENCES

Affordable Care Act (ACA). (2010). 111th Congress, Second Session. Retrieved from http://www.hhs.gov/healthcare/rights/law/index.html

Agency for Healthcare Research and Quality (AHRQ). (2014). *National healthcare disparities report.* Rockville, MD: Author. Retrieved from http://www.ahrq.gov/research/findings/nhqrdr/nhdr13/2013nhdr.pdf

Baker, T. A., & Green, C. R. (2005). Intrarace differences among Black and White Americans presenting for chronic pain management: The influence of age, physical health, and psychosocial factors. *Pain Medicine, 6*(1), 29–38.

Baker, T. A., O'Connor, M. L., Roker, R., & Krok, J. L. (2013). Satisfaction with pain treatment in older cancer patients: Identifying variants of discrimination, trust, communication, and self-efficacy. *Journal of Hospice and Palliative Nursing, 15*(8), 455–463. doi: 10.1097/NJH.0b013e3182a12c24

Becker, W. C., Starrels, J. L., Heo, M., Li, X., Weiner, M. G., & Turner, B. J. (2011). Racial differences in primary care opioid risk reduction strategies. *Annals of Family Medicine, 9*(3), 219–225.

Becker, W. C., Sullivan, L. E., Tetrault, J. M., Desai, R. A., & Fiellin, D. A. (2008). Non-medical use, abuse and dependence on prescription opioids among U.S. adults: Psychiatric, medical, and substance use correlates. *Drug and Alcohol Dependence, 94*(1–3), 38–47.

Bekanich, S. J., Wanner, N., Junkins, S., Mahoney, K., Kahn, K. A., Berry, C. A., et al. (2014). A multifaceted initiative to improve clinician awareness of pain management disparities. *American Journal of Medical Quality, 29*(5), 388-396. doi: 10.1177/1062860613503897

Booker, S. Q. (2014). African Americans' perceptions of pain and pain management: A systematic review. *The Journal of Transcultural Nursing.* Epub ahead of print.

Burgess, D. J., Gravely, A. A., Nelson, D. B., van Ryn, M., Bair, M. J., Kerns, R. D., et al. (2013). A national study of racial differences in pain screening rates in the VA health care system. *Clinical Journal of Pain, 29*(2), 118–123. doi: 10.1097/AJP.0b013e31826a86ae

Burgess, D. J., Grill, J., Noorbaloochi, S., Griffin, J. M., Ricards, J., van Ryn, M., et al. (2009). The effect of perceived racial discrimination on bodily pain among older African American men. *Pain Medicine, 10*(8), 1341–1352. doi:10.1111/j.1526-4637.2009.00742.x

Burgess, D. J., Nelson, D. B., Gravely, A. A., Bair, M. J., Kerns, R. D., Higgins, D. M., et al. (2014). Racial differences in prescription opioid analgesics for chronic noncancer pain in a national sample of veterans. *The Journal of Pain, 15*(4), 447–455. http://dx.doi.org/10.1016/j.jpain.2013.12.010

Burgess, D. J., van Ryn, M., Crowley-Matoka, M., & Malat, J. (2006). Understanding the provider contribution to race/ethnicity disparities in pain treatment: Insights from dual process models of stereotyping. *Pain Medicine, 7*(2), 119–134.

Centers for Disease Control & Prevention (CDC). (2012). Multiple chronic conditions among adults aged 45 and over: Trends over the past 10 years. *National Center for Health Statistics Data Brief, 100.* http://www.cdc.gov/nchs/data/databriefs/db100.pdf

Chan, C. M., & Azman, W. A. (2012). Attitudes and role orientations on doctor-patient fit and patient satisfaction in cancer care. *Singapore Medical Journal, 53*(1), 52–56.

Coelho, K. R., & Galan, C. (2012). Physician cross-cultural nonverbal communication skills, patient satisfaction and health outcomes in physician-patient relationship. *International Journal of Family Medicine,* 376907. doi: 10.1155/2012/376907

Dawson, R., Spross, J. A., Jablonski, E. S., Hoyer, D. R., Sellers, D. E., & Solomon, M. Z. (2002). Probing the paradox of patients' satisfaction with inadequate pain management. *Journal of Pain and Symptom Management, 23*(3), 211–220.

Drwecki, B. B., Moore, C. F., Ward, S. E., & Prkachin, K. M. (2011). Reducing racial disparities in pain treatment: The role of empathy and perspective-taking. *Pain, 152*(5), 1001–1006. doi: 10.1016/j.pain.2010.12.005

Edwards, R. R. (2008). The association of perceived discrimination with low back pain. *Journal of Behavioral Medicine, 31*(5), 379–389. doi: 10.1007/s10865-008-9160-9

Edwards, R. R., Moric, M., Husfeldt, B., Buvanendran, A. M., & Ivankovich, O. (2005). Ethnic similarities and differences in the chronic pain experience: A comparison of African American, Hispanic, and White patients. *Pain Medicine, 6*(1), 88–98.

Field, D. (2004). *Disparities in pain management: An expert interview with Carmen R. Green, MD.* Retrieved from http://www.medscape.org/viewarticle/581003.

Forgiarini, M., Gallucci, M., & Maravita, A. (2011). Racism and the empathy for pain on our skin. [eCollection 2011]. *Frontiers in Psychology, 2*(108). doi: 10.3389/fpsyg.2011.00108

Gaskin, D. J., & Richard, P. (2012). The economic costs of pain in the United States. *The Journal of Pain, 13*(8), 715–724. doi: 10.1016/j.jpain.2012.03.009

Goodin, B. R., Pham, Q. T., Glover, T. L., Sotolongo, A., King, C. D., Sibille, K. T., et al. (2013). Perceived racial discrimination, but not mistrust of medical researchers, predicts the heat pain tolerance of African Americans with symptomatic knee osteoarthritis. *Health Psychology, 32*(11), 1117–1126. doi: 10.1037/a0031592

Goodman, R. A., Posner, S. F., Huang, E. S., Parekh, A. K., & Koh, H. K. (2013). Defining and measuring chronic conditions: Imperatives for research, policy, program, and practice. *Preventing Chronic Disease, 10,* E66. doi: 10.5888/pcd10.120239

Green, C. R., Baker, T. A., Smith, E. M., & Sato, Y. (2003). The effect of race in older adults presenting for chronic pain management: A comparative study of Black and White Americans. *The Journal of Pain, 4*(2), 82–90.

Green, C. R., & Hart-Johnson, T. (2010). The adequacy of chronic pain management prior to presenting at a tertiary care pain center: The role of patient socio-demographic characteristics. *The Journal of Pain, 11*(8), 746–754. doi:10.1016/j.jpain.2009.11.003

Green, C. R., Ndao-Brumblay, S. K., West, B., & Washington, T. (2005). Differences in prescription opioid analgesic availability: Comparing minority and white pharmacies across Michigan. *The Journal of Pain, 6*(10), 689–699.

Hausmann, L. R., Gao, S., Lee, E. S., & Kwoh, C. K. (2013). Racial disparities in the monitoring of patients on chronic opioid therapy. *Pain, 154*(1), 46–52. doi: 10.1016/j.pain.2012.07.034

Henry, S. G., & Eggly, S. (2012). How much time do low-income patients and primary care physicians actually spend discussing pain? A direct observation study. *Journal of General Internal Medicine, 27*(7), 787–793. doi: 10.1007/s11606-011-1960-x

Hewlett, R. (1999). *Pearls of Black wisdom.* White Plains, NY: Peter Pauper Press, Inc.

Hirsh, A. T., Atchison, J. W., Berger, J. J., Waxenberg, L. B., Lafayette-Lucey, A., Bulcourf, B. B., et al. (2005). Patient satisfaction with treatment for chronic pain: Predictors and relationship to compliance. *Clinical Journal of Pain, 21*(4), 302–310.

Institute of Medicine (IOM). (2003). *Unequal treatment: Confronting racial and ethnic disparities in health care.* Washington, DC: National Academies.

Institute of Medicine (IOM). (2011). *Relieving pain in America: A blueprint for transforming prevention, care, education, and research.* Washington, DC: National Academies.

Janssen, S. M., & Lagro-Janssen, A. L. (2012). Physician's gender, communication style, patient preferences and patient satisfaction in gynecology and obstetrics: A systematic review. *Patient Education and Counseling, 89*(2), 221–226. doi: 10.1016/j.pec.2012.06.034

Johnson, T. J., Weaver, M. D., Borrero, S., Davis, E. M., Myaskovsky, L., Zuckerbraun, N. S., et al. (2013). Association of race and ethnicity with management of abdominal pain in the emergency department. *Pediatrics, 132*(4), e851–e858. doi: 10.1542/peds.2012-3127

Joynt, M., Train, M. K., Robbins, B. W., Halterman, J. S., Caiola, E., & Fortuna, R. J. (2013). The impact of neighborhood socioeconomic status and race on the prescribing of opioids in emergency departments throughout the U. S. *Journal of General Internal Medicine, 28*(12), 1604–1610.

Kaseweter, K. A., Drwecki, B. B., & Prkachin, K. M. (2012). Racial difference in pain treatment and empathy in a Canadian sample. *Pain Research and Management, 17*(6), 381–384.

Kenny, S. C. (2007). "I can do the child no good": Dr. Sims and the enslaved infants of Montgomery, Alabama. *Social History of Medicine, 20*(2), 223–241.

Knox, J. B., Orchowski, J. R., & Owens, B. (2012). Racial differences in the incidence of acute low back pain in United States military service members. *Spine, 37*(19), 1688–1692. doi: 10.1097/BRS.0b013e318255a07b

Lavin, R., & Park, J. (2014). A characterization of pain in racially and ethnically diverse older adults: A review of the literature. *Journal of Applied Gerontology, 33*(3), 258–290.

Levin, J., Chatters, L. M., & Taylor, R. J. (2005). Religion, health and medicine in African Americans: Implications for physicians. *Journal of the National Medical Association, 97*(2), 237–249.

Mathur, V. A., Richeson, J. A., Paice, J. A., Muzyka, M., & Chiao, J. Y. (2014). Racial bias in pain perception and response: Experimental examination of automatic and deliberate processes. *The Journal of Pain, 15*(5), 476–484. doi: 10.1016/j.jpain.2014.01.488

Meghani, S. H. (2011). Corporatization of pain medicine: Implications for widening pain care disparities. *Pain Medicine, 12*(4), 634–644. doi: 10.1111/j.1526-4637.2011.01074.x

Meghani, S. H., Byun, E., & Gallagher, R. M. (2012). Time to take stock: A meta-analysis and systematic review of analgesic treatment disparities for pain in the United States. *Pain Medicine, 13*(2), 150–174. doi: 10.1111/j.1526-4637.2011.01310.x

Meghani, S. H., Polomano, R. C., Tait, R. C., Vallerand, A. H., Anderson, K. O., & Gallagher, R. M. (2012). Advancing a national agenda to eliminate disparities in pain care: Directions for health policy, education, practice, and research. *Pain Medicine, 13*(1), 5–28.

Mingo, C. A., McIlvane, J. M., Jefferson, M., Edwards, L. J., & Haley, W. E. (2013). Preferences for arthritis interventions: Identifying similarities and differences among African Americans and Whites with osteoarthritis. *Arthritis Care and Research, 65*(2), 203–211. doi: 10.1002/acr.21781

Morrison, R. S., Wallenstein, S., Natale, D. K., Senzel, R. S., & Huang, L. L. (2000). "We don't carry that"—failure of pharmacies in predominantly nonwhite neighborhoods to stock opioid analgesics. *New England Journal of Medicine, 342*(14), 1023–1026.

Nguyen, M., Ugarte, C., Fuller, I., Haas, G., & Portenoy, R. K. (2005). Access to care for chronic pain: Racial and ethnic differences. *The Journal of Pain, 6*(5), 301–314.

Non, A. L., Rewak, M., Kawachi, I., Gilman, S. E., Loucks, E. B., Appleton, A. A., et al. (2014). Childhood social disadvantage, cardiometabolic risk, and chronic disease in adulthood. *American Journal of Epidemiology, 180*(3), 263–271. doi: 10.1093/aje/kwu127

Parker, S. J., Chen, E. K., Pillemer, K., Filiberto, D., Laureano, E., Piper, J., et al. (2012). Participatory adaptation of an evidence-based, arthritis self-management program. Making changes to improve program fit. *Family and Community Health, 35*(3), 236–245.

Peck, B. M. (2011, October 5). Age-related differences in doctor-patient interaction and patient satisfaction. *Current Gerontology and Geriatrics Research*, 137492. doi: 10.1155/2011/137492

Peek, M. E., Wagner, J., Tang, H., Baker, D. C., & Chin, M. H. (2011). Self-reported racial discrimination in health care and diabetes outcomes. *Medical Care, 49*(7), 618–625.

Rhee, Y. O., Kim, E., & Kim, B. (2012). Assessment of pain and analgesic use in African American cancer patients: Factors related to adherence to analgesics. *Journal of Immigrant Minority Health, 14*, 1045–1051.

Riley, J. L., III, Gilbert, G. H., & Heft, M. W. (2005). Orofacial pain: Patient satisfaction and delay of urgent care. *Public Health Reports, 120*(2), 140–149.

Sartin, J. S. (2004). J. Marion Sims, the father of gynecology: Hero or villain? *Southern Medical Journal, 97*(5), 500–505.

Shapiro, S. E., & Howard, P. K. (2011). Does gender and ethnicity impact initial assessment and management of chest pain? *Advanced Emergency Nursing Journal, 33*(1), 4–7.

Trawalter, S., Hoffman, K. M., & Waytz, A. (2012). Racial bias in perceptions of others' pain. *PLoS ONE, 7*(11), e48546. doi: 10.1371/journal.pone.0048546

Underwood, S. M., Buseh, A. G., Canales, M. K., Powe, B., Dockery, B., Kather, T., et al. (2005). Nursing contributions to the elimination of health disparities among African Americans: Review and critique of a decade of research—Part III. *Journal of National Black Nurses Association, 16*(2), 35–59.

U.S. Census Bureau. (2012). *People Quick Facts.* http://quickfacts.census.gov/qfd/states/00000.html

U.S. Department of Health & Human Services. (2014). 7.1 Million Americans have enrolled in private health coverage under the Affordable Care Act. [Blog] http://www.hhs.gov/healthcare/facts/blog/2014/04/more-7-million-americans-are-signed-private-health-coverage.html

Wandner, L. D., Scipio, C. D., Hirsh, A. T., Torres, C. A., & Robinson, M. E. (2012). The perception of pain in others: How race, gender, and age influence pain expectations. *The Journal of Pain, 13*(3), 220–227.

Williams, D. R., Yan, Y., Jackson, J. S., & Anderson, N. B. (1997). Racial differences in physical and mental health: Socio-economic status, stress, and discrimination. *Journal of Health Psychology, 2*(3), 335–351. doi: 10.1177/135910539700200305

Young, M. F., Hern, H. G., Alter, H. J., Barger, J., & Vahidnia, F. (2013). Racial differences in receiving morphine among prehospital patients with blunt trauma. *Journal of Emergency Medicine, 45*(1), 46–52. doi: 10.1016/j.jemermed.2012.07.088

CHAPTER NINE

Big, Black, and Beautiful Women: Health at Every Size Offers a New Paradigm

E-K DAUFIN

Weight discrimination, aka the war on obesity, has been called the "psychic replacement for old fashioned racism" (Campos, 2004, p. 85). This campaign to make fat people thin is instead making the ineffective diet and weight loss industry richer and fat people sicker. Weight discrimination is used as an excuse to persecute and demean those at higher weights, who are disproportionally African American women.

This chapter seeks to deconstruct the faulty connection between thinness and health, specifically within the Black community. "White" and "male-centric" institutions and worldviews have promoted various factors of racism, sexism, and weightism. For example, the primary issue of patriarchy is that women are usually judged even more harshly than men for their looks. Despite having our first African American family in the White House, racism is alive and well. And weightism is growing significantly in today's society. In other words, many African American women are impacted by all three—racism, sexism, and weightism—making them disproportionately the target of several levels of multiple and intersecting burdens of discrimination.

In a May 2014 Pew Research Center poll, almost 90% of African Americans and 73% of Whites agreed that some racial discrimination still exists against African Americans (Doherty, 2014). Researchers Peter Glick and Susan Fiske, in a 2001 study of more than 15,000 participants in 19 nations, found that sexism still appears to be cross-culturally prevalent. A special report on obesity released in September 2014 suggests that about the same percent of Black and White men were found to be at higher weights, 69% and 71.4% respectively. However, in the same study, 82% of Black women compared to 63.2% of White women were at higher weights. This means that African American women are more likely to be at higher weights compared to any other group in the United States.[1]

As a result, the war on obesity efforts targeted at Black communities only intensify the already present sexism, weight stigma, and racial denigration of the vast majority of African Americans. Diets and exercising with weight loss as the goal have actually been found to increase health risks, rather than permanently transforming participants into Eurocentric beauty ideals of AMA-approved African Americans (Puhl & Heuer, 2010).

In *Psychology Today*, Meg Selig argues against dieting for weight loss. She suggests that dieting is temporary and restrictive, and research has shown that for about 95% of dieters, the weight doesn't stay off in the long run (2009). We know that crash diets, diet pills, and fad diets are harmful, but studies are also finding that dieting itself can be counterproductive. University of Missouri exercise physiologist Steve Ball suggests that the focus on weight loss alone sets people up for regaining the pounds because it slows down metabolism (Maron, 2008).

In this critical discourse analysis, the Health at Every Size (HAES) paradigm is examined. It involves a method of becoming as healthy as possible by eating and moving intuitively for nutrition, pleasure, and social ritual. It involves ending weight stigma by increasing self-esteem and self-acceptance regardless of weight. According to Teun A. Van Dijk, critical discourse analysis is "an effective way to study how social power, abuse, dominance, and inequality are enacted, reproduced, and resisted by text and talk in social and political contexts" (1993, p. 352). Dijk argues that the primary goal of critical discourse analysis is, ultimately, to challenge social and political norms with the hope of bringing about change through critical understanding.

This chapter uses a number of specific definitions. First, "higher weight(s)" is a more neutral and nonjudgmental term used to describe people who are considered to "weigh too much," rather than terms such as "overweight and obese" (Pearce, 2012). The word "fat" may sometimes be used rather than obese because the latter term is a medical diagnosis based on how one looks to the layperson. "Patriarchy" is a prominent view about various structures focusing on how men are normally found in dominating positions while women are often found in oppressive positions. "Weight stigma" is defined as negative or unfair societal beliefs about a group or community concerning size.

Three major myths tied to weightism and African American women will be explored. These three social, cultural, and community myths must be challenged to move toward a more inclusive and equitable society. The first myth suggests that Black culture and individual inferiority make us fat, rather than our genetic slave history and other social factors. The inaccurate assumption is that anyone who is determined can lose weight and keep it off (Bacon, 2010). However, it has been found that most people who lose weight regain it regardless of whether they maintain their diet or exercise program (Mann, Tomiyama, Westling, Lew, Samuels, & Chatman, 2007).

Often people assume that soul food, an important part of African American cultural identity, makes African Americans fat. For example, *Soul Food Junkies* filmmaker Byron Hurt made his documentary because he says his father was gaining a lot of weight and "looking unhealthy" (2012). Hurt equates higher weight with poor health and assumes a soul food diet caused his father's higher weight and death. As one woman says in the film, "You eat. You get big" (Hurt). However, many naturally thin people lead sedentary lives and eat a lot of soul/Southern food, don't get big, but do get sick. These thin members of the Black community don't get the same condemnation when it comes to eating soul/Southern food. It is, therefore, important that thin Blacks begin to deconstruct their own unearned thin privilege because it can be as divisive as other privileges, such as light skin and "good" hair.

Community activists in *Soul Food Junkies* and on other platforms contend that the so-called Black obesity epidemic is not due primarily to soul food indulgences, but actually the "class-based apartheid in the industrialization of our food system" (Hurt). They refer to these segregated areas, in part, as "food deserts," a term commonly used to describe communities with little or no access to affordable, fresh food. In the United States almost 24 million, mostly poor African Americans, live in these areas ("America's Worst 9 Urban Food Deserts," 2001).

Yet these same "predominantly Black neighborhoods have 2.4 fast-food restaurants per square mile compared to 1.5…in predominantly White neighborhoods" and suburbs (Block, Schribner, & DeSalvo, 2004, p. 211). Even African Americans who are fortunate enough to live outside of food deserts may still be constrained by budget to choose the cheaper, more filling, processed foods that are readily available. Bell and Field found that Black people get chastised for "their own (weight) problems" even though junk food is easier and cheaper to access than healthy food (2013).

Moreover, the commercial food industry is motivated to increase large corporate profits rather than produce the most nutrient rich, affordable food for the populace (Bell & Field, 2013). Industrial scale agriculture depletes the soil and requires larger doses of pesticides and chemical fertilizers (Bell & Field). Even if you have the money and access to fresh fruits, vegetables, and meats, they usually contain an inordinate amount of chemicals that accumulate in fat cells, making it difficult, if not impossible, to lose weight and instead contribute to metabolic syndrome and higher weights (Kim, Pellous, Guyot, Tordjman, Bui, Chevallier, et al., 2012, p. 508).

The Black Women's Health Study (BWHS) of Boston University's Slone Epidemiological Center is a major long-term study of Black women's health (2013–2014). In 1995, 59,000 women agreed to participate in the study that does a biannual follow-up covering different topics. The BWHS has found that "genes, diet, socioeconomic status and environmental factors" conspire to make African American women the heaviest group in the United States (Zimmerman, 2012). Notice that genes are listed first. Zimmerman's report notes that experiencing racism and other discrimination as stress also correlates with African American women's higher weights. In addition, the study found that higher levels of childbearing; having less access to safe affordable housing and exercise options; fewer quality affordable and accessible grocery stores; and lower rates of breastfeeding than White women and Latinas were problematic (Zimmerman).

The American Psychological Association (APA) and the Association of Black Psychologists (ABP) report that even though a higher educational status seems "to somewhat protect" White women and Latinas from "rising obesity rates," that same education does not "protect" African American women (Dingfelder, 2013, p. 56). Racial discrimination and patriarchy in American society make it easier to believe that despite higher education, Black women don't eat well and exercise, with the faulty presumption that doing so would make higher weight Black women thin.

The APA and ABP also agree that the "chronic stress of racism and caring for whole family systems" contribute to Black women's higher likelihood of being fat (Dingfelder, 2013). In fact, according to Maes, Neal, and Eves, "genetic factors explain 50% to 90% of a person's weight" (1997, p. 325). Once someone reaches a higher weight, it's pretty much an unchangeable demographic, within a narrow range of about 10–15 pounds in the long term (Aamodt, 2013). This suggests that no matter what dangerous, difficult, and demeaning things a women is willing to do to herself to lose weight, most won't be able to permanently and safely change their size in a significant way.

Today, research suggests that even the typical behavioral, medical, or surgical approaches used to lose that 5–10% of body weight do not work as well for African American women, and it has little to do with compliance (Lynch, Change, Ford, & Ibrahim, 2007, p. 908). A two-year, randomized study of weight loss self-help and structured commercial programs (the latter at great cost to those who try them) found participants maintained an average of 3–9.5 kg weight loss after the first year, and regained from 1.5 to over 3 kg of that small amount after two years (Heshka, Anderson, Atkinson, Greenway, Hill, Phinney, et al., 2003, p. 1797). A longer study may find that participants regained all the weight and more. Our brains are wired to make us gain more weight, to protect against the next weight loss diet which our bodies read as "famine" (Glenville, 2012).

Some foods commonly recommended as "healthy" in weight loss diets may lead to weight gain, including but not limited to processed cereal, Agave syrup, whole wheat bread, prepackaged granola and trail mixes, low fat yogurt, commercial salad dressings, fruit juices, diet soft drinks, organic processed foods, and gluten-free junk foods.[2] Research shows that dieting physiologically makes the dieter hungrier and more "preoccupied with food" (Zheng, Lenard, Shin, & Berthoud, 2009, p. S8). This is not to demonize these or any foods, but to make the point that you can't tell what a person eats by simply looking at her.

It is probably a blessing that Black women are less likely than other women to have bariatric surgery (Lynch et al., 2007). According to the Duke University Medical Center, across race, weight loss surgery recipients are predominantly female, and African Americans comprise only 10% (2009). However, the American Society of Plastic Surgeons indicates that the number of African Americans undergoing weight loss surgery is growing (McGee, 2005, p. 5), despite the fact that weight loss surgery increases actual mortality risks by 700% the first year and by up to 363% over the first four years (Bacon, 2010, p. 63). One study shows up to 36% of weight loss surgery patients may die from the surgery within the first year (Flum, Salem, Elrod, Dellinger, Cheadle, & Chan, 2005, p. 1905).

African American Robyn McGee dedicates her book, *Hungry for More: A Keeping-It-Real Guide for Black Women on Weight and Body Image* to her sister Cathy, who died from gastric bypass surgery at just 49 years old (2005, p. 4). Though the coroner listed the death as "cardiac arrest," after subpoenaing the medical records for a wrongful death suit, the family found that Cathy actually died from a post-surgery infection common in gastric bypass patients. McGee says that she and her sister got their "thick body type from (their) dad," (genetics) and that Cathy tried "pills, powders, Weight Watchers...FenPhen...Atkins, NutriSystem, OPTIFAST, grapefruit diets, and traveling to...Tijuana or Canada to buy miracle appetite injections" (p. 3). Ironically, despite Robyn's observations, the author still attributes her sister's, her own, and all higher weight Black women's larger sizes to overeating and under-exercising, rather than a genetic propensity to simply being larger.

Even if weight loss surgery doesn't kill you, it has about a 90% failure rate and costs nearly $30,000 (Mercola, 2005). Some providers admit that in a conservative estimate of 20–30% of cases, weight loss surgery produces no or inadequate weight loss, and some weight regain (Smart Dimensions Weight Loss, 2014). Also, a meta-analysis of ethnic differences in weight loss surgery finds that despite all the risks and side effects, African Americans lose less weight than other groups (Minnesota Department of Human Rights, 2013).

You may permanently lose some weight with weight loss surgery, but the process almost guarantees lifelong side effects, including but not limited to many other problems such as:

- osteoporosis
- liver failure
- pancreatic impairment
- adhesions
- polyps
- anemia
- arthritis
- pungently odiferous intestinal gas
- fecal and urinary incontinence
- cancer (of the stomach, esophagus, pancreas, and bowel)
- nausea
- chest pain from vomiting
- cold intolerance
- constipation
- depression
- suicide (five times the risk)
- diarrhea
- diverticulitis
- early onset of diabetes and/or hypertension
- erosion of tooth enamel
- excessive stomach acid
- esophageal erosion
- hair loss
- hemorrhoids
- hernia
- hormone imbalances
- need for side-effect drugs
- ulcers
- blood clots
- weakness
- stroke or heart attack
- limb loss
- infertility or complications once impregnated
- infection from leakage into body cavities (peritonitis)
- involuntary anorexia
- irregular body fat distribution (lumpy body)
- body shame for having the lumpy post-operative body and/or excess skin
- new eating disorders
- failure to resolve preoperative eating disorders
- seizures/intense shaking
- shame regarding not being able to lose weight without surgery

- grief that you had to have weight loss surgery in order to receive others' approval, admiration, respect and attention
- pituitary gland malfunction
- nerve and brain damage
- putrid breath, and the list goes on.[3]

Among U.S. adults there can be a high prevalence of cardio metabolic abnormalities in "normal" weight people and a high prevalence of cardio metabolic health in higher weight people (Wildman, Munther, Reynolds, McGinn, Rajpathak, Wylie-Rosett, et al., 2008, p. 1617). In other words, higher weight is not proof of dietary, exercise, intellectual, and/or moral transgression, just as thinness is not a testament to health.

Many argue that African American women's larger bodies may have less to do with their awareness and practice of healthy exercise and eating habits, and more to do with an intrinsic genetic predisposition from ancestors' surviving slavery. Generations of African American slave women had to develop extremely efficient metabolisms to survive working sunrise to sunset, six or seven days a week, year round with little to no accommodations for menstruation, pregnancy, child bearing, birthing, and nursing (Campbell, Miers, & Miller, 2007). They had little to eat, and the psychological stress of sexual imposition/assault, attachment insecurity, and other hardships of the slave industry also took a toll (Barzel, 1977, pp. 92–95).

P. T. Ellison, the editor emeritus of the *American Journal of Human Biology*, believes that the intergenerational genetic and epigenetic mechanisms of slavery still influence weight- and health-related disparities between African Americans and other groups in the United States (2009). He explains, "History may continue to affect not only the social conditions of African American life, but biological and health conditions as well" (pp. 1–2). In other words, the metabolism Black women developed during slavery has been passed down to generations of Black women in today's relatively easier physical work environment.

What is most pernicious about weight discrimination is the false assumption that everyone at a higher weight is so because she is lazy and/or overeats. Internalized and unconscious patriarchy and racism make it easier to believe these negative, inaccurate stereotypes when the highest weight group visible is comprised of African American women. These women are often harassed and discriminated against with impunity, even in their own homes, by family and friends, because fat people are seen as fair game. Sometimes medical doctors, who rarely have more than a few hours of instruction about the treatment of weight issues during their entire seven-year, post-baccalaureate medical education, make the same mistake regarding this myth (Park, 2013).

The second myth is a cultural one that suggests Black women don't suffer from weight stigma in African American and White mainstream culture. There is no insular Black world where Black women are not subject to explicit mainstream White standards of approval. Even in predominantly or completely Black neighborhoods, schools, and churches Black women are judged by White, patriarchal, and popular culture standards.

In pop culture African American attractiveness icons usually have light skin, straight hair, and thin frames. Black women who have comparatively larger sexual features (breasts, buttocks, hips) must be otherwise thin (stomach, arms), such as Michelle Obama, Beyoncé, and Mariah Carrie, to escape the higher weight stigma. Also, Black women who are top-chart recording artists, along with the throngs of Black women in music videos, are relatively thin as well.[4] Plus, Black comedians tend to denigrate higher weight Black women in stand-up acts and feature films such as *Big Momma's House* (2000), the Tyler Perry *Madea* movies (2006–2015), or Eddie Murphy's *Norbit* (2007).

Some scholars have pointed to Queen Latifah as "proof" there's no weight stigma for Black women. Yet, Queen Latifah has capitulated to some White patriarchal standards of beauty. For example, she sometimes sports a long blonde weave rather than the short natural hair she used to wear when she was a rapper. She has also promoted her weight loss plan "to achieve a Hollywood look," but still only managed to shave that 5–10% of her weight as discussed earlier (Queen Latifah, 2014). So, Queen Latifah is still considered "obese" by mainstream medical standards and is constantly presented in ways that reduce her apparent size. Also, because of prejudice against her weight it has been difficult for her to become an accepted leading lady or sex symbol in Hollywood.

Oprah Winfrey's yo-yo dieting and self-hatred for her body is a long, tragic, and public story. Many have tried to lose weight along with Oprah to no avail or have experienced the expected effect that no matter what they do, the weight, plus more, comes back. Yo-yo dieting progressively lowers energy and metabolism, increases body fat while decreasing muscle, and it can induce coronary artery disease, as well as Type 2 diabetes (McNight, 2013).

Also, consider this contrast. The dark chocolate, ultra slim Lupita Nyong'o of *12 Years a Slave* (2013), an African beauty, was celebrated as *People Magazine's* 2014 most beautiful person in the world (Jordan & Coulton, 2014), while the higher weight, also chocolate-colored Gabourey Sidibe, who is a genetic product of the U.S. slave trade, has not been so gloriously received (Vineyard, 2014). Even in Africa, attitudes are changing. Traditionally, in a number of African countries, men who are heavy are seen as successful and women who are heavy are considered beautiful (Birrell, 2014; Engel, 2013). While heavier African women used to be considered more desirable, Western pop culture has influenced many African women, especially younger women, to become more concerned with weight issues (Ferguson, 2011; Morris & Szabo, 2013).

Weight stigma and bias involves negative stereotypes of and attitudes toward those of higher weights. It includes but is not limited to problematic notions such as being lazy, sloppy, incompetent, gluttonous, lacking will power, stupid, ugly, or alternately overly sexual or nonsexual (Puhl, 2014). Weight stigma and bias motivate the unequal, unfair treatment of heavy people at all socioeconomic levels, with women being the most frequent targets (Roehling, 1999). This includes assault, teasing, social exclusion/rejection/isolation; a greater likelihood of being considered guilty in our criminal justice system, bullying or harassment, being denied equitable dating experiences and marriage benefits, adequate medical care, employment, pay equity, job advancement, pay raises, academic and other scholarships, bank loans, housing, public accommodations, insurance, and credit.[5]

One reaction to weight stigmas and bias in Black culture can be seen when the higher weight Black Queens of Comedy make resentful jokes about "skinny" women's unearned thin privilege (Latham, 2001). Another reaction came in 2006 from higher weight comedienne Mo'Nique who executive produced and starred in the film *Phat Girlz* with the DVD tag line, "She's Proving that BIG is Beautiful." The movie shows that this negative notion is not a given in the Black community. However, in the film, which purports to support higher weight Black women, Mo'Nique is constantly binge eating and inordinately focused on food.

Because several higher weight Black female students told him how they were survivors of weight-based bullying, kindergarten through college, historically Black Alabama State University band director Dr. James Oliver founded a plus-sized dance troupe with each participant averaging 230 pounds (Mo'Nique & Likke, 2006). They are called the "Honey Beez" and when they speak at local predominately Black high schools, the girls in the audience often contact the Beez after their appearance to ask for advice on how to survive weight-based bullying (Manning, 2013). Sometimes the predominantly Black audiences for whom they perform cruelly laugh at the larger-sized dancers upon entrance, but by the time the Honey Beez do their signature running cartwheel into a split, most of the jeers turn to cheers.

Disentangling the effects of racial and weight discrimination can be a complicated task (Gee, Ro, Gavin, & Takeuchi, 2008, pp. 493). Though it is often too difficult to prove or enforce, Title VII and other federal laws provide some legal protection against gender, race, color, national origin, religion, creed, and age workplace discrimination or harassment motivated by these factors.[6] But weight is not included in Title VII. Except for the state of Michigan and six cities, it's perfectly legal to discriminate against someone because of weight (Minnesota Dept. of Human Rights, 2013).

Unfortunately, the myth that heavier Black women suffer no weight-based discrimination can lead to Black girls and women being undiagnosed for various health concerns. For example, Stephanie Covington Armstrong, author of the autobiographical *Not All Black Girls Know How to Eat: A Story of Bulimia* (2013), stigmatizes fat bodies in her writing by assuming all fat Black girls overeat. Many dieticians and social workers have said that it's difficult to get treatment for African American female bulimics and anorexics because they present with the disorders at higher weights than White females do.[7]

It is important to note that weight stigmatization is rampant in African American culture as well, even though it usually starts at higher weights. By the author's observation the weight stigma against White women seems to begin around a size 8 and around a size 12 for Black women. Both these sizes are below the average female size of 14 and approximately one third of American women wear a size 16 (Peeke, 2010). So even though weight stigma may begin at a higher level for African American women, proportionally more Black women than White women must deal with internalized weight stigma (see figure 9.1.).

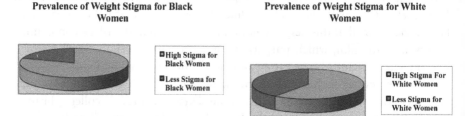

Figure 9.1. Prevalence of Comparative Weight Stigma for Black and White Women.[8]

Finally, there are studies that suggest that Black women are comfortable carrying more weight than White women (Casper & Offer, 1990; Striegel-Moore, Wilfrey, Caldwell, Needham, & Brownell, 2012). I argue these studies suggesting that Black women are subject to no weight stigmas, or are less psychologically affected by weight bias than White women, are based on faulty assumptions.[9] For example, there is intense pressure in the politics of this country for Black women to live up to the myth of the Black Superwoman. It is a guarded survival technique that allows no admission of weakness or pain that leads some Black women to underreport or underperceive weight stigma. Ironically, Michele Wallace in her book, *The Myth of the (Black) Superwoman* (1979), subverts rape with sexuality, and desirability with dominance and violence while enacting weight stigma and ageism when she says that Black women need no longer fear rape only when they are "over sixty" and weigh "two hundred pounds" (p. 60).

The third major myth involves a community issue: the war on obesity. The Black community must stop the war on obesity campaign that only serves to further stigmatize higher weight African Americans. Community organizers and individuals instead should become aware of and adopt the HAES perspective. HAES has five basic tenets: (1) enhancing health, (2) size and self-acceptance, (3) the pleasure of eating well, (4) the joy of movement, and (5) an end to weight bias.[10] HAES is based on the premise that the best way to improve health is to honor your body. It supports people in adopting healthy habits for the sake of their well-being rather than weight control or size change.

People are encouraged to:

- Accept and respect the natural diversity of body sizes and shapes.
- Promote all aspects of health and well-being for people of all sizes.
- Recognize that health and well-being are multidimensional and that they include physical, social, spiritual, occupational, emotional, and intellectual aspects.
- Find the joy in moving one's body and becoming more physically vital.
- Promote individually appropriate, enjoyable, life-enhancing physical activity rather than exercise that is focused on a goal of weight loss.
- Eat in a flexible manner that values pleasure and honors internal cues of hunger, satiety, and appetite.[11]

HAES is not adverse to weight loss, just the counterproductive focus on weight loss. Eating in a flexible manner doesn't mean eating everything you emotionally want but, rather, what you are specifically, physically hungry for at the time. There is a difference. You deal with your emotions directly, not through eating. This is called intuitive eating, and perhaps the best source for learning the practice is *The Diet Survivor's Handbook* (2006), by Judith Matz and Ellen Frankel, both licensed clinical social workers (LCSWs). Even those on restricted diets for diabetes and other conditions can practice intuitive eating. A great introduction to this concept can also be found in the November–December 2010 article, "Intuitive Eating: Enjoy Your Food, Respect Your Body," by Linda Bacon and Matz. Finally, another great beginner's tool is *Health at EVERY Size: The Surprising Truth about Your Weight*, also by Bacon (2010).

There are, of course, obstacles for some in the Black community in order to fully benefit from HAES but they are the same obstacles faced anyway: food deserts, poverty, weight loss pressure, and lack of time, safety, affordable fresh food, stigma-free places to exercise, and the list goes on. Yet, on the most recent edition of Bacon's book, the cover quote from the *New York Times* says, "In the long run the 'Health at Every Size,' approach works better than dieting."

There is considerable free information on the international Association for Size Diversity And Health (ASDAH) website and membership fees are relatively low. Though the ASDAH leadership is becoming more proactive in educating themselves regarding myths that White members may have about African American culture and weight stigma, don't be surprised or thwarted by faulty ideas concerning race. Our cultural health and sanity depend on it.

CONCLUSION

These myths must be overcome if African Americans are to successfully accept the reality of who we are as a people and to thrive. The notion that anybody must be thin in order to be as healthy as possible is simply wrong. Too often the efforts to become thin are demoralizing and ineffective, especially for African American women. This includes weight stigmas that are prevalent in the Black community and the war on obesity campaign, which is proving counterproductive.

According to research, "character and eating flaws" among African Americans who are at higher weights do not make us fat, but instead our genetic slave history, repeated dieting, and stigmatizing social factors do. Higher weight Black women are victims of weight stigma in addition to other forms of discrimination in both the White mainstream and African American culture. One good way to move forward creating better mental and physical health outcomes in the Black community is to adopt and promote a Health at Every Size approach, to honor your body by eliminating the racist, sexist, and weightist stigmas of dieting and exercising in search of Eurocentric standards of slimness.

NOTES

1. *Special Report: State of Obesity*. (2014, September). Race and ethnic disparities in obesity. Retrieved from http://stateofobesity.org/disparities/blacks/
2. All referenced with primary, scientific studies. See Gunnars, K. (2013). Top 11 "diet" foods that make you fat instead of thin. Retrieved July 19, 2014, from http://authoritynutrition.com/top-11-diet-foods-that-make-you-fat/
3. Bacon, L. (2010). *Health at every size: The surprising truth about your weight*. (pp. 63–64). Dallas, TX: BenBella.; Cleveland Clinic. (2014). Risks and complications. Bariatric and Metabolic Institute. Retrieved July 19, 2014, from http://weightloss.clevelandclinic.org/images/file/Risks%20and%20complications%20of%20bariatric%20surgery.pdf; Klein, S. (2013, January 9). Weight loss surgery side effects: Procedure's not-so-glamorous side highlighted by Al Roker's embarrassing story. *Huffington Post*. Retrieved July 19, 2014, from http://www.huffingtonpost.com/2013/01/09/weight-loss-surgery-side-effects-al-roker_n_2441223.html; Mercola, J. (2005, November 3). Dangerous side effects of gastric bypass surgeries. Retrieved July 19, 2014, from http://articles.mercola.com/sites/articles/archive/2005/11/03/dangerous-side-effects-of-gastric-bypass-surgeries.aspx; and Whiteman, H. (2014, February 11). Weight loss surgery: "Not everyone lives happily ever after." *Medical News Today*. Retrieved July 19, 2014, from http://www.medicalnewstoday.com/articles/272432.php

4. Just one of many such studies: Simmons, A. (2008). Black womanhood, misogyny, and hip-hop culture: A feminist intervention. *Cultural Landscapes, 1*(2), 27–48.

5. A vast body of research supports these separate indices. For an overview of many of them see Morrison, M. (2013, 27 September). Humans: 10 frightening ways we discriminate against fat people. Retrieved July 14, 2014, from http://listverse.com/2013/09/27/10-frightening-ways-we-discriminate-against-fat-people/

6. Title VII of the Civil Rights Act of 1964. Retrieved July 13, 2014, from http://www.eeoc.gov/laws/statutes/titlevii.cfm ; Race/Color Discrimination. Retrieved July 13, 2014, from http://www.eeoc.gov/laws/types/race_color.cfm ; and Protected Classes. Retrieved July 15, 2014, from http://www.oshr.nc.gov/Guide/EEOS/Resources/Protected%20Classes.pdf

7. Konstantinovsky, M. (2014, March 20). Eating disorders don't discriminate. Slate.com. Retrieved from http://www.slate.com/articles/double_x/doublex/2014/03/eating_disorders_and_women_of_color_anorexia_and_bulimia_are_not_just_white.html; see also Gordy, C. (2011, April 28). Blacks with bulimia: A secret in plain sight. The Root. Retrieved from http://www.theroot.com/articles/culture/2011/04/black_women_bulimia_affects_them_too.html

8. Daufin (2015), based on statistics from An, R. (2014). Prevalence and trends of adult obesity in the U.S. 1999–2012. *Obesity*, http://dx.doi.org/10.1155/2014/185132

9. I presented on some of the methodological flaws of studies that purport to support the hypothesis that Black women experience no weight stigma, bullying, harassment, or psychological effect at the April 2014 National Popular Culture/American Culture Conference in Chicago.

10. Health at Every Size, http://www.haescommunity.org/

11. Association for Size Diversity and Health, www.sizediversityandhealth.org

BIBLIOGRAPHY

Aamodt, S. (2013, June). Why dieting usually doesn't work. *Ted Talks*. Retrieved January 15, 2014, from http://www.ted.com/talks/sandra_aamodt_why_dieting_usually_doesn't_work.html

America's worst 9 urban food deserts. (2011, September). NewsOne: For Black America. Retrieved July 18, 2014, from http://newsone.com/1540235/americas-worst-9-urban-food-deserts/

Armstrong, C. S. (2013, February 20). Room for debate: One size does not fit all. *New York Times*. Retrieved from http://www.nytimes.com/roomfordebate/2012/05/07/women-weight-and-wellness/one-size-does-not-fit-all-8nytimes.com

Bacon, L. (2010). *Health at every size: The surprising truth about your weight*. Dallas, TX: BenBella.

Bacon, L., & Aphramor, L. (2011). Weight science: Evaluating the evidence for a new paradigm shift. *Nutrition Journal, 10*(9). Retrieved from http://www.nutritionj.com/content/pdf/1475-2891-10-9.pdf

Bacon, L., & Matz, J. (2010, November–December). Intuitive eating: Enjoy your food, respect your body. *Diabetes Self-Management*, 44–61.

Barzel, Y. (1977, April). An economic analysis of slavery. *Journal of Law and Economics, 20*(1), 92–95.

Bell, B., & Field, T. (2013, March 27). The true cost of industrialized food. *Other Worlds*. Retrieved July 18, 2004, from http://otherworldsarepossible.org/true-costs-industrialized-food

Birrell, I. (2014, September 21). Obesity: Africa's new crisis. *The Guardian*. Retrieved from http://www.theguardian.com/society/2014/sep/21/obesity-africas-new-crisis

Block, J. P., Scribner, R. A., & DeSalvo, K. B. (2004, October). Fast food, race/ethnicity, and income: A geographic analysis. *American Journal of Preventative Medicine, 27*(3), 211.

Boston University, Slone Epidemiology Center. (2014). *Black Women's Health Study*. Boston: Author. Retrieved from http://www.bu.edu/bwhs/

Campbell, G., Miers, S., & Miller, J. (2007). *Women and slavery. Vol. 2: The modern Atlantic*. Athens: Ohio University Press.

Campos, P. F. (2004). *The obesity myth: Why America's obsession with weight is hazardous to your health*. New York: Penguin.

Casper, R., & Offer, D. (1990, September). Weight and dieting concerns in adolescents: Fashion or symptom. *Pediatrics, 86*(3), 384–390.

Center for Disease Control. (2012). Table 68. Healthy weight, overweight, and obesity among adults aged 20 and over. Retrieved from http://www.cdc.gov/nchs/data/hus/2012/068.pdf

Dingfelder, S. (2013, January). African American women at risk. *American Psychological Association Monitor, 44*(1), 56.

Doherty, C. (2014, June 28). *For African Americans, discrimination is not dead*. Pew Research Center. Retrieved July 10, 2010, from http://www.pewresearch.org/fact-tank/2013/06/28/for-african-americans-discrimination-is-not-dead/

Duke University Medical Center. (2009, July 6). Large-scale analysis finds bariatric surgery relatively safe. *Science Daily*. Retrieved from www.sciencedaily.com/releases/2009/06/090624153104.htm

Ellison, P. T. (2009, January). Developmental plasticity in a biocultural context. *American Journal of Human Biology, 21*(1), 1. doi: 10.1002/ajhb.20841

Engel, P. (2013, May 23). Women in poor West African country are force-feeding themselves for beauty's sake. *Business Insider*. Retrieved from http://www.businessinsider.com/women-force-feeding-in-mauritania-2013-5

Ferguson, C. (2011). *The relationship between American media exposure and Trinidadian female adolescents' body image satisfaction*. Graduate Theses and Dissertations. Retrieved from http://scholarcommons.usf.edu/etd/3100

Flum, D., Salem, L., Elrod, J. A., Dellinger, E. P., Cheadle, A., & Chan, L. (2005). Early mortality among Medicare beneficiaries undergoing bariatric surgical procedures. *Journal of the American Medical Association, 294*(15), 1903–1908.

Gee, G. C., Ro, A., Gavin, A, & Takeuchi, D. T. (2008, March). Disentangling the effects of racial and weight discrimination on body mass index and obesity among Asian Americans. *American Journal of Public Health, 98*(3), 493–500.

Glenville, M. (2012). How to lose weight naturally. Retrieved from http://www.marilynglenville.com/womens-health-issues/weight-control/

Glick, P., & Fiske, S. T. (2001, February). An ambivalent alliance: Hostile and benevolent sexism as complementary justifications for gender inequality. *American Psychologist, 56*(2), 117.

Gunnars, K. (2013). Top 11 "diet" foods that make you fat instead of thin. AuthorityNutrition. Retrieved on July 19, 2014, from http://authoritynutrition.com/top-11-diet-foods-that-make-you-fat/

Heshka, S., Anderson, J. W., Atkinson, R. L., Greenway, F. L., Hill, J. O., Phinney, S. D., et al. (2003, April 9). Weight loss with self-help compared with a structured commercial program: A randomized trial. *Journal of the American Medical Association, 289*(14), 1792–1798. doi:10.1001/jama.289.14.1792

Hurt, B. (Director). (2012). Soul food junkies: Family, food & tradition. [Television series episode]. In L. Vossen (Producer), *Independent Lens Film*. United States.

Jordan, J., & Coulton, A. Y. (2014, April 23). Lupita Nyong'o is People's most beautiful. *People.* Retrieved from http://www.people.com/people/package/article/0,,20360857_20809287,00. html

Kim, M. J., Pelloux, V., Guyot, E., Tordjman, J., Bui, L.-C., Chevallier, A., et al. (2012, April). Inflammatory pathway genes belong to major targets of persistent organic pollutants in adipose cells. *Environmental Health Perspectives, 120*(4), 508–514.

Latham, W. (Producer) & Purcell, S. (Producer/Director). (2001). *The Black queens of comedy* [Motion picture]. United States: Paramount Pictures.

Lynch, C. S., Chang, J. C., Ford, A. F., & Ibrahim, S. A. (2007). Obese African-American women's perspectives on weight loss and bariatric surgery. *Journal of General Internal Medicine, 22*(7), 908–914.

Maes, H., Neale, M., & Eaves, L. (1997, July), Genetic and environmental factors in relative body weight and human adiposity. *Behavioral Genetics, 27*(4), 325–351.

Mann, T., Tomiyama, A. J., Westling, E., Lew, A. M., Samuels, B., & Chatman, J. (2007). Medicare's search for effective obesity treatments: Diets are not the answer. *American Psychologist, 62*, 3, 220–233.

Manning, T. (2013). Meet the Honey Beezs. *The Montgomery Advertiser.* http://www.montgomery advertiser.com/VideoNetwork/2224226585001/Meet-the-Honeybeez

Maron, D. F. (2008, July 7). Dieting can be counterproductive. *The Boston Globe.* Retrieved from http://www.boston.com/news/science/articles/2008/07/07/dieting_can_be_counterproductive/

Matz, J., & Frankel, E. (2006). *The diet survivor's handbook: 60 lessons in eating, acceptance and self-care.* Naperville, IL: Source.

McGee, R. (2005). *Cathy's slim hopes, hungry for more: A keeping-it-real guide for Black women on weight and body image.* Emeryville, CA: Seal.

McNight, C. (2013, October 27). Health risks of yo-yo dieting. Livestrong.com. Retrieved July 21, 2014, from http://www.livestrong.com/article/353915-health-risks-of-yoyo-dieting/

Mercola, J. (2005, November 3). Dangerous side effects of gastric bypass surgeries. Retrieved from http://articles.mercola.com/sites/articles/archive/2005/11/03/dangerous-side-effects-of-gastric-bypass-surgeries.aspx

Minnesota Department of Human Rights. (2013). Weight bias: Fast facts: Where it's illegal. Retrieved July 14, 2014, http://mn.gov/mdhr/education/articles/rs10_2where.html

Mo'Nique (Producer) & Likké, N. (Director). (2006). *Phat Girlz* [Motion picture]. United States: Fox Searchlight.

Morris, P. F., & Szabo, C. P. (2013). Meanings of thinness and dysfunctional eating in Black South African females: A qualitative study. *African Journal of Psychiatry, 16*, 338–342.

Park, A. (2013, October 10). The need for better obesity education—in medical schools. *Time.* Retrieved July 15, 2014, from http://healthland.time.com/2013/10/10/the-need-for-better-obesity-education-in-medical-schools/print/

Pearce, T. (2012, 10 September). Is "obesity" a dirty word even for doctors? *The Globe and Mail.* Retrieved from www.theglobeandmail.com/life/the-hot-button/is-obesity-a-dirty-word-even-for-doctors/article620602/

Peeke, P. (2010, June 24). Pondering the plus-size phenomenon [Blog]. Web MD. Retrieved from http://blogs.webmd.com/pamela-peeke-md/2010/06/pondering-the-plus-size-phenomenon.html

Pisani, J. (2014, November 18). Business is seeing big bump in curve craze. *Fayetteville Observer.* Retrieved from http://www.fayobserver.com/living/business-is-seeing-big-bump-in-curve-craze/article_d9ee718d-436d-5276-b11a-8ddadcc7e128.html

Puhl, R. (2014). Weight discrimination: A socially acceptable injustice. Retrieved July 10, 2014, from http://www.obesityaction.org/wp-content/uploads/Obesity-Discrimination.pdf

Puhl, R., & Heuer, C. A. (2010). Obesity stigma: Important considerations for public health. *American Journal of Public Health, 100*, 1019–1028.

Queen Latifah weight loss: How did she do it? (2014). Retrieved from http://www.queenlatifahweightloss.com/

Roehling, M. V. (1999, December). Weight-based discrimination in employment: Psychological and legal aspects. *Personnel Psychology, 52*(4), 969–1016.

Selig, M. (2009). *Changepower: 37 Secrets to habit change success.* New York: Routledge.

Smart Dimensions Weight Loss. (2014). Revision surgery for failed bariatric surgery in Los Angeles, CA. Retrieved on July 19, 2014, from http://www.smartdimensions.com/failed-bariatric-surgery-revision-los-angeles/

Striegel-Moore, R., Wilfley, D., Caldwell, M. B., Needham, M. L., & Brownell, K. D. (2012). Weight-related attitudes and behaviors of women who diet to lose weight: A comparison of Black dieters and White dieters. *Obesity Research, 4*(2), 109–116.

Van Dijk, T. A. (1993). Principles of critical discourse analysis. *Discourse and Society, 4*(2), 249–283.

Vineyard, J. (2014, May 2). Read Gabourey Sidibe's wonderful speech from the Ms. Foundation gala. Retrieved on July 21, 2014, from http://www.vulture.com/2014/05/read-gabourey-sidibes-ms-gala-speech.html

Walker, K. (2012, July 31). The Black Barbie syndrome. *Ebony Magazine.* http://www.ebony.com/style/the-black-barbie-syndrome-article687#axzz3TLr4qkjo

Wallace, M. (1979). *Black macho & the myth of the super woman.* New York: Dial.

Whiteman, H. (2014, February 11). Weight loss surgery: "Not everyone lives happily ever after." *Medical News Today.* Retrieved July 19, 2014, from http://www.medicalnewstoday.com/articles/272432.php

Wildman, R., Muntner, P., Reynolds, K., McGinn, A P., Rajpathak, S., Wylie-Rosett, J., et al. (2008). The obese without cardiometabolic risk factor clustering and the normal weight with cardiometabolic risk factor clustering. *Journal of American Medicine: Internal Medicine, 168*(15), 1617–1624.

Zheng, H., Lenard, N. R., Shin, A. C., & Berthoud, H.-R. (2009). Appetite control and energy balance regulation in the modern world: Reward-driven brain overrides repletion signals. *International Journal of Obesity (London), 33*(Suppl 2), S8–S13. doi: 10.1038/ijo.2009.65

Zimmerman, R. (2012, November, 29), Common health: Why are 4 out 5 Black women obese, overweight? WBUR's Common Health Reform & Reality. Retrieved 14 July, 2014 from http://www.commonhealth.wbur.org/2012/11/why-are-four-out-of-five-black-women-obese

Birds of a Feather? Black Men's Experiences and Behavior in Marriage and Romantic Relationships

ARMON R. PERRY, DERRICK R. BROOMS,
AND SIOBHAN E. SMITH

INTRODUCTION

Over the last 50 years major changes have occurred in perhaps the most often discussed Black social, cultural, and community issue—the family structure. Currently, slightly more than one third of all African American adults are married (Chambers & Kravitz, 2011), African American cohabiting couples are less likely to marry than cohabiting couples of other ethnicities (Rinelli & Brown, 2010), more than two thirds of African American children live away from their fathers (Aird, 2003), and an unprecedented number of African Americans are involved in either same sex (Gates & Newport, 2012; Kastanis & Gates, 2012) or interracial relationships (Newport, 2013; U.S. Census Bureau, 2012).

The evolving nature of Black romantic relationships has brought a dramatic shift to Black culture and experience in the 21st century. Perry and Brooms (2013) examined Black men's perceptions and experiences with commitment in marriage and romantic relationships. Analyzing qualitative interview data from a diverse sample of African American men, the researchers found that counter to many studies focused on African Americans, the majority of their participants desired marriage and were able to articulate the benefits they derive from it. In this chapter, we extend that work by examining the extent to which the friends of African American men have similar or dissimilar experiences with marriage, as well as the influence of these experiences on men's attitudes and behaviors in their own marriages and relationships.

ENVIRONMENTAL CONTEXTS IMPACTING BLACK MARRIAGES

The research on Black marriages and romantic relationships has always examined the influence of environmental contexts on individual's attitudes and behaviors. Early work discussed discriminatory policy regimes and social institutions that forced Blacks to either spiral into a so-called tangle of pathology characterized by unstable, matriarchal family structures (Clark, 1965; Frazier, 1939; U.S. Department of Labor, 1965) or adopt nontraditional family structures featuring extended family networks in an attempt to remain resilient in the face of oppression (Martin & Martin, 1978; Stack, 1974).

Later, researchers began to focus on other macro issues, including shifts in the economy that led to increases in African American male unemployment or underemployment (Hall, Livingston, Henderson, Fisher, & Vines, 2007; Malveau, 2004; Wilson, 2012). Attention has also been paid to the war on drugs and the ways in which it has contributed to the mass incarceration of Black men (Alexander, 2010). This has had the effect of either removing Black men from their communities while incarcerated or, due to the invisible punishments that accompany the aftermath of incarceration, making them largely undesirable marriage mates. Combined, the loss of low-skilled manufacturing jobs and the increase in the number of incarcerated Black men have led researchers to conclude that the Black male-female sex ratio is unbalanced, making it difficult for Black women, especially highly educated Black women, to find a comparable Black male marriage mate (Davis, Williams, Emerson, & Houard-Bryant, 2000; Ferguson, Quinn, Eng, & Sandelowski, 2006).

BLACK MEN AND PEER GROUPS

The socialization process is an important component of peer groups, usually consisting of friends and associates who are similar in age and social status. In discussing same-sex peer relationships among Black men, Harris (1999) notes that peer norms exert a significant degree of influence over members' behaviors. Additionally, these relationships help individuals meet intrapersonal and interpersonal needs while also offering support for activities and companionship. Thus, the quality of peer relationships is important throughout the life cycle.

In various studies on subsections of Black men, researchers theorize that social networks and capital (Young, 1999) along with the impact of cultural norms

(Anderson, 1999; Furstenberg, 2001; Liebow, 1967) have a significant impact on the lives of Black males—especially those in major urban areas. Young (1999), in his study of 26 poor Black men in Chicago, suggests that family background, educational experiences, and social relations provide a significant source of explanatory power for the repositories of capital that the men maintained in their lives. Even further, the capital that the men accumulated was specific to their lived experiences and the "alternative" capital helped them to navigate their more immediate circumstances (p. 202).

Given the context of neighborhood relations, peer associations were unstable, risky, and precarious. Anderson (1999), in his study of inner-city Black America, describes the code of the street as "a set of prescriptions and proscriptions, or informal rules of behavior organized around a desperate search for respect that governs public social relations" (p. 10). This desire and demand for respect impacts peer and familial relations as well. Thus, an adherence to a code of the streets, or an affinity for a cool masculinity (Majors & Billson, 1993), or the streets as a socializing agent (Oliver, 2006) often pose challenges for Black males' intimacy and relationships. Majors and Billson (1993) use "cool pose" (cool masculinity) to describe a coping strategy employed by young Black males as a way of surviving in a restrictive society—one that proves problematic for Black males' racialized and gendered identities. They posit that cool pose "may be a factor in frustrating love relationships and violence in the home and on the streets" (p. xi). Similarly, Oliver (2006) argues that Black men who routinely participate in street-related activities may position themselves as "less desirable as husbands and long-term intimate partners" (p. 931). Therefore, many urban Black males realize that they do not have the capacity to fulfill the roles ascribed to being a husband so they express little interest in committing themselves to marriage (Anderson, 2008). Moreover, they realize that attempting to commit to marriage forces them to the margins of their peer group (Anderson, 1990). Taken collectively, the peer group and one's socialization are important factors that impact Black men's relationship experiences, habits, and possibilities.

While the aforementioned research has certainly advanced our knowledge regarding the state of Black male-female relationships and the influence of the peer group, the disproportionate emphasis placed on uneducated, chronically jobless, adolescent and young adult men means that there is a crucial gap in the literature. Additionally, there has been increasing media interest in Black men's peer groups and their influence on marriage attitudes and behavior, including movies such as *The Wood* (1999); *The Brothers* (2001); *The Best Man* (1999); *How to Be a Player* (1997); *Act Like a Lady, Think Like a Man* (2012); and *About Last Night* (2014). The popularity of these movies suggests that research on the influence of Black men's peer groups is likely to resonate with both academic and lay audiences. Therefore, the purpose of this chapter is to fill a gap in the academic literature and contribute to the burgeoning pop culture conversation on Black male-female relationships by (1) determining if there is a relationship between Black men's marital status and that of their peer group and (2) examining the influence of that relationship on Black men's attitudes and behavior toward marriage.

MIXED METHODS STUDY

The data for this chapter were collected as part of a mixed methods study funded by the National Center on Marriage and Family Research to examine Black men's attitudes toward marriage. Data collection involved survey questionnaires and in-depth interviews. In an attempt to recruit a diverse cross-section of Black adult males, potential participants were recruited from a local university, social service agencies, barbershops, and philanthropic organizations, employing a targeted community-based sampling procedure (Waters & Biernacki, 1989), with the primary criteria being the participants' race and gender.

On average, the men were 41.00 (sd = 15.88) years old, had 1.96 (sd = .63) biological children, and had a reported annual income of $40,674 (sd = 1000.04). Fifteen (45.45%) of the men held either a high school diploma or a GED, 13 (39.39%) held a college degree, 1 (3.03%) held neither a high school diploma nor a GED, and 4 (12.12%) did not report their level of educational attainment. At the time of data collection, 14 (42.42%) of the men were married to their first-and-only wife, 9 (27.27%) were single and had never married, 7 (21.21%) were single as a result of being divorced, and 3 (9.09%) were divorced and remarried. With regard to the participants' peer groups, the men reported having an average of 10.8 (sd = 10.1) close friends (i.e., members of their inner circle), of which 4.30 (sd = 1.3) were married. Thus, 39.8% of the participants' close friends were married at the time of data collection, which is slightly lower than reports estimating that 42% of African American adults are married (Chambers & Kravitz, 2011).

With regard to data analysis, the quantitative analysis involved a chi-square cross tabulation designed to determine if there was a relationship between the percentage of the participants' peer group that was married and the participants' marital status.[1] The qualitative analysis included 33 in-depth interviews audio-recorded to ensure accuracy,[2] and the data were interpreted per the guidelines of Creswell (1998) and Strauss and Corbin (1998). The coding process helped to tease out many of the nuances in the participants and their peers' concepts of marriage and romantic relationships.[3]

FINDINGS—FLOCKING TOGETHER

The preliminary analysis for this study was designed to determine if there was a relationship between the percentage of the participants' peer group that is married and the participants' marital status. As indicated by the chi square frequency cross-tabulation analysis, there is a statistically significant relationship between the percentage of the peer group that is married and the participants' marital status.[4] After establishing that there was indeed a relationship between the percentage of the participants' peer group that is married and the participants' marital status, we analyzed the qualitative interview data to better understand the nuances of these relationships. In doing so, three salient themes emerged including: Flocking Together (e.g., discussions of marriage and peer associations); What's the Vibe? (e.g., the climate in the peer group related to marriage); and Boys to (Married) Men (e.g., peer groups in transition with regard to their receptivity to marriage).

Many of the men in this study framed their understanding about marriage and romantic relationships through their interactions with peers. In discussing their peer relations, interactions, and influences, the men highlighted how their romantic relationship decisions were affected by peer group connections. The following section highlights the significant roles that the peer group played for many of the men. Peabo, a 35-year-old married man, reported that five of his eight friends were married, explaining:

> I was thinking birds of a feather flock together…It was funny, I called one of my partners up and I said man I'm getting married and it blew his mind. He said out of all our crew, I figured me and you would be the last ones to get married 'cause we are kindred spirits and we don't half do nothing. When we do something, we do it.

Peabo recalls the conversation he had with one of his friends about getting married, which took his friend by surprise. The conversation suggests they shared a lifestyle pattern that did not seem likely to change at the time, thus, among their friendship circle, they "would be the last ones to get married." Peabo continued:

> The way we met was in church. Our parents went to the same church. They were apostolic, which me, I never did embrace that lifestyle but I appreciate the values that I learned from it. But, uh, his girlfriend at the time he said was uh…she had joined the church and he broke up with her because he didn't want to be a hindrance to her progression because he knew he wasn't ready for that. It was funny because the next year, probably because he saw me growing up and maturing a little bit, he started to re-evaluate his life and now he and his wife got married.

Peabo began his reflection by offering that like-minded people usually associate with each other, in providing a context for his "birds of a feather flock together" statement. Since he and his friend are kindred spirits they figured that they would approach romantic relationships similarly. In recounting their friendship, he noted they met in church and his friend's girlfriend attended the church as well. As a testament to the influence of their friendship, Peabo noted that his friend witnessed his own growth and maturation, which may have influenced him to reevaluate his life and contributed to his decision to get married.

Similarly, Victor, a married 58-year-old, acknowledged his association with other peers who were married and how these friendships lend motivation to romantic relationships. He stated:

> Just about everybody I associate with is married. I have one, two. There's two that aren't married but everybody else is.... I think that we've talked about this before and they think that they're too young to be married even though they have some age on them. There are some things that they wanted to do before getting married and they weren't able to do all of it.

Victor shared that almost everyone he associates with is married, which is consistent with Peabo's affirmation that "birds of a feather flock together." Victor highlights the influence of the peer group. The point here is not necessarily to convince his friends to get married, but more so that his marriage provides an arena for him to engage in a conversation with his peers about their current and future relationships.

Another participant, Jayden, a married 64-year-old who reported that all 15 of his closest friends were married, discussed how he thought his peer group would talk about marriage:

> [They would say the] same thing I said. Because I guess like-minded people hang out together. And uh...I guess people in my age group, we had to go to church whether you wanted to or not and you were brought up through the church and you tried to do the right thing.

The idea that similar people stayed connected is strengthened by Jayden's account. In addition to sharing that all 15 of his closest friends were married, he offered that they all would probably say the same things as him about marriage. He suggests that their ideas are probably connected to the similarities of their early socialization by going to church and trying to behave in ways that denote appropriateness and responsibility. Many of the participants in this study offered some insight on how their friends helped them discuss and think about romantic relationships. Additionally, peers in this group provided the men with a support network that had social, emotional, and personal benefits.

WHAT'S THE VIBE?

The participants also shared their thoughts about the more abstract and intangible vibe around marriage that existed in their respective peer groups. As corroborated by the quantitative analysis, in most cases, the marriage vibe within the peer group was consistent with the participants' marital status. For many of these men, the vibe around marriage was generally favorable, which served to create environments that fostered fellowship and bonding around the common experience of being married. Consider Steve, a 33-year-old married man, who reported that three of five friends were married:

> Iron sharpens iron. Like one of my friends, you know he's younger than me but if he has any marital problems, he may confide in me and I'll tell him what I think. Also, if I have any particular issues I can talk to him. The other friend, we don't really discuss marriage because he's a newlywed so he hasn't had any issues yet. But the other guy, yeah, we bounce ideas off each other and talk about things that go on.

Steve's comments illustrate the sentiments expressed by several participants related to how being surrounded by other married men provides an additional layer of social support helping them during the ups and downs of marriage. As Steve mentions, this support manifests itself in many ways, including having other men to talk to about relationship issues and challenges. Thus, for many of the study participants, having peer groups largely populated by married men created a culture, or vibe, in which marriage was not only acceptable but also preferred. The quote from Steve's interview is representative of the men whose peer group included mostly married men in its identification of social support and resources to navigate their own marriages.

However, in other cases being a member of a group was characterized as having less favorable attitudes and created an apprehensive vibe around marriage. For many of these men, words and phrases like "chaotic," "it's hard," and "they don't want to be tied down" were offered when they were asked to describe their friends' perceptions of marriage. Most of the single men in this position espoused opinions suggesting that they were, at best, not ready for marriage and, at worst, reluctant and suspicious. Aidan, a 27 year-old newlywed, explained how he decided to change his peer group in an attempt to surround himself with people who would be more supportive of his current trajectory.

> Um...I just changed my peer group here recently but of my previous peer group, none of them were married....They turned off by it. I know they are. Even with me being married, they're astonished, like I did something impossible. That's the way they treat it.... It's so far from where they are presently...Because none of their parents are married and they don't really respect the covenant. Plus, it's been normalized. Having children out of wedlock has

been normalized, just multiple relationships with women is normalized. It's ok, women are accepting it and men are accepting it.

Unlike Steve, who reported that most of his friends were married, Aidan, and others like him whose peer groups were disproportionately populated by unmarried men, shared stories characterizing the vibe around marriage as hesitant and reluctant. As was the case with Aidan's former peer group, the apprehensive vibe could be attributed to men's firsthand experiences or knowledge of others' negative experiences with marriage. Yet for some of the younger men, the apprehensive vibe around marriage was not related to negative experiences, but could instead be attributed to the fact that the men and their peer groups were in periods of transition.

BOYS TO (MARRIED) MEN

The third theme that emerged from the analysis was the transition that some of these men experienced from enjoying the single life to seeking a marriage partner. This transition was illustrated by one man's diminishing interest in the "playboy lifestyle" giving way to his gradual adoption of a mindset that viewed marriage as desirable. Nate, a remarried 43-year-old who reported two of his seven close friends were married, offered:

> We had started talking about marriage. We had started talking about giving up this playboy lifestyle, settling down, you know. So we were all in that mindset, we were getting ready to have kids, we were 25-, 26-years-old so I was just ready. I really was.

This notion was quite tangible to peer group members and was accepted by the other members of the group. Participants in the study like Nate felt that this period was "the time to settle down":

> We, we opened ourselves up to be able to talk about those types of things. So for whatever reason, we were all at the same point in our lives at about the same time. We were all ready, because we had experienced so much at the age of 26 to 28, we were all like now is the time to settle down.

Nate describes the necessary discussion during his transitional period and a general agreement among all of his peers that they were ready to engage in more serious relationships. Reflecting on his past, Cameron, a married 60-year-old, said that for him, this transitional period was marked with a tension between the values of his bachelor life and his ready-to-settle-down mentality, and that his friends noticed the tension: "They could see in me that there was something a little different and so that conflict of values was there for me."

James, a 22-year-old with a serious girlfriend, echoes Cameron's sentiments, expressing a conciliatory tone within his peer group:

> One of my friends just recently got married. He was one of the guys in our rat pack and uh...I mean we were all really happy for him. I don't think any of us were having, you know, adverse reactions. But there definitely is a sense that our world is changing. The one who got married, he doesn't hang out much anymore. Although I don't think anyone would vocalize it, but we all know he's not the same. You know, there's no more staying out drinking all night no more.

In this excerpt, James describes a "sense that our world is changing," and like Cameron, he understands that the changes not only have individual implications, but they are felt by all members of the peer group. In the same vein, Peabo characterizes the impact of his marriage as sparking "a spiritual revelation" in his friend, leading him to embrace the notion of being married:

> Yup. I really do [think that my marriage had an influence on my crew]. I mentioned my one friend and to say this...I don't mean to say that we were all ladies' men, but we didn't have any problems, and my one friend, it woke him up to more of a spiritual revelation to where he wanted to be and what he wanted to get out of life.

In sharing their narratives, several study participants and their peer groups agreed that a new receptivity started with one of its members embracing marriage. As the experiences of Nate, Cameron, James, and Peabo show, the vibe around marriage can induce change representing a shift in values and priorities, ultimately leading the flock in a new direction.

DISCUSSION

The purpose of this chapter was to determine if there was a relationship between Black men's marital status and that of their peer group. The results of the quantitative analysis revealed that there was a statistically significant relationship between Black men's marital status and the values/beliefs of the majority of their peer group. The in-depth qualitative interview data also uncovered some of the nuances related to the ways in which the men's marital status influences the attitudes and behaviors of their peer group and vice versa. These analyses yielded three emergent themes that centered on how the men associated with their peer group, the general culture and vibe of the group about marriage, and how some of the men were in transition regarding their receptivity toward marriage.

The men in our study agreed that their friends influenced many of their romantic relationships. Several of the men asserted that most of their closest friends and other people that they associate with shared the same relationship status to the extent that they basically "flocked together." For many of the men, this shared status offered them a support group to share their experiences, listen to critical feedback, and to assess their own relationships. Thus, the peer group can serve as a powerful socializing agent in helping these men think about their behaviors and attitudes toward marriage and how they might imagine their respective futures. The bonds of friendships allowed some of the men to lean on each other for social support and personal growth; it also revealed the sanctity of their friendships. However, for others, membership in peer groups that were disproportionately populated by single men contributed to a culture of apprehension toward marriage. For these men, there was very little support and encouragement for marriage. Instead, the men in these groups perceived the failed relationships and negative experiences of those around them as cautionary tales, making them reluctant to embrace marriage.

In addition to the participants whose peer groups had an established vibe related to marriage, some of the men offered narratives suggesting that their groups were in a transition phase regarding their receptivity toward marriage. This was mostly true of younger men. Older participants retrospectively recalled the events and experiences leading their peer group to shift its thinking about marriage. This occurred as those who once described themselves and their friends as "players or ladies' men" experienced or witnessed a core member of the peer group settle down with one woman. As a consequence of the changing group perspective, the men began to reflect and subsequently view marriage more favorably. Ultimately, this perspective metamorphosis triggered a chain reaction within the peer group, such that others also considered marriage.

In many ways, the findings from this study are consistent with the results of previous research on Black men (Anderson, 2008; Majors & Billson, 1993; Oliver, 2006; Young, 1999) in that they point to the prominent role that the peer group plays in shaping men's attitudes and behaviors within their relationships. However, our study represents a departure from previous studies in that many of our study participants and their peers were either married or reported being in the process of embracing marriage as a realistic and desirable option. It is likely that differences between the findings of previous research and our study can be explained by the demographic differences in the respective study samples. The work of Anderson (1990, 1998, 2008), Wilson (2012), and Young (1999) feature low-income Black men whose economic disadvantages contributed to their relationship and familial challenges. Contrarily, our sample was more socially and economically diverse and featured men spanning the age, socioeconomic, and educational attainment continua. Also, many of the men in our study grew up in married, two-parent homes or espoused values suggesting that their religious beliefs shaped their attitudes and behaviors toward marriage.

When analyzing the findings of this study, there are some limitations that should be considered. Although we were successful in collecting data from a diverse cross-section of African American men, the sample was not random and, thus, there is no assumption that the findings are generalizable. Also, given that there was only one data collection wave, we cannot account for changes in the men's experiences and behavior over time. Finally, we did not triangulate the qualitative interview data by interviewing members of the participants' peer groups. Therefore, our analyses were limited to the perspectives and recollections of the specific participants.

Despite the limitations, the findings of this study advance the literature on Black men and relationships. As a matter of fact, they may have implications for future research examining marriage attitudes, experiences, and behaviors. The primary contribution of this study is that it gives voice to a diverse sample of Black men sharing their own experiences and the meanings they ascribe to them. Given that research on Black men is disproportionately deficit-centered, this study also serves to bring some balance to this important body of research.

In advancing the state of knowledge, future research should continue to recruit diverse groups of Black men into studies that empower them to demonstrate agency in the telling of their own narratives. Beyond the implications for academic research, the findings from this study may also contribute to pop culture and public discourses on Black men and their behavior within relationships and family. In recent years, books and movies about finding and keeping a good Black man have become a cottage industry. Given the popularity of these media, it may be that the findings from these types of studies can inform future media portrayals by featuring authentic representations of Black culture and experience.

ACKNOWLEDGMENT

This research was supported by the National Center for Family and Marriage Research, which is funded by a cooperative agreement, grant number 5 U01 AE000001-03, between the Office of the Assistant Secretary for Planning and Evaluation, U.S. Department of Health and Human Services, and Bowling Green State University. The opinions and conclusions expressed herein are solely those of the author and should not be construed as representing the opinions or policy of any agency of the federal government.

NOTES

1. Specifically, participants were asked how many men made up their inner circle of close friends. Subsequently, the men were also asked how many of those men were married. In employing the chi-square analysis, a 2 x 2 cross-tabulation table was developed consisting of rows (i.e., participant married or not married) and columns (i.e., less than 50% of the peer group married or 50% or more of the peer group married).

2. Interviews followed a semi-structured format and were conducted at times and locations of the participants' choosing. On average, each interview lasted 42 minutes. All of the interviews were transcribed and coded using QSR International's NVIVO8. Per the tenets of the phenomenological approach, after the interviews were transcribed and the texts were coded for emerging themes, they were later grouped into meaning units that led to an overall description of the participants' conceptualizations of marriage and the significant life events and experiences that shaped those conceptualizations.

3. Specifically, as they were articulated throughout the interviews. Subsequently, the participants and their peers' narratives were illuminated featuring their experiences and epiphanies along with the contexts in which they occurred to present the patterns, processes, and unique aspects of their lives.

4. $(X^2 (1, 28) = 5.038, p = .025)$

BIBLIOGRAPHY

Aird, E. (2003). Making the wounded whole: Marriage as a civic right and civic responsibility. In O. Clayton, R. Mincy, & D. Blankenhorn (Eds.), *Black fathers in contemporary society: Strengths, weaknesses, and strategies for change* (pp. 153–164). New York: Russell Sage.

Alexander, M. (2010). *The New Jim Crow: Mass incarceration in the age of colorblindness.* New York: New.

Anderson, E. (1990). *Sex codes and family life among Northon's youth. Streetwise: Race, class, and change in an urban community.* Chicago: University of Chicago Press.

Anderson, E. (1999). *Code of the street: Decency, violence, and the moral life of the inner city.* New York: Norton.

Anderson, E. (2008). Facing the situation of young, Black men in inner cities. In E. Anderson (Ed.), *Against the wall: Poor, young, Black and male* (pp. 1–27). Philadelphia: University of Pennsylvania Press.

Chambers, A. L., & Kravitz, A. (2011). Understanding the disproportionately low marriage rate among African Americans: An amalgam of sociological and psychological constraints. *Family Relations, 60*(5), 648–660.

Clark, K. B. (1965). *Dark ghetto: Dilemmas of social power.* New York: Harper & Row.

Creswell, J. W. (1998). *Qualitative inquiry and research design: Choosing among five traditions.* Thousand Oaks, CA: Sage.

Davis, L. E., Williams, H., Emerson, S., & Hourd-Bryant, M. (2000). Factors contributing to partner commitment among unmarried African Americans. *Social Work Research, 24*(1), 4–16.

Ferguson, Y. O., Quinn, S. C., Eng, E., & Sandelowski, M. (2006). The gender ratio imbalance and its relationship to risk of HIV/AIDS among African American women at historically Black colleges and universities. *AIDS Care, 18*(4), 323–331.

Frazier, E. F. (1939). *The Negro family in the United States*. Chicago: University of Chicago.

Furstenberg, F. F. (2001). The fading dream: Prospects for marriage in the inner city. In E. Anderson & D. S. Massey (Eds.), *Problem of the century: Racial stratification in the U.S.* (pp. 224–246). New York: Russell Sage.

Gates, G. J., & Newport, F. (2012, October 18). *Special report: 3.4% of U.S. adults identify as LGBT*. Retrieved from http://www.gallup.com/poll/158066/special-report-adults-identify-lgbt.aspx

Hall, R. E., Livingston, J. N., Henderson, V. V., Fisher, G. O., & Hines, R. (2007). Postmodern perspectives on the economics of African American fatherhood. *Journal of African American Studies, 10*(4), 112–123.

Harris, S. M. (1999). Black male masculinity and same sex friendships. In R. Staples (Ed.), *The Black family: Essays and studies* (6th ed., pp. 77–85). Belmont, CA: Wadsworth.

Kastanis, A., & Gates, G. J. (2012). *LGBT African-Americans and African American same sex couples*. Los Angeles: Williams Institute, UCLA School of Law.

Liebow, E. (1967). *Tally's corner: A study of Negro street corner men*. New York: Little Brown.

Majors, R., & Billson, J. M. (1993). *Cool pose: The dilemmas of Black manhood in America*. New York: Touchstone.

Malveau, J. (2004). The real deal on Black unemployment. *Black Issues in Higher Education, 21*, 33.

Martin, E. P., & Martin, J. M. (1978). *The Black extended family*. Chicago: University of Chicago Press.

Newport, F. (2013, July 25). *In U.S., 87% approve of Black-White marriage, vs. 4% in 1958*. Retrieved from http://www.gallup.com/poll/163697/approve-marriage-blacks-whites.aspx

Oliver, W. (2006). "The streets": An alternative Black male socialization institution. *Journal of Black Studies, 36*(6), 918–937.

Perry, A. R., & Brooms, D. R. (2013). Commitment, partnership and family: African American men's concepts of marriage and meaning. *Spectrum: A Journal on Black Men, 1*(2), 55–82.

Rinelli, L. N., & Brown, S. L. (2010). Race differences in union transitions among cohabitors: The role of relationship features. *Marriage & Family Review, 46*(1–2), 22–40.

Stack, C. (1974). *All our kin: Strategies for survival in a Black community*. New York: Harper & Row.

Strauss, A., & Corbin, J. (1998). *Basics of qualitative research: Techniques and procedures for developing grounded theory*. Thousand Oaks, CA: Sage.

U.S. Census Bureau. (2012). *2010 Census shows interracial and interethnic married couples grew by 28 percent over decade*. http://www.census.gov/newsroom/releases/archives/2010_census/cb12-68.html

U.S. Department of Labor. Office of Policy Planning and Research. (1965). *The Negro family: The case for national action*. Washington, DC: Government Printing Office.

Waters, J. K., & Biernacki, P. (1989). Targeted sampling: Options and considerations for the study of hidden populations. *Social Problems, 36*(4), 416–430.

Wilson, W. J. (2012). *The truly disadvantaged: The inner city, the underclass, and public policy* (2nd ed.). Chicago: University of Chicago Press.

Young, A. A. (1999). The (non)accumulation of capital: Explicating the relationship of structure and agency in the lives of poor Black men. *Sociological Theory, 17*(2), 201–227.

CHAPTER ELEVEN

Fifty Shades of Brown: Understanding the Social, Sensual, and Sexual Lives of Black American Women

ASHER PIMPLETON AND NIKITA MURRY

Research is clear in the ways in which Black American women are paid less, required to work harder, and experience higher rates of disease compared to their counterparts. There is no impact that is greater than another; however, the ramifications of sorrowful sexual identities present themselves as forerunners to the list of challenges—many pejorative—that the Black American woman must navigate. For instance, one of the most unfortunate consequences of this has been evident in the rates of sexually transmitted diseases within this particular population.

In general, women bear the brunt of sexually transmitted diseases (STDs) and sexually transmitted infections (STIs) for diagnosis both globally and nationally (CDC, 2010; WHO, 2011). In a 2001 global report, an estimated 50 million women were diagnosed with chlamydia compared to nearly 42 million men. On a national scale, women are almost three times more likely to contract chlamydia than men (CDC, 2010). These differences are even more pronounced when the data are analyzed according to ethnicity and gender. Black American women are disproportionately affected when it comes to many STDs and STIs (CDC, 2010). For example, in 2009 infection rates for chlamydia among Black American women were approximately eight times higher among their White counterparts (CDC, 2010).

In the same study, Black American female adolescents between the ages of 15 to 19 received a positive diagnosis for gonorrhea, 16.7 times more frequently than White females in this subpopulation (CDC, 2010). Infection rates for syphilis among Black American women ages 15- to 24-years-old more than doubled between 2005 and 2009 (CDC, 2010). This increase was greater among Black American adolescent girls between the ages of 15- to 19-years-old, who had infection rates that were nearly 29 times higher than those of White adolescent girls in the same category (CDC, 2010).

Conditions such as these only compound the impact that STDs and STIs, especially HIV and AIDS, have on a community that can often already be fiscally disadvantaged in various ways. Infection rates continue to demonstrate a need for improved educational, informational, and medical services. However, sexual health, decision making, and other overemphasized depreciatory positions concerning the deficiency and morality of behavior has plagued Black American women in the research literature (Jenkins, 2007; Murry, 2010, Pimpleton, 2012; Williams, 2005). The common portrayal of Black American women is a caricature who is promiscuous, other-dependent, uneducated or poorly educated, unmarried, and diseased.

Even at the dawn of a new millennium, research across disciplines continued to present Black American women within the context of teen pregnancy, HIV/AIDS and other sexually transmitted infections, unemployment rates, poverty, loose sexual behaviors, and domestic violence or other abuses (Williamson, 2007). While these topics are important, they are also one-sided and carry overtones of perpetual despondency and deficiency. For example, a preponderance of the mental health literature stayed wedded to a vocational philosophy, as evidenced by the wealth of research that addresses the coexistence of Black American women's mental health, work, and the workplace.

With the millennium underway, the new question becomes are Black American women participating in the construction of their own negative script when it comes to decision making in areas such as sexuality? Additionally, to what degree have the cultural dynamics that are unique to these women been addressed and incorporated into best mental health practices, as well as the prevention and educational efforts that have so often been targeted toward them. The pathway to answering these questions begins with a brief historical literature review of Black American women through the lenses of feminism and power. More specifically, it is critical to explore how these two forces have helped to shape sexuality and sensuality for the Black American woman.

BLACK AMERICAN WOMEN AND FEMINISM

Initially presented to fit all women, the classic feminist ideology of the 1960s and 1970s has expanded into postmodern or diversity feminism, which strives to address gender concerns within the context of contemporary issues, race and ethnicity, and sexual orientation (Enns, Sinacore, Ancis, & Phillips, 2004). Feminism, as a movement, has evolved from a concept focused on equality and empowerment for women through political engagement into a form tailored toward differing goals among women. Herlihy and Corey (2005) note at least three waves of feminist perspectives, with each shift providing a response to the expanding needs of the women represented. Early feminist therapy confronted the oppression of women and largely mirrored the worldview of middle-class White women. Modern feminism has shifted the emphasis toward multiculturalism and multiple forms of oppression, as current feminists accept that gender and other forms of identity oppression are partners in the quest for emancipation (Herlihy & Corey).

It is also necessary to acknowledge the work of Gilligan (1982), who offers one of the most notable critiques on the developmental differences between men and women by challenging Erikson's stage theory of identity development over the lifespan. It is here where a developmental portrait of women is painted that establishes them as relationally oriented, morally driven, and valuing mutuality, respect, and caring. These issues, Gilligan argues, are at the core of women's existence compared to men, who value individuation and separation.

Outside of work in the areas of feminism or womanist identity development, explanations for how Black American women across the lifespan perceive themselves slowly emerges as part of the new research landscape, particularly related to mental health (Murry, 2010). Black American women have a history that is unavoidably defined by centuries of slavery, oppression, and various forms of violence. Within the goal of providing counseling intervention that is ethical, appropriate, and beneficial, two questions arise: How can the impact of dehumanization based on race go ignored as an experiential factor with the potential to affect the psyche of Black American women? Moreover, how can the methods by which Black American women demonstrate resiliency go unexamined? These questions are especially important if counselors, educators, and others involved in prevention efforts sincerely desire to conceptualize Black American women in the most complete ways possible. The first step to accurately answering these questions is to better understand the cultural factors that may influence how these women perceive and construct their roles as sexual beings, in conjunction with other psychological factors that serve as main ingredients in the sexual decision-making process.

SEXUAL DECISION MAKING: RACE, GENDER, AND PSYCHOLOGICAL FACTORS

Although the previously discussed issues are valid factors in the decision-making process, research suggests that cultural issues such as gender, communication with partner(s), and an unequal balance of power in the relationship also play important roles, particularly for Black American women (Collins, 1986, 2005; Davidson & Marcano, 2010; Foreman, 2003; Stephens & Phillips, 2005). Psychological and emotional connections, such as intimacy, a desire for long-term commitment, and pleasure for themselves or their partners were found to be dominant and reoccurring themes when discussing how they make the decision to engage in safe or unsafe sex (Foreman). Moreover, Black American women reported a higher rate of risky behavior, such as having unprotected sex, in efforts to obtain and maintain a serious relationship. This type of behavior suggests that there could be a link between safe or risky decision making, particularly when it comes to sex and issues surrounding self-efficacy and the locus of control.

An equally plausible argument is that these factors manifest in ways that are rooted in cultural identity and personal experience. For example, there are studies indicating that some Black Americans perceive themselves as lacking a strong level of personal or internalized control compared to their White counterparts (Shaw & Krause, 2001; Bandura, 1969). Experiences with repeated encounters of oppression mean that Black American participants also tend to report a higher level of externalized locus of control. In other words, despite persistent attempts to advance, participants believed that these efforts were disrupted due to circumstances outside of their personal control, such as racism or systemic barriers among others (Rotter, 1966; Wade, 1996; Bruce & Thornton, 2004).

Consequently, issues related to perceived power and control could be heightened or exacerbated for Black American women for a variety of reasons, including fewer Black American partnership options. For example, the ratio of Black American men to Black American women more strongly favored toward men. According to the 2010 U.S. Census Bureau report, for every 87 Black American men, there are 100 Black American women. According to the Sentencing Project (http://www.sentencingproject.org/template/page.cfm?id=122), it is likely that at least one out of every three Black American men will be incarcerated during his lifetime. Therefore, one could speculate that these circumstances could lead to perceptions of gender and power imbalance among Black American women. In other words, the apparent scarcity of available Black American men may result in a stronger willingness for Black American women to engage in unsafe sexual behavior or decision making. Another harmful element to decision making as it relates to power and control is the willingness to accept physical, sexual, and psychological abuse in order to maintain a relationship, even one that is unhealthy.

Previous research indicates that these issues appear to be important variables when it comes to negotiating safer sex practices for Black American women (Ferguson, Quinn, Eng, & Sandelowski, 2006; McNair & Prather, 2004). The literature defines gender and power imbalance primarily within two constructs (Ferguson et al.; McNair & Prather). First, gender imbalance is defined as an unequal ratio of

Black American men to Black American women (Ferguson, et al.). Because there are more Black American women than men, there are fewer partnership options for Black women within the Black American community (Ferguson, et al.). Consequently, these women may be more willing to take risks in efforts to secure relationships, which contributes to the power imbalance (Ferguson, et al.). This type of perceived power differential could also play a role in the lack of communication that appears to occur between Black American women and their partners. For example, if the female partner feels as though she has less power in the relationship, she may be less willing to communicate her needs to her partner. This could be especially true when it comes to asserting one's rights within the relationship, particularly as it relates to sexual decision making and safer sex practices. This has also been a point of discussion in the literature.

The literature indicates that for some HIV-infected Black American women, partners' willingness to use condoms is an important factor when deciding to engage in sexually risky behavior (Bedimo, Bennett, Kissinger, & Clark, 1998). In addition, participants reported it to be more difficult, if not impossible, for a condom to be used during intercourse if partners were opposed to wearing it (Bedimo et al.). Unfortunately, the results of the Bedimo study suggest that undeveloped negotiation skills regarding condom use with partners resulted in an absence of condom use or in unsafe sexual practices. In the same study this appeared to be even truer of Black American adolescent female participants. Similar research suggests that while women may initiate the conversation about safer sex, men appear to exercise more control over the couple's actual use of condoms (Gentry, Elifson, & Sterk, 2005). Therefore, a woman's decision to value affective connections more than her safety, personal rights, and physical well-being could be influenced by differences in partnership power, emotional dependence, or fear of losing love (Jarama, Belgrave, Bradford, Young, & Honnold, 2007). These are delicate and difficult issues to try to successfully negotiate with a partner without having the skills and training to do so.

SEXUAL DECISION MAKING IN ADOLESCENCE AND YOUNG ADULTHOOD

Adolescence is not only a time of biological, emotional, and psychological development, but it is also the beginning of sexual and sensual exploration and development as well. In addition to the developmental factors that are at work during the sexual decision-making process, cultural factors may also be in play. Studies indicating that Black American adolescent and adult females may be at a higher risk for engaging in sexually risky behavior help to support this idea (Bartlett,

Buck, & Shattell, 2008; Ford & Norris, 1993; Neff & Crawford, 1998). In a 2008 study conducted by Bartlett, Buck and Shattell, both Black American and Hispanic adolescent girls were more likely to have sexual intercourse without birth control compared to their White counterparts. Black American adolescent girls in the study were more likely to engage in sexual behavior with multiple sexual partners as compared to both Hispanic and White girls. However, self-esteem for Black American adolescent girls in the study was higher than both Hispanic and White adolescent girls. Given some of the previously discussed research, this aspect of the study is confounding and suggests that there may be other factors contributing to these participants' willingness to engage in sexually risky behavior and decision making.

McCabe and Killackey's 2004 study found a link between young women's intention to participate in sexual behavior and the degree of perceived personal control they believed they had in doing so. However, previous sexual experiences were not predictors of present intentions to engage in sexual behavior. Norms from participants' peers and parents were also found to be significant predictors of engagement for sexual behaviors. The socialization aspect (peer and parental norms) of the sexual decision-making process for these participants clearly emerges. Although perception of personal control along with family and peer norms appear to be predictors regarding intentions to engage in sexual behavior, the authors suggest that the decision to engage in sexual behavior appears to be shaped more strongly by emotions and thoughts that occur in the present moment of sexual behavior versus a more objective stance to sexual decision making that may occur outside of the "heat of the moment." However, heat of the moment type of sexual decision making has not only emerged as a theme among adolescent and adult women, but also with middle-aged and older women.

In a 2012 study by Pimpleton self-efficacy and locus of control were examined as risk factors in sexual decision making for Black American women enrolled in Midwestern college institutions. The construct of self-efficacy was assessed using the New General Self-Efficacy Scale (Chen, Gully, & Eden, 2001). Locus of control was measured using the Internality, Powerful Others and Chance subscales (Robinson, Shaver & Wrightsman, 1991). Finally, sexual behaviors and decision making were assessed using the Sexual Risks Scale, which is comprised of the following six subscales: (1) Attitudes about Safer Sex, (2) Normative Beliefs, (3) Intentions to Try to Practice Safe Sex, (4) Expectations about the Feasibility of Safer Sexual Activity, (5) Perceived Susceptibility to HIV/AIDS, and (6) Substance Use (DeHart & Birkimer, 1997). The results indicate that there were only significant predictors for two out of the six subscales used to assess sexual decision making for the Black American women in this sample. Both internal and external forms of locus of control (Chance and Powerful Others) were significant predictors of participants' normative beliefs regarding safer sex practices above and beyond self-efficacy (Pimpleton, 2012).

Additionally, there was a significant interaction between self-efficacy and both internal and external loci of control as predictors for participants' Intentions to Try to Practice Safe Sex (Pimpleton, 2012). These factors combined played a significant role in participants' efforts to engage in safer sexual behavior and decision making. So, although locus of control may influence these participants' beliefs regarding safer sexual practices, these beliefs did not translate into actual behavioral changes. Similarly, the combination of locus of control and self-efficacy probably played a role in the intentions for safer practices for this sample.

Like participants in other samples, the women in this study reported a relatively strong sense of self-efficacy, yet this was not a significant predictor for sexual decision making for this particular group. Participants demonstrated a strong externalized locus of control, which aligns with previous literature (Pimpleton, 2012).

Cultural and developmental factors influence the results of this study and others like it. The level of individual's advancement in their biopsychosocial and identity development certainly would play a role in which aspects of sexual decision making would be most important. This point may also explain some of the similarities and differences in the results of various studies when examining sexuality, sexual decision making, and sexual identity across the lifespan. One could argue that many behaviors and cognitive frameworks that emerge during middle and late adulthood often began forming during adolescence and therefore need continued exploration and examination over the life cycle.

SEXUAL BEHAVIOR, BELIEFS, AND IDENTITY DEVELOPMENT FOR BLACK AMERICAN WOMEN: MIDDLE AND LATE ADULTHOOD

The call for informative research that explores Black American womanhood is not a new one. As early as 1973, Foster wondered when researchers would undertake the task of presenting the African American woman in ways that identify her collective self. Helms raised a similar question in 1979. Foster launched a call for interdisciplinary efforts to view African American women beyond the homogeneous lens of sameness and consider the reality that while Black women may be united racially, they are not uniform in their ways of giving meaning to their life experiences and how that life is lived as a Black woman in the United States. Few to date have explored gender identity development for Black American women (Wallace & Wilchins, 2013). That is to say, primarily qualities of the sociopolitical and biological nature have surfaced in discussions about Black American women, across multiple disciplines. However, the mental health field is relatively void of positions that explore a Black woman's worldview. More important, few scholars have asked Black women how they define themselves as individuals, let alone as sexual and sensual beings (Gushue & Constantine, 2003).

A content review of major journals of the counseling profession indicates that mental health professionals are slow to advance literature that specifically speaks to the question of how Black women determine their womanhood, or what variables might serve as contributing influences of the development of a womanhood identity. For example, Nilsson, Love, Taylor, and Slusher (2007) conclude from their content analysis of quantitative research articles published in the *Journal of Counseling and Development* from 1991 to 2000 that few articles focused primarily on people of color. White participants comprised the majority of research participants in these studies. The authors suggested that one possible cause for the lack of racial-ethnic representation in research samples was due to the demographics of the populations from which participants were selected. Nevertheless, Nilsson et al. recognized the lack of racial representation within scholarly research as an ongoing concern.

So, there is a need for more balanced ethnic and gendered representations within the literature, specifically, pertaining to the identity development of Black American women. Qualitative research provides a unique opportunity for these women to construct their own narrative. While the quantitative literature may help to identify factors that play a role in certain behaviors, qualitative work helps to provide insight into the scripts and scenarios that may have made certain factors significant. For example, in a 2010 study conducted by Murry, women told their stories of how they defined themselves as Black American women and sexual beings through interviews and focus groups. For these participants, ages 35 and older, three major themes emerged: becoming a woman, qualities of Black American womanhood, and Black women in contemporary America. The emergence of a womanhood identity occurred through motherhood, other lifecycle transitions, maternal family influences, and by cultivating wisdom through life experiences and formal education. Qualities associated with womanhood included responsibility, independence, self-sacrifice, overcoming challenges and resilience, spirituality and faith, and sexuality. Participants also pointed to contemporary culture and history for examples of how Black women are viewed in the United States. Interview participants described an existence in mainstream culture marked by messages that either uplift or weigh down one's sense of self as a Black woman in contemporary America.

In some ways, this finding was consistent with previous literature on female identity development (Moradi, 2004). Based on the findings from this study, womanhood also includes a transition in attitude or ideology such that personal beliefs about character, self-motivation, and self-awareness are prominent. This process can differ for each Black American woman.

Considerable overlap exists between direct experiences and external influences in realizing how Black American women come to identify themselves as women. As an example, motherhood is significant to the research findings because some participants move into that role and consider it a leading reason for seeing themselves as women. However, what made childbirth a relevant experience was the responsibility that accompanied the role and not necessarily motherhood itself. For example, Brenda, a 57-year-old interview participant, explained how the role of a mother crystallized when she became a parent. "Then it just really sunk in. This is what she did. This is the love that she gave me." Therefore, motherhood was associated with becoming a woman because it also involved responsibility and care for the comprehensive well-being of a dependent child. This prototype of Brenda, a Black American woman, helps create the image of a protective, strong, and caring individual (Sharp & Ispa, 2009), who also recognizes the need to raise children, particularly daughters, with skills that will allow them to become self-determinant and self-sufficient (Mandara, Varner, & Richman, 2010).

However, different themes emerge as participants discuss their sexual identity (Murry, 2010). Black American women between the ages of 35 to 62 perceive the time in which they became women as a process shaped by life experiences, significant events, and milestones. The development of a sexuality-based identity, however, was not prominent among the factors. Arriving at a definition of womanhood collectively was not solely dependent upon a single event or commonly lauded milestones such as achieving professional or academic accolades, reaching a certain age of maturity, or embarking upon traditional roles of spouse or caregiver. Murry (2010) notes that while some Black American women may recognize sexuality as a component of their identity as women, there remains a lack of comfort with discussing issues related to sexuality, whether that includes sexual development, sensuality, or sexuality within intimate relationships. Open discussion of sexuality could prove discomforting for this population of women for several reasons. First, social norms in the Black American community discourage such matters as "personal business." An African American male focus group participant recalled family lectures during which his mother reminded him to safeguard his "private parts."

A considerable amount of socially constructed baggage exists related to sexuality and Black American women. The history of Black women includes a legacy of sexual exploitation, specifically culturally, where American sexuality remains politicized around issues such as birth rate, HIV infection rates, and perceptions of promiscuity (Townsend, 2008). But this is not to say that Black American women do not consider themselves as sexual beings or reject sexuality as part of their identity as women.

Furthermore, the patterns of communication across generations leave unanswered questions concerning the ways in which information learned by Black women ages 35 and older is passed on to younger Black American women. More specifically, when considering age, one might explore what teachings older women share with younger females to assist them toward developing a womanhood identity. This is a piece of data that is of interest and worthy of further exploration by scholars, researchers, mental health professionals, and educators interested not only in contributing to the literature but also in helping to provide a more balanced and representative point of view.

RESEARCHERS, EDUCATORS, AND PRACTITIONERS IN THE PIPELINE

There is an apparent lack of racial representation among potential researchers within the counseling and helping professions. According to the National Science Foundation (NSF, 2009) 2008 Survey of Earned Doctorates, Black Americans accounted for 32 of the 215 doctorates awarded in counselor education/counseling and guidance, and 36 of the 418 doctorates earned in counseling psychology. Overwhelmingly, more Whites earned doctorates in those fields than any other racial group, with 275 and 129 degrees awarded respectively. Overall, for the same year, Black American women accounted for 0.05% of the 22,496 doctorates awarded to women. Given the opportunity, Black American women counseling professors can have a healthy impact on the counseling and helping professions and subsequent attitudes toward multicultural issues (Bryant, Coker, Durodoye, McCollum, Pack-Brown, Constantine, et al., 2005). In order to access these opportunities, openings are needed for Black American female counselor educators to step into roles other than nurturing figures for minority students (Bryant et al.) While women in general face considerable challenges in academia, such as dissatisfaction in the workplace, Black American women have been noted to experience treatment that is different and more complex than their ethnic and/or gendered counterparts (Hill, Leinbaugh, Bradley, & Hazier, 2005).

Alternatively, the outlook is encouraging for African American counselors in the work environment. These points are relevant to this discussion because they address the professional climate in which research is conducted by and about people of color, namely Black Americans. Furthermore, this has a direct impact on the clinicians, educators, and other helping professionals that these scholars will be training in a number of ways. For example, having a more balanced representation of any minority population, coupled with significant involvement in training and education should facilitate more culturally competent and aware practitioners. As a result, the influence of more minority educators and researchers would not only be apparent in the classroom and the literature but also in the community. Concerning issues of personal and sexual identity development and other matters that influence health and wellness, professionals are better equipped to effectively work with Black American women and other populations when armed with proper training.

IMPLICATIONS FOR RESEARCH, EDUCATION, AND PRACTICE

This chapter contributes to the basic understanding of Black American women's decision-making process across their lifespan, focusing on areas of relevance with an interest on race, sexuality, and mental health. The contributions of literature highlighted in this chapter emphasize the need for a more fundamental understanding of Black American women as potential clients as they seek therapy.

For counselors, educators, and prevention specialists, it is important to understand how race, sexuality, and mental health play a role in what Black American women believe about safer sex practices. When working with diverse populations, particularly around issues of sexual behavior and beliefs, it is critical that the racial aspect of culture be given significant consideration within an integrated clinical practice. In essence, those who train mental health and other helping professionals may be able to more effectively and ethically train them to work with clients who present with issues about identity, sex, and sexuality. In addition, the facilitators of dialogue surrounding sexual decision making should not be comprised solely of designated resources, such as those who work as sex and sexuality educators and therapists. Yet, even those who specialize in sexuality issues will be better equipped to facilitate this conversation within a more culturally appropriate context.

BIBLIOGRAPHY

Bandura, A. (1969). *Principles of behavior modification*. New York: Holt, Rinehart, & Winston.

Bartlett, R., Buck, R., & Shattell, M. M. (2008). Risk and protection for HIV/AIDS in African American, Hispanic and White adolescents. *Journal of National Black Nurses Association, 19*(1), 19–25.

Bedimo, A. L., Bennett, M., Kissinger, P., & Clark, R. (1998). Understanding barriers to condom usages among HIV-infected African American women. *Journal of the Association of Nurses in AIDS Care, 9*(3), 48–58.

Bruce, M. A., & Thornton, M. C. (2004). It's my world? Exploring Black and White perceptions of personal control. *The Sociological Quarterly, 45*, 597–612.

Bryant, R. M., Coker, A. D., Durodoye, B. A., McCollum, V. J., Pack-Brown, S., Constantine, M. G., et al. (2005). Having our say: African American women, diversity, and counseling. *Journal of Counseling and Development, 83*(3), 313–319.

Centers for Disease Control & Prevention (CDC). (2011). Health disparities in HIV/AIDS, viral hepatitis, STDs, and TB: African Americans/Blacks. Retrieved September 30, 2011, from http://www.cdc.gov/stdconference/2000/media/AfAmericans2000.htm.

Centers for Disease Control & Prevention. (2010). HIV in the United States: An overview. Retrieved September 16, 2011, from http://stacks.cdc.gov/view/cdc/11978/

Centers for Disease Control & Prevention. (2011). HIV in the United States. Retrieved September 30, 2011, from http://www.cdc.gov/hiv/resources/factsheets/PDF/us.pdf

Centers for Disease Control & Prevention. (n.d.). HIV/AIDS facts among women. Retrieved October 7, 2008, from http://ww.gov/hiv/topics/women/resources/factsheets/pdg/women.pdf

Chen, G., Gully, S. M., & Eden, D. (2001). Validation of a new general self-efficacy scale. *Organizational Research Methods, 4*(1), 62–83.

Collins, P. H. (2005). *Black sexual politics: African Americans, gender and the new racism*. New York: Routledge/Taylor & Francis.

Collins, P. H. (1986). Learning from the outsider within: The sociological significance of Black feminist thought. *Social Problems, 33*(6), S14–S32.

Davidson, M. G., & Marcano, D. L. (2010). *Convergences: Black feminist and continental philosophy*. Albany: State University of New York.

DeHart, D., & Birkimer, J. C. (1997). Trying to practice safer sex: Development of the Sexual Risks Scale. *The Journal of Sex Research, 34*(1), 11–25.

Enns, C. Z., Sinacore, S. L., Ancis, J. R., & Phillips, J. (2004). Toward integrating feminist and multicultural pedagogies. *Journal of Multicultural Counseling and Development, 32*, 414–427.

Ferguson, Y. O., Quinn, S. C., Eng, E., & Sandelowski, M. (2006). The gender ratio imbalance and its relationship to risk of HIV/AIDS among African American women at historically Black colleges and universities. *AIDS Care, 18*(4), 323–331.

Ford, K., & Norris, A. E. (1993). Knowledge of AIDS transmission, risk behavior, and perceptions of risk among urban, low-income, African-American and Hispanic youth. *American Journal of Preventative Medicine, 9*, 297–306.

Foreman, F. E. (2003). Intimate risk: Sexual risk behavior among African American college women. *Journal of Black Studies, 33*(5), 637–653.

Foster, F. S. (1973). Changing concepts of the Black woman. *Journal of Black Students, 4*(3), 433–454.

Gentry, Q. M., Elifson, K., & Sterk, C. (2005). Aiming for more relevant HIV risk reduction: A Black feminist perspective for enhancing HIV intervention for low-income African American women. *AIDS Education and Prevention, 12*(3), 238–252.

Gilligan, C. (1982). *In a different voice*. Cambridge, MA: Harvard University.

Gushue, G. V., & Constantine, M. G. (2003). Examining individualism, collectivism, and self-differentiation in African American college women. *Journal of Mental Health Counseling, 25*, 1–16.

Helms, J. E. (1979). Black women. *The Counseling Psychologist, 8*(1), 40–41. Retrieved April 1, 2008, from http://tcp.sagepubs.com/subscriptions

Herlihy, B., & Corey, G. (2005). Feminist therapy. In G. Corey (Ed.), *Theory and Practice of Counseling & Psychotherapy* (7th ed., pp. 339–373). Belmont, CA: Brooks Cole-Thomson Learning.

Hill, N. R., Leinbaugh, T., Bradley, C., & Hazier, R. (2005). Female counselor educators: Encouraging and discouraging factors in academia. *Journal of Counseling and Development, 83*(3), 374–380.

HIV Surveillance by Race/Ethnicity (through 2009). Retrieved November 17, 2011, http://www.cdc. gov/hiv/pdf/HIV_2013_RaceEthnicitySlides_508.pdf

Holcomb-McCoy, C., & Addison-Bradley, C. (2005). African American counselor educators' job satisfaction and perceptions of departmental racial climate. *Counselor Education and Supervision,* 45(1), 2–15.

Jarama, S. I., Belgrave, F. Z., Bradford, J., Young, M., & Honnold, J. A. (2007). Family, cultural and gender role aspects in the context of HIV risk among African American women of unidentified HIV status: An exploratory qualitative study. *AIDS Care, 13*(3), 307–317.

Jenkins, C. M. (2007). *Private lives, proper relations: Regulating Black intimacy.* Minneapolis: University of Minnesota Press.

Jones, C., Hohenshil, T., & Burge, P. (2009). Factors affecting African American counselors' job satisfaction: A national survey. *Journal of Counseling and Development, 87*(2), 152–158.

Mandara, J., Varner, F., & Richman, S. (2010). Do African American mothers really "love" their sons and "raise" their daughters? *Journal of Family Psychology, 24*(1), 41–50.

McCabe, M. P., & Killackey, E. J. (2004). Sexual decision making in young women. *Sexual Relationship Therapy, 19*(1), 15–27. doi: 10.1080/14681990410001640808

McNair, L. D., & Prather, C. M. (2004). African American women and AIDS: Factors influencing risk and reaction to HIV disease. *Journal of Black Psychology, 30*(1), 106–123.

Moradi, B., Yoder, J. D., & Berendsen, L. L. (2004). An evaluation of the psychometric properties of the Womanist Identity Attitudes Scale. *Sex Roles, 50,* 253–266.

Murry, N. (2010). *A qualitative exploration of African American womanhood: Implications for counseling and counselor education.* Doctoral dissertation. Retrieved from ProQuest. (Order No. 3440813).

National Science Foundation, Division of Science Resources Statistics. (2009). Doctorate recipients from U.S. universities: Summary report 2007–08. Special Report NSF, 10–309. Arlington, VA.

Neff, J., & Crawford, S. (1998). The Health Belief model and HIV risk behaviors: A causal model analysis among Anglos, African-Americans and Mexican-Americans. *Ethnicity & Health, 3*(4), 283–299.

Nilsson, J. E., Love, K. M., Taylor, K. J., & Slusher, A. L. (2007). A content and sample analysis of quantitative articles published in the *Journal of Counseling & Development* between 1991 and 2000. *Journal of Counseling & Development, 85*(3), 357–363.

Pimpleton, A. M. (2012). *Exploring self-efficacy and locus of control as risk factors in sexual decision making for African American women.* Doctoral dissertation. Retrieved from ProQuest. (Order No. 3543900).

Racial disparity. (n.d.). *In the sentencing project.* Retrieved from http://www.sentencingproject.org/ template/page.cfm?id=122

Robinson, J. R., Shaver, P. R., & Wrightsman, L. S. (1991). Locus of control. *Measures of Personality and Social Psychological Attitudes. Vol. 1: Measures of Social Psychological Attitudes* (pp. 427–428). San Diego, CA: Academic.

Rotter, J. B. (1966). Generalized expectancies for internal versus external control of reinforcement. *Psychological monographs: General and applied, 80*(1), 1–29.

Sharp, E., & Ispa, J. (2009). Inner-city single Black mothers' gender-related childrearing expectations and goals. *Sex Roles, 60*(9–10), 656–668.

Shaw, B. J., & Krause, N. (2001). Exploring race variations in aging and personal control. *Journals of Gerontology Series B: Psychological Sciences & Social Sciences, 56B*(2), S119–S125.

Stephens, D. P., & Phillips, L. (2005). Integrating Black feminist thought into conceptual frameworks of African American adolescent women's sexual scripting processes. *Sexualities, Education and Gender, 7*(1), 37–55.

Townsend, T. (2008). Protecting our daughters: Intersection of race, class and gender in African American mothers' socialization of their daughters' heterosexuality. *Sex Roles, 59*(5–6), 429–442.

U.S. Department of Justice. (2000). Correctional populations in the United States, 1997. Retrieved from http://www.bjs.gov/index.cfm?ty=pbdetail&iid=691

Wade, J. T. (1996). An examination of locus of control/fatalism for Blacks, Whites, boys and girls over a two-year period of adolescence. *Social Behavior and Personality, 24*, 239–248.

Wallace, S., & Wilchins, R. (2013). *Gender norms: A key to improving health and wellness among black women and girls.* TrueChild.Org Executive Summary, The Heinz Endowment Foundation. http://www.truechild.org/Images/Interior/findtools/heinz%20report.pdf

Williams, C. B. (2005). Counseling African American women: Multiple identities—multiple constraints. *Journal of Counseling and Development, 83*(3), 278–283.

Williamson, M. (2007, May 28). Women, HIV and employment, CDC Statistics. Retrieved from http://aia.berkeley.edu/media/pdf/women_hiv_and_employment.pdf

World Health Organization (WHO). (2011). *Sexually transmitted infections (STIs).* Retrieved September 29, 2011, from http://www.who.int/mediacentre/factsheets/fs110/en/

Interracial Relationships: Attitudes among Heterosexual College-Educated African American Women

DANIELLE M. WALLACE AND SONJA PETERSON-LEWIS

INTRODUCTION

> Although I have seen many, I never saw much positive in the relationships between White men and Black women...So I admit that I am a bit amused by the way they portray the relationship between Olivia and Fitz.... I am not impressed that she is seeing a married man, but it [the relationship] is amusing because most people are not used to seeing men treat Black women with love and open respect—and especially not White men.... So watching that relationship is kind of strangely amusing.[1]

In April 2012, the network television show *Scandal* premiered. A political thriller, *Scandal* focuses on Olivia Pope, owner of a crisis management firm and former communications director for the president of the United States. Much of the series focuses on the romantic relationship between Olivia and married President Fitzgerald "Fitz" Grant. In some parts of the country, viewers are said to have *Scandal* viewing parties due in part to the show's placement of an African American woman as the central figure, but also because of its portrayal of a respectful interracial relationship. The show has sparked a conversation about the overall acceptability of interracial dating, as well as a discussion about Black women's willingness to date men who are not Black.

Although the 2010 U.S. Census revealed that one out of every four African American male newlyweds married a non-Black partner, a study by the Pew

Research Center (2012) shows that, historically, heterosexual African American women tend to be less receptive to interracial relationships and show a strong and often exclusive preference for Black partners. This preference for Black male partners does not necessarily translate into opportunities for positive, constructive relationships. Census data revealed a Black sex ratio of 86.6—meaning that for ages 15 and above, there are roughly 87 Black men to every 100 Black women (U.S. Census, 2003). Numerous sociopolitical considerations and personal preferences among both men and women can further lower this ratio. On college campuses where the proportion of Black women can easily exceed that of Black men by four to one, Black women's singular preference for finding Black partners can greatly lower not only their probability of finding a suitable life mate but also their probability of having any appreciable dating or courtship opportunities during their college years.

LITERATURE REVIEW

At its most basic level, mate selection in the United States tends to operate on the basis of homogamy—that is, people tend to marry others of similar race, religion, age, education level, and socioeconomic status (Kerckhoff, 1964, 1976; Regan, 2003). Homogamy occurs in large part because people tend to live, work, and socialize near those who are like themselves. Homogamous pairings are typically thought to be more satisfying than heterogamous ones because these types of pairings are expected by society and are, therefore, sanctioned and supported (Kerckhoff, 1976). Homogamous partners are allowed to participate in society without the reprimand or reproach frequently dealt out to those in heterogamous relationships (e.g., interracial, interreligious, or intercultural). The latter are often denied the social approval and benefits that can be gained from inclusion in a particular group (Homans, 1958).

Homogamy is closely linked to propinquity, or geographic nearness, which plays a role in marriage markets.[2] The people to whom one is geographically closest become "the 'field of availables,' those whom one has the greatest chance of meeting and marrying" (Kerckhoff, 1976, p. 263). Often, people meet those similar to them in institutional settings such as school, work, or religious networks. However, demographics and sex ratios can complicate the process of meeting potential mates with whom stable relationships can be formed. As noted earlier, the sex ratio is a calculation of the number of men per 100 women in a particular area. A low sex ratio indicates that there are more women than men; a high sex ratio indicates that there are more men than women. Imbalanced sex ratios have the ability to greatly affect stable relationship formation, particularly among African Americans.

EFFECTS OF DISPARITIES IN BLACK MALE-FEMALE RATIO

Various authors (Cox, 1940; Guttentag & Secord 1983; Jackson, 1971) have argued that the sex ratio is directly related to the marriage rates among African Americans and directly contributes to the mate selection processes of Black women and men. More specifically, Cox found that sex ratio imbalance had the most influence on the marriage rates of Black women—a group whose relationship habits are greatly shaped by mate availability and the conditions of the marriage market. As a result of the low sex ratio, Black women who prefer Black mates are at a disadvantage in the marriage market because many Black men have the option of choosing mates on their own terms and therefore have more choices of desirable mates than do Black women (Aldridge, 1991; Braithwaite, 1981; Chapman, 2007; Harford, 2008; Johnson & Staples, 2005; McClintock, 2010; South, 1993).

Educational institutions are traditionally one of the venues in which individuals meet future spouses (Blossfield & Timm, 2003; Kalmijn, 1998; Kerckhoff, 1976). Research (Ganong, Coleman, Thompson, & Goodwin-Watkins, 1996; Ross, 1997) shows that college-educated women tend to prefer college-educated mates, in part because they expect that similarity in education will result in more shared goals and more supportive relationships (Mundy, 2012; Sullivan & Coltrane, 2008). However, in colleges and universities, as in the larger society, Black women tend to outnumber Black men. As of 2010, there were just over 1.7 million Black women enrolled in four-year colleges as compared to roughly 983,000 Black men (U.S. Department of Education, 2010). Due to the numerical disparities, if every one of these college-educated Black women were looking to marry a college-educated Black man, and these men were looking to marry Black women, roughly 42% of the women would be without mates.

However, just as pursuing a college education helps to shape individuals' aspirations for themselves, it also shapes the qualities they desire in a serious relationship partner. The college educational experience brings individuals into proximity with a variety of personalities, nationalities, races, classes, and interest groups and, as such, can broaden individuals' exposure to, interactions with, and perspectives on others who were previously outside one's sphere of familiarity. This social broadening aspect of college life raises the question of whether acquiring a college education affects attitudes toward relationships with other races. This chapter investigates how college completion status affects Black women's attitudes toward interracial relationships at three levels—casual dating, steady dating, and marriage.

INTERRACIAL DATING AND MARRIAGE ATTITUDES
OF BLACK WOMEN

Porter and Bronzaft (1995), in interviews with Black female college students found that, overwhelmingly, the women indicated a desire to date and marry Black men and did not date men from other racial groups. Those who did date men from other racial groups indicated that they did not find those relationships more fulfilling or rewarding than relationships they had with Black men. Respondents also felt that Black men were more supportive of their career and educational goals than other men from other groups and they were easier to communicate with.

Like Porter and Bronzaft, McClintock (2010) found that African American female students were less willing than their male counterparts to engage in interracial sexual or romantic partnerships, expressing a preference for same race mates in all levels of relationships. Some researchers have examined racial group–related factors that affect dating practices and preferences among college students. In a longitudinal study of students' attitudes toward interracial dating on college campuses, Levin, Taylor, and Caudle (2007) found that intergroup dating on college campuses was negatively related to in-group identification. Thus, high in-group identification meant lower levels of intergroup dating. Conversely, students who exhibited lower levels of in-group bias and identification were more likely to date members of other ethnic and racial groups during college. These findings suggest that the higher one's level of racial consciousness or racial group commitments, the lower one's receptiveness to interracial dating.

McClintock (2010) found that in general, Black and Asian students tended to have more segregated social networks. However, within these two groups, African American men and Asian women engaged in interracial hookups—casual, unplanned intimate encounters (Bogle, 2008; Sassler, 2010)— and dating at higher rates than African American women and Asian men, a trend that mirrors gender differences in interracial marriage statistics. This finding raises the possibility that the preference for a partner's race may change with the level of relationship commitment, specifically, the more intimate the relationship an individual seeks, the more likely he or she may be to seek out same-race partners—particularly if they have high in-group identification/consciousness. Given that the quest for serious relationships is often correlated with age or one's stage in life, we might expect that as individuals grow older and/or move to more stable life stages (i.e., progress toward completing their educations and earn degrees), their receptiveness to interracial relationships change.

Another issue shaping individuals' attitudes toward relationships is the types of messages received from parents and family regarding marriage-related issues. Research has shown that children often adopt their parents' ideals and attitudes about marriage, relationships, and family (Kapinus, 2004; Moen, Erickson, & Dempster-McClain, 1995). In addition, Cunningham and Thornton (2006) have found that parents' marital quality can influence children's attitudes about marriage-related issues such as divorce, premarital sex, and cohabitation. Given that parents have the ability to shape children's attitudes toward marriage and family through socialization and modeling, a question that should be explored is how the nature of parental love relationships and the model of marriage and other intimate relationships to which they exposed their children affected those children's attitudes toward and expectations of relationships.

INTERRACIAL MARRIAGE PATTERNS OF BLACK MEN AND WOMEN

Although most American marriages follow patterns of racial homogamy, the incidence of racial intermarriage has increased since the 1967 *Loving v. Virginia* U.S. Supreme Court decision, which declared laws prohibiting interracial marriage unconstitutional. By 2010, interracial and interethnic heterosexual married couple households had increased from 7% to 10% in 2000 (Pew Research Center, 2012; U.S. Census Bureau, 2012a). In total, interracial and interethnic married couples numbered more than 5.3 million in 2010 (U.S. Census Bureau, 2011).

The percentage of Black newlyweds who married interracially increased from 15.5% in 2008 to 17.1% in 2010 (Pew Research Center, 2012). As of 2010, 24% of Black male newlyweds compared to 9% of Black female newlyweds married a non-Black spouse (Pew Research Center, 2012). Blacks tend to intermarry most with Whites, then Latinos, then Asians (U.S. Census Bureau, 2012b).

Sex ratio imbalances result in the more populous gender either not being in relationships, or in their looking to out-groups for potential mates (Guttentag & Secord, 1983; Qian, 1999). Most often, one finds that racial intermarriage is most common among the women of a particular group. This has been especially true among Asian women, who out-marry at higher rates than any other group of women (Tucker & Mitchell-Kernan, 1990). However, the opposite phenomenon has occurred within the Black community. The tendency among Black men to seek non-Black partners more often than do Black women results in a larger population of potential spouses for Black men and a diminished source of eligible spouses for those Black women who prefer Black mates.

Even in the face of drastic sex ratio imbalances, Black women out-marry at lower rates than all other race-gender groups (Qian & Lichter, 2011), and tend not to view interracial marriage as a viable option. This, then, raises the question of what factors affect Black women's attitudes toward interracial relationships.

THE PRESENT STUDY

Motivated by the statistics on availability of eligible Black partners and literature on interracial relationships, this study examines how four variables or factors affect Black women's attitudes about interracial relationships. The four variables are:

1. Respondents' college graduation status—divided into those who have completed studies at or above the bachelor's level versus those who have not yet completed college.
2. Respondents' life stage—divided into age groups 18–23 (baccalaureate years) and 27–30 (early career years).
3. Sex ratio consciousness—whether or not respondents agreed, were unsure, or disagreed that there were adequate numbers of eligible Black mates available as their potential partners.
4. Perceptions of love relationships observed during formative years as happy, mixed, or unhappy.

The respondents included 102 heterosexual women who came from two major populations: students currently enrolled as graduate or undergraduate students at an urban university in the Northeast, and postgraduate women who learned of the study via academic/professional organizations or through snowball sampling. Participants fell into the following age groups: 18–21 (n = 60), 22–26 (n = 26), 27–30 (n = 9), 31–34 (n = 3), and 35 and older (n = 4). In regard to education level, the participants fell into two groups: those who had completed some college (n = 54), and those who had completed bachelor's and graduate degrees (n = 46). The data were collected both in face-to-face settings and through an online survey. All face-to-face administration of the instrument took place on the university campus at which participants were enrolled. Preliminary analyses revealed no significant differences between in-person and online responses; thus, we combined data from all sources for this chapter.

The original study from which our data come (Wallace, 2014) examined a sample of Black men's and women's attitudes about marriage, perceptions of their own and others' marriageability, and a number of other relationship-related issues, including their level of receptiveness to intraracial and interracial relationships. The Perceptions of Interracial Dating section of the instrument used an adaptation of Bogardus's social distance scaling (1933) to measure participants' yes-no receptiveness to entering five levels of social contact—friendship, dating, steady relationship, sexual relationship, and marriage—with opposite sex members of four racial groups—Asian, White, Latino/a, and Black. Because casual dating, steady dating, and marriage better reflect the meaning of relationship than do friendships and purely sexual relationships, we have chosen to focus on these three relationship levels for this study.[3]

Effects of College Graduation Status on Receptiveness to Interracial Relationships

Prompted by the literature suggesting a relationship between certain socio-demographic variables and individuals' attitudes about interracial relationships, our first question was, "Does college completion status affect Black women's attitudes toward entering romantic interracial relationships at the casual dating, steadily dating, or marriage levels?" To conduct this analysis, we grouped respondents into two college completion groups: (1) those currently working toward a college degree (non-completers) and (2) those who had earned bachelor's degrees or higher. Of the 102 women in the study, 99 had data that qualified them for inclusion in this analysis. Of those 99, 54 (54.5%) had not yet completed college and 45 (45.5%) had completed college.

Receptiveness to Casual Interracial Dating: Effects of College Graduation Status

The question we are seeking to answer here is, "Is there a predictable relationship between women's college completion status and their willingness to enter casual dating relationships with Asian, White, or Latino males?" The results of Chi-square analysis appear in table 12.1 below.[4]

Table 12.1. Women's Receptiveness to Casual Interracial Dating by College Completion Status.

Ethnicity of prospective Casual Dating partner	Percentage of women respondents by college completion status indicating willingness to enter into a casual dating relationship with members of the specified "racial" group				
	Women who had not completed college (n=54)	Women who had completed college with bachelor's or higher (n=45)	Chi-Square	d.f.	Sig. Level (p values)
Asian (Avg. 66%)	61% (33/54)	71% (32/45)	1.089	1	.297
White (Avg. 77%)	80% (43/54)	73% (33/45)	0.546	1	.460
Latino male (Avg. 88%)	89% (48/54)	87% (39/45)	0.114	1	.736

Note: An asterisk marks p values that are statistically significant at the .05 level.

As table 12.1 shows, respondents' college completion status did not predict their receptiveness to casual interracial dating. In fact, regardless of college completion status, the majority of women—between 61% and 89%—were willing to participate in casual interracial dating. With an average of 88% approval, Latinos were most favored for casual interracial dating, followed by Whites (76.5%). Although the 66% average receptiveness to casually dating among Asian men is lowest of the groups, it appears socially significant that well over half the Black women in this analysis, regardless of college education status, indicated that they were receptive to casual interracial dating.

Receptiveness to Steady Interracial Relationships: Effects of College Completion Status

Steady dating represents a level of commitment above casual dating. Our question here is, "Does women's college completion status affect their receptiveness to being in a steady interracial relationship?" The results of this analysis appear below in table 12.2.

Table 12.2. Women's Receptiveness to Steady Interracial Relationships by College Completion Status.

Ethnicity of prospective steady partner	Percentage of women respondents by college completion status indicating willingness to enter a steady relationship with members of the specified "racial" group				
	Women who had not completed college (n=54)	Women who had completed college with bachelor's or higher (n=45)	Chi-Square	d.f.	Sig. Level (p values)
Asian (Avg. 47.5%)	46%	49%	.066	1	.797
White (Avg. 56%)	63%	49%	1.98	1	.163
Latino (Avg. 75%)	83%	67%	3.713	1	.05*

Note: An asterisk marks p values that are statistically significant at the .05 level.

As the table shows, there is a statistically significant effect of college completion status on respondents' receptiveness toward having steady relationships with Latinos; specifically, women without college degrees were significantly more receptive (87%) to dating Latinos than were those with college degrees (67%). This same relationship held toward steady dating relationships with Whites but was not statistically significant. Findings suggest an opposite trend for attitude toward dating Asian men, with college graduates (49%) being slightly more receptive than non-graduates (46%).

Receptiveness Toward Interracial Marriage: Effects of College Completion Status

Our final question regarding effects of college completion status was, "Does respondents' college completion status affect their receptiveness to interracial marriage?" The results of this analysis revealed no significant differences for any of the groups by college completion status. However, there were two notable trends in respondents' receptiveness to interracial marriage. First, nongraduates were, in all cases, more open to interracial marriage than were college graduates. Second, percentages followed a trend such that both non-graduates and graduates gave highest endorsement to Latinos (70% and 61%, respectively), followed by Whites (54% and 42% respectively), and then Asians (39% and 38%, respectively).

EFFECTS OF LIFE STAGE ON RECEPTIVENESS TO INTERRACIAL RELATIONSHIPS

Our second major question was whether respondents' stage in life affected their receptiveness to various levels of interracial relationships. In our observation as college teachers, the late teens to middle twenties are traditionally the baccalaureate degree–seeking years—the times when individuals are trying to establish a sense of themselves, their strengths, and interests. On the other hand, the late twenties to early thirties often bring concerns about establishing careers, long-term intimate relationships, home, and family life—at least for individuals who desire these features. These concerns were evident among subjects in this study, and therefore for this analysis, we divided respondents into two groups or life stages—those 18–23 years, a group we associate with baccalaureate years—and those 27 and older, a group we associate with the early career years. In order to create more distinct divisions between these two stages, we completely omitted from analysis respondents who were in the 24-to-26 age range because they are often in between the two life stages.

Receptiveness to Casual Interracial Dating: Effects of Life Stage

We first examined the relationship between life stage and attitude toward casual interracial dating. The results of this analysis appear below.

Table 12.3. Women's Receptiveness to Casual Interracial Relationships by Life Stage.

Ethnicity of Prospective Casual Dating Partner	Percentage of women respondents by life stage indicating willingness to enter a casual dating relationship with members of the specified "racial" group				
	18-23 (n=78)	27 and older (n=16)	Chi-Square	d.f.	Sig. Level (p values)
Asian male (Avg. 62%)	68%	56%	0.809	1	.368
Caucasian male (Avg. 69%)	82%	56%	5.05	1	.024*
Latino male (Avg. 80%)	91%	69%	5.91	1	.015*

Note: An asterisk marks p values that are statistically significant at the .05 level.

Table 12.3 reveals that receptiveness to casual interracial dating was higher among persons in the 18–23 year-old group than among the early career, 27 and older group. This difference between groups was true across all ethnic groups, but was statistically significant only for White and Latino dates. Specifically, Black women 18 to 23 were significantly more receptive to casual dating with Latinos (91%) and Whites (82%) than were women 27 and older. Receptiveness to Latino dates (69%) and White dates (56%) was significantly lower for the older group. We note that regardless of age group/life stage, respondents' receptiveness toward casual interracial dating was over the 50% mark.

Receptiveness to Steady Interracial Dating: Effects of Life Stage

Table 12.4 below shows the results of life stage on women's receptiveness to having a steady ("boyfriend") interracial relationship. Chi-square analysis revealed a significant effect of life stage on respondents' receptiveness to having a steady relationship with White males ($\chi^2(1) = 5.90$, $p < .05$). Specifically, compared to early career women 27 and older, twice as many women in the 18 to 23 age (baccalaureate) range were receptive to steady interracial relationships with White males. The life stage groups did not differ significantly from each other in their receptiveness to steady relationships with Latino or Asian men. As with previous relationships, the trend in order of acceptance was Latino first, followed by White, then Asian.

Table 12.4. Women's Receptiveness to a Steady Interracial Relationship by Life Stage.

Ethnicity of Prospective Steady Partner	Percentage of women respondents by life stage indicating willingness to enter a steady relationship with members of the specified "racial" group				
	18-23 Baccalaureate Years (n=78)	27 and older Early Career Years (n=16)	Chi-Square	d.f.	Sig. Level (p values)
Asian male (Avg. 51%)	46%	56%	0.54	1	.461
White male (Avg. 47.5%)	64%	31%	5.90	1	.015*
Latino male (Avg. 70%)	77%	63%	1.45	1	.23

Note: An asterisk marks p values that are statistically significant at the .05 level.

Receptiveness to Interracial Marriage: Effect of Life Stage

Table 12.5 revealed no statistically significant differences between life stage groups in terms of their percentage acceptance of interracial marriage; however, comparing the marriage-receptive percentages to casual interracial dating percentages and steady interracial relationship percentages reveals that as the level of relationship commitment increases, lower percentages of respondents are receptive to interracial relationships. Despite being lower than other relationships and non-significant, the percentages again show a trend toward greatest favorability toward Latinos, followed by Whites.

Table 12.5: Women's Receptiveness to Interracial Marriage by Life Stage.

Ethnicity of Prospective Interracial Marriage Partner	Percentage of women respondents by life stage indicating willingness to enter interracial marriage				
	18-23 (n=78)	27 and older (n=16)	Chi-Square	d.f.	Sig. Level (p values)
Asian male (Avg. 42%)	40%	44%	.088	1	.766
White male (Avg. 46%)	54%	38%	1.420	1	.233
Latino male (Avg. 61%)	65%	56%	.480	1	.488

Note: An asterisk marks p values that are statistically significant at the .05 level.

EFFECTS OF RESPONDENTS' PERCEPTION OF AVAILABILITY OF ELIGIBLE BLACK MATES

The third major area we explored is whether Black women's attitudes about interracial relationships are affected by their perception of the availability of Black males as mates. That is, does the perceived Black male shortage affect Black women's receptiveness to being in interracial relationships? To explore this issue, we created the independent variable "Perception of Availability of Eligible Black Men" by recoding into three categories the responses to one question, "There are plenty of eligible Black men available for women like me to marry." We first collapsed the original five-point Likert-type response scale into three categories—(1) No, I do not believe there are enough eligible Black mates; (2) I am not sure whether there are enough eligible Black mates, and (3) I believe there are enough eligible Black mates. Table 12.6 below shows the results of this analysis for casual interracial dating.

Effects on Casual Interracial Dating

The analysis in table 12.6 revealed that whether women perceived there to be available Black mates had a statistically significant effect on their receptiveness to casually dating White males ($\chi^2(2) = 6.08$, $p < .05$). The trend in percentages shows that among Black women who said they believed there were enough eligible Black males to marry, 96% were willing to casually date Whites. Among those who were unsure as to whether there were enough eligible Black mates, 73% were willing to casually date Whites. Among those who believed there were not enough eligible Black males for them to find a suitable partner, 70% were receptive to casual dates with Whites. The general trend—lower willingness to date interracially as perceived numbers of eligible Black males decrease—holds for receptiveness to casually dating Asian and Latino males but is not statistically significant. This finding runs counter to intuition in that we would expect that the fewer the number of eligible Black males respondents believe are available, the *more* receptive those respondents would be to relationships with non-Black males. Instead, among these respondents, the greater the belief in the shortage of eligible Black male partners for themselves, the lower their willingness to date interracially.

Table 12.6. Women's Receptiveness to Casual Interracial Dating by Perception of the Availability of Eligible Black Male Mates.

Ethnicity of Prospective Casual Dating Partner	Percentage of respondents receptive to entering casual interracial dating relationships by perceived availability of eligible Black male mates					
	No; I do not believe there are enough eligible Black mates (n=43)	I am not sure whether or not there are enough eligible Black mates (n=33)	Yes; I believe there are enough eligible Black mates (n=23)	Chi-Square	d.f.	Sig. Level (p values)
Asian male (Avg. 62%)	63%	61%	78%	2.15	2	.341
White male (Avg. 71.5%)	70%	73%	96%	6.083	2	.048*
Latino male (Avg. 85.5%)	86%	85%	96%	1.73	2	.422

Note: An asterisk marks p values that are statistically significant at the .05 level.

Effects on Steady Relationships

Table 12.7 below reveals that respondents' level of belief as to whether there were adequate numbers of eligible Black mates had no significant effect on their receptiveness to steady relationships with any of the ethnic groups. However, despite lack of statistical significance, the percentages generally suggest that, contrary to our expectations, respondents' perception of a shortage of marriage-eligible Black males lowered respondents' willingness to be in relationships with men from other racial groups.

Table 12.7. Women's Receptiveness to Steady Interracial Relationship by Perception of the Availability of Eligible Black Male Mates.

Ethnicity of Prospective Steady Partner	Percentage of respondents receptive to entering steady interracial relationships by perceived availability of eligible Black male mates					
	No; I do not believe there are enough eligible Black mates (n=43)	I am not sure whether or not there are enough eligible Black mates (n=33)	Yes; I believe there are enough eligible Black mates (n=23)	Chi-Square	d.f.	Sig. Level (p values)
Asian male (Avg. 47%)	42%	52%	52%	.963	2	.618
White male (Avg. 52%)	51%	52%	74%	5.67	2	.160
Latino male (Avg. 72%)	77%	67%	87%	3.08	2	.245

Note: An asterisk marks p values that are statistically significant at the .05 level.

Effects on Marriage

Analysis using perceived availability of eligible Black males as the predictor variable and receptiveness toward interracial marriage as the outcome variable (table 12.8 below) reveals that respondents' belief as to whether there were adequate or inadequate numbers of eligible Black mates and their receptiveness to marriage with Whites approached statistical significance ($p = .087$) but was not significant. There was no significant effect of perceived availability on receptiveness toward Latinos or Asians, suggesting that respondents' perception of whether there are or are not enough marriage-eligible Black males is related to their holding White males to a different standard than they hold Latino or Asian males. In other words, among respondents in this study, the perception that there is a shortage of marriage-eligible Black males is related to a decrease in percentage receptiveness to relationships with men from other racial groups. Although difference is present for all groups, it approaches significance only for White males.

Table 12.8. Women's Receptiveness to Interracial Marriage by Perception of the Availability of Eligible Black Male Mates.

Ethnicity of Prospective Marriage Partner	Percentage of respondents receptive to entering interracial marriage by perceived availability of eligible Black male mates					
	No; I do not believe there are enough eligible Black mates (n=43)	I am not sure whether or not there are enough eligible Black mates (n=33)	Yes, I believe there are enough eligible Black mates (n=23)	Chi-Square	d.f.	Sig. Level (p values)
Asian male (Avg. 39%)	35%	39%	44%	.489	2	.783
White Male (Avg. 51%)	37%	52%	65%	4.88	2	.087
Latino male (Avg. 67%)	61%	67%	74%	1.224	2	.542

Note: An asterisk marks p values that are statistically significant at the .05 level.

Because the findings in Table 12.8 run counter to logic, we ran correlational analyses to examine the relationship between (A) items testing female respondents' perceptions of the level of availability of Black mates and (B) respondents' receptiveness toward interracial marriage. Correlational analysis using the full five-point Likert-type responses revealed positive correlations between women's responses to the item, "There are plenty of eligible Black men available for women like me to marry," and their receptiveness to marrying members of other racial groups. Although this correlation, like others tested here, was positive for all groups, it was statistically significant only for respondents' receptiveness to White men (r (99) = .276, $p < .01$). This finding suggests that among these respondents, perceiving there to be available Black men was related to respondents being significantly more receptive to marriage with White males.

Consistent with the above finding, we found a positive correlation between respondents' responses to "There are many available Black men that I would want to marry" and their attitudes toward marrying non-Black men, but significantly so—(r(99) = .254, $p < .05$)—only for receptiveness to marrying White men. Finally, consistent with the previous two correlational findings, we found a negative correlation between responses to "Eligible Black women outnumber eligible

Black men" and respondents' receptiveness to marrying non-Black males, with the correlation again being significant only for receptiveness to marrying White males, (r(99) = -.232, p < .05). In the discussion section, we discuss what we think may underlie these counterintuitive findings.

RELATIONSHIP BETWEEN OBSERVING HAPPY RELATIONSHIPS AMONG PRIMARY ADULTS AND ATTITUDES ABOUT INTERRACIAL RELATIONSHIPS

The final issue we explored for this study is whether the level of happiness women observed in love-based relationships among adults in their household during their formative years affected women's attitudes toward interracial relationships. To answer this question, we recoded into three categories—"happy, mixed, and unhappy"—the respondents' original five-point Likert-type response to the question, "Overall, how would you characterize the love relationships between the adults in your family as you were growing up?" and examined whether or not this had an impact on their receptiveness to interracial relationships at the casual dating, steady dating and marital levels.

Effects on Casual Dating

Again, as with the other analyses, the percentage trend favoring Latinos first followed by Whites for interracial relationships continued. Chi-square analysis examining the relationship between level of happiness observed between adults in respondents' household of origin and attitude toward casually dating Latino males revealed a marginally significant relationship (χ^2(3) = 5.083, p < .079); here, observing higher happiness was related to greater receptiveness to casually dating Latinos. The chi-square statistic was not significant for respondents' attitudes toward dating White or Asian males. Without directly asking the participants, we cannot speculate on the reasons underlying these findings.

Table 12.9. Women's Receptiveness to Casual Interracial Dating by Level of Happiness Observed among Adults in Formative Years.

Ethnicity of Prospective Casual Dating Partner	Percentage of women respondents receptive to entering casual interracial dating relationships by Level of Happiness Observed among Adults in Formative Years					
	Observed Unhappy Relationships among Adults in Household (n=18)	Observed Mixed Happiness and Unhappiness among Adults in Household (n=60)	Observed Happy Relationships among Adults in Household (n=21)	Chi-Square	d.f.	Sig. Level (*p* values)
Asian male (Avg. 61.5%)	56%	67%	71%	1.15	2	.562
White Male (Avg. 73.5%)	67%	80%	76%	1.39	2	.500
Latino male (Avg. 81.5%)	72%	92%	91%	5.083	2	.079

Note: An asterisk marks *p* values that are statistically significant at the .05 level.

Steady Dating and Marriage

We forego showing tables for the two remaining "Effects of Observing Happiness" analyses because of lack of statistical significance. However, we must note that across all analyses using happiness observed in families of origin as a predictor variable, we found that, generally, having observed happy relationships among adults while growing up was related to respondents' higher receptiveness to interracial relationships at all three levels—casual dating, steady partnership, and marriage. However, none of the differences was statistically significant.

DISCUSSION AND IMPLICATIONS

This chapter examined the relevance of several social variables in predicting Black women's attitudes about entering interracial relationships at the casual dating, serious dating, and marriage levels. The predictor variables of interest were (1) women's college completion status, (2) women's life stage as assessed by age group, (3) women's perception of availability of eligible Black males, and (4) women's perception of the happiness level of relationships between adults in their lives.

Results show that, overall, respondents were receptive to interracial relationships given that receptiveness percentages ranged from 30% to 86%, depending upon which predictor variable, which type of relationship, and which ethnic group was under consideration. Thus, no less than about one third of the women in this study indicated that they would be receptive to some type of interracial relationship. Consistent with Childs (2005), the respondents' receptiveness to the various levels of interracial relationships decreased as the seriousness of the relationship increased; thus, the percent of women receptive to casual interracial dating was higher than the percent receptive to having a steady interracial relationship, and the percentage receptive to interracial marriage was lower than both of these.

Although the respondent variables we examined—women's college completion status, life stage, perceived availability of eligible Black mates, and level of happiness observed in primary relationships—did not consistently predict these respondents' attitudes about interracial relationships, we noticed three trends that are important to acknowledge and to examine in future research. First, although about one third of the respondents in this study were receptive to an interracial relationship, the women in this study were consistently more receptive to relationships with Latino men first, followed by White men and then Asian men. Without asking the respondents, we cannot know the definite reason for this trend. However, in speculating based on other aspects of the study not covered here, we believe this greater receptiveness to Latinos may be related to at least two issues. First, Latinos can be of any race or skin color—including Black. Given the research literature's consistent finding of Black women's traditional preference for Black mates, the favorability toward Latinos may be a hidden reflection of a racial preference. Second, and perhaps more important, Black women may expect Latinos to share or at least be able to identify with the social experiences and social concerns that tend to befall or disproportionally affect people of color—issues related to discrimination, employment, economics, housing, education, social justice, police harassment, and so on. Thus, the expectation of alignment in experiences and identification may underlie the respondents' greater receptiveness to Latino males.

We believe that respondents' comparatively lower receptiveness scores for Asian men reflect that the majority of African Americans have little social interaction, and therefore, little real familiarity with people of Asian descent. Much of Black American–Asian interaction takes place in the context of Asian-owned businesses located in Black communities, and these interactions have been fraught with tension, often due to each group's lack of knowledge about the other's culture. We believe that as a greater number of younger Black and Asian people interact, traditional stereotypes will be reduced, aiding in the development of constructive associations.

A finding that appears to run contrary to logic and previously established mate selection and marriage theory (Guttentag & Secord, 1983; Qian, 1999) bears discussion. Logic would dictate that the fewer eligible mates one believes there are within one's preference group, the greater would be one's willingness to date beyond one's group. For respondents in this study, however, this assumption did not apply. Specifically, respondents who believed there were too few eligible Black mates for relationships were less rather than more receptive than their counterparts to entering relationships with White males.

Without asking each participant the reasons for their responses, we cannot be sure what this trend in percentages means; however, comments that several respondents made on open-ended items and/or during the focus group phase of the study suggest that some women perceive policies and practices promoted by and for White society—and by White men in particular—as being responsible for the low availability of marriage-eligible Black men. Our present findings may possibly reflect the concept of group survival thrust, that is, the fact that Black women generally are concerned about the welfare and survival of Black men not merely as potential suitors, but also as their sons, brothers, fathers, uncles, cousins, and friends. Black women's all-inclusive concern for Black men makes it probable that respondents in this study were thinking not merely about Black males as potential mates but also about the status, survival, and condition of Black males in general. If, as previous research suggests, these respondents perceived Whites as having some level of responsibility for the relatively disadvantaged and often endangered condition of Black men, then as such, they might perceive having close relationships with Whites—and more specifically with White men—as a form of affiliating with the enemy.

Finally, although respondents' attitudes toward relationships with Black men were not among the central questions in this study, Wallace (2014) examined this receptiveness as part of a larger study of relationship attitudes of college-educated Blacks. It is interesting to note that at every level of every predictor variable in this study (i.e., college graduate versus nongraduate status, happy home versus unhappy home, and so on) and at every relationship level (i.e., casual dating, steady dating, or marriage) no fewer than 96% of the women in this study were receptive to relationships with Black mates. Thus, this study found no evidence that education level, life stage, perceived availability of eligible Black men, or the nature of original home environment formed a basis by which Black women rejected relationships with Black men. If there were data to support past speculation suggesting that Black women set their standards too high for marriage based on their education levels or other social factors similar to those we examined here, the data from this study show no support of that speculation.

NOTES

1. Interviewee speaking with second author about television's portrayal of an interracial relationship between character Oliva Pope (portrayed by actress Kerry Washington) and U.S. President Fitzgerald Grant (portrayed by actor Tony Goldwyn) on the ABC television series *Scandal*.

2. The concept of marriage markets is related to the economic understanding of marriage in which people compete for mates in the same way that people compete for money and commodities in the larger monetary markets (Becker, 1981). Oppenheimer (1988) compares marriage markets to job markets by arguing that one will search for a mate who has specific characteristics in much the same way one would search for a job with a required amount of benefits and/or perks.

3. Because we (1) assessed receptiveness to various levels of relationships on a yes-no scale, and (2) recoded respondents' responses to the above variables into two or three discrete categories reflecting yes-no or yes-maybe-no, we have used the Chi-square statistic throughout for most analyses. The Chi-square statistic allows us to determine whether there is a dependent (predictable) relationship between two or more variables. Thus, for example, in this study, a statistically significant Chi-square value would mean that one can predict women's receptiveness toward a particular type of interracial relationship based solely on knowing their status on the predictor variable such as whether or not they graduated from college, their life stage, and so on. We present findings based on the four independent variables in the order presented above. Although the usual practice is to present only tables that show statistically significant results, we present some tables for nonsignificant results when (1) the results run contrary to expectations or to established theory, or (2) when we believe it will be helpful for the reader to see and compare patterns in responses.

4. The reader should note that although we, for the sake of simplicity, show only the percentage of yes responses, the Chi-square analyses compared percentage of yes responses to the percentage of no responses at each combination of ethnicity and education status. Readers wanting to know the percentage of no responses need only subtract the percentage of yes responses from 100 percent.

BIBLIOGRAPHY

Aldridge, D. P. (1991). *Focusing: Black male-female relationships*. Chicago, IL: Third World.

Becker, G. (1981). *A treatise on the family*. Cambridge, MA: Harvard University Press.

Blossfield, H. P., & Timm, A. (Eds.). (2003). *Who marries whom?: Educational systems as marriage markets in modern societies*. Boston, MA: Kluwer Academic.

Bogardus, E. S. (1933). A social distance scale. *Sociology & Social Research, 17*, 265–271.

Bogle, K. A. (2008). *Hooking up: Sex, dating and relationships on campus*. New York, NY: New York University Press.

Braithwaite, R. L. (1981). Interpersonal relations between Black males and Black females. In L. E. Gary (Ed.), *Black men* (pp. 83–97). Newbury Park, CA: Sage.

Chapman, A. B. (2007). In search of love and commitment: Dealing with the challenging odds of finding romance. In H. P. McAdoo (Ed.), *Black families* (4th ed., pp. 285–296). Thousand Oaks, CA: Sage.

Childs, E. C. (2005). Looking behind the stereotypes of the "angry Black woman": An exploration of Black women's responses to interracial relationships. *Gender & Society, 19*(4), 544–561.

Cox, O. (1940). Sex ratio and marital status among Negroes. *American Sociological Review, 5*(6), pp. 937–947.

Cunningham, M., & Thornton, A. (2006). The influence of parents' marital quality on adult children's attitudes toward marriage and its alternatives: Main and moderating effects. *Demography, 43*(4), 659–672.

Ganong, L. H., Coleman, M., Thompson, A., & Goodwin-Watkins, C. (1996). African American and European American college students' expectations for self and future partners. *Journal of Family Issues, 17*(6), 758–775.

Guttentag, M., & Secord, P. F. (1983). *Too many women?: The sex ratio question.* Beverly Hills, CA: Sage.

Harford, T. (2008). *The logic of life: The rational economics of an irrational world.* New York, NY: Random House.

Homans, G. C. (1958). Social behavior as exchange. *American Journal of Sociology, 63*(6), 597–606.

Jackson, J. J. (1971). But where are the men? *The Black Scholar, 3*(4), 34–41.

Johnson, L. B., & Staples, R. (2005). *Black families at the crossroads: Challenges and perspectives.* San Francisco, CA: Jossey-Bass.

Kalmijn, M. (1998). Intermarriage and homogamy: Causes, patterns, trends. *Annual Review of Sociology, 24,* 395–421.

Kapinus, C. A. (2004). The effect of parents' attitudes toward divorce on offspring's attitudes: Gender and parental divorce as mediating factors. *Journal of Family Issues, 25,* 112–135.

Katz, A. M., & Hill, R. (1958). Residential propinquity and marital selection: A review of theory, method and fact. *Marriage and Family Living, 20*(1), 27–35.

Kerckhoff, A. C. (1964). Patterns of homogamy and the field of eligibles. *Social Forces, 42,* 289–297.

Kerckhoff, A. C. (1976). Patterns of marriage and family formation and dissolution. *Journal of Consumer Research, 2,* 261–275.

Levin, S., Taylor, P. L., & Caudle, E. (2007). Interethnic and interracial dating in college: A longitudinal study. *Journal of Social and Personal Relationships, 24*(3), 323–343.

McClintock, E. A. (2010). When does race matter? Race, sex and dating at an elite university. *Journal of Marriage and Family, 72*(1), 45–72.

Moen, P., Erickson, M. A., & Dempster-McClain, D. (1995). Their mothers' daughters? The inter-generational transmission of gender attitudes in a world of changing roles. *Journal of Marriage and the Family, 59,* 281–93.

Mundy, L. (2012). *The richer sex: How the new majority of female breadwinners is transforming sex, love and family.* New York, NY: Simon & Schuster.

Oppenheimer, V. K. (1988). A theory of marriage. *American Journal of Sociology, 94*(3), 563–591.

Pew Research Center. (2012). *The rise of intermarriage: Rates, characteristics vary by race and gender.* Washington, DC: Pew Research Center Social & Demographic Trends.

Porter, M. M., & Bronzaft, A. L. (1995). Do the future plans of educated Black women include Black mates? *The Journal of Negro Education, 64*(2), 162–170.

Qian, Z. (1999). Who intermarries? Education, nativity, region, and interracial marriage, 1980 and 1990. *Journal of Comparative Family Studies, 30*(4), 579–597.

Qian, Z., & Lichter, D. T. (2011). Changing patterns of interracial marriage in a multiracial society. *Journal of Marriage and Family, 73*(5), 1065–1084.

Regan, P. (2003). *The mating game: A primer on love, sex and marriage.* Thousand Oaks, CA: Sage.

Ross, L. E. (1997). Mate selection preferentials among African American college students. *Journal of Black Studies, 27*(4), 554–569.

Sassler, S. (2010). Partnering across the life course: Sex, relationships and mate selection. *Journal of Marriage and the Family, 72*(3), 557–575.

South, S. J. (1993). Racial and ethnic differences in the desire to marry. *Journal of Marriage and the Family, 55*(2), 357–370.

Sullivan, O., & Coltrane, S. (2008). *Men's changing contribution to housework and childcare.* The Council on Contemporary Families, Miami, FL. Retrieved from https://contemporaryfamilies.org/mens-changing-contribution-to-housework-and-childcare-brief-report/

Tucker, M. B., & Mitchell-Kernan, C. (1990). New trends in Black American interracial marriage. *Journal of Marriage and the Family, 52,* 209–218.

U.S. Census Bureau. (2003). *Women and men in the United States: March 2002.* Washington, DC: U.S. Government Printing Office.

U.S. Census Bureau. (2011). *Age and sex composition: 2010.* Washington, DC: U.S. Government Printing Office.

U.S. Census Bureau. (2012a). *Households and families: 2010.* Washington, DC: U.S. Government Printing Office.

U.S. Census Bureau. (2012b). *Hispanic origin and race of wife and husband in married-couple households for the United States: 2010.* Washington, DC: U.S. Government Printing Office.

U.S. Department of Education. (2010). *Total fall enrollment in degree-granting institutions, by level of student, sex, attendance status, and race/ethnicity: Selected years, 1976 through 2010.* Washington, DC: U.S. Government Printing Office.

Wallace, D. M. (2014). *The search for "the one": The dating, marriage and mate selection ideals of college-educated Blacks.* (Doctoral dissertation), Retrieved from ProQuest Dissertation and Theses Full Text. (Accession No. 3623300).

CHAPTER THIRTEEN

Cultural Racism and Violence in African American Communities

WILLIAM OLIVER

INTRODUCTION

The high rates of intra-racial violence is among the most significant contemporary challenges confronting not just the African American community but the larger American society as well. As far back as 1979, *Ebony Magazine* devoted a special issue to the causes and consequences of Black-on-Black crime. Since that time, politicians, criminal justice agencies and practitioners, academic researchers, public policy institutes, media, public schools, community leaders, and community organizations have put forward a variety of viewpoints and implemented numerous policies and programs to address the causes, consequences, and solutions to violence in the African American community. Unfortunately, what has emerged in America is a self-perpetuating urban violence–focused industrial complex with stakeholders manifesting varying degrees of commitment toward the development of substantive solutions. While millions of dollars have been allocated, more recent violent crime data suggest that the independent and collective efforts of these various stakeholders and interest groups have not yet sufficiently mitigated the problem of violence in the African American community.

The position adopted in this chapter is that many violence prevention efforts are insufficient because they are not informed by a comprehensive understanding of the various factors that converge and give rise to high rates of intergenerational violence among disadvantaged African Americans. As such, this chapter suggests that to fully understand the causes of the high rates of violence among African Americans and, to prevent that violence, public policymakers and community leaders must become familiar with how intergenerational exposure to cultural racism is associated with and provides the cultural and situational context for these disproportionate rates. More specifically, I argue that cultural racism is a largely unexplored factor in efforts to explain and prevent these high rates of interpersonal violence among African Americans.

VIOLENCE AMONG AFRICAN AMERICANS

As of 2013, African Americans constituted 13.2% of the U.S. population, but are disproportionately represented among violent crime offenders and victims. For example, the Federal Bureau of Investigation (2012) reports that in 2012, African Americans accounted for 31% of persons arrested for assault, 34% of persons arrested for aggravated assault, 32.5% of persons arrested for rape, 49.4% of persons arrested for murder, and 54% of persons arrested for robbery. Furthermore, it is important to note that violent crime in America primarily involves an intraracial victim-offender relationship pattern. That means violent crime victims are generally targeted by members of their same racial or ethnic group. For example, in 2012, 91% of Black murder victims were killed by Black offenders. Similarly, the majority of White murder victims (83%) were killed by White offenders (Federal Bureau of Investigation, 2012).

The disproportionate representation of African Americans among violent crime offenders and victims is most dramatically illustrated in current homicide data indicating that, for every age range, African American males and females have higher rates of death resulting from homicide than any other racial or ethnic group. In 2010, for instance, Black males, all ages combined, had a homicide rate (8.7/100,000) nearly three times the White male rate (3.3/100,000). The most telling indicator of racial disparities in homicide rates is evident in the disparate rates of Black and White males ages 15–24. The National Center for Health Statistics (2013) reports that in 2010 Black males in that age range had a homicide rate (71/100,000) that was 17 times greater than the rate (4.1/100,000) among White males (National Center for Health Statistics, 2013).

While it is common for the popular media to cast the problem of violence as an African American male problem, in terms of describing the demographic characteristics of persons most at risk, it is important to note that African American females are also disproportionately represented among homicide victims compared to White females. For example, in 2010, Black females, all ages combined, had a homicide rate (5/100,000) two and a half times greater than the homicide rate

(1.8/100,000) of White females. Furthermore, among the age range 25–44, in which females are most likely to be murdered, African American females had a homicide rate (7.4/100,000) that was three times greater (2.4/100,000) than that of White females (National Center for Health Statistics, 2012).

THE TRADITIONAL CAUSATION BOX

Over the course of the past 50 years criminologists and others who address questions related to the causes of crime and violence have increasingly focused their attention on criminal offending and victimizing among African Americans (Cloward & Ohlin, 1960; Wolfgang & Ferracuti, 1967; Curtis, 1975; Sampson & Wilson, 1995; Green & Gabbidon, 2000; Unnever & Gabbidon, 2011). Theoretical explanations of the causes of crime and violence among African Americans have tended to adopt a cultural or structural perspective.

Proponents of cultural explanations of crime and violence among African Americans lean toward causal explanations that focus on social processes in which African Americans at risk for violent crime offending and victimizing internalize values and norms that condone violence as a means of resolving disputes (Wolfgang & Ferracuti, 1967). In addition, some proponents of cultural explanations of causation make reference to various indicators of social and community disorganization, such as the high rates of poverty, the high rates of joblessness (particularly among African American males), the high rates of teen pregnancy and children born out of wedlock, and the low rates of participation in formal and voluntary organizations. These indicators serve to erode the supervision of youth and to weaken community control over adolescent and young adult peer groups, thereby providing a context for their adoption and enactment of values, norms, and behaviors that increase their risk of criminal offending and victimizing (Sampson, 1993).

In contrast to the cultural perspective, there is also a long tradition in criminology and the social sciences of attributing the high rates of crime and violence among African Americans to a legacy involving intergenerational exposure to adverse structural conditions, including racial oppression in the form of slavery, legal segregation, and racially based discrimination designed to subordinate African Americans by limiting their access to political participation, education, employment, capital, and housing (Du Bois,1899/1973; Clark, 1965; Curtis, 1975). Furthermore, proponents of structural explanations of the causes of crime and violent crime among African Americans tend to argue that violence and collateral behaviors that increase the risk of violent crime are often a means to cope with blocked access to legitimate opportunities for upward mobility and material deprivation (Merton, 1938).

THE STRUCTURAL CULTURAL PERSPECTIVE

A major innovation in the development of criminological theory seeks to enhance understanding of "the causes" of the high rates of violent crime offending and victimizing among African Americans. It involves the construction of theoretical explanations that place emphasis on both structural and cultural factors. Toward this end I have proposed the structural-cultural perspective to specifically examine how various structural and cultural factors converge and contribute to the violence among African Americans, particularly African American males. The primary claim of the structural-cultural perspective is that the high rates of disproportionately high rates of violent crime offending and victimization among African Americans is a direct result of the convergence of adverse structural pressures and dysfunctional cultural adaptations (Oliver, 2003). In other words, there are three distinct structural pressures that serve as a catalyst for the high rates of interpersonal violence among African Americans: (1) institutional racism, (2) race-neutral transformation of the American economy, and (3) cultural racism.

INSTITUTIONAL RACISM

Intergenerational exposure to institutional racism is a major structural factor contributing to the high rates of interpersonal violence among African Americans. The term "institutional racism" is used here to refer to the systematic deprivation of equal access to conventional and legitimate opportunities in the form of political participation, education, vocational training, employment, capital, and housing (Knowles & Prewitt, 1968). The historic and contemporary practice of racial discrimination has functioned to disadvantage many African Americans and contribute to significant racial disparities in levels of educational achievement, income, the accumulation of wealth, and family stability (Wilson, 1996; Patterson, 1998). As such, historic and contemporary practices designed to block African Americans access to legitimate opportunities has functioned as a major source of racial disadvantage and social structural stress that predisposes some marginalized African Americans to engage in alternative means (e.g., robbery, burglary, theft, drug dealing, gang affiliation) of acquiring status conferring material goods and social esteem (Venkatesh, 2006). However, these alternative means of acquiring material goods and social esteem increase the risk of interpersonal conflict and violence (Oliver, 1998; Jacobs & Wright, 2006).

RACE-NEUTRAL TRANSFORMATION OF THE ECONOMY

The second structural pressure that is addressed in the structural-cultural perspective is race-neutral transformation of the U.S. economy. Beginning in the 1970s, a major trend, that has impacted the American economy with major risk factors is chronic unemployment and concentrated poverty. These factors associated with high levels of violence in disadvantaged urban communities involve deindustrialization and the subsequent loss of hundreds of thousands of low-skill, high-wage industrial manufacturing jobs, particularly as a result of innovations in the modes of production. In addition, decreasing the number of low-skill, high-wage manufacturing jobs has been linked to the outsourcing of jobs to third world countries that offer American companies access to low-paid non-unionized workers enhancing corporate profits at the expense of American workers and society as a whole (Wilson, 1996). The race-neutral transformation of the economy has had a devastating impact on the capacity of lower and working-class African American men to assume the economic responsibilities associated with adulthood, marriage, and fatherhood.

CULTURAL RACISM

Within academic literature that seeks to explain the high rates of violence among African Americans there is a long tradition of attributing these high rates of exposure to racism and racial discrimination along with related collateral consequences. However, what is unique and also problematic about this literature is that the discussion of racism is often limited to institutional racism, that is, the systematic deprivation of equal access to legitimate opportunities (Merton, 1938; Curtis, 1975; Wilson, 1987). In contrast to much of the existing literature that argues that there is a direct or indirect association between institutional racism (e.g., racial discrimination, relative deprivation, and/or income inequality) and the high rates of intrapersonal violence among African Americans, I argue that the concept of institutional racism as it is generally defined and operationalized in academic research, as well as public policy, does not describe the breadth nor the impact of racism as a social practice that adversely affects African Americans. Thus, while it is important to consider and account for the various ways in which exposure to institutional racism across generations provides a legacy and context for antisocial behavior, in order to enhance the understanding of how racism and violence interact among African Americans it is also important to consider the effects of cultural racism.

The term "cultural racism" expands the definitional range of racism as a concept and a form of problematic social practice in order to address the complexity of African American exposure to racism and the manner in which that exposure provides a psychological and social context for violent crime offending and victimizing among African Americans. The term "cultural racism" is used here to refer to the systematic manner in which the White majority as a group has established its primary cultural institutions (e.g., education, mass media, and religion) to elevate and glorify European physical elements, achievement, and character while, at the same time, denigrating the physical elements, achievement, and character of non-White people (Oliver, 2001). The primary distinction between institutional racism and cultural racism is that institutional racism has been implemented as a social practice that seeks to block or deny equal access to legitimate opportunities that facilitate survival, upward mobility, and racial equality in American society. In contrast, cultural racism functions as a social practice that is designed to diminish the cultural image and integrity of other groups, particularly African Americans (Akbar, 1994; Welsing, 1974).

A major example of cultural racism as a problematic social practice has been the conspicuous absence of a substantive representation and discussion of African Americans in the K–12 social studies curricula. This is important because all societies and cultures use their history to celebrate their achievements and promote a positive personal and collective identity as a people (Commager, 1970). As such, the conspicuous absence of African Americans in history and social studies textbooks serves to reinforce and promote racial stereotypes while eroding the self-concept of African Americans (Clark & Clark, 1947, 1980; Schaefer, 1993).

Cultural racism has also been promoted in television shows and film. For example, in his comprehensive survey of African Americans in film, Bogle (1974) found that in the first 50 years of American film, African Americans were primarily portrayed as Toms, coons, tragic mulattoes, mammies, and violent bucks. The primary purpose of the stereotypical portrayal of African Americans in television and film has been to entertain Whites by stressing their innate inferiority (Bogle, 1974; Schaefer, 1993). Berry (1996) argues that in contemporary society issues of racialism can be found in media images and messages for similar reasons perpetuating insensitivity, negative bias, stereotypical beliefs, as well as hostility and resentment toward African Americans.

The cultural subordination of African Americans by means of American cultural practices has also been perpetuated by the unique manner in which Christianity has been practiced in America through the projection of European images of both God and Christ. This practice contributes to the cultural subordination of African Americans because African Americans are vulnerable to internalizing the belief that those who look like the European image of God are superior and those who do not are inferior (Welsing, 1980).

CONSEQUENCES OF EXPOSURE TO CULTURAL RACISM

Intergenerational exposure to cultural racism has contributed to what Karenga (1988) refers to as a "cultural crisis" among African Americans. Cultural racism, as a larger societal practice, impacts the failure of African Americans as a group to institutionalize an affirming cultural agenda. The lack of such an agenda to counteract exposure to cultural racism has led to an African American cultural crisis that is characterized by: (1) loss of historical memory, (2) lack of appreciation of the physical characteristics and functional cultural practices of African Americans and Africans in the diaspora, and (3) the lack of cultural competence. Collectively, these elements within the African American cultural crisis are manifested as cultural disorganization—that is, the erosion of the capacity to develop and utilize culturally based institutions and culturally focused practices promoting not only survival but also functional and cumulative progress across each successive generation (Welsing, 1974; Madhubuti, 1990).

Another major consequence of exposure to the combined effects of institutional and cultural racism is the distortion of the individual and collective self-concept, personality, and mental health of African Americans (Clark & Clark, 1980; Baldwin, 1984). Many African American researchers in the field of psychology support Baldwin's (1984) observation that psychological misorientation is a common state of disorder in the black personality. As such, African American psychologists, particularly those who maintain membership in the Association of Black Psychologists, ascribe to the view that African Americans' exposure to racial oppression is a major factor contributing to mental disorders. For example, Baldwin uses the term "psychological misorientation" to generally describe a personality disorder that exists among African Americans as a result of their exposure to problematic social processes and social institutions. Educational structures, mass media, and religion too often disseminate anti-Black political rhetoric, socialization messages, and negative images.

Akbar (1981) has described several specific African American mental health disorders emerging from the general condition of psychological misorientation, including: (1) anti-self disorder, (2) alien-self disorder, and (3) self-destructive disorder. According to Akbar, anti-self disorder is a mental disorder in which African Americans manifest overt and covert hostility toward other African Americans and, by implication, toward themselves. As such, the individuals experiencing anti-self-disorder identify with the majority's projected hostility toward African American culture. In addition, Akbar uses the term "alien-self disorder" to describe an increasing number of African Americans who have been socialized to pursue materialistic goals. Akbar suggests that these individuals focus on materialism and evaluate their worth by the prevalence of material possessions. They are encouraged to ignore racial disparities associated with racial oppression and instead live their lives as if racism and oppression never existed. They adopt the perspective of the dominant wealthy members of society even if it means condemnation of self. Akbar includes "self-destructive disorder" in his typology of mental disorders associated with exposure to institutional and cultural racism because victims of self-destructive disorders tend to engage in self-defeating attempts to survive in a society that systematically (via both structural and cultural forces) tend to frustrate conventional efforts. African Americans manifesting self-destructive disorder, according to Akbar, are typified by various types of street hustlers (e.g., prostitutes, drug users, drug dealers, etc.).

CULTURAL RACISM, CULTURAL CRISIS, AND VIOLENCE

The failure of African Americans to establish an affirming cultural agenda is problematic because it has hindered African Americans' capacity to develop a narrative that assists individual resistance and rejection to the internalization of self-defeating beliefs regarding racial group membership and the adoption and enactment of problematic roles and lifestyles (Oliver, 1989). Furthermore, the persistent institutionalized practice of cultural racism, including its ultimate goal of establishing African Americans as functional inferiors, serves as a powerful structural factor contributing to high rates of interpersonal violence among African Americans (Welsing, 1974). As such, this failure of African Americans to institutionalize collective resistance to cultural racism by developing an affirming cultural agenda and cultural practices has facilitated the emergence of cultural disorganization. In addition, the subsequent adoption and enactment of problematic role orientations and lifestyles lead to a broad range of disruptive behaviors, including acts of interpersonal violence, particularly among those who are concentrated in disadvantaged urban areas (Anderson, 1994; Wilson, 1994).

As a consequence of the achievements of the Civil Rights Movement, great strides have been made in dismantling overt institutional racism in the United States. However, the upward mobility and the exodus of advantaged African Americans from racially segregated communities have served to weaken African American culture, particularly in economically disadvantaged urban neighborhoods. The dismantling of overt racial discrimination has served to highlight the fact that individualism and materialism have emerged as dominant concerns of African Americans to the exclusion of establishing a collective cultural agenda and consensus regarding forward movement in an era characterized by deindustrialization, globalization, and postracial rhetoric (Wilson, 1987; Wise, 2010). For example, during the slavery era, there was consensus around the desire to become free. During the Jim Crow era there was consensus around the desire to achieve full first-class citizenship. In contemporary America, following the dismantling of overt racial discrimination, there does not appear to be a collective agenda around which African Americans rally to promote the forward movement and strength of African Americans as a distinct group within the larger society (Madhubuti, 1990).

The practice of cultural racism and the resulting cultural disorganization that it creates functions as an unexamined aspect of the network of factors precipitating the disproportionate rates of violent crime offending and victimizing among African Americans. It is my view that cultural disorganization, precipitated by the converging effects of institutional and cultural racism, has provided a space in which marginalized African American males and females pursue social esteem and material success through the adoption and enactment of problematic role orientations and lifestyles. Hence, the lack of an institutionalized, affirming cultural agenda to socialize African American children, youth, and young adults with values that contribute to economic independence based on engagement in legitimate activities, family stability, political participation, and the collective progress of African Americans has allowed "the streets" to emerge as an alternative site facilitating the enactment of problematic roles (e.g., gang members, drug users, drug dealers, robbers, thieves, prostitutes, etc.) and lifestyles that increase the likelihood of interpersonal conflict and violent crime offending and victimizing (Oliver, 1998; Wright & Decker, 1997; Sterk, 1999; Jacobs & Wright, 2006).

CONCLUSION AND RECOMMENDATIONS

With regard to the fight to achieve human and civil rights, the actor and civil rights activist Paul Robeson once said, "The battle front is everywhere and there is no sheltered rear" (1958, p. 52). This statement is equally applicable to efforts to prevent and reduce the disproportionate rates of violent crime offending and victimizing among African Americans. The high rates of violence that plague African American communities are the product of multiple causes (e.g., inadequate public education, concentrated poverty, chronic unemployment, drug use, access to weapons, willingness to use violence to resolve disputes, inadequate supervision of youth, the proliferation of street gangs) and therefore require multiple solutions. The causal argument put forward in this chapter does not suggest that exposure to cultural racism is the singular cause of violence among African Americans. Rather, I argue that criminologists and others who conduct research on violence or who are involved in crafting public policy and responses to violence among African Americans have neglected to consider and account for the problematic and crimiogenic effects of exposure to cultural racism.

Therefore, it is my view that the African American community itself must become fully engaged in the prevention of violence by addressing the deleterious effects of intergenerational exposure to cultural racism. One means of facilitating cultural-based intervention is to develop strengths-based racial socialization models of childrearing. That is, the institutions that African Americans control (e.g., churches, mosques, community centers, sororities, fraternities, and other civic organizations) must move toward developing parenting education, responsible fatherhood, and mentoring programs that include emphasis on positive racial socialization assisting African American children, youth, and young adults in developing the resiliency to counteract exposure to both institutional and cultural racism. According to Lesane-Brown (2006), children who have not experienced positive racial socialization may be more vulnerable to internalizing the negative images embedded within racial stereotypes.

Furthermore, Unnever and Gabbidon (2011) report that African Americans are more likely to offend if their parents inadvertently fail to fully prepare them to fight the toxic effects of racial injustices. What is needed is cultural socialization that seeks to prepare children, youth, and young adults to successfully negotiate the broad range of challenges associated with life in America, specifically being African American in America. Consistent with this view Nicolas et al. (2008) indicate that the goal of cultural socialization of African American youth should involve enhancing "the capacity of Black youth to use racial identity and critical consciousness skills and resources to recognize racism and discriminatory experiences and to value themselves and resist personal and institutional racism in their lives and their environmental contexts" (p. 271).

BIBLIOGRAPHY

Akbar, N. (1981). Mental disorder among African Americans. *Black Books Bulletin, 72*, 18–25.

Akbar, N. (1994). *Chains and images of psychological slavery.* Jersey City, NJ: New Mind Productions.

Baldwin, J. A. (1984). African self-consciousness and the mental health of African Americans. *Journal of Black Studies, 15*, 177–194.

Berry, V. (1996) *Introduction in mediated messages and African American culture: Contemporary issues* (V. Berry & C. Manning-Miller, Eds.). Thousand Oaks CA: Sage.

Bogle, D. (1974). *Toms, coons, mulattoes, mammies, and bucks: An interpretive history of blacks in American films.* New York: Bantam.

Clark, K. B. (1965). *Dark ghetto.* New York: Harper & Row.

Clark, K. B., & Clark, M. P. (1947). Emotional Factors in Racial Identification and Preference in Negro Children. *The Journal of Negro Education, 9*(3), 341–350.

Clark, K. B., & Clark, M. P. (1980). What do Blacks think of themselves? *Ebony, 36*(1), 176–183.

Cloward, R., & Ohlin, L. (1960). *Differential opportunity theory: A theory of delinquent gangs.* New York: Free.

Commager, H. S. (1970). *Meet the U.S.A.* New York: Institute for International Education.

Curtis, L. A. (1975). *Violence, race and culture.* Lexington, MA: Lexington.

Du Bois, W. E. B. (1899/1973). *The Philadelphia Negro. A social study.* Milwood, NY: Kraus-Thomson.

Federal Bureau of Investigation. (2012). *Crime in the United States*. Washington, DC: U.S. Department of Justice.

Greene, H. T., & Gabbidon, S. L. (2000). *African American criminological thought*. Albany: State University of New York.

Jacobs, B. A., & Wright, R. (2006). *Street justice-retaliation in the criminal underworld*. New York: Cambridge University.

Karenga, M. (1988). Black studies and the problematic of paradigm: The philosophical dimension. *Journal of Black Studies, 18*, 395–414.

Knowles, L. L., & Prewitt, K. (1968). *Institutional racism in America*. Englewood Cliffs, NJ: Prentice Hall.

Lesane-Brown, C. L. (2006). A review of race socialization within black families. *Developmental Review, 26*, 400–426.

Madhubuti, H. (1990). *Black men: Single, dangerous and obsolete*. Chicago: Third World.

Merton, R. (1938). Social structure and anomie. *American Sociological Review, 3*, 672–682.

National Center for Health Statistics. (2013). *Health, United States, 2012*. Hyattsville, MD: U.S. Department of Health and Human Services.

Nicolas, G., et al. (2008). A conceptual framework for understanding the strengths of black youths. *Journal of Black Psychology, 34*, 261–280.

Oliver, W. (1989). Black males and social problems: Prevention through Afrocentric socialization. *Journal of Black Studies, 20*, 15–39.

Oliver, W. (1998). *The violent social world of Black men*. San Francisco: Jossey-Bass.

Oliver, W. (2001). Cultural racism and structural violence: Implications for African Americans. *Journal of Human Behavior and the Social Environment, (2001) 4*, 2/3, 1–26.

Oliver, W. (2003). The structural-cultural perspective: A theory of Black male violence. In D. F. Hawkins (Ed.), *Violent crime: Assessing race & ethnic differences* (pp. 280–302). New York: Cambridge University Press.

Patterson, O. (1998). *Rituals of blood: Consequences of slavery in two American centuries*. New York: Basic Civitas.

Robeson, P. (1958). *Here I stand*. New York: Beacon.

Sampson, R. J. (1993). Family management and child development: Insights from social disorganization theory. In J. McCord (Ed.), *Facts, frameworks and forecasts; Vol. 3, Advances in criminological theory* (pp. 63–94). New Brunswick, NJ: Transaction.

Sampson, R. J., Wilson, W. J. (1995). Toward a theory of race, crime and urban inequality. In J. Hagan and R. D. Peterson (Eds.), *Crime and urban inequality* (pp. 37–54). Stanford, CA: Stanford University Press.

Schaefer, R. J (1993). *Racial and ethnic groups*. New York: HarperCollins.

Sterk, C. E. (1999). *Fast lives: Women who use crack cocaine*. Philadelphia: Temple University Press.

Tucker, M. B., & Michell-Kernanm, C. (1995). *The decline in marriage among African Americans*. New York: Russell Sage.

Unnever, J. D., & Gabbidon, S. L. (2011). *A theory of African American offending: Race, racism and crime*. New York: Routledge.

U.S. Census Bureau. (2013). *State and county quick facts*. Retrieved from http://quickfacts.census.gov/qfd/states/00000.html

Venkatesk, S., A. (2006). *Off the books:The underground economy of the urban poor*. Cambridge, MA: Harvard University Press.

Welsing, F. C. (1974). The conspiracy to make Blacks inferior. *Ebony, 29*, 84–95.

Welsing, F. (1980). The concept and color of God and Black mental health. *Black Books Bulletin, 7,* 27–29.

Wilson, A. N. (1994). *Understanding Black adolescent male violence.* New York: Afrikan World Info.

Wilson, W. J. (1996). *When work disappears: The world of the new working poor.* New York: Vintage.

Wilson, W. J. (1987). *The truly disadvantaged, the inner city, the underclass, and public policy.* Chicago: University of Chicago Press.

Wise, T. (2010). *Color-blind: The rise of post-racial politics and the retreat from racial equity.* San Francisco: City Lights.

Wolfgang, M. E., & Ferracutti, F. (1967). *The subculture of violence: Towards an integrated theory in criminology.* London: Tavistock.

Wright, R. T., & Decker, S. H. (1997). *Armed robbers in action: Stickups and street culture.* Boston: Northeastern University Press.

Part 3:
Media, Pop Culture, and
Technology Issues

CHAPTER FOURTEEN

The Rise of Urban Fiction

KRISTINA GRAAFF AND VANESSA IRVIN

STREET LITERATURE'S HISTORICAL SPACES

Urban fiction, also known as street lit, is a contemporary literary genre that focuses on the city experiences of 21st-century African Americans and Latinos. The current iteration of urban fiction, however, has roots in the literary traditions of yesteryear, stemming as far back as the 16th and 17th centuries. In fact, the original street literature publications were in the form of large, poster-sized printouts called broadsides that were sold on city streets more than 400 years ago (Shepard, 1973). Early authors, such as Daniel Defoe, were pamphleteers and journalists creating broadside publications, long before their narratives were published in the novel format. In London streets large, poster-sized, two-sided newsprints of local news, events (e.g., executions), poetry, gossip, stories, and ballads, often about affairs and other improprieties, were popular (Shepard; Collison, 1973).

Defoe's work *Roxana* (1724) is an early example of narrative realism novels depicting the harsh, gritty stories of city living of that time. The character of Roxana is reminiscent of popular current-day street lit protagonist, Winter Santiaga, of the 1999 groundbreaking novel, *The Coldest Winter Ever*. Like Winter, Roxana's story begins with her as a wealthy woman and then, through adversity, she loses her fortune and social standing. The story focuses on Roxana's exploits as she seeks to maintain her standard of living by any means necessary, including multiple marriages, pregnancies, and prostitution. Like our modern Winter, the 18th-century Roxana seeks her financial solutions through her relationships with various men. Seeking the comfort and protection of men is all Roxana knows, akin to the agency of Winter Santiaga. Urban fiction characters either come from or become intimately familiar with the uncompromising world of the streets, having to make crucial life decisions. As women in a patriarchal world, Roxana and Winter are strong female characters living transgressive lifestyles in response, and in rebellion, to a male-dominated society.

Realistic narratives continued to depict the experiences of European immigrants to American city life during the late 19th and early 20th centuries by authors such as Stephen Crane, who inspired the Naturalism literary movement (Campbell, 2010). Crane self-published his debut publication, the novella *Maggie: A Girl of the Streets*, in 1893. The book was "refused by all publishers that it was submitted to because of its brutal and sexual realism" (back cover of *Maggie*, Digireads, classic edition). *Maggie* is the example of a gritty tale being self-published and, decades later, another similar story comes from Teri Woods, who not only self-published her first novel, the 1999 street lit classic, *True to the Game*, but also started a successful self-publishing company for urban fiction.

During the third immigration wave to the United States (1881–1920) (Shirey, 2012), many novels were published that depicted the ghetto lives of European immigrants (Irvin Morris, 2012). Street literatureesque titles published during that time include *Yekl: A Tale of the New York Ghetto* by Abraham Cahan (1896), *Sister Carrie* by Theodore Dreiser (1900), and Frank Norris's *McTeague* (1899). Together with Crane's *Maggie*, these works contributed to the literary genre called realism or naturalism.

Simultaneously, the great Northern migration of southern-based African Americans to northern cities brought stories of the early 20th-century urban African American experience. One salient title that tells this story is *The Sport of the Gods*, authored by esteemed African American poet Paul Laurence Dunbar in 1902. In *Sport of the Gods*, a southern family is forced to move up north to Chicago. Their transition from southern life to the glitz, glam, and mayhem of city life proves to be a traumatic evolution for the entire family, just as immigration proved to be a traumatic transition for the characters in *Yekl*, *Sister Carrie*, and *McTeague*.

The Harlem Renaissance gave rise to urban fiction stories during the postnaturalism movement with works such as Richard Wright's *Native Son* (1940) and Ann Petry's, *The Street* (1946). In 1965 Claude Brown's coming-of-age novel *Manchild in the Promised Land* was published, along with Malcolm X's autobiography. These books tell the story of the plight of the African American man coming of age from boyhood to manhood in the streets of American cities. These works were popular during the mid-1960s and continue to be must reads today. In turn, the Black Power literary movement of the 1970s (e.g., Donald Goines' *Iceberg Slim*) gave rise to other urban popular culture, such the birth of the musical genre Hip Hop.

Hip hop was created in 1972 by DJ Cool Herc (Chang, 2005). It gave voice to the realities of contemporary urban living as a fallout shelter for people coming from wars of that time: the Korean War, the Vietnam War, and the escalating war on drugs in low-income minority neighborhoods (Lusane, 1999; Loury, 2008; Alexander, 2010). The elements of hip hop—DJing (musical performance), B-boying (hip hop dance), graffiti (artistic expression), and MCing (oral expression)—all worked in tandem to create not just a musical genre but also an urban artistic culture and lifestyle representing human experience. Today's street lit can be considered the written-literary expression of hip hop culture.

As a form of hip hop lit, today's urban literature has particularly impacted African American leisure reading habits, especially as authors responded to reader feedback for more appropriate content for teen readers. To meet this need, urban literature emerged. Young adult urban literature by pioneering Black authors included Walter Dean Myers, Sharon Flake, and Nikki Grimes. Newer young adult authors like NiNi Simone, L. Divine, and Kashambah Williams also came to prominence. These authors created book content and packaging specifically targeted to savvy African American urban teens with popular series such as Drama High, Platinum Teen, and the Ni Ni Girl Chronicles, to name a few.

Black literature expanded as other literary forms developed: sistah lit that include early contributors Terry McMillan, Eric Jerome Dickey, and Bebe Moore Campbell; urban erotica, an adult fiction movement spearheaded by author Zane; Christian fiction, which grew with popular authors Victoria Christopher Murray and Jacqueline Thomas; and finally, street lit itself moved forward through Vickie Stringer, Omar Tyree, Shannon Holmes, Carl Weber, and K'wan Foye.

Black literature has been pivotal to giving voice to the late 20th-and early 21st-century experience. But specifically, street lit authors bring the ills and concerns of today's urban citizens, particularly the low-income citizenry, to mainstream discourse. Their novels address daily survival practices in low-income neighborhoods, emphasizing the important role that the streets play in survival. Also written as a response to the war on drugs, now a full-fledged war on the poor, many plots deal with the issues of race-related law enforcement and mass incarceration. Streets and prisons are thus the most important narrative locations in much of today's street lit.

THE STREETS AND THE PRISON SYSTEM:
STREET LITERATURE'S NARRATIVE SPACES

Most plots in street lit revolve around the characters' involvement in the local drug trade, which is usually portrayed as the most accessible source of income in areas that are otherwise devoid of mainstream employment opportunities. Since the selling of drugs commonly takes place outdoors, the streets are an important narrative location. This becomes apparent in titles such as *Street Dreams* (K'wan, 2004), *The Streets Keep Calling* (Chunichi, 2010), or *Married to Da Streets* (Silk, 2006). Many book covers depict characters in photos or illustrations on street corners. Most narratives focus on male protagonists and how they transform the streets into a business platform for their entrepreneurial subsistence practices. While fewer novels display women drug dealers or hustlers (see, e.g., Jones, 2008; Stringer, 2009), most female characters ensure their share in the trade by getting involved with one of the key figures. Many street literature novels thus promote traditional gender roles and maintain heterosexual relationships as a norm.

Contrary to the actual drug trade—a petty income practice most dealers can barely survive on—protagonists in street literature often occupy a position in the higher ranks of the business and generate vast sums of money. Once characters hold a leading position in the drug business and indulge in hyperbolic and meticulously depicted acts of conspicuous consumption, only a constant influx of money allows them to maintain their lifestyle. The streets, where the drug money is drawn, are therefore not only the main spatial-economic resource on site but are also a highly contested space that opposing characters fight over.

Many novels emphasize the social and economic know-how that is necessary to navigate the urban streets, including the manual work of product preparation, customer retention, and leader authority (Benjamin, 2010; K'wan, 2004; Souljah, 1999). While this approach often ignores the devastating effects that drug selling has on Black communities, it evaluates and illustrates the complexity of daily survival practices in disadvantaged areas.

At the same time, the protagonists' needs to survive through limited entrepreneurial practices reflect upon the U.S. shift to a neoliberal regime that holds the individual "responsible and accountable for his or her own actions and well-being" (Harvey, 2005). In many narratives, characters embrace ideologies of entrepreneurial freedom out of necessity, such as the protagonist Malik in J. M. Benjamin's *My Manz and 'Em* (2010) when commenting on his return to the drug businesses after failing to obtain a job in the "regular" economy:

> I don't need an interview with no boss. I'm my own boss, make my own hours, and I pay myself. I know, ain't no longevity in this shit..., I'm just trying to stack some paper, so I can live comfortably. (p. 178)

In some stories characters are successful in making it out of the marginalizing setting. However, caught in highly segregated urban areas and subjected to permanent police surveillance, many characters are eventually arrested. Prisons are thus the second major narrative space, and many storylines are defined by the characters' back-and-forth movement between the two places.

Although they do not always contain explicit political messages, street literature narratives often comment on the persistence of racial discrimination through storylines. Taking place in small geographic perimeters of inner-city neighborhoods, the genre illustrates the confining effect of urban segregation. In their emphasis on illicit entrepreneurialism as a main source of income, the stories testify to the existing discrimination in the job market. The characters' common exposure to police controls reflects the omnipresence of racial profiling, while their oscillation between urban neighborhoods and prisons speaks to state interventions that have been described as "the New Jim Crow" (Alexander, 2010).

Experiences of racial bias on all levels of the justice system, especially how they play out since the introduction of the war on drugs, are a central topic in many narratives. Once arrested, characters are faced with sentencing disparities, enforced guilty pleas, and mandatory minimums for offenses that are mainly persecuted in minority neighborhoods (Benjamin, 2010; Jihad, 2004). For example, as the protagonist Corey in Shannon Holmes' *Never Go Home Again* dryly observes, "It would take more than just luck or well-wishing for a minority to get a fair shake in any courtroom in America. Contrary to popular beliefs, the system of justice isn't blind; it sees very well the color of a man's skin" (2004, p. 10). While the majority of incarcerated characters in street literature are male, we also find prison portrayals of women, like Jaz, one of the protagonists in Wahida Clark's *Thugs and the Women Who Love Them* (2004). Jaz's account details her first day in confinement:

> By the time I shower, it's time to get in the lunch line. I can't believe what's supposed to be lunch. They give me a small metal cup with a metal spoon and tell me not to lose it. The cup has some watered down Kool-Aid in it. One gulp and it's gone. They give us a metal tray, divided into sections. One section holds four cold French fries, one holds a dried-up hot dog and the other has what I guess is chocolate pudding. I sure did take the free world for granted. I can't eat the hot dog, because no one's sure if it's pork or not. I do eat the four French fries, but I'm scared to eat the chocolate pudding. I walk over and sit down at the metal table and stool that are bolted down to the floor. (2004, p. 175)

As the quote illustrates, despite being works of fiction, street literature narratives usually comment on the current system of mass incarceration in American society (see also Graaff, 2010). Many storylines reflect on recent changes in the U.S. prison system, in particular privatization, cuts of rehabilitative offers, and overcrowding.

Therefore, street literature can also be considered one of the most recent contributions to the genre of prison literature.[1] Aside from placing these novels in a genre of urban literature, they can also be read in the historical continuum of writings about incarceration.

STREET LITERATURE'S SPACES OF PRODUCTION, DISTRIBUTION, AND CONSUMPTION

Street literature's ties to the urban streets and the prison system are not only expressed within the narratives, they are also essential locations where the novels are produced, marketed, and consumed. Much of the 20th and 21st-century urban fiction was first sold on the streets of low-income neighborhoods, especially in New York City and Philadelphia. Established publishers initially rejected this type of writing because they did not consider it commercially viable at the time. Today, despite the acceptance in traditional publishing, street vending continues to play an important role in the genre's distribution and often guarantees its availability in urban areas that lack bookstores (Graaff, in press). Since the (re)emergence of street literature coincided with affordable desktop publishing and electronic printing techniques, many of the genre's first authors self-published their novels. The street literature market is still largely engineered by self-published books and independent presses (e.g., Cash Money Content, W. Clark Publishing, or A New Quality Publishing). Additionally, now that mainstream publishers have recognized the profit that can be generated with the genre, they are now actively publishing major authors who regularly appear on bestselling publishing lists such as *The New York Times*.

Since more affordable production and printing techniques have lowered the threshold for entering the self-publishing business, street literature has led to an entrepreneurial boom in the U.S. book market. While viewed by some as a democratization of the literary scene, others consider it an indicator for increasing neoliberalization in the cultural sphere (Chiles, 2006, 2009; Early, 2009). Among the most outspoken critics is the author Nick Chiles, who not merely dismisses the popular narratives on grounds of propriety but also for economic reasons. As he explains, street literature has "impacted the life and work of every working Black writer in America," especially since the novels have been taken up by commercial publishers. Himself under contract with Penguin Books, a publisher that so far has no street literature imprint, Chiles claims that it is primarily because many street literature authors supplement their publishers' marketing strategies with street-related promotion that has prompted commercial publishers to generally reduce their "marketing and publicity budgets for black books" (para. 10). In other words, from his perspective, street literature's entrepreneurialism fosters already existing tendencies in the publishing industry to shift more responsibility to the authors by expecting them to successfully market their own products.

Simultaneous to its emergence in urban landscapes, street literature appeared in the U.S. prison system as well, which not only holds the largest population per capita in the world, but also disproportionately incarcerates people of color due to the aforementioned racially biased law enforcement and penal policies (Alexander, 2010; Walmsley, 2011). Out of the 2 million people currently imprisoned, more than 900,000 are Black (West, 2010), and many of them stem from neighborhoods comparable to those portrayed in such narratives. Street literature is a popular genre among inmates who apply a variety of reading strategies to the narratives. Sweeney's study (2010) on the reading practices of female inmates illustrates how prisoners use street literature in many different ways. First, it serves as an entertaining distraction, where the genre allows readers to mentally leave the correctional faculty. Second, since many of the stories are cautionary tales, readers also use them to reflect on their own experiences. Third, for many of the inmates in Sweeney's study, street lit is also a "reminder of home" (p. 148).

Street literature is not only widely read in prison but a number of novels are also written by inmates. For some of these inmate authors, the writing of street literature serves a therapeutic function, enabling them to come to terms with former street activities (Jihad, personal communication, December 2, 2009). Others use it to "write themselves out" of the prison environment, which is usually characterized by constant noise and lack of privacy (W. Clark, personal communication, December 15, 2009). Many imprisoned authors, however, see street literature as an additional source of income. They begin to write the popular narratives in the hope that it might allow them to supplement their commissary accounts, cover legal fees, or financially prepare them to earn an income after their release (J. M. Benjamin, personal communication, June 24, 2010; W. Clark, personal communication, December, 15, 2009; Jihad, December 2, 2009). While only few authors are able to eventually live off their books, the motivations of many inmates to venture into the writing business in the first place speaks to the recent restructuring of the social state and prison systems. The system of mass incarceration has become more punitive with the responsibility for a successful reintegration after release increasingly shifting to the individual. Writing is thus often considered as a supplement to the downsized rehabilitation programs. So, to some these books are viewed as an asset that might, at least partially, cover for abolished state funding.

The fact that prison authorities often respond with harsh repercussions to the inmates' writing and reading practices is thus highly problematic in light of the many functions that street literature fulfills for the population.[2] Censorship practices that frequently ban street literature written by Black authors from prisons on the grounds that the novels might incite violence, while accepting comparable works by White authors (Sweeney, 2010, pp. 43, 143f.), are reminiscent of antebellum practices denying literacy to the Black population. They are also destructive in that they undermine one of the few ways that inmates can navigate and potentially overcome their confining environment.

CONCLUSION: STREET LITERATURE GIVES RISE TO INTERPRETIVE SPACE IN BLACK CULTURE

Contemporary street literature exists along a historical literary continuum of hard-luck city stories that tell tales about how the streets serve as a stage where low-income residents live out their entrepreneurial and survival lifestyles. Characters are portrayed as articulating the confining aspects of low-income culture and living in a city environment controlled by a hegemonic, capitalistic infrastructure marginalizing the poor, as well as people of color. Street literature has emerged as a response to spatial, social, economic, and political exclusion. With confinement a key aspect of inner-city living and in cyclical fashion, various activities performed on the streets result in prison time for too many citizens. In turn, when confined in prison, inmates gain comfort and inspiration from reading and writing street lit.

As a literary genre that brings visceral and real outcomes from readers' interactions with stories, street lit should always be examined beyond moral categorizations and beyond the binary of "good" versus "bad" fiction. In fact, the question becomes good or bad fiction for whom? Readers? Schools? Libraries? Publishers? Authors? Street lit, since its renaissance publications of the 1990s (*Flyy Girl, Coldest Winter Ever*, and *True to the Game*), has proven that there are positive outcomes. The genre offers a "good" way for schools and libraries to spark the reading habit of many students and teen readers (Morris, Agosto, Hughes-Hassell, & Cottman, 2006; AUSL, 2012). Street lit has been "good" for authors who entered the genre via entrepreneurial means and/or progressed on to full-time publishing contracts with mainstream publishers (Kilgannon, 2006). And the publishing industry has profited, via mainstream publishing, as a number of street lit titles have appeared on the coveted *New York Times* Bestsellers List.

Finally, we must also consider the analysis of power relations and how they are expressed in censorship in the acquisition, access, reading, and writing of street literature texts. For educators have, for the most part, been resistant to fully engaging with street literature or in gaining a true understanding of what the genre does for its readers (Irvin Morris, 2012). Public intellectuals have decried the genre, citing that stories perpetuate negative stereotypes of low-income Black and Brown citizens.

Yet it can be argued that there is always some truth to fiction and some universality in articulated human experience. Readers have continued to be very clear about what truths work and don't work for today's street literature. For example, in social media and active author book tours, readers have access to authors like never before. So, it is particularly important to note that street lit authors are incredibly interactive with their readers on social media platforms such as Instagram, Twitter, and Facebook, often marketing promotions for their new titles with chapter releases in e-book format as teasers for upcoming novels. Book trailers (book promotion videos) today can be as sophisticated as the next hip hop video. Amazon and YouTube have become a platform where readers review their favorite titles and authors respond to readers' concerns. For example, street lit author Treasure E. Blue often sponsors reading contests to stay connected with his readers. Authors K'wan Foye and Wahida Clark both facilitate Facebook groups where they market their book signings and solicit reader feedback for character development and plot evolution in upcoming stories. In fact, because of reader response to most of his stories, K'wan has written novels that ultimately became blockbuster series.[3] Authors are essentially reading and writing with their readers in mind, adding depth and agency in innovative ways.

In other words, negative stereotypes about street lit become moot when the stereotype of "Black people don't read" is squashed with the voraciousness of street lit readers and the prolific outcomes of street lit authors and publishers to satisfy the demand. In truth, Black people do read, Black people do write, and Black people engage in such literacy practices with passion, commitment, and appreciation for the reading experience.

Aside from the literary constrictions and controversies that street lit provokes, questions are raised about ways in which street lit has become an additive expression of Black culture. Readers and writers use these words to gain reflective understandings of their lived worlds, making street lit a testament to the experiences of low-income African American and Latino city residents. The stories in urban fiction create a safe space in which all stakeholders can explore, tell, retell, discuss, write, and publish truth to represent the conditions and circumstances upon which Black culture continues to evolve and thrive.

NOTES

1. Most scholarship on contemporary prison writing does not consider the literary form of street literature (see H. Chevigny, 2011; B. H. Franklin, 1998a, 1998b; Levi & Waldman, 2011; Miller, 2005). Exceptions are Justin Gifford's book *Pimping Fictions* (2013) and Megan Sweeney's monograph *Reading is My Window* (2010), that both elaborate on street literature as a form of prison writing. Also in his introduction to the April 2015 edition of the American Book

Review—a special edition dedicated to prison writing—Gifford acknowledges street literature as a form of fiction written inside correctional facilities (Gifford 2015, p. 3). In his contribution to the same journal edition, H. Bruce Franklin also makes mention of street literature (Franklin, 2015, p. 4). None of the articles, however, further elaborate on the popular literary form. The same goes for Franklin's article "Can the Penitentiary Teach the Academy How to Read?" (2008) in which the author briefly refers to street literature. However, Franklin only addresses it in order to stress the continuing importance that the novels by Donald Goines have on prisoners in gaining literacy (p. 646).

2. Repercussions usually entail solitary confinement, destruction of manuscripts, and transfers to other facilities. All authors I interviewed confirmed to have experienced punishment in response to their writing (Benjamin, personal communication, June 24, 2010; Clark, personal communication, December 15, 2009; Jihad, personal communication, December 2, 2009). For a recent settlement between the American Civil Liberties Union of North Carolina Legal Foundation and the N.C. Department of Correction on the writing of street literature manuscripts in North Carolina state prisons view Coble (2010) and ACLU (2010).

3. For example, K'wan's 2012 novel *Animal* has progressed into the following installments: *Animal II: The Omen* (2013), *Animal III: Revelations* (2014), *Ghetto Bastard: The Beginning* (a prequel) (2014).

BIBLIOGRAPHY

ACLU. (2010, March 8). ACLU-NC legal foundation announces successful settlement of lawsuit against North Carolina prison officials for violating free speech rights of published author/prisoner. Retrieved from http://acluofnc.org/EasyBlog/aclu-nclf-successfully-settles-lawsuit-against-nc-prison-officials-who-violated-free-speech-rights-of-published-author-inmate.html

Alexander, M. (2010). *The New Jim Crow: Mass incarceration in the age of colorblindness*. New York: New.

AUSL. (2012). An interview with AUSL library media specialist, K. C. Boyd. Retrieved from http://auslchicago.org/blog/post/32

Benjamin, J. M. (2010). *My manz and 'em*. (2nd. rev. ed.). Plainfield, NJ: New Quality.

Brown, C. (1965). *Manchild in the Promised Land*. New York: Macmillan.

Cahan, A. (1896). *Yekl: A tale of the New York ghetto*. New York: Appleton.

Campbell, D.M. (2010). Naturalism in American Literature. *Literary Movements*. Dept. of English, Washington State University. Retrieved from http://public.wsu.edu/~campbelld/amlit/natural.htm

Chang, J. (2005). *Can't stop won't stop: A history of the Hip Hop generation*. New York: Picador.

Chevigny, H. (Ed.). (2011). *Doing time: 25 years of prison writing*. New York: Skyhorse.

Chiles, N. (2006, January 4). Their eyes were reading smut. *New York Times*. Retrieved from http://www.nytimes.com/2006/01/04/opinion/04chiles.html

Chiles, N. (2009). Interview: A critical look at street lit, conducted by Taylor Nix. Retrieved from http://theubs.com/interviews/nick-chiles.php

Chunichi. (2010). *The streets keep calling*. West Babylon, NY: Urban.

Clark, W. (2004). *Thugs and the women who love them*. New York: Dafina.

Coble, C. (2010, April 16). ACLU and North Carolina Department of Corrections reach settlement over prisoner publications. Newsroom law blog. http://www.newsroomlawblog.com/2010/04/

articles/first-amendment-1/aclu-and-north-carolina-department-of-corrections-reach-settle ment-over-prisoner-publications/

Collison, R. (1973). *The story of street literature*. New York: Little Hampton.

Crane, S. [Johnston Smith, pseud.]. (1893). *Maggie: A girl of the streets*. Self-published.

Defoe, D. (1722). *The fortunes and misfortunes of Moll Flanders*. London: Chetwood.

Defoe, D. (1724). *Roxana: The fortunate mistress*. London: Chetwood.

Dreiser, T. (1900). *Sister Carrie*. New York: Doubleday.

Dunbar, P. L. (1902). *The sport of the gods*. New York: Dodd, Mead.

Early, G. (2009, February 5). What is African-American literature? *eJournal USA: Multicultural Literature in the United States Today 14*(2), 17-20. U.S. Department of State. Bureau of International Information Programs. Retrieved from http://iipdigital.usembassy.gov/media/pdf/ejs/0209.pdf

Franklin, H. B. (1998a). *Prison literature in America: The victim as criminal and artist*. New York: Oxford University.

Franklin, H. B. (Ed.). (1998b). *Prison writing in 20th-century America*. New York: Penguin.

Franklin, H. B. (2008). Can the penitentiary teach the academy how to read? *PMLA, 123*, 643–649.

Franklin, H. B. (2015). Prison literature, then and now. *American Book Review 36*(3), 4.

Gifford, J. (2013). *Pimping fictions: African American crime literature and the untold story of Black pulp publishing*. Philadelphia: Temple University Press.

Gifford, J. (2015). Introduction to focus: Prison writing. *American Book Review 36*(3), 3.

Graaff, K. (2010). Reading street literature, reading America's prison system. *Pop Matters*. Retrieved from http://www.popmatters.com/feature/119786-reading-street-literature-reading-americas-prison-system/

Graaff, K. (in press). Ethnic contestations over African American fiction: The street vending of street literature in New York City. In K. Graaff & N. Ha (Ed.), *Urban street vending in 273 the neoliberal city: A global perspective on the practices and policies of a marginalized economy*. New York: Berghahn.

Harvey, D. (2005). *A brief history of neoliberalism*. New York: Oxford.

Holmes, S. (2004). *Never go home again*. New York: Atria.

Irvin Morris, V. (2012). *Reading in mirrors: Using street literature to facilitate practitioner inquiry with urban public service librarians*. Doctoral dissertation, University of Pennsylvania.

Jihad. (2004). *Street life*. Deer Park, NY: Urban.

Jones, B. (2008). *Loyalty*. New York: Holley.

Kilgannon, C. (2006, February 14). Street lit with publishing cred: From prison to a four-book deal. *New York Times*. Retrieved from http://www.nytimes.com/2006/02/14/books/14rele.html

K'wan. (2004). *Street dreams*. New York: St. Martin's Griffin.

K'wan. (2012). *Animal*. New York: Cash Money Content.

K'wan. (2013). *Animal 2: The Omen*. New York: Cash Money Content.

K'wan. (2014a). *Animal 3: Revelations*. New York: Cash Money Content.

K'wan. (2014b). *Ghetto bastard: The beginning*. New York: Write 2 Eat Concepts.

Levi, R., & Waldman, A. (Eds.). (2011). *Inside this place, not of it: Narratives from women's prisons*. San Francisco: McSweeney's.

Loury, G. C. (2008). *Race, incarceration, and American values*. Boston: MIT.

Lusane, C. (1999). *Pipe dream blues: Racism and the war on drugs*. Boston: South End.

Miller, Q. (Ed.). (2005). *Prose and cons: Essays on prison literature in the United States*. Jefferson, NC: McFarland.

Morris, V. J., Agosto, D. P., Hughes-Hassell, S., & Cottman, D. T. (2006). Street lit: Flying off teen fiction bookshelves in Philadelphia public libraries. *Journal of Young Adult Library Service, 5*(1), 16–23.

Norris, F. (1899). *McTeague: A story of San Francisco*. New York: Doubleday & McClure.

Petry, A. (1946). *The street*. New York: Houghton Mifflin.

Shepard, L. (1973). *The history of street literature: The story of broadside ballads, chapbooks, proclamations, news-sheets, election bills, tracts, pamphlets, cocks, catchpennies, and other ephemera*. Detroit, MI: Singing Tree.

Shirey, W. (2012). Immigration waves. Immigration in America. Retrieved from http://immigra tioninamerica.org/603-mmigration-waves.html

Silk, W. (2006). *Married to da streets*. Laveen, AZ: Good2Go.

Souljah, S. (1999). *The coldest winter ever*. New York: Pocket.

Stringer, V. (2009). *Let that be the reason*. New York: Atria.

Sweeney, M. (2010). *Reading is my window. Books and the art of reading in women's prisons*. Chapel Hill: University of North Carolina.

Walmsley, R. (2011). *World prison population list* (9th ed.). International Centre for Prison Studies. London: King's College. Retrieved from http://www.idcr.org.uk/wpcontent/uploads/2010/09/ WPPL-9-22.pdf

West, H. (2010). *Prison inmates at midyear 2009*. Bureau of Justice Statistics. http://www.bjs.gov/ index.cfm?ty=pbdetail&iid=2200

Woods, T. (1999). *True to the game: A novel*. Havertown, PA: Meow Meow.

Wright. R. (1940). *Native son: A novel*. New York: Harper & Brothers.

CHAPTER FIFTEEN

An Affair to Remember: Hip Hop and the Feminist Perspective

DONNETRICE C. ALLISON

I never considered myself a feminist—in my late twenties when I was head-nodding to the *Money, Cash, Hoes* collaboration of Jay Z and DMX; and I didn't consider myself a feminist a year later, when I agreed to a "traditional" marriage, took my husband's last name and promised to love, honor and "obey" him. Although I had two degrees by that time and was working on a third—and he only had one—I agreed that he would head the household and I would take the lead on rearing our future children. I was in love, and I was happy with that arrangement. It made perfect sense to me as an African American female born and raised in the 70s. The messages I received early on were of "Black power" and "Black beauty." I grew up on *Soul Train, Good Times* and *The Jefferson's.* My four older sisters wore their hair natural—beautiful afros, like crowns; my mom bought products like Afro-Sheen and read *Jet* magazine; my dad drove a Cadillac and smoked Winston 100s; we saw every "Blaxploitation" movie ever made, and cheered for the hero who inevitably managed to "stick it to Whitey." So, I never considered myself a feminist and neither did anyone I knew.

For me, the faces of feminism were Gloria Steinem and Betty Friedan. The issues were specific to White, middle class women who wanted the "right" to work the job of their choosing, rather than be restricted to staying home and raising children. They wanted to use their fancy degrees, rather than hang them on the wall. They wanted to climb the corporate ladder and, in general, they didn't even seem to like men! The problem was that no one that I knew in my working class neighborhood in Massachusetts had those kinds of problems. No woman I knew had the option to stay home and raise her children full-time! In fact, my mother often worked two jobs! No woman I knew had a college degree; certainly none were positioned to work in Corporate America, much less "climb its ladders." Therefore, I disregarded most of what they said and presumed that it only applied to the "privileged."

In 1989, I entered college as a freshman, with aspirations of becoming a fiction writer. I majored in English and was taught about the writings of Ralph Waldo Emerson, Mark Twain, Henry David Thoreau and other New England Renaissance writers by predominantly White male professors. Late into my sophomore year a Black female English professor was hired by the small New England university I attended. I was ecstatic and I rushed to find her office. I found her and immediately registered for her Black Literature class that was being offered the following semester. It was in that class that I learned about Langston Hughes, Claude McKay, Countee Cullen, Zora Neale Hurston, and eventually bell hooks. *Ain't I a Woman* was my first introduction to a Black woman's perspective on feminism. The book confirmed what I had already suspected; early feminism did not take into account the needs and aspirations of Black women. In the book, hooks (1981) stated: "White women saw Black women as a direct threat to their social standing—for how could they be idealized as virtuous goddess-like creatures if they associated with Black women who were seen by the White public as licentious and immoral" (p. 131)? As a result, Black women were not welcomed to the table in the early feminist movement. Another Black female author I read during that course was Alice Walker. In her book, *In Search of Our Mothers' Gardens*, she introduced the term Womanist and referred to it as a "Black feminist or feminist of color." Walker (1983) went on to explain that the phrase "acting womanish" was often used in the Black community to describe a young girl who was "outrageous, audacious, courageous or willful...acting grown up." Simply put, she stated that "womanist is to feminist as purple is to lavender."

Once in graduate school at Howard University, I was introduced to the work of Clenora Hudson-Weems and Patricia Hill Collins. In her book, *Africana Womanism: Reclaiming Ourselves*, Hudson-Weems (1993) coined the term "Africana Womanism" as more separate and distinct from feminism than Walker's "Womanism." She stated:

> Africana Womanism is not Black Feminism...or Walker's Womanism...Africana Womanism is an ideology created and designed for all women of African descent. It is grounded in African culture, and therefore, it necessarily focuses on the unique experiences, struggles, needs, and desires of Africana women. (p. 24)

In the book, *Black Feminist Thought: Knowledge, Consciousness and the Politics of Empowerment,* Collins (1991) grapples with the term "Black Feminist," as it makes presumptions about race as a biological category that creates oneness and the notion that Black women, by virtue of their Blackness, have an automatic feminist consciousness. For me, this was certainly untrue. In fact, while these scholars did impact my perspective on an intellectual level, they did not influence me to perceive myself as either a Feminist, Womanist, Black Feminist or Africana Womanist.

It was not until 2003 that my perception of myself changed significantly. That year, I gave birth to an 8 pound, 15 ounce little girl after 30 hours of labor, and my world was turned upside down. My perspective changed, my perception changed, and my voice changed. Although she was not my first child—just 18 months earlier I'd given birth to a son—there was something different about this experience. I believe that when my son was born, I became a mother—with all that that role entails. I became second in my own life and my heart grew twice its size. But when my daughter was born I became a woman. Everything was different about the experience of bringing her into the world. My son was born by emergency C-section and spent 8 days in intensive care; my daughter was born after hours of pushing, and she was so large that a plunger-like device was used to assist her exit. It was completely exhausting, yet invigorating. I felt powerful, and strong, and amazing! My body did what God created it to do!

Having her forced me to re-examine everything that I stood for, everything that I represented, the way I carried myself, the things I said, and the way I said them. Why? Because I knew that I would soon become her mirror, and I did not want to tarnish her reflection. I knew that I would soon become her measuring stick, and I did not want her to miscalculate herself or her worth. I knew that whatever I loved she would potentially claim as her own. And one of the things I loved most was music—especially hip hop!

I was about eight or nine-years-old when *Rapper's Delight* hit the airwaves. I remember my older brother, who was about 15 or 16, walking around the house chanting the lyrics. It drove my mother crazy, but to me, it was cool. To me, my brother was cool, so if rap was cool to him it was cool to me. My brother was a star high school basketball player. He was popular, and he loved this new thing called rap music. It wasn't until I was about 15 or 16 myself, however, that I developed my own love affair with hip hop. Rakim was my first love. "I was a fiend, before I became a teen, I melted microphones instead of cones of ice cream, music orientated so when hip hop was originated, fit it like pieces of puzzle, complicated" (Eric B. & Rakim, 1987). Now, I was the one walking around chanting lyrics, and I knew every word of Rakim's music. He epitomized creativity to me, because he used words, and rhymes, and metaphors in ways that no one before him had. For instance, he commonly used alliteration in his rhymes with awe-inspiring speed: "Music mixed mellow maintains to make melodies for MC's motivates the breaks" and "Vocals, vocabulary, your verses, you're stuck in. The mic is a Drano, volcanoes erupting." Verses like those flowed from his lips with ease. Then, he'd metaphorically describe his rhymes as a powerful force that was overwhelming his audience and other MC's alike. I was attracted to this, because of my own interest in writing. Almost as soon as I learned to spell, I began writing poems and short stories; and by high school, I was an honor student and member of the literary magazine. So I knew Rakim wasn't like the others. He used intellectual words and phrases, and very little street slang. He said, "In this journey you're the journal I'm the journalist. Am I Eternal? Or an eternalist?" To this day, I believe he is one of the best.

My next love was for De La Soul. They were different—maybe even a little grungy—but again, for me it was all about the creativity. They had no designer jeans or sneakers like Run-DMC, no gold chains like Slick Rick. Their hair wasn't in perfectly shaped high top fades, like Kid 'N' Play. In fact, their fades were crooked and half dreadlocked. The darkest of the three—who I thought was the sexiest—wore glasses and looked wise. All of this added to their uniqueness, and their attraction. I knew every word of every song on their first album, *3 Feet High and Rising*, including the comic interludes. There were 24 tracks on the album—more than any rap album I'd heard before—and nearly half of those tracks were like commercial breaks between songs. Track 10—*Take It Off*—urged listeners to stop wearing played out fashions like colored eye-contacts, Converse, Jordache jeans, Kangols, and Gazelles. It was imaginative and witty, yet at the same time the whole album offered an important message "Be yourself."

My third—and dare I say my strongest and truest love—came during the year that I graduated high school and began college—1989. Throughout my high school years I dealt with self-esteem issues. I had trouble loving myself; my African features—large lips, chocolate brown skin, thick thighs and a shapely butt. I couldn't stand those features, and in all of the short stories that I wrote, I would change them to light skin, long hair and a model's waistline. See, in the '80s, notions of "Black Power" and Black beauty had shifted dramatically. Brown girls with natural hair were no longer the flavor of the month; long weaves and bleaching cream had taken over. Then came Chuck D. "Here it is, BAM, and you say 'Goddamn, this is the dope jam!'" (Public Enemy, 1988). He was energy and voice and message all wrapped in one. His voice was booming, and his message was in your face. He never minced words, or bit his tongue. He said things no one else would. He epitomized Black pride and condemned racism: "Elvis was a hero to most but he never meant shit to me, you see straight up racist that sucker was simple and plain." "Mother-fuck him and John Wayne," hype-man Flavor Flav chimed in (Public Enemy, 1990). So during this love affair, I had my fist in the air cursing injustice and celebrating my Blackness. Public Enemy, I believe, served as a catalyst to my freshman year involvement with groups like the Black Student Union, the Peer Mentors program, and a literary magazine that featured the works of Black students and Black historical authors. I attended a predominantly White university and we fought often for change, diversity, and improved representation, all the while chanting, "Don't believe the hype," and "Fight the Power." It was an inspiring time for me, a time when I truly believed that my peers and I could change the world. Chuck D and Public Enemy represented hip hop at its finest: A no-holds-barred, agent of change.

I had a few flings after Chuck, but never to that intensity. They were mostly for amusement. For a while, I enjoyed the jibber-jabber of Das Effect, "Bum Stickety Bum Stickety Bum" (Das EFX, 1992). Although on the surface they didn't seem to be saying much, they made reference to many of the cartoons and sitcoms that my generation grew up on. So in some ways, my love was based on nostalgia. "Thunder, thunder, thunder cats, whoah!" After Das Effect, the Pharcyde caught my attention. Their lyrics were comical; and their videos were innovative and artistic. My favorite song was *She Keeps Passing Me By*, about the girl that got away. The popularity of music videos also impacted my love of Hip Hop back then. I remember in the Pharcyde video that as each M.C. rapped about his dream girl, they would hang upside down, seemingly from the clouds. Last, but certainly not least, during my pursuit of whimsy, I came across my most animated love—Busta Rhymes.

I was about 25 the year that Busta Rhymes released his first solo album, after parting from the group Leaders of the New School. I had finished my Master's degree the year before and ended a two-year relationship; so I was alone in the middle of—what seemed like nowhere to me—teaching at a predominantly White university in rural Virginia. There were no single Black men for miles; there was no place to party where I wouldn't run into my undergraduate students; and my Blockbuster card was on fire from the constant use. What a welcome relief was *Woo Hah! I Got You All in Check* (Busta Rhymes, 1996). Hearing that song and watching him jump around in the video with his colorful jackets and matching hats made me laugh out loud after a long day of trying to prove myself in the ivory tower. I also had another fling that year with a foursome—known as, The Lost Boyz. They too had a "feel-good" vibe, even though they talked about some harsh realities of the ghetto. They had a jovial camaraderie and their voices played well off of one another, particularly the way Freaky Tah's harsh and raspy voice came in on the background of Mr. Cheek's slick verses. In fact, the university where I was teaching sponsored a concert featuring both Busta Rhymes and The Lost Boyz. It was one of the most entertaining live hip hop shows I'd ever attended. Busta and his sidekick, Spliff Star, bounced around on stage and climbed the support beams as they rapped. Then, The Lost Boyz danced around one another in a circle chanting "Music Makes Me High" from their debut album, *Legal Drug Money* (1995).

My last hip hop love affair jumped off between late 1997 and early 1998, right around the time that I met my future husband. He was a dark and tortured soul, who said things like: "I'ma rob this nigga. And when I'm done, I'ma slay him for bein' stupid like, comin' through after 1 or 2 and havin' a gun that he couldn't get to (DMX, 1998).

He came across as violent and even psychotic, but I looked deeper and listened closer, and heard other things like:

Lord why is it that, I go through so much pain
All I saw was black, all I felt was rain.
(DMX, 1998)

I felt genuinely sorry for him, for his pain. He seemed to have demons deeper than any I'd ever known, and his life was harder than anything I'd ever experienced. So I needed to support him and his music. See, I had a "savior" complex back then. Meaning, in all of my previous relationships, I was drawn to men who had problems of some sort. I believed that if I saved them, they would need me. I would be their hero, and in turn, they would love me. And, judging from his lyrics, DMX really needed to be saved, and I loved that about him.

In fact, for a while, my attraction to this broken man created a bit of tension in my real-world relationship. My fiancé was five and half years my senior and he never caught the hip hop bug, so he could not understand my relationship with DMX. Why would an educated young woman from New England be attracted to such violence and negativity? He just didn't see what I saw. He didn't hear the creative word plays; he didn't feel the energy and excitement of a crowd of hip hop lovers when the D.J. would blend a mix of the hottest tracks; he didn't feel the bass and treble through his soul; he didn't understand the voice and the way in which it spoke to us and for us; and he didn't see anything positive about the messages—particularly the messages DMX delivered. So we debated, and I continued to defend all those I loved before him.

Today, after 15 years of marriage, we battle less. My passion has decreased and I just can't defend what I now see and hear, the way I could then. In short, the love I have for popular hip hop music today has dwindled considerably from that of yesterday. It began to dwindle the day that a new, far more powerful love entered my life—my three children. The process was gradual, but with each birth, my feelings about hip hop changed, most dramatically when my one and only daughter was born. When my first son was an infant and we would ride around in the car, I would play nursery rhymes while he was awake, and then switch to rap music once he fell asleep. And when I was alone, I would still blast Jay Z, DMX and a few others who were hot at the beginning of the millennium. I honestly never thought about the denigration of women in hip hop (at least not in a way that I took personally) because, since I was so far removed from the lifestyles that many of these artists claimed to lead, I just thought, "they aren't talking about me, or any woman that I know for that matter." In fact, I even used to chuckle when an artist would say something like:

I got no patience
And I hate waitin.
Hoe get yo' ass in here
And let's RI-I-I-I-IDE.

(Jay Z, 1999)

Then my daughter was born and I looked at her little chocolate brown face that looks so much like mine and it became my mission to make sure that she never questioned herself and her worth the way I did as a teen. She loves music, just as I did. She especially loves to sing, and I encourage her talents. My question is—does the music love her as much as she loves it? I would argue that today—it doesn't. In a span of three years women went from "Black woman, mother of my earth; Black woman, you gave me birth," (Jungle Brothers, 1989) to "hoes and tricks"—and apparently we remain that to this day. Snoop says, "We don't love them hoes," and Dre (1992) added, "Bitches ain't shit but hoes and tricks!" Today, in any given club in anywhere, U.S.A, young men and women are chanting "these hoes ain't loyal" (Chris Brown & Lil' Wayne, 2014). It has become the new anthem of sorts—one of the hottest songs and most problematic ideologies currently permeating the industry, and the message tends to be most specifically directed at women of color, given that it starts off with: "Black girl with a big booty" (Chris Brown & Lil' Wayne, 2014).

So, as my children grew and became more interested in music and popular culture, I stopped playing hip hop on the radio—at least nothing that was produced in the new millennium; and I do not watch, or allow them to watch, music videos. I believe the visual message is even more potent than the audio message; and the visual message is clear, women are purely sexual objects and for every one man there are 20–30 of them vying for his attention. I do not wish for my daughter to receive that message, nor do I wish for her to learn how to dance like a stripper, which is essentially all the young women in videos today are doing. Similarly, the female artists are no different than the video vixens—just better paid. Granted, some might argue that they are empowered and free to express their sexuality but, as the mother of a teen son and pre-teen daughter, I disagree. It is more empowering to let your talent speak for you without needing to be half-naked on stage.

At the 2014 BET Awards, Nicki Minaj accepted her 5th trophy in five years for "Best Female Hip Hop Artist," and in her acceptance speech she stated, "I thank God that I have been able to do something and represent women in a culture that is so male driven." This statement really bothered me, because if she is the primary representation for women in hip hop today, then I feel that the message to young women interested in the genre becomes: surgically enhance your body and leave very little to the imagination when you are on stage. During Nicki's performance on that same awards show, she did just that. She came on stage riding on the back of a motorcycle—to ensure that the audience had a good view of her derriere, wearing what looked like black leather bikini bottoms, cut high in the back like thong underwear. She also wore a large gold chain—just barely covering her breasts—as a top, fishnet stockings, and knee-high strappy leather boots. She performed her latest hit, *Pills and Potions*, where she rapped:

> I see the envy when I'm causin' a frenzy
> So I pop pills for em
> Cop cribs in the hills on 'em.
>
> (Nicki Minaj, 2014)

It has become somewhat of an anthem for overcoming the pain of a broken heart, but as I listened deeper and took a look at the visual images in the music video, I heard messages of drug addiction and materialism. In the music video, Nicki wore a fur vest and leather bikini bottoms, bunny ears—reminiscent of the Playboy Bunny—and Xs taped across her nipples. Likewise, she featured a shirt-less man with a full torso of tattoos and washboard abs—today's image of masculinity—as her love interest. What I didn't see was anything that I would want my daughter—or sons—to emulate.

In addition to re-examining my love of hip hop after the births of my children, I also had to re-examine my views on feminism. I came to understand that in addition to advocating for equal pay and equal rights, feminists rallied against male chauvinism and the sexual objectification of women, and they spoke out against the trivialization of women's roles in the social order as "trophies," "trinkets," or other spoils of conquest. And while I still believe that traditional feminism tends to discount the voices of women of color, I now see that it can be a valid barometer by which to measure hip hop culture. Part of that realization came to me through Joan Morgan's breakthrough book, *When Chicken-Heads Come Home to Roost: A Hip-Hop Feminist Breaks it Down* (1999). There was so much in that book that I could relate to, and she too questioned feminism and its place with women of color and women of the Hip Hop generation. Morgan (1999) also coined the term "hip hop feminist." She explained that our generation (those who were coming of age when rap music first hit the airwaves) "need a feminism committed to keeping it real." Morgan went on to say:

> We need a voice like our music—one that samples and layers many voices, injects its sensi-bilities into the old and flips it into something new, provocative and powerful. And whose occasional hypocrisy, contradictions, and trifleness guarantee us at least a few trips to the terror-dome, forcing us to finally confront what we'd rather all hide from.
>
> (Morgan, 1999, p. 62)

As is the case for America in general, the hip hop industry has always been male-driven, but the early female M.C.s that I admired—M.C. Lyte, Monie Love and Queen Latifah—were fully clothed and serious about the message in their lyrics, and they spat messages with more noble/laudable themes. In their hit song, *Ladies First*, they described women as:

> Strong, stepping, strutting, moving on
> Rhyming, cutting, and not forgetting
> We are the ones that give birth
> To the new generation of prophets because it's Ladies First.
>
> (Queen Latifah, 1989)

Groups like Salt-n-Pepa and TLC pushed the envelope a little further by talking about safe sex and female satisfaction. Salt-n-Pepa, I would describe as more "fly" and feminine than Lyte, Latifah and Monie, because they had the fancy hairstyles, and they wore the latest fashion and jewelry. Similarly, members of TLC were cute and quirky. They wore baggy clothes and loud colors. Yet none of them were sexualized.

The expectation for female M.C.s changed in the '90s, during the bling era. M.C.s like Foxy Brown and Lil' Kim came on the scene; songs with messages like *Get Money* topped the charts. Now, more important than lyrical ability, was material wealth, and—for the female M.C.—sex appeal. In Kim's verse on *Get Money*, she rapped:

> Used to bring work outta town on Greyhound
> Now I'm Billboard bound, niggaz press to hit it
> Play me like a chicken, thinkin' I'm pressed to get it.
>
> (Junior Mafia, 1996)

Of course, one cannot examine women's images in hip hop today without discussing Queen Bey—one half of hip hop's royal couple—Beyonce Knowles-Carter. As a mother, I must admit, I struggle with her role as queen of the industry. In 2011, Beyonce fired her father as her manager and purported to "take control" of her own brand. More than two years later—December 2013—she released her fifth solo album, *Beyonce*, directly to her fans in digital format, without promotion. The album had to be purchased as a complete set, because no singles were released, and each song included a music video. It was a smashing success and debuted at Number 1 on the Billboard 200 chart (Billboard.com).

So why do I struggle with the Queen Bey brand? Yes, she is talented. Yes, she is beautiful. Yes, she commands the stage. Yes, she is business savvy. And she has also been labeled a feminist by many, because she is known for songs like: *I'm a Survivor*—with Destiny's Child, *Irreplaceable, Listen, If I Were a Boy, Single Ladies*, and *Run the World (Girls)*, which included the chorus: "My persuasion can build a nation; endless power, the love we can devour; you'll do anything for me; who run the world—girls" (Beyonce, 2011).

Yet her on-stage persona, which she calls Sasha Fierce, is overtly sexual. For many, this is female empowerment at its best. She is perceived to have it all. She is married to a mogul, who is arguably one of the most influential rap artists in the industry. She is in control of her business and her brand; and she is doing and saying whatever she pleases. But is she a role model? Is she an artist whom I would encourage my daughter to emulate, as an aspiring artist herself? I would have to say no—especially given the recent release of *Beyonce*. While she has always been provocative on stage, the recent music and performances that I have seen associated with this album are even more overt. So much so that while watching her perform *Drunk in Love* with her husband—Jay Z—on the 2014 Grammy Awards, my young daughter asked, "why is she almost naked?" I certainly didn't have a justifiable answer, all I could say was, "I guess that is what she chooses to do." Then she asked, "And her husband is okay with everyone seeing his wife's body?" So it seems, because Jay Z rapped:

Foreplay in a foyer, fucked up my Warhol
Slid the panties right to the side

And Beyonce sang:

(I want your body right here, daddy, I want you, right now)
Can't keep your eyes off my fatty.
(Jay Z & Beyonce, 2013)

As I see it, the Carters went from an intensely private couple, who never talked about their relationship—to flaunting their sexual prowess. Is it empowerment or industry demand? This is the question I struggle with. Is Beyonce empowered or is she a pawn? If she—and only she—chose to write, produce and release her recent album with all the alcohol-driven, profanity-laced, sexual innuendo it entails, then, I guess she is empowered. But if any other entity—her husband, PR team or management team—encouraged her to produce this material and create this image, then she is a pawn. Either way, I choose not to expose my daughter to much of the Queen Bey brand.

As for my two sons, I am also concerned about the messages they receive about masculinity in hip hop culture. As such, I do not expose them to the music of today either. My eldest son is very much attracted to the bravado of hip hop. Three of his favorite songs are *I'm Bad*, by LL Cool J; *How Ya Like Me Now*, by Kool Moe Dee; and *Ain't No Half Steppin,'* by Big Daddy Kane. Of course, all of these songs are three decades old—by design. My children know far more about "old School" hip hop, than current hip hop. I suspect, however, that if I allowed him to listen to Lil' Wayne, Young Jeezy, Wiz Khalifa and 2 Chainz, he would enjoy their bravado as well. Hip hop music—and its culture in general—was founded on bravado.

That is one of the things I grew to love. Back then, they were bragging about lyrical ability. Who was the hottest M.C. on the mic? Today, most typically, they are bragging about their sexual conquests, drug use, criminal exploits, and material wealth. None of those are messages that I want my son to admire.

My youngest son, on the other hand, is attracted to the bravado on the dance floor. He loves the idea of stepping out in front and challenging another through movement. B-boying, as it is known, is one of the four pillars of hip hop. And I must admit, I love that he loves it because it is purely about movement and physicality; I believe that it is still fairly pure to its origins—on the cardboard laid down on the streets in NYC. Granted, I still don't allow him to watch many music videos, because they rarely portray pure dance; they primarily show images of drugs, violence, sex and materialism. However, I have taken him to see films like *Battle of the Year* (2013), which attempts to depict the continuing legacy of competitive B-boying.

Now, I do not say all of this in an attempt to argue that old school hip hop was flawless—without violence or misogyny; nor do I attempt to argue that I was always conscious of the potential impact of these messages and images. In fact, the opposite is the case. I had no problem with Lil' Kim's first album release, with the widely circulated poster of her spread eagle, wearing a leopard-print bikini. Although I never attempted to emulate her sexualized image, I knew the songs from *Big Momma Thang* word-for-word. Such as:

> That's how many times I wanna cum, twenty-one
> And another one, and another one, and another one
> 24 carats nigga
> That's when I'm fuckin wit' the average nigga.
> (Lil' Kim, 1996)

So, am I now a feminist or womanist whose just hating on hip hop? I don't have a membership card, or bumper sticker proclaiming myself to be. In fact, I rarely use the term in my social life or scholarly discourse. However, I can say unequivocally that I do not want my daughter to become another nameless, faceless brown body gyrating on the stage or screen for the gratification of others. I do want her to have voice and agency and respect—for herself and from others. I want her to have relationships with people who honor her worth, respect her body, and hear her voice. I want her to have opportunities that are based on what she knows, and not what she has; I want her to appreciate her own natural beauty and God-given assets. What I want for my sons is not significantly different. I want them to know and understand their worth and the worth of others—particularly the women around them, and I do not want them to pursue material wealth above all else. I agree with Collins (2005) when she says that:

Depicting African American women as bitches; the sexual use of African American women's bodies by circulating images of Black women's promiscuity; derogating the reproductive capacities of African American women's bodies...all work to obscure the closing door of racial opportunity in the post-civil rights era. (p. 137)

I also agree with Hudson-Weems (1993) that there are certain issues that are unique to women of African descent, and one of those is our treatment and portrayal in hip hop music and culture. And, finally, I agree with Morgan (1999) when she says that, "If feminism intends to have any relevance in the lives of the majority of Black women, if it intends to move past theory and become functional it has to rescue itself from the ivory towers of academia...to be as helpful to Shequanna on 142nd as it is to Samantha at Sarah Lawrence" (p. 76).

If my agreement with these feminist and womanist scholars makes me a feminist/womanist myself, then I am proud to be! And as for my love affair with hip hop, it is not completely over; it has simply been surpassed by the love I have for my children. So, now our relationship consists of occasional visits from behind bars. You see, I believe that today's hip hop has become a prisoner to capitalism. Sometimes I visit him, putting my hand up against the thick security glass, and a tear rolls down my face in memory of what we once had. I used to love him.

REFERENCES

Beyonce. (2013). *Beyonce*. New York, NY: Columbia.

Beyonce. (2011). 4. New York, NY: Columbia.

Billboard.com (2014).

Brown, Chris. (2013). *Loyal*. New York, NY: RCA.

Busta Rhymes. (1996). *The Coming*. New York, NY: Elektra.

Collins, P. H. (1991). *Black Feminist Thought: Knowledge, Consciousness, and the Politics of Empowerment*. Vol. 2. New York, NY: Routledge.

Collins, P. H. (2005). *Black Sexual Politics: African Americans, Gender, and the New Racism*. New York, NY: Routledge.

Common. (1994). *Resurrection*. New York, NY: Relativity.

Das EFX. (1992). *Dead Serious*. New York, NY: East West America.

De La Soul. (1989). *3 Feet High and Rising*. New York, NY: Tommy Boy.

DMX. (1998). *It's Dark and Hell is Hot*. New York, NY: Def Jam.

Dr. Dre (1992). *The Chronic*. Los Angeles, CA: Death Row Records.

Eric B. & Rakim. (1988). *Follow the Leader*. New York, NY: 4th and Broadway.

Eric B. & Rakim. (1987). *Paid in Full*. New York, NY: 4th and Broadway.

hooks, b. (1981). *Ain't I a Woman: Black Women and Feminism*. Boston, MA: South End Press.

Hudson-Weems, C. (1993). *Africana Womanism: Reclaiming Ourselves*. Troy, Michigan: Bedford Publishers, Inc.

Jay Z. (2004). *Fade to Black*. Hollywood, CA: Paramount Home Entertainment.

Jay Z. (2000). *The Dynasty Roc la Familia*. New York, NY: Roc-A-Fella.

Jay Z. (1999). *Vol. 3: Life and Times of S. Carter*. New York, NY: Roc-A-Fella.

Jungle Brothers. (1989). *Done by the Forces of Nature*. Burbank, CA: Warner Bros.

Junior Mafia. (1995). *Conspiracy*. New York, NY: Big Beat.

Lil' Kim (1996). *Hardcore*. New York, NY: Big Beat.

The Lost Boyz. (1995). *Legal Drug Money*. New York, NY: Uptown/Universal.

Morgan, J. (1999). *When Chicken-heads Come Home to Roost: A Hip-Hop Feminist Breaks it Down*. New York: NY: Touchstone.

Nicki Minaj. (2014). *Pills N Potions*. New Orleans, LA: Young Money.

The Pharcyde. (1992). *Bizarre Ride II the Pharcyde*. Los Angeles, CA: Rhino Records.

Public Enemy. (1990). *Fear of a Black Planet*. New York, NY: Def Jam.

Public Enemy. (1988). *It Takes a Nation of Millions to Hold Us Back*. New York, NY: Def Jam.

Queen Latifah. (1989). *All Hail the Queen*. New York, NY: Tommy Boy.

The Sugar Hill Gang. (1980). *The Sugar Hill Gang*. New York, NY: Sugar Hill.

Walker, A. (1983). *In Search of Our Mothers Gardens*. New York, NY: Harcourt Brace Jovanovich, Publishers.

CHAPTER SIXTEEN

(Un)Comfortable Contact? Viewing Race and Interaction in 25 Years of Super Bowl Commercials through the Lens of Social Distance

ERNEST L. WIGGINS AND KENNETH CAMPBELL

INTRODUCTION

Blacks have progressed significantly in television commercials over the years, going from nearly complete absence to relative parity when compared to their proportion of the population (Dominick & Greenberg, 1970; Bush, Solomon, & Hair, 1977; Licata & Biswas, 1993; Coltrane & Messineo, 2000; Mastro & Stern, 2003; Henderson & Baldasty, 2003). It is indeed rare in the 21st century not to see a Black character in at least one of every three commercials on network television (Entman & Rojecki, 2000). Their presence cuts across all types of commercials such as food, soft drinks or alcoholic beverages, or for financial services or vehicles (Taylor & Stern, 1997; Wilkes & Valencia, 1989; Licata & Biswas), and in all types of programming including the most watched of all, the annual Super Bowl (Campbell, Jeter, & Wiggins, 2008; Crupi, 2014). However, this progress is tempered by a shortage of Blacks as primary characters in Super Bowl and other commercials and questions arise about their roles and relationships with other characters (Taylor & Stern; Wilkes & Valencia; Campbell, Jeter, & Wiggins). The mere fact that Blacks are more likely to appear as background characters rather than main characters, who are the focus in the ad and could be argued to represent power, is worthy of exploration. We use social distance theory to analyze Super

Bowl commercials from 1989 to 2014, addressing the question of Black presence and interracial interaction.

The importance of the social and cultural roles advertising plays in American society has been well established by scholars who posit that advertisements communicate and shape cultural values and ideology (Leiss, Kline, & Jhally, 1986; Paek & Shah, 2003). The contents of commercials—the images and values—are selected because they communicate quickly and effectively, which generally means images of Blacks must be palatable to the broader, predominantly White audience (Staples & Jones, 1985; Humphrey & Schuman, 1984; Wilson, Guiterrez, & Chao, 2013). Gray (1995) argues that advertisements are one of the key cultural sites in the "struggle for 'blackness,'" specifically, the complex process in society of giving meaning to blackness. Commercials reflect how those who create them see reality and how they perceive the reality of the consumer. The consequences can be significant, especially when there are narrow and consistent representations such as those connecting race and social distance, a sociological construct that seeks to measure the amount of contact between individuals or groups (Parrillo & Donoghue, 2005). The world in commercials can influence how people see themselves and others, particularly those with whom they have little contact (Gerbner, 1998; Leiss, Kline, & Jhally; Sinclair; Goffman, 1976; Kassarjian, 1969). Goffman suggests that advertisements contain numerous social cues used in daily life to make sense of members of society and to impose frames on others, their actions, and the situations in which they are encountered. These images also serve as a sociocultural mirror reflecting the degree to which a group, such as Blacks, is accepted into the mainstream culture (Humphrey & Schuman), or a distorted mirror reflecting a particular level of acceptance (Pollay, 1986).

Though not expressly an application of social distance theory, Entman and Rojecki's (2000) analysis of 1,600 commercials in prime time argues that commercials that present characters of various races positively and meaningfully interacting might produce some effect on the White viewing audience's perceptions of people of color. However, Entman and Rojecki explain, "We are not claiming that viewing these images has a massive impact on Whites. But we do believe ads provide uniquely appropriate indicators of the culture's racial heartbeat." Advertising agencies, they continue, "could be stretching culture limits, exercising a potential to nudge Whites toward racial comity. Treating Blacks and Whites equivalently, showing them in comfortable contact across and within racial groups, could both reflect and spur such progress" (p. 162).

This idea of "comfortable contact across and within racial groups" contains within it the sociological concept of "social distance." As defined by Robert Park in 1924, social distance is "an attempt to reduce to something like measurable terms the grades and degrees of understanding and intimacy which characterize personal and social relations generally." Park was a student of pioneering social theorist

Georg Simmel, who coined the term "social distance" while seeking a definition of "race consciousness" and a measurement of "race relations" (1924). Park contends that "the terms 'race consciousness' and 'class consciousness,' with which most of us are familiar, describe a state of mind in which we become, often suddenly and unexpectedly, conscious of the distances that separate, or seem to separate, us from classes and races whom we do not fully understand" (p. 340).

Park's student Emory Bogardus (1925) created a metric, the Social Distance Scale, in an attempt to measure how comfortable group members would be interacting with members of other racial or ethnic groups. Subjects (initially White male college students) were asked to report their degree of comfort with members of specified racial or ethnic groups by indicating on a continuum of social distance the subject's comfort with the specified group. Degrees ranged from allow members to enter the country, the highest degree of social distance, to allow members to marry into the family, the lowest degree of social distance. Despite some criticism (Ethington, 1997), social distance has been administered regularly since the 1920s and judged by many researchers to be a reliable measure of prejudice (Brickerhoff & Mackie, 1986; Kleg & Yamamoto, 1998; Lee, Sapp, & Ray, 1996; Weinfurt & Moghaddam, 2001). Parrillo and Donoghue (2005) updated Bogardus's Social Distance Scale in 2002 to account for demographic and cultural shifts in the population and found that even though distance still existed between racial, ethnic, and religious groups, it had indeed decreased measurably by the 21st century.

The concept of social distance is useful in the evaluation of the interactions of characters in television commercials and can lend insight into meaning and understanding communicated about social conventions, especially as they relate to interracial interactions. The social distance (both physical and metaphorical) between characters of different races in television commercials (1) might suggest the advertisers' view of the public they're trying to reach and (2) might offer a measure of the nation's "racial heartbeat," as Entman and Rojecki suggest. The presence of social distance constructs in Entman and Rojecki's discussion of the nature and duration of interactions among characters in commercials is relevant. They analyzed instances of physical proximity, touching and intimate caressing or kissing between and among characters (physical contact), and instances when characters directly addressed audience members. They found "overt conventional stereotyping diminished," yet White characters were about three times more likely to appear in contact with other models (almost exclusively White) or directly addressing the audience (p. 168).

Guided by literature that suggests that the presence and portrayals of Blacks in television commercials have improved significantly over time, and by Parrillo and Donoghue's finding of reduced social distance at the turn of the century, this chapter addresses social distance and race in Super Bowl Commercials. The focus is on primary characters; a primary character is the one in the commercial determined to have the most time or the central role. The assumption is that the greater the interaction within and between the races, the lesser the degree of social distance present. So this research explores six hypotheses:

- H1: A significantly greater proportion of Black primary characters will be speaking to other Black characters compared to White primary characters speaking to other White characters.
- H2: A significantly greater proportion of Black primary characters will have no contact interaction with other characters compared to White primary characters having no contact with other characters.
- H3: A significantly greater proportion of Black primary characters will have contact interaction with other Black characters compared to White primary characters having contact interaction with other White characters.
- H4: A significantly greater proportion of Black primary characters will be speaking to White characters during the second half of the 25-year time frame.
- H5: A significantly greater proportion of Black primary characters will have contact interaction during the second half of the 25-year timeframe than during the first half.
- H6: A significantly greater proportion of Black primary characters will have contact interaction with White characters during the second half of the 25-year timeframe than the first half.

METHODOLOGY

This study coded and examined interactions of Black primary characters and White primary characters only. Interactions of secondary and background characters were not included in the coding. Coders were instructed to code only one character as primary; if two were coded, only the first one coded was used in the analysis.

Interaction was operationalized as a character speaking, singing, or making an otherwise meaningful vocalization to one or more persons in the commercial since it involves a form of exchange. Speaking to the TV audience was not considered interaction. Also, interaction was operationalized as visible physical contact, such as a handshake, an embrace, kissing, or pat on the back. Implied contact was not coded. Commercials that did not have an identifiable person (e.g., ones with animated figures or that featured a product with only a voice-over) were not included in the study. Consistent with previous studies, movie trailers, network promotions, and public service announcements were not coded.[1]

RESULTS

Table 16.1. Speaking Interaction.

Primary Character	Yes Frequency	Yes Percentage	No* Frequency	No* Percentage	Total
Black	109	70.8	45	29.2	154
White	547	68	258	32	805
Total	656	68.4	303	31.6	959

*Includes primary characters who talk to TV audience. Chi square .479 $df=1$; $p=.489$

The expectation was to find that a significantly greater proportion of Black primary characters would not be speaking in the commercials compared to White primary characters. While this expectation does not directly address interracial social distance and therefore was not stated as a hypothesis, the premise is that a lack of speaking on the part of a Black character is an indication of social distance. The data showed that about the same percentage of Black and White primary characters spoke in the commercials studied, and the difference—70.8% of Blacks speaking versus 68% of Whites—was not statistically significant (table 16.1). Speaking, then, as an interaction, was spread throughout the groups. Since it was frequent this suggested a low degree of social distance.

To assess social distance as measured through speaking across racial lines, we hypothesized that when speaking, a greater proportion of Black primary characters would be addressing other Blacks in the commercials compared to White primary characters who would be addressing other Whites.

Table 16.2. Speaking Interaction by Race.

Primary Character	Same Race Frequency	Same Race Percentage	Different* Frequency	Different* Percentage	Not Speaking Frequency	Not Speaking Percentage	Total
Black	33	21.4	33	21.4	88	57.1	154
White	291	36.1	84	10.4	430	53.4	805
Total	324	33.8	117	12.2	518	54.0	959

*Different race or group including more than one race. Chi square 21.430; $df=2$; $p=.000$

In other words, the expectation here was that Whites, as primary characters, would talk across racial lines but not Blacks, which would be an indication of social distance between Black primary characters and Whites. The hypothesis was not supported. A significantly greater proportion of White primary characters (36.1%)

was found to be talking to other Whites compared to Black primary characters talking to other Blacks (21.4%). In fact, only 10.4% percent of White primary characters talked across racial lines, suggesting a clear case of social distance. For Blacks, the same percentage of primary characters (21.4%) that talked to other Blacks also talked across racial lines. Perhaps the greatest indicator of social distance was that a majority of Blacks (57.1%) and Whites (53.4%) did not address anyone in the commercials; rather, they talked indirectly, spoke to the TV audience, or did not speak at all (table 16.2).

Further explored was the interaction in the Super Bowl commercials through an analysis of physical contact. Smaller proportion of Black primary characters having contact interaction with other characters compared to White primary characters having contact interaction with other characters was expected. The data did not support this hypothesis either.

Table 16.3. Contact Interaction.

Primary Character	Yes		No		
	Frequency	Percentage	Frequency	Percentage	Total
Black	38	24.7	116	75.3	154
White	190	23.6	615	76.4	805
Total	228	23.8	731	76.2	959

Chi square .082; $df=1$; $p=.774$

There was little physical interaction among the primary characters, within or between races, and when present, it was nearly the same percentage. Just 24.7% of Black primary characters and 23.6% of White primary characters were involved in physical contact, a difference that was not statistically significant. Thus, the expectation of finding greater social distance based on contact by primary characters was not found (table 16.3).

It was also hypothesized that when there was contact, a significantly greater proportion of Black primary characters would have contact interaction with other Black characters compared to White characters having contact interaction with other White characters. This revealed that Black primary characters were equally as likely to be in contact with other Blacks as across racial lines, 12.3% in each case. Whites tended to have contact with other Whites almost exclusively. Only 3.6% of Whites were involved in interracial physical interaction (table 16.4). In other words, the third hypothesis suggested—that a greater proportion of Blacks would be interacting with Blacks, which would reflect greater social distance for Blacks—and it was not supported. However, the expectation of a lack of interracial physical interaction is supported particularly given the results for White primary characters.

Table 16.4. Contact Interaction by Race.

Primary Character	Same Race Frequency	Same Race Percentage	Different Frequency	Different Percentage	N/A* Frequency	N/A* Percentage	Total
Black	19	12.3	19	12.3	116	75.3	154
White	161	20	29	3.6	615	76.4	805
Total	180	18.8	48	5.0	731	76.2	959

*N/A=Primary Character is not involved in contact. Chi square 23.770; df=2; p=.000

To facilitate a longitudinal analysis that examines interactions in the commercials over the 25-year period, we divided the timeframe into a first period (1989–2001) and a second period (2002–2014), each made up of 13 years. There were 399 commercials (41.6%) in the first period and 560 (58.4%) in the second (table 16.5).

The number of Black primary characters who were speaking increased between the two periods from 41 to 68, a 65.9% difference. Both the number and percentage of White primary characters speaking also showed a large increase, from 217 to 330, representing a 52.1% increase. However, the proportion of Black primary characters talking remained essentially the same during the two periods, 69.5% and 71.6% respectively. And although there was a greater percentage of White primary characters speaking during the latter period, 63.8% versus 71%, none of the differences were statistically significant (table 16.5).

Table 16.5. Speaking Interaction by Time Period.

Primary Character	Yes Frequency	Yes Percentage	No* Frequency	No* Percentage	Total
Black					
1st period	41	69.5	18	30.5	59
2nd period	68	71.6	27	28.4	95
White					
1st period	217	63.8	123	36.2	340
2nd period	330	71	135	2.9	465
Total					
1st period	258	64.7	141	35.3	399**
2nd period	398	71.1	162	28.9	560***

*Includes Primary Characters who talk to the TV audience. **Chi square .707; df=1; p=.400
*** Chi square .014; df=1; p=.905 Total Chi square .479; df=1; p=.489

Table 16.6. Speaking Interaction by Race by Time Period.

Primary Character	Same Race		Different*		Not Speaking		
	Frequency	Percent	Frequency	Percent	Frequency	Percent	Total
Black							
1st period	5	8.5	14	23.7	40	67.8	59
2nd period	28	29.5	19	20	48	50.5	95
White							
1st period	90	26.5	27	7.9	223	65.6	340
2nd period	201	43.2	57	12.3	207	44.5	465
Total							
1st period	95	23.4	42	10.3	269	66.3	406**
2nd period	229	40.9	76	13.6	255	45.5	560***

*Different race or group including more than one race. Chi square 19.071; $df=2$; $p=.000$
***Chi square 7.758; $df=2$; $p=.021$ Total Chi square 21.430; $df=2$; $p=.000$

Specifically addressing hypothesis #4—that a significantly greater proportion of Black primary characters will be speaking to White characters in the second period than during the first period—nearly a quarter (23.7%) of Black primary characters were speaking across racial lines during the first period. A slightly smaller proportion, 20%, did the same in the second period. This decrease does not support the hypothesis. The percentage of White primary characters speaking across racial lines increased slightly between the two periods, from 7.9% to 12.3%. At the same time, the percentages of Black primary characters speaking to other Blacks increased from 8.5% to 29.5%, and the percentage of White primary characters speaking to other Whites increased from 26.5% to 43.2%, suggesting greater social distance rather than reduced. These differences were statistically significant (table 16.6).

Table 16.7. Contact Interaction by Time Period.

| Primary | Yes | | No | | |
Character	Frequency	Percentage	Frequency	Percentage	Total
Black					
1st period	18	30.5	41	69.5	59
2nd period	20	21.1	75	78.9	95
White					
1st period	73	21.5	267	78.5	340
2nd period	117	25.2	348	74.8	465
Total					
1st period	91	22.8	308	77.2	399**
2nd period	137	24.5	423	75.5	560***

*Chi square 2.333; $df=1$; $p=.127$ **Chi sq .721; $df=1$; $p=.174$ ***Total chi sq .082; $df=1$; $p<.774$

Exploring social distance between the two periods involved examining contact interaction during the second half of the 25-year timeframe. However, the proportion of Blacks involved in contact interaction did not increase as expected, but actually dropped—going from 30.5% to 21.1%. Thus, the fifth hypothesis was not supported. The number of interactions by Black primary characters increased by just two between the two periods although the number of commercials with Black primary characters increased slightly from 36, or 37.9%. The percentage of White primary characters also increased very little from the first period to the second, going from 21.5% to 25.2%. The differences were not statistically significant (table 16.7).

Table 16.8. Contact Interaction by Race by Time Period.

| Primary | Same Race | | Different Race | | N/A* | | |
Character	Frequency	Percent	Frequency	Percent	Frequency	Percent	Total
Black							
1st period	9	15.3	9	15.3	41	69.5	59
2nd period	10	10.5	10	10.5	75	78.9	95
White							
1st period	62	18.2	11	3.2	267	78.5	340
2nd period	99	21.3	18	3.9	348	74.8	465

	Same Race		Different Race		N/A*		
Primary Character	Frequency	Percent	Frequency	Percent	Frequency	Percent	Total
Total							
1st period	71	17.8	20	5.0	308	77.2	399**
2nd period	109	19.5	28	5.0	423	75.5	560***

*N/A=Primary Character is not involved in contact Chi square 15.272; df=2; p=.000
**Chi square 11.860; df=2; p=.003 ***Total Chi square 23.770; df=2; p=.000

Finally, exploring changes in social distance over time, we hypothesized that a significantly greater proportion of Black primary characters would have contact interaction with White characters during the second half of the 25-year timeframe than the first half. We found that during the first period, an equal—although small—percentage (15.3%) of Black primary characters was involved in contact with other Blacks and with Whites and other minorities. In comparison, during the second period the percentage of Black primary characters involved in contact interaction was again equal and the number was relatively small—10.5%, just 10 individuals each, for same race and interracial physical interaction. The percentages for the interactions were actually lower than during the first period, which was the opposite of what we expected. The differences were statistically significant; thus, the hypothesis was also not supported (table 16.8).

Overall, the data shows that during the first period, 18.2% of White primary characters were involved in contact with other Whites, but only 3.2% were involved in contact with Blacks. During the second period, the percentages for interaction increased slightly to 21.3% for same race interaction, but remained particularly low for interracial reaction at 3.9%. Again, the differences were statistically significant (table 16.8). So both results, for Blacks and Whites, suggest an increase in social distance.

DISCUSSION AND CONCLUSION

This study found that social distance between Blacks and Whites is evident in the Super Bowl commercials. While the commercials feature more Black primary characters, these characters remain at a distance, both physically and metaphorically, from White characters. Despite our expectations, there did not appear to be more comfort showing interracial interaction in the second period than during the first. In other words, significant improvement, measured by an increase in interracial interactions, was not found.

The most evident social distance might be reflected in the relationship we did not seek to measure but that was clearly evident in these results, that is, the fact that the large majority of primary characters of both races did not speak to or interact with each other. This might be a way to avoid putting Blacks in positions of higher status over Whites or in intimate situations, two areas where social distance is still a matter of preference in today's society. Given that commercials are a powerful force in shaping culture and cultural values, the implications of social distance reflected in the Super Bowl commercials are clear. These commercials present a reality, even in the 21st century, that suggests Blacks and Whites ostensibly inhabit separate worlds and have little to say to each other. Such messages do nothing to normalize cross-racial exchanges or interactions.

Creators of Super Bowl advertising messages might take a lesson from the producers of popular television series who are consistently "stretching cultural limits" by casting across racial and ethnic groups, portraying interracial friendships, courtships, and marriages (the most intimate of social distances), and challenging social constructs that suggest comfort is only to be found in the familiar. This points to a real need to have more African Americans as advertising producers and creators. The Cheerios 2014 Super Bowl commercials featuring an interracial couple and their daughter is a step in the right direction, although only a timid step. The parents do not touch in the commercial and they barely occupy the same frame. When the Black father and biracial daughter are shown sitting at the kitchen table, a silhouette of the mother's lower body can be seen apparently standing near the stove. Later, a frame of the mother's face is shown as she reacts to the conversation between father and daughter about a new baby. This indication of social distance in the commercial was followed up in real life with both negative and positive reaction on social media (Colbert, 2014). This suggests greater, not lesser, social distance—at least in the advertisers' view of the public—and a racial heartbeat that might have weakened over time.

There are limitations to the study, particularly our focus on only primary characters. In some commercials, there is considerable activity involving other background characters. This activity often includes a Black character. This research shows that just over half of the commercials contain at least one Black character, although previous research suggests many are in token roles (Bristor, Lee, & Hunt, 1995). Future research should address the full range of Black characters in Super Bowl commercials as well as the struggle for Blackness—to use Gray's terminology—in other cultural sites. Gray (1995) argues that representation of Blacks in any one aspect of television—in this case commercials—must be read in combination with representations in other programming and "other cultural sites of the society, as well as the social locations and conditions in which people live and how they make meanings from television" (p. 9). Finally, it is acknowledged that there are limitations to quantitative analysis when addressing interactions; thus, a separate textual analysis is already underway to give a more nuanced analysis of Blacks and interaction in Super Bowl commercials.

NOTE

1. After preliminary coding of commercials not involved in the study and revisions to the coding sheet, two graduate students coded the commercials, with each assigned half of the years. Both coded three years of commercials for intercoder reliability. Using Holsti's formula, the result was an intercoder reliability coefficient of .84. In the analysis, some categories of responses were combined, which reduced the number of decisions by coders and theoretically increased the intercoder reliability score. Due to the unavailability of the graduate students, one of the authors who trained the coders coded three years of the commercials.

BIBLIOGRAPHY

Bogardus, E. S. (1925). Measuring social distance. *Sociology and Social Research, 9*, 299–308.

Brickerhoff, M., & Mackie, M. (1986). The applicability of social distance for religious research: An exploration. *Review of Religious Research, 28*(2), 151–167.

Bristor, J. M., Lee, R. N., & Hunt, M. R. (1995). Race and ideology: African-American images in television advertising. *Journal of Public Policy & Marketing, 14*(1), 48–59.

Bush, R. F., Solomon, P. J., & Hair, J. F. (1977). There are more Blacks on TV commercials. *Journal of Advertising Research*, 21–25.

Campbell, K., Jeter, P. J., & Wiggins, E. (2008, August). *Representations of African Americans in Super Bowl commercials, 1989–2006: An analysis of primary and secondary characters.* Paper presented at Association for Education in Journalism and Mass Communications, Chicago, IL.

Colbert, H. (2014, February 5). Diversity, inclusion theme of this year's Super Bowl ads. Retrieved from http://www.insightnews.com/news/11851-diversity-inclusion-theme-of-this-years-super-bowl-ads

Coltrane, S., & Messineo, M. (2000). The perpetuation of subtle prejudice: Race and gender imagery in 1990s television advertising. *Sex Roles, 42*(5–6), 363–389.

Crupi, A. (2014, February 3). Nielsen overturns earlier call: Super Bowl XLVIII is most-watched, ever. *Adweek.* Retrieved from http://www.adweek.com/news/television/nielsen-overturns-earlier-call-super-bowl-xlviii-most-watched-ever-155461

Dominick, J. R., & Greenberg, B. S. (1970). Three seasons of Blacks on television. *Journal of Advertising Research, 10*, 21–27.

Entman, R. M., & Rojecki, A. (2000). *The Black image in the White mind: Media and race in America.* Chicago: University of Chicago Press.

Ethington, P. J. (1997, September 16). The intellectual construction of social distance: Toward a recovery of Georg Simmel's social geometry. *CyberGeo, 30.*

Gerbner, G. (1998). TV as storyteller: The distorted world of TV. Retrieved from https: www.media ed.org/assets/products/111/studyguide_111.pdf/

Goffman, E. (1976). *Gender advertisements.* Cambridge, MA: Harvard University Press.

Gray, H. (1995). *Watching race: Television and the struggle for "Blackness."* Minneapolis: University of Minnesota Press.

Hall, S. (1997). *Representation: Cultural representations and signifying practices.* Thousand Oaks, CA: Sage.

Henderson, J. J., & Baldasty, G. J. (2003). Race, advertising, and prime-time television. *The Howard Journal of Communications, 14*(2), 97–112.

Humphrey, R., & Schuman, H. (1984). The portrayal of Blacks in magazine advertisements: 1950–1982. *Public Opinion Quarterly, 48*(3), 551–563.

Kassarjian, H. H. (1969, February). The Negro and American advertising, 1946–1965. *Journal of Marketing Research, 6*(1), 29–39.

Kleg, M., & Yamamoto, K. (1998). As the world turns: Ethno-racial distances after 70 years. *Social Science Journal, 35*(2), 183–191.

Lee, M., Sapp, S. G., & Ray, M. C. (1996). The reserves social distance scale. *The Journal of Social Psychology, 135*(1), 17–25.

Leiss, W., Kline, S., & Jhally, S. (1986). *Social communication in advertising: Persons, products, and images of well-being.* New York: Methuen.

Licata, J. W., & Biswas, A. (1993). Representation, roles, and occupational status of Black models in television advertisements. *Journalism Quarterly, 70*(4), 868–882.

Mastro, D. E., & Stern, S. R. (2003, December). Representations of race in television commercials: A content analysis of prime-time advertising. *Journal of Broadcasting and Electronic Media, 24*(4), 638–647.

Paek, H. J., & Shah, H. (2003). Racial ideology, model minorities, and the "not-so-silent partner": Stereotyping of Asian Americans in U.S. magazine advertising. *The Howard Journal of Communications, 14*(4), 225–243.

Park, R. (1924, July–Aug.). The concept of social distance. *Journal of Applied Sociology, 8*(6), 339–344.

Parrillo, V. N., & Donoghue, C. (2005). Updating the Bogardus Social Distance Studies: A new national survey. *Social Science Journal, 42*(2), 257–271.

Pollay, R. W. (1986). The distorted mirror: Reflections on the unintended consequences of advertising. *Journal of Marketing, 50*(2), 18–36.

Sinclair, J. (1987). *Images incorporated: Advertising as industry and ideology.* New York: Croom Helm.

Staples, R., & Jones, T. (1985). Culture, ideology & Black television images. *The Black Scholar, 16*(3), 10–21.

Taylor, C., & Stern, B. (1997). Asian-Americans: Television advertising and the "model minority" stereotype. *Journal of Advertising, 26*(2), 47–60.

Weinfurt, K. P., & Moghaddam, F. M. (2001). Culture and social distance: A case study of methodological cautions. *The Journal of Social Psychology, 141*(10), 101–111.

Wilkes, R. E., & Valencia, H. (1989). Hispanics and Blacks in television commercials. *Journal of Advertising, 18*(1), 19–25.

Wilson, C. C., Gutierrez, F., & Chao, L. M. (2013). *Racism, sexism, and the media: Multicultural issues into the new communications age.* Thousand Oaks, CA: Sage.

CHAPTER SEVENTEEN

The Construction of Black Diasporic Identities in News Discourse on Immigration in the U.S. Black Press

ILIA RODRÍGUEZ

Recent mediated debates on immigration policy reform have constituted sites of discursive struggles over the meaning of national and diasporic identities. This chapter focuses on coverage of immigration in the U.S. Black press between 2006 and 2014 to examine how those discourses activated can construct positions of identification for members of the African diaspora.[1] A central argument in this chapter is that U.S. newspapers produced for U.S.-born African Americans, as well as for African, Jamaican, Haitian, and other immigrant communities from the Caribbean, contribute to the enduring, historical legacy of the Black Atlantic. This is most evident in the ways the Black press gives visibility and voice to emigrants from Africa and the Caribbean, and provides common referents and solidarity among members of the African diaspora. By approaching contemporary Black newspapers in the English language as interpretive communities of publishers, editors, journalists, sources, and readers (Lindlof, 1988; Zelizer, 1993), this research explores their role as actors in a transnational circuit of ideas, activism, and political discourses on immigration. The analysis presented here highlights the ways in which news coverage of immigration inscribes certain identities onto social groups by constructing boundaries of inclusion and exclusion and by constituting discourses on interethnic relations in the United States.

THE BLACK ATLANTIC AND AFRICAN DIASPORIC IDENTITIES

Gilroy (1993) conceptualizes the Black Atlantic as a cultural and political forma-tion created by African diasporic peoples who suffered from the Atlantic slave trade and its enduring historical consequences in Europe, the Americas, and the Caribbean. Gilroy's work calls attention to the historical development of a modern, Western Black culture that is not specifically African, American, Carib-bean, or British, but a hybrid formation and cultural exchange sharing themes and experiences that transcend ethnicity and nationality.[2] In elucidating the Black subject position, Gilroy builds on Du Bois' theory about double consciousness and challenges narrow notions of cultural nationalism to describe Black identity as an ongoing process of travel and exchange across the Atlantic Ocean. He discusses three themes that have historically given a sense of continuity to key dimensions of the Black Atlantic. First is the sailing ship as a symbol that evokes: (1) the middle passage of the slave trade as an "organizing symbol," (2) the experience of migrations within and across national boundaries, (3) the multiple "projects for redemptive return to an African homeland" across time, (4) the "circulation of ideas and activists," and (4) the "movement of key cultural and political artifacts: tracts, books, gramophone records, and choirs" (p. 4). A second theme is slavery, a shared experience and memory of terror for peoples in Black diasporic communi-ties across the Atlantic, and a key component of the transnational trade that made it possible for Western modernity to attain economic and cultural hegemony. A third theme is the saliency of intellectual connections (literary, political, cultural), music, and performance as important fields for cultural exchanges.

My approach to the construction of Black identities in news discourse was also informed by the notion of Diasporic identities. Drawing on Hall (1996) and Glissant (1989), identity is defined as a fragmented and unfixed sense of self that is historically constructed through difference and within discursive formations and social relations of power. Identities are "fragmented and fractured; never singu-lar but multiply constructed across different, often intersecting and antagonistic, discourses, practices and positions" (Hall, 1996, p. 4).[3] The concept of diaspora, used initially to refer to forced displacements of Jews and Armenians, is currently applied to the study of "various forms of dispersion and levels of transnational consciousness" (Drzewiecka, 2002, p. 3). Diaspora groups often invoke identity narratives of shared roots, ethnic heritage, historic homeland, and new environ-ments while they are simultaneously engaging competing discourses on national-ity, ethnicity, and race, among others. For these groups, diasporic identity is one dimension of their sense of cultural distinctiveness, and it is communicated within and across dominant national cultures, often in service of political commitments and projects.[4] In this chapter, the concepts of Black Atlantic and diasporic identity provide a framework to analyze how discourses produced by African American newspapers build or maintain identity positions across borders through a wide spectrum of ideologies.

COVERAGE OF THE BLACK ATLANTIC IN THE AFRICAN AMERICAN PRESS

Research on migration and immigration has focused primarily on the historical migrations of African Americans to the north and west of the United States.[5] More recent scholarship has explored discourses on Black transnational migrations in the Black press at different historical junctures, and a few scholars have incorporated the concept of the Black Atlantic in their work (Gilroy, 1993; Clarke, 2013; Razi, 2013). For example, Razi examines Black transnationalism in Jamaican print culture of the early 19th century. In approaching early Black Anglophone newspaper culture, he underlines transnational connections that are often overlooked in studies of the early Black press in the United States, which are predominantly national in scope. For instance, he notes that John Russworm, co-editor of the first U.S. African American newspaper in 1827, was a Jamaican-born free man of color. Razi focuses on Jamaica's first Black, antislavery newspaper (1829–1836) and discusses how the paper's editors used the rhetoric of "crown loyalism" to denounce the "planter-dominated colonial government's refusal to implement the civil rights that the British Crown had extended to the island's free Black and slave population prior to the Slavery Abolition Act of 1833" (p. 105). Further, Razi explains how the newspaper, even after the colonial government repeated attempts to suppress it, fostered a transnational network of solidarity and influence for Jamaica's free and enslaved Afro-Creole population and provided a sustained critique of colonial elites. Drawing on Gilroy and others, he explores how U.S. African American journalists were "decidedly aware" of the antislavery and political campaigns for Black citizenship of Caribbean editors in Jamaica, St. Kitts, and Barbados in the mid-19th century (pp. 106–107).

In Arenson's (2013) study of the return migration of African North Americans from Canada to the United States during the Reconstruction Era, he discusses social and political pressures that forced slaves and free Blacks to migrate north, the impact of U.S. president Abraham Lincoln's Emancipation Proclamation, and the experiences of life in Canada in relation to return migration. Looking at the late 19th century, Karcher (2005) offers a transnational perspective on African American journalist Ida B. Wells' antilynching campaign in 1893 and 1894. She focuses on Wells' alliance with White American writer Albion W. Tourgée and British Quaker, anti-imperialist Catherine Impey, as they sought to mobilize British public opinion against lynching in the United States. Karcher shows how the three sought to create "imagined communities" that could work together for universal equality, yet each articulated a distinctive form of transnational consciousness and rhetoric.

Shifting the focus to the 20th century, Mislan (2013) examines how the *Negro World*, the official newspaper of Marcus Garvey's United Negro Improvement Association, fostered Black internationalism. She analyzes editorials from 1924 to 1926 and argues that calls for liberation from European colonialism and capitalism did not exclude an embracing of Western ideals of progress applied to communities of color around the world. Her study also underscores how Black journalism in the early 20th century promoted solidarity throughout the Black Atlantic world. Tillery and Chresfield (2012) analyze the portrayal of first-wave West Indian immigrants to the United States in four African American newspapers from 1910 to 1940. Their findings indicate that a majority of articles, editorials, and letters portrayed West Indians as (1) in affinity with the U.S. African American community, (2) a part of the broader U.S. Black community, and (3) model minorities with high levels of education.

Other approaches to Black transnationalism are offered by Broussard and Paul (2014), who examine the writings of Ollie Stewart, the Paris-based foreign correspondent for the *Afro-American* newspaper from 1949 to 1977. They point out how his reporting incorporated a broad range of topics, particularly racism, U.S. foreign policy, national politics, and the achievements and activities of Blacks abroad. Along these lines, Broussard's (2013) book on African American correspondents highlights how these Black journalists play an advocacy role for African Americans and also persist in comparing the status of Blacks across nations in hopes of advocating for racial equality in the United States. In another study, Pendaz (2005) focuses on an African American newspaper in Minneapolis-St. Paul to analyze coverage of Africa from 1965 to 1975. The author found that content highlighted southern Africa liberation struggles and progressively developed a sole focus on South Africa. Coverage also reflected the concerns of the Black nationalists and Black power movements and celebrated historical liberation struggles and victories. These findings support theories of collective memory that suggest that engagement with Africa reflects both past and present political aims of Black peoples across national boundaries. This chapter contributes to this conversation by examining the historical legacy of the Black press in the context of contemporary discussions of immigration policy in the United States.

DISCOURSE ANALYSIS

This research explored the power of discourse to constitute transnational and national identities through the symbolic construction of cultural boundaries and relations between self-other. Drawing on models of critical discourse analysis of news media (Fairclough, 1995; Richardson, 2000; Reisgl & Wodak, 2001), particular attention is given to thematic clusters in coverage and within these to the rhetorical constructions and referential strategies used in news discourse to avow and ascribe positions of identification.[6] The discussion that follows is based on a thematic analysis of 2,161 items and close linguistic analysis of 98 articles—news reports, features, and advice columns—on the subject of immigration published between 2006 and 2014.[7] English-language newspapers serving U.S. African Americans as well as Haitian, Jamaican, greater Caribbean, and African immigrant communities in the United States and Canada were chosen.[8] The research questions guiding the analysis were: How does news coverage of immigration in African American newspapers construct geospatial mappings, identity boundaries, and cultural referents for members of the African diaspora? How does coverage maintain the legacy of the Black Atlantic?

THE "MAPPINGS" OF AN IMAGINED BLACK ATLANTIC IN IMMIGRATION COVERAGE

Reporting on immigration maintains the historical role of the Black newspapers. They inform, educate, advocate, and interpret the impact of immigration policies from a Black perspective.[9] These roles are performed through: (1) news reporting that informs on policy developments and relevant events and resources for Caribbean and African immigrants; (2) legal advice columns (prominent in newspapers serving immigrants from the Caribbean—*The Weekly Gleaner*, *Haitian Observateur*, *Caribbean Today*);[10] (3) columns, features, and editorials that politicize and racialize immigration policies from a Black perspective and offer advocacy for Black immigrants; and (4) personality profiles and historical features that cultivate collective memories of displacement, racial pride, and solidarity among Black peoples. These newspapers also allow Black immigrants to articulate their diverse individual and collective predicaments and range of positions in the complex structures of immigration. The overlapping "maps" explained below construct a Black transnational formation and ascribe identity positions to those inside and outside of it.

GEOSPATIAL MAPPING AND IDENTITY POSITIONS: "US" AND "THEM"

The naming of the national origins of the sources cited in news stories, as well as the countries and regions mentioned as exemplars in coverage, suggest a geospatial mapping of an imagined Black transnational formation of interest to the Black press and its readers. This spatial map incorporates African American communities affected by various immigration patterns and policymaking.[11] In each newspaper examined, the linking of the U.S., the Caribbean, Canada, Africa, and Afro-Hispanic groups reproduced historical circuits associated with the Black Atlantic.

Who are the social actors inhabiting this geographical construction? Through referential strategies, journalists populate this imagined space with social categories that construct an opposition between a Black diasporic "us" and "them." This labeling of "us" gives a sense of cohesion and shared identity to the diversity of groups from the United States, the Caribbean, African nations, Canada, and Afro-Latinos that make up the African diaspora in immigration coverage. In addition to an inventory of labels for racial identification, other markers of inclusion in this identity formation are lived stories of forced or voluntary displacement and migration due to economic hardship or political violence, discrimination, racism, marginalization, and victimization at different times in history. Also noteworthy are the themes of racial pride, personal triumph over obstacles, and aspirations to live a not-so-accessible American dream as discursive avenues to create Black diasporic identification across groups. Coverage of in-group tensions, such as ethnic rivalries among Black peoples, gender inequality, and class difference within "us" was not salient. The only salient instances of antagonism within the Black diaspora refer to the differentiation between legal or "law abiding" Black immigrants and "illegals" or "undocumented" Black immigrants.

"Us" is defined in relation to institutions and groups that are positioned as antagonists or competitors in the reporting. They are "them" because they represent: (1) economic competition (as in the contestation of the idea that African American laborers lose low-wage jobs to undocumented Mexican workers); (2) preferential treatment by the U.S. government (as in the case of Cuban versus Haitian immigrants); (3) political advantages (as in the case of Cubans and Hispanics in Florida displacing African Americans, Haitians, and West Indian communities; or the influence of the Latino vote on the partisan Republican and Democratic parties); (4) the practice of institutionalized racism by government agencies (through unfair immigration quotas, denial of refugee status, or excessive rules); (5) economic exploitation of Black peoples (from plantation economies to low-wage agricultural work in Florida, human trafficking, or "scamsters" who take advantage of immigrants) either in present times or in history; and (6) undocumented individuals in contrast to citizens or noncitizens with legalized status. Appendix 17.1 shows how referential and naming strategies used by journalists create both alliances (vertical) and tensions (horizontal) between social categories constructed in news coverage.[12]

MAPPING THE RACIAL POLITICS OF IMMIGRATION POLICYMAKING

Within this thematic cluster, news stories focus the attention on the racialization of immigration policies—particularly through discussion of (1) inter-ethnic tensions caused by migration patterns and immigration rules, (2) the unfair or racist treatment of Black immigrants, and (3) the calls for solidarity and interest convergence among "Black and Brown folks."

Inter-ethnic tensions involve African Americans and undocumented Mexican immigrants. One such tension is the competition between Mexican undocumented immigrants and working-class African Americans. For example, in April 2006, when millions of immigrants across the nation were marching to mark the National Day of Action on Immigrants' Rights, an article in the *Philadelphia Tribune* framed the event as tension between African Americans and "Latinos," although the term "Latino" is used in reference to undocumented emigrants from Mexico and Latin America and not U.S. Latino citizens. The piece opened with a quote from an unemployed African American house cleaner from Atlanta who was "unable to muster empathy or sympathy for the demonstrators." The source told the reporter: "I do not hate them...I just feel they took over" (Simpson & Ingram, 2006). In another piece, *The Philadelphia Tribune* posed the question directly: "Are illegals taking jobs from Blacks?" The writer cited economists, statistical data, and workers to affirm that the combination of high illegal migration, unemployment numbers for African American workers, and competition for jobs "should sound some kind of alarm." The writer noted that since 1970, less than 2% of illegal migration has come from Sub-Saharan Africa while 28% has originated in Mexico. A construction worker, a "Black man in his 30s," is quoted as an exemplar of how undocumented "Latino" laborers had driven wages down for African Americans: "I have been doing construction on and off for the last year, and when I first started, I saw some Black faces other than me...But when I got some work at another site...Almost everybody was Latino...If it's not discrimination, if it's not racism, what the hell would you call it?" The writer also cited statistics to indicate that "40 percent of native-born Blacks work in high-immigrant occupations—cleaning, food preparation, manufacturing, and transportation—this in comparison to 22.9 percent of Whites in the same fields." A quotation from an economics professor put it succinctly: "Arguably the most racist policy in this country for the past quarter century has been that of immigration...An onslaught of poorly educated, mostly Hispanic immigrants has severely hindered attempts of African Americans to climb the economic ladder" (Ingram, 2006b).

In 2010, the debates over the proposed Development, Relief, and Education for Alien Minors (DREAM) Act activated a particular angle within the theme of

Black-Latino conflict. *The Tennessee Tribune*, echoing conservatives and Republicans, reported on "birth tourism" and "anchor babies" to question whether the 14th Amendment "really" requires state and federal governments to recognize as "full-fledged citizens" the "babies whose only connection to this country is the fact that their mother was in the country unlawfully at the moment of their birth." The editorial favored state action to challenge the use of the 1868 amendment, designed to ensure citizenship to former slaves and recognize undocumented children ("Time of Limit," 2010). *The Weekly Gleaner* advocated the opposite view, citing statistics that show that the trend labeled "birth tourism" is "not as dramatic" as immigration opponents claimed and is "extraordinarily rare for immigrants to come to the U.S. just so that they can have babies and get citizenship" ("Birth Tourism," 2010).

Unfair treatment of Black immigrants was another major theme concerning the "unfair" or "racist" treatment of African and Caribbean immigrants by U.S. immigration policies and authorities. Emphasis is placed on comparing the case of Haitian and Cuban immigrants (e.g., Terrell, 2006; Adams, 2007; Weatherspoon, 2007; Uttley, 2007). Stories in the *Haiti Observateur*, the *Weekly Gleaner*, and the *Miami Times* suggest that "immigration rules are unjust and unfair" because they allow Cubans to be granted status of political refugees from Fidel Castro's "dictatorship" upon "washing up on American soil" while Haitians are treated as economic refugees and deported even though they have endured brutal dictators (Uttley).

Discussion of the immigration status of Haitians also leads to a debate on how Cuban and Hispanic immigrants in South Florida are displacing African Americans and other immigrants from the Caribbean. For example, in the *Miami Times*, a street poll showed the opinions of African Americas who expressed discomfort with the growth of the "Hispanic" population in Miami. One saw the immigration policy toward Haitians as "discrimination" that does not give "a Black man" a "fighting chance." Others saw the growth of the "Hispanic" community as a force that is displacing African Americans out of Miami, where "Blacks cannot even get jobs today unless they are bilingual" and where Hispanics "have a lot of control over everything in our government system negating what the Blacks say" (Terrell, 2006). In the same newspaper, a street poll in 2007 asked more specifically: "Do you think Cubans are taking over Liberty City?" Six out of six people consulted answered "yes" and added: "We don't have anywhere to stay; they are moving in and pushing us out"; "not necessarily Cubans, but everyone is taking over Liberty City"; "Look at Haitians and Blacks, we don't receive any of the benefits that they do": "a lot of illegal Cubans have commercial licenses…but when Blacks go out for the same benefits they get the runaround"; "Cubans know how to band together… Black people have to learn that once you get something, you help people out" (Weatherspoon, 2007).

In another piece in *Caribbean Today*, a writer cited census statistics that show that the "Caribbean population" in Miami-Dade and Broward County shows a "notable drop" in the number of residents with "West Indian ancestry" between 2006 and 2008. He also cited a casual survey of "Caribbean-born South Florida residents," claiming that "some have relocated to, or are in the process of moving to areas like Atlanta, New York and the Carolinas in search of cheaper housing, higher paying jobs, and lower cost of living" (Davis, 2009). An article, titled "Color of Neglect," focuses on "disparities" in immigration quotas granted to Haitians and Cubans. The writer stresses "the feelings of discrimination against Haitians" and refers to other "anomalies" in the immigration process: the extremely low numbers of visas granted to Africans, who often face political repression, when compared to European nations like Poland (Ingram, 2006b).

In the *Louisiana Weekly*, readers learned that of "the 3 million Black immigrants," about "two-thirds are from the Caribbean and Latin America, mostly Jamaica." If from the African continent, most are from Nigeria, Ethiopia, and Ghana. In the context of the debates on the DREAM Act, the writer explained, these groups are labeled as "barely a footnote" in an "immigration conversation that is usually framed as a Mexican-border issue." Sources in the piece asserted that Black immigrants have "a harder time": "People who go against the norm of what Americans are 'supposed to look like' and that generally includes Black people, have more difficulty…Also a fair number of African immigrants are Muslim, putting them in a suspect category" (Gordy, 2011). Likewise, an article in *the Afro-American* labeled immigration policy "unfair to people of color," who have not experienced Ellis Island like the overwhelming majority of White European immigrants from 1892 to 1954. Wright (2009) notes how African Americans can claim ancestors who "arrived by way of the infamous slave trade" and likened their forced incorporation within the nation to the political situation of Latinos, who lost their land and civil rights after the U.S.-Mexican War, or the "Chinese, who came to the United States after the 1849 gold rush" to work in mines and other subordinate positions.

At the time of the debate on Arizona's SB 1710 immigration law, a columnist argued that the legislation reflected "White racial anxiety" and "the sense of entitlement that Whites have always enjoyed is being challenged by demographic data showing the growth of Black and Brown" populations. According to the column, the law was labeled "racist" by an Afro-Latina activist and a labor organizer as it "legalized racial profiling." Also quoted in the article is a university professor who suggests that racial profiling of any group is particularly relevant to African Americans because of their history as victims of it (Muhammad, 2010).

The last example above suggests an alternative to the theme of inter-ethnic tension to that of solidarity and interest convergence between Latinos and African Americans. Offered primarily by activists and local politicians, two propositions entered the discourse. First, it is "unfair that the two groups [Latinos and African Americans] have to be pitted against one another" for the sake of political candidates running on anti-immigration platforms. Second, illegal immigration affects both Latinos and African American citizens (Simpson & Ingram, 2006). This position is the central focus of seven articles in the study ("Rev. Dr. Derrick," 2014; Ingram, 2006a; Simpson & Ingram, 2006; Gordy, 2011; Muhammad, 2010; Bournea, 2011; Gallaher, 2013) and is a secondary theme in a few others. In 2011, coverage of a keynote address by Pulitzer Prize–winning journalist Sonia Nazario in the *Call & Post* cited the author's call for solidarity: "Nazario said the desire for immigrants to find a better life in the United States is similar to the journey that millions of African Americans took during the Great Migration of the 20th century. Just as African Americans left the segregated South to find opportunity in the North, many Latin Americans are leaving their native countries to do the same" (Bournea). In the *Chicago Defender*, coverage of a panel on Black-Latino communities quoted sources stressing that "similarities between Black and Latino groups began at the start of American history, with the institution of slavery"; "(America has) relied forever on a subordinated lower class that has been racially marked"; and the two communities were "forced to migrate into America" by forces like U.S. trade agreements" (Gallaher).

MAPPING CULTURAL MARKERS OF THE BLACK DIASPORA

This second thematic cluster includes columns, features, and profiles that constructed three broad cultural markers of the Black diaspora: stories of racial pride upon overcoming discrimination; the struggles of Black peoples to achieve an elusive American dream; and the construction of collective memory via references to slavery, a contemporary economy where Blacks are exploited and forced to migrate for jobs, modern human trafficking, the middle passage, the plight of African immigrants trying to reach the United States and Europe, European colonialism, and nostalgic images and symbolic returns to Africa.

The cultural marker of overcoming discrimination and promoting racial pride is constructed most explicitly through personality profiles that promoted racial pride and positive models. The profiles introduced civic-minded individuals who were volunteers, community and political activists, cultural organizers, artists, high-achieving students, and successful professionals. For example, the *New York Amsterdam News* published the story of a 19-year-old undocumented emigrant from Senegal who had struggled alone since age 14 after his mother was deported. A bright student who won a robotics competition in high school, he was attending college with a student visa in 2007 and serving as tutor to other immigrant youth ("Immigrant City," 2007). Other individuals profiled were: the 76-year-old Jamaica honorary consul in Philadelphia who served, unpaid, the interests of the Jamaican community—with a PhD in entomology, he had lived a professional life as a research biologist and civic leader with the NAACP and other Black professional associations (Welles, 2006); a labor organizer who tells stories of discrimination and activism in Canada (Tanna, 2008); a Cape Verdean surgeon who immigrated to the United States at age 14 with low English-language fluency and became a pioneer in the field of minimally invasive surgery ("From Minimal English," 2009); a successful Colombia-born fashion designer in New York who was the first in his family to graduate from college (White, 2008); an Ethiopia-born doctoral fellow at Harvard University who first went to school at age 14 and rose to be the first Ethiopian woman to earn a PhD in Israel (Simmonds, 2009); a Somali immigrant serving as park ranger at Lincoln Memorial Park ("Naturalized Citizen," 2009); a Guyana-born account manager (Lamb, 2010); a U.S.-born reverend appointed national director of Faith Outreach for the Democratic Convention Committee ("Rev. Dr. Derrick," 2014); and finally, an undocumented chemical engineer born in Nigeria who graduated at the top of her class and was a DREAM Act activist (Gordy, 2011). In their life stories, there were four recurrent themes: the overcoming of some form of adversity (in the form of poverty, racism, immigration bureaucracy, or political violence); the valuing of education as a path to success; the record of hard work and success; and the involvement in civics, activism, or community service.

In addition to profiles of individuals, other pieces fomented collective pride. For example, a feature article countered the stereotype of Black youth as criminals by citing a national poll:

> African American young people are 'most likely to vote regularly, belong to groups involved with politics, donate money to candidates or parties, display buttons or signs, canvass and contact the broadcast or print media'. The study also showed that Black people between ages 15–25 were most likely to raise money for a charity, tying with Asian Americans. (Bullock, 2006)

In another example, a news report about a symposium on Frank Yerby "introduced" this historical novelist to "the Black community" with the concern that he is not "over time" "remembered as a White man" ("Why Is Frank," 2006).

An elusive or differentiated experience of the American dream offered profiles of success and pride featuring narratives of discrimination, economic hardship, or cultural adaptation that made the American "dream" difficult to attain or perennially elusive (e.g., "For Koreans," 2010; "From West Africa," 2007; Hester, 2012; Mbatogu, 2010; Reid, 2011; Sanders, 2010; Simpson & Ingram, 2006; Strickland, 2008). In some cases, Black immigrants tell stories of unfulfilled expectations, downward mobility, and cultural isolation. For example, a feature about teenage emigrants from West Africa living in the Bronx highlighted their disappointment with U.S. society. Rather than reasserting the ideology of the American dream, the six teens profiled spoke of "America" as a "rotten place," where life was "kind of hard" or "harder than" life in their native countries, where there is "too much noise outside," discrimination against Muslims, violence and drug use on the streets, classmates that made fun of or picked on them, parents who "work all the time," and impoverishment. Some of them spoke of life in their countries as easier, safer, with more personal freedom to go out with friends and girlfriends and to have fun. Two teens wanted to return to Africa ("From West Africa," 2007). Other features described African elders in Phoenix as "Arizona's neglected immigrants" facing cultural isolation, barriers, unemployment, and lack of services (Sanders, 2010) and Africans in Chicago as underserved (Hester, 2012).

Also on the margins were "Native-born African-American Muslims" facing discrimination and hostility that "doesn't stop with Muslims of Arab extraction." The reporter noted that "42 percent of all American Muslims are Black." They were "largely ignored" before September 11 attacks but now faced racism with the added "burden of religious persecution." One source quoted indicted Black churches for disseminating anti-Muslim bias. Another source referred to the problem of separation by race among Muslims: "African-American Muslims often feel a great disconnect between them and their brother and sister Muslims who are not Black" (Simpson & Ingram, 2006). Another counternarrative of the American dream is present in the story of a 63-year-old Jamaican immigrant farm laborer in Florida who, after 26 years in the United States, was living a life plagued with hardship and poverty. The company that hired him eventually closed and left the laborers without a work permit. After September 11, he could not find work and learned the trades of mason and carpenter, but his salary and legal status still did not allow him to return to Jamaica when his wife died and to see his family. The man explained: "I have 10 kids in Jamaica; the last one was three years old when I left. I haven't been back since. Now they are big men and women and hardly know me." He also said he had "six grandkids I haven't seen. Every day I promise them that I am coming home, but I can't. It's real embarrassing" ("Tales of Hope, Despair," 2008). The man's story echoes the hardships of African slaves and their descendants in the New World economies to activate collective memory.

Within Black collective memory are stories that offer perspectives on current trends or on historical processes that have shaped common experiences among members of the African diaspora. The stories referred or alluded to slavery, ships and boats, displacement, forced migration, and human trafficking (e.g., "Black History Timeline," 2009; Buyessse, 2010; "ICES Gives Voice to Victims," 2010; Judith, 2007; Julal & Davis, 2006; Murray, 2007; "Tales of Hope," 2008; "Trafficking in Persons," 2010; Williams, 2011). For example, in a piece about the Caribbean immigrant population in Philadelphia, the reporter states: "Much like African-Americans, Caribbean people are first and foremost Africans brought to the New World in slave ships to work on sugar plantations" (Julal & Davis). In another piece, members of the African diaspora in the Caribbean and South, Central, and North America are labeled "disenfranchised peoples" whose contributions to national cultures are neglected while European colonialism is exalted. A column titled "Illegal Immigration and the Black Economy" depicts the U.S. "black economy" as one of "neglect," where there are many categories of jobs with U.S.-born African Americans competing with immigrants or where—even when they have college degrees—African Americans are not hired. As a solution, the sources suggest that African Americans "build their own communities and stop trying to integrate" (Williams-Gibson, 2006). In sum, through references like these, news discourse on immigration activates a repertoire of images identified as unifying themes of the Black Atlantic.

CONCLUSION

This analysis of immigration coverage provides evidence of the enduring historical role of the Black press in the constitution of the Black Atlantic through a geospatial mapping of immigration circuits that link Africa, the United States, Canada, the Caribbean, Afro-Latin America, and, to a lesser extent, Great Britain. Within this space, news discourse also suggests diasporic identity boundaries that group Black peoples of different nationalities on the basis of racial identification, lived experiences of displacement, migration due to economic hardship or political violence, discrimination, racism, marginalization within national cultures, and victimization in present or historical times. Other cultural markers of the Black diasporic identity are racial pride upon overcoming discrimination; the struggles of Black peoples to achieve an elusive American dream; and the construction of collective memory. In this sense, contemporary coverage of immigration in the Black press features some of the central themes identified by Gilroy (1993) as themes that have historically given a sense of continuity to the Black Atlantic.

NOTES

1. I use the term "Black press" to denominate newspapers produced in the United States for U.S.-born African American readers as well as for emigrants from Africa and the Caribbean. See list of newspapers and target audiences in note 7 below.
2. Gilroy (1993) calls this formation a counterculture that has been constitutive of and constituted by European modernity, as Black intellectuals and writers have "come to terms with their inherently ambivalent relationship to the West and its dubious political legacies" (p. 47).
3. Hall's (1990) conceptualization of cultural identity situates identity along dual vectors of (1) similarity-and-continuity and (2) difference-and-rupture. Similarity-and-continuity allow

communities to find a grounding in the past, while the second vector of difference-and-rupture accounts for the diversity within colonized and oppressed communities whose cultures were not acknowledged by the colonizers or dominant sectors of society.

4. According to Brah (1996), the concept of diaspora "centers on the configurations of power which differentiate diaspora internally as well as situate them in relations to one another" (p. 183).

5. For instance, Cronin (2000) examined four Oklahoman Black newspapers and discussed the influence of African American editors on westward migration from 1891 to 1915. She shows how the promotional devices used by Black editors to encourage migration reproduced popular Black middle-class beliefs (borrowed from Whites) in Victorian morality and social order. Oklahoma's Black editors sought sober, moral, hard-working citizens who sought economic prosperity and, eventually, equality through land ownership and wealth accumulation rather than political agitation. They also used themes of self-help, group solidarity, and race pride, along with the promise of a safe haven, as promotional devices to attract and keep settlers. Likewise, Desantis (1998) examined coverage of the Great Migration (1915–1919) and found that the *Chicago Defender* actively tried to persuade discontented southern Blacks to migrate to the North through recurring rhetorical appeals to the American dream mythology. However, Jones and McKern (2004) found that the *Chicago Defender* during 1929–1940 reversed its stance on migration, when it discouraged Blacks from moving north as the nation faced the Great Depression. Without the economic lure that the North had provided in the past, the press had to confront and alert readers of the issues of racism that existed everywhere, including the North.

Black (2013), on the other hand, examines how the Black press educated migrants in Progressive Era Chicago on matters of settlement, local law, citizenship, and struggles for racial equality. In a weekly column titled "Legal Helps," attorney Richard Westbrooks answered questions about commercial practices, domestic life, civil rights, and residential conditions. Westbrooks' answers advocated a theory of African American citizenship that was rooted in the implied equality of local law rather than in the decreed equality of constitutional law. According to Black, he challenged the theory of individual citizenship to articulate both individual and collective equality and partial and comprehensive statuses. His advocacy, amid criticism and discrimination of the White legal establishment, revealed a bottom-up legal consciousness rooted in everyday encounters and social practices of racism.

6. Referential strategies refer to the choices made by writers in the selection of names or labels to describe people and create and organize social categories. According to Reisgl and Wodak (2001), choosing to describe an individual or group in one way or another serves social, political, or psychological purposes.

7. The database Ethnic News Watch—for African American, Caribbean and African newspapers circulating in the United States and Canada—was used to identify articles. An initial search using the term "immigration" as subject heading produced 2,161 items in various document types (reports, biographies, advertisements, articles, bibliography, reviews). This initial sample was examined and coded for general thematic patterns. For close linguistic analysis, I reduced the selection to 98 items by narrowing the search to newspaper "articles" only.

8. The selection of 98 news items includes articles from 24 news outlets: *Philadelphia Tribune, Indianapolis Recorder, Oakland Post, Miami Times, Bay State Banner* (Boston), *Boston Banner, Call and Post* (Cleveland, Ohio), *Chicago Defender, Michigan Chronicle* (Detroit), *Tennessee Tribune, Los Angeles Sentinel, New York Amsterdam News, New York Beacon, Culvert Chronicles* (New York

City), *Louisiana Weekly, Sun Reporter* (San Francisco), *Sacramento Observer, Precinct Reporter* (San Bernardino, California), *Afro-American Red Star* (Washington, D.C.). I also included papers serving particular Black diasporic communities in the United States: *The Weekly Gleaner*, North American edition—an edition of a Jamaican newspaper that is published in New York— *Boston Haitian and Haiti Observateur* (Brooklyn, NY), *African Times* (Los Angeles), *Caribbean Today* (Miami).

9. Research on African American and other ethnic newspapers has privileged the national context and a functionalist approach to the roles of these media in the construction of cultural identities in contestation with the dominant White press. For instance, Wilson, Gutiérrez, and Chao (2003) have documented the similarities across media serving U.S. ethnic minorities. In their historical approach, they found that all ethnic media emerged to provide news and alternative views from communities of color not covered by the dominant White press; play an advocacy role against conditions of discrimination and oppression; counter stereotyping, ridicule, and negative coverage in mainstream media. In the particular case of the African American press, researchers have, likewise, pointed out its importance as a corrective force against racial bias in the mainstream; as an alternative and trustworthy source of coverage, interpretation, and opinions; as an advocate and promoter of community development; and to present advertisers with a space and a message (Washburn, 2006; Wolseley, 1990; Dates & Barlow, 1993; Brown, 2013).

10. Whether in the form of Q&A columns where attorneys and immigration resource centers answered readers' questions, or in columns and features focusing on a single topic, this coverage provided practical and legal advice and advocacy on a wide range of topics, from the most basic to the more complex. Among these topics were visa overstays, emergency travel to the United States, passport requirements, how to prepare for the U.S. citizenship test, do's and don'ts of social security, student visas, sex offenders status under immigration law, dual citizenship, naturalization process, medical examinations required for the green card, tax residency status, how to open bank accounts, rules for air travel, permanent resident status, passport book and passport card explained, extended stay, work permits, how to detect discrimination on the job or in job interviews, free legal clinics announced, getting a green card through a job offer, status of returning residents (to the Caribbean), and how to avoid scams and abuses of immigrants.

11. The South [of the United States], the [U.S.] "third border" [i.e., the Caribbean], the U.S. Virgin Islands, the West Indies, the Caribbean, Jamaica, Haiti, Cuba, Puerto Rico, Dominican Republic, Afro-Colombia, St. Vincent, Barbados, Grenada, St. Kitts, Belize, Trinidad and Tobago, Guyana, Latin America, Africa, Sub-Saharan Africa, Cameroon, Cape Verde, Chad, Mauritania, Comoros, Swaziland, Mali, Ethiopia, Ghana, West Africa, Sierra Leone, Liberia, Nigeria, Sudan, Somalia, South Africa, Guinea, Ivory Coast, Democratic Republic of Congo, Senegal, Rwanda, Tanzania, Canada, and Great Britain.

12. Read vertically, the "Us" column in appendix 17.1 outlines the contours of a Black transnational and diasporic community that presents great diversity and fragmentation. Read horizontally, it presents the terms that appeared in contrast, tension, or opposition to the groups identified as "us" within the stories and that suggest identity positions and social relations. Terms on the table are reproduced verbatim from stories analyzed. I added the phrases in brackets for clarification and context.

Appendix 17.1. Referential Strategies and Relational Statements: "Us" and "Them"

"Us"	"Them"
African Americans	Immigrants, poorly educated, mostly Hispanic immigrants
Americans	Illegal immigrants [who take "our" limited resources and jobs]
Blacks	Whites
Black collective	White mainstream culture
Black community	White mainstream
Black exodus [Reconstruction Era]	White people
Black folks	Illegal aliens, Mexican immigrants, illegals, and Latinos
Black migration [after abolition of slavery]	
Black youth	Asian American, White and Latino youth
Blacks in Miami-Dade	Cubans in Miami-Dade
Brown folks [U.S. citizens and legal residents]	Illegals
Native-born blacks, Latinos, Asians, mainly Chinese [U.S.,19thC]	American mainstream (white) culture
Native-born [U.S.] African American Muslims	U.S. society, Black churches, Muslims who are not Black
Neo African Americans [African, Caribbean, Afro Latinos]	
New Americans [African immigrants in U.S.]	
People of color [no Ellis Island for them]	Whites, overwhelming majority…came through Ellis Island
Southern blacks	White nationalism, white supremacy
Afro-Latinos	Europeanized national cultures
Afro-Colombians	U.S. imperialism
Puerto Ricans	Non-citizens
Caribbeans	
Caribbean Americans	
Caribbean-born immigrants	
Caribbean-born South Florida residents	People of other ethnicities in Florida
Caribbean deportees, aliens from the Caribbean	U.S. government
Caribbean immigrant population in Philadelphia	
Law-abiding Caribbeans	Illegal Caribbeans
West Indian ancestry [displaced from South Florida]	Hispanic community
Haitians	Cubans
Haitians and African Americans in South Florida	Cubans in South Florida
Haitian refugees	Cuban refugees
Dominicans	
American citizens	Undocumented, illegal immigrants, aliens
Africa	Europe, Poland, Mexico, China, India, Vietnam, Arabs, Philippines, Middle East

"Us"	"Them"
African community [in Columbus, Ohio]	
African children born African Americans	
African Diaspora	
African Dreamers	Latino Dreamers
African elders [in Phoenix, Arizona]	
African immigrants	Immigration authorities
African immigrants who are Muslim	U.S. government
African youth in the Bronx	The Bronx [as hostile environment to African immigrant youth]
West Africans	
Refugees	U.S. immigration system and rules
Lost Boys of Sudan	
Senegalese youth	Police
African Canadian community	
Jamaican nurses [unable to reach the Canadian dream]	Canadian government rules
The only black member of the Government in Ontario [Canada]	
Blacks, Jews, Europeans displaced after World War II in Canada	White Canadians [in the 1940s]
African Americans	Democratic and Republican parties seeking Latino votes
Jewish women born in Ethiopia	
Immigrant-friendly cities	Cleveland, Ohio, cultural incompetence, insensitivity
Immigrant victims	Dishonest, incompetent lawyers, scamsters targeting immigrants
Victims of human trafficking	Traffickers
Disenfranchised people	European colonialism
Immigrant babies, anchor babies	Birth tourism
Children of color	
Coalition of immigrants, workers, the young, the poor, and people of color	Tea Party, immigration hardliners
Former slaves [beneficiaries of the 14th Amendment]	Children born to foreign mothers not even lawfully in the country

BIBLIOGRAPHY

Adams, A. (2007, September). The burden of deportees. *The Weekly Gleaner*. Retrieved from http://search.proquest.com/docview/369054155?accountid=14613

Arenson, A. (2013). Experience rather than imagination: Researching the return migration of African North Americans during the American Civil War and Reconstruction. *Journal of American Ethnic History, 32*(2), 73.

"Birth tourism" a tiny portion of immigrant babies. (2010, September). *The Weekly Gleaner*. Retrieved from http://search.proquest.com/docview/756209378?accountid=14613

Black, J. E. (2013). A theory of African-American citizenship: Richard Westbrooks, the Great Migration, and the *Chicago Defender*'s "Legal Helps" column. *Journal of Social History, 46*(4), 869–915.

Black history timeline. (2009, February 10). *Philadelphia Tribune*. Retrieved from http://search.proquest.com/docview/337824719?accountid=14613

Bournea, C. (2011, January). Capital's MLK program features music, art, discussion. *Call & Post*. Retrieved from http://search.proquest.com/docview/854570476?accountid=14613

Brah, A. (1996). *Cartographies of diaspora: Contesting identities*. New York: Routledge.

Broussard, J. C. (2013). *African American foreign correspondents: A history*. Baton Rouge: Louisiana State University Press.

Broussard, J.C., & Paul, N. (2014). Ollie Stewart: An African American looking at American politics, society and culture. *Journal of Pan African Studies, 6*(8), 228–246.

Brown, D. (2012, August). Beware of scamsters. *The Weekly Gleaner*. Retrieved from http://search.proquest.com/docview/1039135999?accountid=14613

Brown, P. A. (2014). Book reviews: *African American foreign correspondents: A history. American Journalism, 31*(1), 127–129. doi: 10.1080/08821127.2014.875370

Brown, R. (2013). *Framing the second decade: A content analysis of African-American newspaper coverage of people of color*. A Report from the Center for the Integration and Improvement of Journalism. San Francisco: San Francisco State University.

Bullock, Lorinda. (2006, October 11). Study: Young Blacks are most politically engaged. *New Pittsburgh Courier*. Retrieved from http://search.proquest.com/docview/367994588?accountid=14613

Buysse, C. Y. (2010, March 11). The age of neo-African Americans. *The Boston Banner*. Retrieved from http://search.proquest.com/docview/367267949?accounti

Clarke, K. (2013, August). Notes on cultural citizenship in the Black Atlantic world. *Cultural Anthropology, 28*(3), 464–475.

Cronin, M. M. (2000). A chance to build for ourselves. *Journalism History, 26*(2), 71.

Dates, J. L., & Barlow, W. (1993). *Split image: African Americans in the mass media*. Washington, DC: Howard University Press.

Davis, D. A. (2009, December). U.S. census 2010 holds key to welfare of Caribbean Americans. *Caribbean Today*. Retrieved from http://search.proquest.com/docview/196913893?accountid=14613

DeSantis, A. D. (1998). Selling the American dream myth to Black Southerners: The Chicago 'Defender' and the great migration of 1915–1919. *Western Journal of Communication*, (4), 474.

Drzewiecka, J. A. (2002). Reinventing and contesting identities in constitutive discourses: Between diaspora and its others. *Communication Quarterly, 50*(1), 1–23.

Fairclough, N. (1995). *Media discourse*. London: Bloomsbury Academic.

Fernández, V. (2011, September). Boycott against Arizona is not over, say grassroots groups. *The Louisiana Weekly*. Retrieved from http://search.proquest.com/docview/897130590?accountid=14613

For Koreans, the issue is assimilation, not immigration. (2010, October). *The Tennessee Tribune.* Retrieved from http://search.proquest.com/docview/763651689?accountid=14613

From minimal English to minimally invasive surgery. (2009, February). *The Culvert Chronicles.* Retrieved from http://search.proquest.com/docview/427347884?accountid=14613

From West Africa to the Bronx, U.S. expectations shift for teens. (2007, March). *New York Amsterdam News.* Retrieved from http://search.proquest.com/docview/390406145?accountid=14613

Gallaher, J. (2013, March). Black and Latino communities share similar struggles, say panelists. *Chicago Defender.* Retrieved from http://search.proquest.com/docview/1346948961?accountid=14613

Gaudio, R. P. (2011). The Blackness of "broken English." *Journal of Linguistic Anthropology, 21*(2), 230–246. doi: 10.1111/j.1548-1395.2011.01108.x

Gilroy, P. (1993). *Black Atlantic: Modernity and double consciousness.* Cambridge, MA: Harvard University Press.

Glissant, E. (1989). *Caribbean discourse: Selected essays.* Charlottesville: University Press of Virginia.

Gordy, C. (2011, June). Black immigrants join the debate. *The Louisiana Weekly.* Retrieved from http://search.proquest.com/docview/872843984?accountid=14613

Habtu, H. (2009, May). Comprehensive immigration reform to be or not to be? *African Times.* Retrieved from http://search.proquest.com/docview/218364067?accountid=14613

Hall, S. (1990). Cultural identity and diaspora. In J. Rutherford (Ed.), *Identity: Community, culture, difference* (pp. 222–237). London: Lawrence & Wishart.

Hall, S. (1996). Introduction: Who needs identity? In S. Hall & P. du Gay (Eds.), *Questions of cultural identity* (pp. 1–17). London: Sage.

Hester, I. (2012, March). Africa to Chicago. *Chicago Defender.* Retrieved from http://search.proquest.com/docview/1013877997?accountid=14613

ICE gives voice to victims of human trafficking. (2010, January). *Michigan Chronicle.* Retrieved from http://search.proquest.com/docview/390324752?accountid=14613

Illegal, law abiding Caribbean immigrants will not be deported. (2011, August). *The Weekly Gleaner.* Retrieved from http://search.proquest.com/docview/896364232?accountid=14613

Immigrant city tech student gives back by helping high school students excel. (2007, June). *New York Amsterdam News.* Retrieved from http://search.proquest.com/docview/390302336?accountid=14613

Immigration Q&A. (2007, January). *Boston Haitian Reporter.* Retrieved from http://search.proquest.com/docview/368883888?accountid=14613

Ingram, M. L. (2006a, April 9). Broken border. *Philadelphia Tribune.* Retrieved from http://search.proquest.com/docview/337828394?accountid=14613

Ingram, M. L. (2006b, May 21). Color of neglect. *Philadelphia Tribune.* Retrieved from http://search.proquest.com/docview/337753004?accountid=14613

Jones, R., & McKerns, J. P. (2004). Depression in "The Promised Land": *Chicago Defender* discourages migration, 1929–1940. *American Journalism, 21*(1), 55–73.

Judith, W. C. (2007, February). Educating the Afro-Caribbean diaspora. *The Weekly Gleaner.* Retrieved from http://search.proquest.com/docview/369248931?accountid=14613

Julal, B., & Davis, C. (2006, July 9). Caribbean currents. *Philadelphia Tribune.* Retrieved from http://search.proquest.com/docview/337755284?accountid=14613

Karcher, C. L. (2005). Ida B. Wells and her allies against lynching. *Comparative American Studies, 3*(2), 131–151. doi: 10.1177/1477570005052526

Lamb, D. (2010, August). Patrick Hendricks: City agency account manager. *New York Beacon*. Retrieved from http://search.proquest.com/docview/792321021?accountid=14613

Lindlof, T. R. (1988). Media audiences as interpretive communities. *Communication Yearbook, 11*(1988), 81–107.

Mgbatogu, I. (2010, October). Immigrant PAC hosts forum for endorsed candidates. *Call & Post*. Retrieved from http://search.proquest.com/docview/814791559?accountid=14613

Mislan, C. (2013). An "Obedient Servant." *Journalism History, 39*(2), 115–125.

Muhammad, C. (2010, May 20). An America for Whites only? What is behind the anti-immigration push and who are the next targets? *Sun Reporter*. http://search.proquest.com/docview/367179649?accountid=14613

Murray, L. A. (2007, March). 14 Senegalese men search for economic freedom. *New York Amsterdam News*. Retrieved from http://search.proquest.com/docview/390361522?accountid=14613

Naturalized citizen honored. (2010, May). *Afro-American Red Star*. Retrieved from http://search.proquest.com/docview/346127025?accountid=14613

Pendaz, S. (2005). Minneapolis/St. Paul African American's engagement with Africa, 1965–1975: Using a local case to explore the transnational. Conference Papers, American Sociological Association, 1.

Razi, A. (2013). "Coloured citizens of the world": The networks of empire loyalism in emancipation-era Jamaica and the rise of the transnational Black press. *American Periodicals, 23*(2), 105–124.

Reid, T. (2011, June). The Canadian dream? *The Weekly Gleaner*. Retrieved from http://search.proquest.com/docview/873876678?accountid=14613

Reisigl, M., & Wodak, R. (2001). *Discourse and discrimination: Rhetorics of racism and anti-Semitism*. London: Routledge.

Rev. Dr. Derrick Harkins to address the Christian business league. (2014, February). *Call & Post*. Retrieved from http://search.proquest.com/docview/1511406462?accountid=14613

Richardson, J. E. (2007). *Analysing newspapers*. New York: Palgrave.

Sanders, D. (2010, June). Arizona's neglected immigrants—African elders. *The Louisiana Weekly*. Retrieved from http://search.proquest.com/docview/609821874?accountid=14613

Simmonds, Y. J. (2009, October). Ethiopian scholar visits the *Sentinel. L.A. Sentinel*. Retrieved from http://search.proquest.com/docview/369310961?accountid=14613

Simpson, W. P., & Ingram, M. L. (2006, April 16). Should U.S. have counted illegals? *Philadelphia Tribune*. Retrieved from http://search.proquest.com/docview/337794753?accountid=14613

Strickland, L. N. (2008, April). Children of color spotlight immigrant heritage week 2008. *New York Amsterdam News*. Retrieved from http://search.proquest.com/docview/390263040?accountid=14613

Tales of hope, despair. (2008, June). *The Weekly Gleaner*. Retrieved from http://search.proquest.com/docview/369085896?accountid=14613

Tanna, L. (2008, May). His early years facing discrimination in Canada. *The Weekly Gleaner*. Retrieved from http://search.proquest.com/docview/369239842?accountid=14613

Terrell, C. (2006, May). Street talk. *Miami Times*. Retrieved from http://search.proquest.com/docview/363142535?accountid=14613

Tillery, A., & Chresfield, M. (2012). Model Blacks or "Ras the exhorter": A quantitative content analysis of Black newspapers' coverage of the first wave of Afro-Caribbean immigration to the United States. *Journal of Black Studies, 43*(5), 545–570. doi: 10.1177/0021934712439065

Time of limit 14th Amendment "anchor baby" language. (2010, August). *The Tennessee Tribune.* Retrieved from http://search.proquest.com/docview/751592019?accountid=14613

Trafficking in persons (pt. 1). (2010, April). *The Weekly Gleaner.* Retrieved from http://search.pro quest.com/docview/314195096?accountid=14613

Uttley, J. (2007, May). Five "life-saving" tips for transforming U.S. immigration. *Haiti Observateur.* Retrieved from http://search.proquest.com/docview/369014712?accountid=14613

Walker, R. (2008, July). Are Cleveland's doors really open to everyone? *Call & Post.* Retrieved from http://search.proquest.com/docview/238529292?accountid=14613

Washburn, P. S. (2006). *The African American newspaper: Voice of freedom.* Evanston, IL: Northwestern University Press.

Weatherspoon, T. (2007, May). Street talk. *Miami Times.* Retrieved from http://search.proquest.com/docview/363179399?accountid=14613

Welles, E. (2006, July 30). Honorary consul looks after Jamaican interests. *Philadelphia Tribune.* Retrieved from http://search.proquest.com/docview/337801777?a

White, R. M. (2008, July). D'Angelo's showroom opens in Harlem. *New York Amsterdam News.* Retrieved from http://search.proquest.com/docview/390370351?accountid=14613

Why is Frank Yerby Symposium important? (2006, April). *Oakland Post.* Retrieved from http://search.proquest.com/docview/367395756?accountid=14613

Williams, S. (2011, February). Black townships and migration. *Afro-American.* Retrieved from http://search.proquest.com/docview/858409483?accountid=14613

Williams-Gibson, J. (2006, April 07). Illegal immigration and the Black economy. *The Recorder.* Retrieved from http://search.proquest.com/docview/367528515?accountid=14613

Wilson, C. C., Gutierrez, F., & Chao, L. (2003). *Racism, sexism, and the media: The rise of class communication in multicultural America.* Thousand Oaks: Sage.

Wolseley, R. E. (1990). *The Black press.* Ames: Iowa State University.

Wright, J. (2009, February). Immigration policy unfair to people of color. *Afro-American.* Retrieved from http://search.proquest.com/docview/367314865?accountid=14613

Zelizer, B. (1993). Journalists as interpretive communities. *Critical Studies in Media Communication, 10*(3), 219–237.

CHAPTER EIGHTEEN

Now You See Me: The Visibility of Whiteness in Black Context Films

OMOTAYO O. BANJO

After decades of scholarly inquiry and critique, it has become indisputable among scholars, media critics, and audiences that the media display biased and limiting representations of racial and ethnic minorities. Research continues to reveal imbalanced representations of African Americans in news, primetime television, film, and popular culture altogether (Bogle, 2001; Dixon & Linz, 2000; Gray, 1989; Mastro & Greenberg, 2000; Watts & Orbe, 2002). Arguably, the media help to reproduce ideologies associated with racial constructs, and thus, such investigations are critical to unpacking social and political attitudes toward Blacks. For example, Oliver, Jackson, Moses, and Dangerfield's (2004) research demonstrates that Whites are more likely to criminalize Afrocentric-looking individuals. Mastro, Lapinski, Kopacz, and Behm-Morawitz (2009) found that Black suspects are more likely to receive a guilty verdict and the longest sentencing time compared to White suspects. Furthermore, their research found that participants are more likely to report negative attitudes toward Blacks after exposure to newscasts featuring Blacks as criminals. In addition, Ramasubramanian (2010) suggests that poor perceptions of Blacks based on television stereotypes are negatively correlated with support for affirmative action policies.

Much of the current research supports the interrelations between media portrayals and attitudes about race. However, identity theories generally posit that groups are defined in contrast to one another, and race specifically is a hierarchical category wherein European/White Americans are positioned above all other groups. Much of the scholarship on race has overlooked an integral component to the racial hierarchy, which motivates our research questions. Although some whiteness scholars point out that White people are also products of the sociopolitical construct of race, little empirical attention has been given to the portrayals of Whites in media and specifically in ethnic-oriented media, where whiteness is most conspicuous (Foster, 2003; Gabriel, 1996). The purpose of this chapter is to establish Black entertainment as a significant cultural site through which race and media scholars can effectively deconstruct whiteness.

RACE: AN "EQUAL OPPORTUNITY" SOCIAL CONSTRUCT

Cultural theorists contend that race is a sociopolitical construct—that is, race is a classification system by which people are essentially organized by their physical and biological traits. For example, one group may be the benefactor of a political system while others are disadvantaged. Anthropologists once classified people based on physical features such as the size and shape of an individual's nasal cavity, skull, or teeth. Physical features were then associated with personal aptitude, which served to support oppressive and thus "racist" systems. White Americans have historically been deemed the superior and advantaged racial group, while Black and Brown Americans were seen as oppressed and disadvantaged groups.

In all societies, however, people are grouped or classified in some way. Stuart Hall (1997) describes this phenomenon as a "cultural impulse," whereby humans are compelled to understand our social world by organizing people into groups. Burke and Stets (2000) contend that people are generally defined within contrasting categories—that is, groups often lie within a relational hierarchy such that one is above or superior to another. Social identity theory (Tajfel & Turner, 1979) posits that we group ourselves with individuals with whom we share similar characteristics and dissociate from those who have different characteristics. Subsequently, we ascribe value to ourselves based on our group membership within a given social category. Race is one such category through which we seek to define ourselves and find meaning. According to Hall (1997), the meaning of race is subject to the "shifting relations of difference" and therefore "can never be finally fixed."

Although most of the literature on race addresses the political construction of disenfranchised racial and ethnic groups, it is also important to acknowledge the construction of the counterpart by which racial minorities are defined. Painter (2010) explicates a history of the creation of the White race and points to an ancient system that classified people groups not by physical characteristics but by geographic location. For example, Painter notes,

Vague and savage notions had lodged in the Greek mind concerning Scythians and Celts, who lived in what is now considered Europe. Voicing broad ethnic generalizations, Greeks had words—Skythai and Keltoi—to designate far distant barbarians. Scythian, for instance, simply meant little known northeastern illiterate...and Celts denoted hidden people, painted people, strange people and barbarians to the west.... Ancient Greeks did not think in terms of *race*; instead Greeks thought of *place*. (pp. 4–5)

Mystical and superior characteristics were associated with people groups originating east of the Black Sea in the Caucuses regions, from which the term "Caucasian" is derived. According to Painter, artists, clergymen, and scientists negotiated the boundaries of these Caucasians over time, even at one point including North Africa and excluding Russia. The shifting boundaries of the White social group as defined by individuals and institutions demonstrate the extent to which even White racial identity is socially constructed.

With consideration for the lumping together of Europeans, it seems reasonable to consider White racial identity as a product of the sociopolitical construction of race. To be sure, race is a classification system of power and White people are benefactors of such a system, and thus, the social construction of race is not actually "equal." Nonetheless, whiteness (the presumed culture of White people) is also a social construct subject to the shifting of relational meaning and is therefore ripe for interrogation.

THE INVISIBILITY OF WHITENESS

For more than 20 years, critical theorists have examined how institutions and policies work to favor and normalize the practices of White racial groups, therefore perpetuating an ideology of whiteness. Within the normativity of whiteness exists the practice of universal assumptions, cultural appropriation, superiority, entitlement, and privilege (Martin, Krizek, Nakayama, & Bradford, 1996; McIntosh, 1990; Painter, 2010). Lewis (2004) characterizes whiteness as ignorant of itself, plus the concept of racial hierarchy, and it is therefore blind to difference while presuming authority over what is different. Although whiteness studies primarily examine how cultural belief systems disadvantage some groups over others, it has many implications for White racial identity.

Ruth Frankenberg (1995) argues that, as with all social identities, people are not necessarily born with a sense of superiority, but acquire these belief systems through social networks and political systems that protect racial ideologies. Carter, Helms, and Juby (2004) maintain that while much scholarship has examined Whites' social attitudes toward other minority groups, insufficient attention has been given to how Whites come to identify as *White*. Based on William Cross's (1971) theory of Nigresence, Helms and Carter (1991) propose a stage development theory of White racial identity, and contend that White Americans' reactions and interactions with Black Americans largely depended on their personal resolutions toward their own racial identity. The first three stages describe Whites' obliviousness to the meaning of race in everyday interactions and identification with White superiority. The latter two stages, Pseudo-independence and Autonomy, describe Whites' rationalization about their social position and an ultimate decision to distance oneself from White supremacist ideology. It may be possible to observe these identity negotiations in contexts where whiteness stands out.

The intersections of race and class also work together to embellish the ideal of whiteness. White racial identity is articulated as normative and homogenous except in the case of social class (Foster, 2003; Roediger, 1991). Portwood-Stacer (2007) lays out a history of eugenics studies that argues that poor Whites were biologically inferior to "normal" Whites and, therefore, the term "poor White trash" was developed to socially distance Whites who did not fit the cultural aesthetics of whiteness from what true whiteness is crafted to mean. Growing scholarship on the portrayals of "White trash" point to the criminalization and demoralization of poor Whites, often linking them with racial minorities (Newitz & Wray, 1997; Toti, 2010).

In contexts where whiteness is made visible this reality may not be hidden. When approaching race as a socially constructed classification system it is arguable that racial minorities are not the only individuals who are impacted by the ideology of race. We recognize the media as participatory institutions in the meanings of race in our social world. As Stuart Hall (2000) argues, "Media construct for us a definition of what race is, what meaning the imagery of race carries, and what the problem of a race is understood is to be" (p. 273). Not only do media help to define perceptions of Black culture, but also it helps to reinforce the majority (or White) culture in many ways.

There have been a number of studies on the portrayals of whiteness in mainstream media—that is, from a White-dominated perspective (Dyer, 2003); however, Lewis (2004) contends that newer scholarship should explore how people of color interpret whiteness. Specifically, she states that because "[racial minorities'] lives have been contained, limited, [and] excluded [by whiteness], racial minorities are one potential source of insight into an effort to understand how whiteness works today" (p. 639). Wise (2011) points out the invisibility of privilege as it perpetuates the problem of racial construction and racial injustice and, therefore, must be made conspicuous. Essentially, since whiteness is described in relation to what is non-White, it seems fitting to explore whiteness in non-White contexts, such as Black entertainment.

BLACK ENTERTAINMENT AS A CULTURAL SITE

African Americans have historically been featured as minor characters in films produced by and targeting the White majority. In very early media history, Blacks were portrayed as servile, subordinate, unintelligent, and low-status individuals in both film and television (Bogle, 2001). Entman and Rojecki (2000) establish that mainstream media portray an unbalanced representation of Blacks, and this repackaging of Black culture is reflective of Whites' sociopolitical attitudes toward Blacks. Film scholars generally agree that D. W. Griffith's *Birth of a Nation* (1915) was the earliest recorded history of representations of blackness in film. In this film, blackness—illustrated by a White male in blackface—was characterized as inferior and threatening to white purity. Hall (2001) notes that films have always shed insight into Black and White relations; therefore, films like *Birth of a Nation* reflect the ideological sentiment of Jim Crow laws.

Soon African American writers and directors took the characterization of Blacks and Black culture into their own hands, by producing film narratives that more accurately reflect their lived experiences and the tensions within their community. For example, George and Noble Johnson are acknowledged as early pioneers of the Black film industry in 1915 (Cutler & Klotman, 1999). Having acquired resources to produce and distribute films, the Johnson brothers created films showing Blacks as educated and skillful individuals who faced and overcame racial discrimination and adversity. Writer and director Oscar Micheaux is perhaps most prominently known for producing films that portray Black Americans as intelligent and prosperous, yet addressing dissensions in the Black community (Diawara, 1993). However, limited financial resources and limited access to Hollywood ultimately resulted in the demise of the independent Black film industry and continues to be an obstacle to its growth (Rhines, 1996; Cutler & Klotman, 1999).

During the 20th century, race films specifically targeted Black audiences providing an alternative to the poor representations of Blacks in mainstream films. In these films, White characters were often cast in authoritative roles and sometimes portrayed as prejudiced, oppressive and secretly lustful for Black women (Butters, 2000). In some cases, Whites were featured as allies and friends. During the Civil Rights and Black Power era, Blaxploitation films emerged and included content that challenged White domination (Squires, 2009). Independent filmmakers increased during the 1980s and 1990s where Black directors like Spike Lee, F. Gary Gray, John Singleton, and the Hughes Brothers told narratives that addressed frustration with systemic bias and the ghettoizing of Black and Brown neighborhoods (Hall, 2001). During this era, most narratives primarily centered on crime and living in the ghetto (Guerrero, 1993; Jones, 1996).

Contemporary Black-context films have increasingly become difficult to define with the evolution of culture and symbiotic dependency. Ideally, Black-context films are written, directed, and produced by an African American and focus on the Black cultural experience. However, the imbalance in ownership and the disparity in distribution power make it difficult to produce and promote such films. The most recent diversity report released by the Federal Communications Commission (FCC) reveals that Black ownership of commercial stations has decreased significantly since 2011 with Blacks owning around 6 stations nationwide and Asians and American Indians owning more than 10 stations (Eggerton, 2014). As a result of limited power in the industry, some Black context media have been and continue to be produced by non-Blacks (Johnson, 2010). Nonetheless, most scholars agree that Black entertainment is distinguished and best classified by its racial representation and cultural thematic content (Berry & Berry, 2001; Reid, 2005).

In order to increase access, quality, and profitability, Black creatives must widen their appeal. Many films popular in the Black community have been produced and directed by Whites. Presumably, White directors are able to tell Black narratives more objectively, thereby increasing its marketability (Squires, 2009). The necessary symbiotic relationship between the varying industry arms—which may or may not be owned by non-Blacks—complicates a conceptualization of Black films. On one hand, there is the effort of Black creatives to create opportunities for Black actors, writers, and directors, as well as to give voice to some aspect of the Black cultural experience. On another hand, Black creatives do not want to be defined or limited by race, contending that their films must be universal narratives featuring African Americans (Cole, 2013). In other words, although Black-context films do achieve box-office success, Black filmmakers are strategically including White characters into their films in order to broaden their appeal (Squires, 2009).

With the increase of White characters in Black entertainment, it seems fitting to explore an oft-overlooked question of identity in Black context films. Scholars suggest that stereotypes are most obvious within an ethnic context because ethnic identity is most salient to racial minorities (Ford, 1997). Whereas some Black narratives seem to focus on the Black cultural experience, the inclusion of White characters can shed some insight into how Whites are seen in this experience. To date, most scholarship on Black media has examined religion, sexuality, colorism, and issues of gender and class inequality (Burks, 1996), but scholarship on White representation in Black contexts is scarce. This chapter will examine how race emerges in Black contexts, specifically answering two questions: (1) How are White minority characters in Black-context films portrayed? (2) What potential insights into the meaning of whiteness can be traced based on these portrayals?

THE VISIBILITY OF WHITENESS

To date, there are few empirical studies examining the portrayal of whiteness in films with a majority minority cast. Gabriel (1996) argues that whiteness can be portrayed as having status, expressing discomfort with multiculturalism, and being patriotic, exclusive, and territorial. Critiques of films centered on urban narratives like *Dangerous Minds* (1995), *We Are Marshall* (2006), or *Freedom Writers* (2007) identify the position of White characters as saviors in relation to a majority minority cast (Foster, 2003; Jones, 2007; Vera & Gordon, 2003). For example, in *Freedom Writers* (2007), Erin Gruwell (Hilary Swank), a newly minted teacher, ventures off from her suburban home to teach at-risk minority students in Long Beach, California. Although initially met with resistance, ultimately Gruwell wins the students over by helping them find their voices. Although many urban narratives featuring White heroes are based on true accounts and, as such, are noteworthy stories, it is also valuable to note the overrepresentation of these White-centric narratives in mainstream cinema compared to other true stories that feature similar dedication to underprivileged youth by more than just Black athletic coaches, but also Black educators.

Tierney (2006) examines the portrayals of whiteness in Asian-context films, including *The Last Samurai, Bulletproof Monk*, and *Kill Bill*, and points out that though White characters in these films face challenges with cultural inclusion, they generally emerge as accepted appropriators and masters of Asian culture. Tierney contends that the portrayal of Whites as superior is practically impossible without positioning White characters to Asian characters (the Other). Tierney adds, "The proof of the White characters' viability as a master of an Asian martial art is inscribed by his or her defeating an Asian practitioner" (p. 610). These findings are similar to Oh and Banjo's (2012) analysis of the television series *Outsourced*, in which Rajiv's social critiques of Western imperialism were often muted by alienating him from the other Indian characters and making him the butt of the joke. In Tierney's words, "Hostility towards Whites is not allowed" (p. 610).

Historically, White characters are simply background or minor characters and rarely a main character in a Black-context film; however, in recent times, White character inclusion has increased. Banjo and Fraley (2014) argue that in contexts in which Blacks are the majority, three typologies of Whites are likely to emerge. The Man typology is the authority figure type. This character is typically an officer, a boss, a judge, prison guard, or is in some position of authority to a Black character in the film. In the Wayans brothers' *Don't Be a Menace to South Central While Drinking Your Juice in the Hood* (1996), a parody of popular Black films during the 1990s, characters Loc Dog (Marlon Wayans) and Ashtray (Sean Wayans) enter a convenience store and are suspected of robbery by the Asian owners. Unbeknown to the owners, a White character dressed in a button-down shirt and tie conspicuously stuffs a sack with merchandise, which he does not intend to pay for. While the Asian owners are distracted by their suspicion, the White character opens the cash register and takes all the money. After a dispute between the Black customers and the Asian owners, the White character reemerges with a gun and shoots the owner. Having no weapons Loc Dog and Ashtray are surprised to discover the White character with a gun. Ashtray and Loc Dog turn to each other and expressly announce the nameless White character as "The Man!" who is surreptitiously responsible for framing other Black men such as Michael Jackson and O. J. Simpson for crimes they presumably did not commit. The Man typically knows he benefits from his whiteness and makes decisions that often cost Black characters.

Black films that center on historical contexts, such as *Sarafina* (1992), *Rosewood* (1997), *A Time to Kill* (1996), *Life* (1999), *Hotel Rwanda* (2004), or *12 Years A Slave* (2013), often feature Whites as slave masters, racist bigots, supervisors, and as holding supremacist ideals. Such depictions usually reflect the Black-White relations of the era in which the narrative is situated. For example, the comedy *Life* is set in 1932 where New Yorkers Ray Gibson (Eddie Murphy) and Claude Banks (Martin Lawrence) head to Mississippi for a business deal, but are eventually accused of a murder committed by a White sheriff (Ned Vaughn) and are sent to the Mississippi State Penitentiary for life. In the historical drama *Hotel Rwanda*, Nick Nolte plays Colonel Oliver, who is charged with keeping peace in Rwanda during the 1994 civil war. Here we see a White character in a majority minority cast in a leadership position. Exemplifying how historical contexts featuring White characters depict Black-White relations during a given period, Oliver expresses to the manager of the hotel Paul Rusesabagina (Don Cheadle) that, though he is bright, Mr. Rusesabagina could never own the hotel because he is Black. A conscience-torn Oliver confesses that the West views Africans as less than "niggers" and are, thus, less likely to offer relief. Such representation reifies the authority and power that aligns with the construct of whiteness.

The Man typology also emerges in films that specifically address racial tensions such as *Higher Learning* (1995) or *Do the Right Thing* (1989). For example, in the romantic drama *Higher Learning*, White freshman Remy (Michael Rappaport) looks for a place to belong and inevitably joins a neo-Nazi group. The film portrays a series of attacks on Blacks, gays, and interracial couples, which ultimately leads to the death of freshman Malik's (Omar Epps) girlfriend. Here the majority of White characters are portrayed as violent and holders of supremacist ideologies. In more contemporary contexts, The Man character is not always overtly racist but is generally portrayed as a marker of upward social mobility and either possesses the power or thinks he has the power to decide the fate of a Black character. Banjo and Fraley (2014) reference Jorge (Kevin Bacon) in the film *Beauty Shop* (2005), in which Jorge is the salon owner and Regina's (Queen Latifah) employer. Upon hearing of her desire to own and operate her own shop, Jorge tries everything he can, although unsuccessfully, to obstruct her success.

The second typology proposed by Banjo and Fraley is the Wannabe, a character who identifies with Black culture and yet is often not accepted by other White and, sometimes, Black characters. The character Isaac Rosenberg in *Barbershop* (2002) is a classic example of the Wannabe, where Isaac is the singular White barber in the shop and in the film. He identifies with hip hop culture and speaks in what is considered to be African American language (i.e., Ebonics). The Black characters in the film often poke fun at him, interrogating his authenticity, and, although he is in a Black space, he is never fully assimilated. A recent example of the Wannabe can be found in the *Think like a Man* franchise where comedian Gary Owen plays a character (Bennet) that sometimes vacillates between Ebonics—distinguishing his association with Black culture—and standard English, accentuating his whiteness. His friends, who are mostly Black, consistently criticize any commentary he offers, and when he uses Ebonics or references Black culture, he becomes a target of racial humor. Although he engages with his friends as a team, it is not always reciprocated. For example, when playing a game of basketball, Bennet lifts his hands to extend a high-five to his teammates, but he is ignored and left hanging.

Last, Banjo and Fraley (2014) propose that White characters in Black films can also be portrayed as ignorant of Black culture, wanting to fit in but doing so in a way that emphasizes their difference. Unlike the Wannabe, they do not identify with Black culture; neither have they adopted any Black cultural aesthetics. However, they may occasionally reference Black cultural objects to communicate or connect with a Black character. The Whitebread character may not necessarily want to be accepted, but interactions with Black characters make him uncomfortable. For example, in the film *Boomerang* (1992), a salesperson interrogates three Black male shoppers about their ability to afford the merchandise in the store. The character, Marcus (Eddie Murphy) remarks that White people are naturally "programmed to fear Black people." In a more recent film, *The Best Man 2* (2013), the White character (Eddie Cibrian) fits within the context of the plot as Nia Long's boyfriend, who is professional, articulate, and uses standard English. However, it is obvious to the characters and audience that he feels a slight discomfort around her Black friends and is not fully accepted into that Black space.

Recently, Banjo, Jennings, Dorsett, and Fraley (2014) conducted a content analysis of more than 30 Black films released across two decades. Findings revealed that White characters in Black movies tend to be articulate, intelligent, and even-tempered, and were more so when interacting with Black characters compared to other White characters. White characters were also more likely to wear professional dress and have a higher job authority in relation to Black characters. In support of the typology of the Whitebread, White characters were depicted as keenly aware of racial differences, but also uneasy about race, cultures, or ethnicities, which range from mild distrust to violence against others. In addition, White characters were more likely to dress in a way that did not match the context, thereby highlighting their racial difference.

To be sure, film allows for character development that could move White characters from these proposed limited characterizations. There exists a range of typologies beyond the three proposed by Banjo and Fraley (2014), but without further investigation, such representations are yet to be uncovered. Films such as *Remember the Titans* (2000), *The Family that Preys* (2008), and *Django Unchained* (2012) invert the buddy film or magical Negro stereotype for Blacks such that White characters facilitate the main plot and/or exist simply to assist a major Black character's development. For example, Quentin Tarantino's *Django Unchained* features Dr. Schultz (Christoph Waltz) as the White savior archetype; however, although the Black slave Django (Jamie Foxx) needs Schultz's help to safely enter the home of the slave owner holding his wife captive, Schultz is killed and Django is able to save both himself and his wife.

Power continues to be associated with whiteness and, thus, although welcome (whether for morale or marketability), White characters in Black-context films are not fully embraced in Black cultural space. Even though their friendship may be valued, their racial acceptance is not completely validated as they will likely become the target of a joke or will not be given equal status. The relationships between Blacks and Whites in mainstream film sometimes promulgate a racial utopia that affirms Martin Luther King's dream, but the fact that White characters are not fully immersed or accepted into many Black-context films suggests that underlying tensions may still exist.

CONCLUSIONS

Undoubtedly films that highlight the Black cultural experience and are written, and/or produced, and/or directed by African Americans give voice to Black Americans and are produced to shed insight into a Black American cultural experience. Among them is the way "blackness" interacts with the dominant culture; it can be subversive, but not necessarily contentious. It can be inclusive, but also disparaging. Sharing its origins with the birth of American film history, Black-context films are part of the fabric of American cultural arts. Studying Black-context films yields both theoretical and practical implications. First, Black-context films are a cultural site through which race scholars can unpack aspects of whiteness from the Other's perspective. On a practical level, Black context films may serve as a barometer for existing Black-White relations in the United States.

Recent controversies surrounding whiteness in Black space emphasize Blacks' relation to Whites. For example, Miley Cyrus's appropriation of common Black cultural aesthetics, such as twerking, led to much criticism of her motives by virtue of her whiteness. In addition, the criticism surrounding Ryan Lewis and Macklemore's Grammy win as the Best Hip Hop artist in 2013 revealed some murmurs of racial irreconciliation. It seems obvious from these interactions that there continues to be certain ideas, rules, and expectations regarding White people in Black-dominated spaces. At times, these tensions emerge in film and, thus, it may be useful to expand research on the portrayals of Whites in Black film.

Berry (1996) argues that "racialism flows through the media in direct response to the presentation of America's racial experience" (p. ix). Here, the author argues for the ways in which mainstream media use stereotypical imagery to reproduce racist ideologies; however, one might also contend that essential attitudes regarding all racial groups—including the White majority—are communicated through the media and are a direct reflection of the American racial experience. Both mainstream and Black media construct and reinforce racial typologies, but as Blacks become more accepted into dominant spaces and Whites into Black spaces, it could have a positive impact on race relations. Black-produced media content can provide a space through which Black audiences can reconcile their racial attitudes concerning majority members. Similarly, it can also become a space through which White individuals feel connected with and exercise their interactions with non-Whites.

To date, a large volume of expository research on Black films exists; however, there is little to no empirical scholarship on the White representations and social effects in Black entertainment that help to establish the genre as a valuable cultural site for scholarly inquiry. Scholars interested in race in film are encouraged to seriously consider how whiteness is conveyed in varying racial contexts. Examining Whiteness in racial contexts allows for a more inclusive and expansive discussion on the construction and meaning of race.

The popularity of Black context media continues to ebb and flow. The Black film industry continues to move between independent and Hollywood (mainstream) production, and, therefore, a comparative analysis of whiteness in independent versus mainstream productions may yield meaningful results. Some of the references used in this chapter are situated in Africa and may pose some theoretical debate among scholars on possible distinctions between African media compared to Black media. Future research should entertain this potential question of differences and examine the positioning of White characters in various Black contexts.

As has been demonstrated there are a plethora of research questions waiting to be explored concerning the meanings of race, the work of film in conveying its meaning, and the value of Black-dominated spaces in unpacking the meaning of race. By approaching Black-produced films as meaningful sites of scholarly inquiry beyond defending blackness, we may help to move the genre from the periphery and integrate Black film into the larger American cultural sphere.

REFERENCES

Banjo, O. O., & Fraley, T. (2014). The Wannabe, The Man, and Whitebread: Portrayals of whiteness in Black films. *Western Journal of Black Studies, 38*(1), 42–52.

Banjo, O. O., Jennings, N., Dorsett, N., & Fraley, T. (2014, August). *Content analysis of portrayal of Whites in Black-context films.* Paper presented at the annual conference of Association for Education in Journalism and Mass Communication, Montreal, Canada.

Berry, S. T., & Berry, V. T. (2001). *The 50 most influential Black films: A celebration of African-American talent, determination, and creativity.* New York: Citadel.

Berry, V. T. (1996). Introduction. In V. T. Berry & C. L. Manning-Miller (Eds.), *Mediated messages and African American culture* (p. ix). Thousand Oaks, CA: Sage.

Bogle, D. (2002). *Toms, coons, mulattoes, mammies and bucks: An interpretive history of Blacks in American films.* New York: Continuum.

Bogle, D. (2001). *Primetime blues: African-Americans on network television.* New York: Farrar, Straus and Giroux.

Burke, P. J., & Stets, J. E. (2000). Identity theory and social identity theory. *Social Psychology Quarterly, 63*(3), 224–237.

Burks, R. E. (1996). Intimations of invisibility: Black women and contemporary Hollywood cinema. In V. T. Berry & C. L. Manning-Miller (Eds.), *Mediated messages and African American culture* (pp. 24–39). Thousand Oaks, CA: Sage.

Butters, G. R., Jr. (2000). From homestead to lynch mob: Portrayals of Black masculinity in Oscar Micheaux's *Within Our Gates. Journal of Multi-Media History.* http://www.albany.edu/jmmh/vol3/micheaux/micheaux2.html

Carter, R. T., Helms, J. E., & Juby, H. L. (2004). The relationship between racism and racial identity for White Americans: A profile analysis. *Journal of Multicultural Counseling and Development, 32*(1), 2–17. doi: 10.1002/j.2161-1912.2004.tb00357.x

Cole, O. (2013). Why *The Best Man Holiday* isn't "race-themed." Retrieved from http://www.huffingtonpost.com/olivia-cole/the-best-man-holiday-race_b_4295853.html

Cross, W. E., Jr. (1971). The Negro-to-Black conversion experience. *Black World, 20*(9), 13–27.

Cutler, J. K., & Klotman, P. R. (1999). Introduction. In P. R. Klotman & J. K. Cutler (Eds.), *Struggles for representation: African American documentary film and video* (p. xiii). Bloomington: Indiana University Press.

Diawara, M. (Ed.). (1993). *Black American cinema.* New York: Routledge.

Dixon, T. L., & Linz, D. (2000). Overrepresentation and underrepresentation of African Americans and Latinos as lawbreakers on television news. *Journal of Communication, 50*(2), 131–154.

Dyer, R. (2003). The matter of whiteness. In M. Kimmel & A.L. Ferber (Eds). *Privilege: A reader* (pp. 21–32). Boulder, CO: Westview Press.

Eggerton, J. (2014). FCC releases ownership diversity report. *Broadcasting & Cable.* Retrieved from http://broadcastingcable.com/news/washington/fcc-releases-ownership-diversity-report/132112#.U64e5sGI6Rg.facebook

Entman, R., & Rojecki, A. (2000). *The Black image in the White mind.* Chicago: University of Chicago Press.

Ford, T. E. (1997). Effects of stereotypical television portrayals of African-Americans on person-perception. *Social Psychology Quarterly, 60*(3), 266–278.

Foster, G. (2003). *Performing whiteness: Postmodern re/constructions in the cinema.* New York: SUNY.

Frankenberg, R. (1995). *The social construction of whiteness.* Minneapolis, MN: University of Minnesota Press.

Gabriel, J. (1996). What do you do when minority means you? *Falling Down* and the construction of "whiteness." *Screen, 37*(2), 129–151. doi: 10.1093/screen/37.2.129

Gray, H. (1989). Television, Black Americans, and the American dream. *Critical Studies in Media Communication, 6*(4), 376–386. doi: 10.1080/15295038909366763

Guerrero, E. (1993). *Framing Blackness: The African American image in film.* Philadelphia: Temple University Press.

Hall, S. (2000). Racist ideologies and the media. In P. Marris & S. Thornham (Eds.), *Media studies: A reader* (pp. 271–282). New York: New York University Press.

Hall, S. (2001). The spectacle of the other. In M. Wetherell, S. Taylor, & S. J. Yates (Eds.), *Discourse theory and practice: A reader* (pp. 324–344). London; Thousand Oaks, CA: Sage.

Hall, S. (Lecturer), & Jhally, S. (Ed.). (1997). *Race, the floating signifier* [Documentary film]. United States: Media Education Foundation.

Helms, J., & Carter, R. T. (1991). Relationships of White and Black racial identity attitudes and demographic similarity to counselor preferences. *Journal of Counseling Psychology, 38*(4), 446–457.

Johnson, M. (2010). Incorporating self-categorization concepts into ethnic media research. *Communication Theory, 20*(1), 106–125. doi: 10.1111/j.1468-2885.2009.01356.x

Jones, J. (1996). The new ghetto aesthetic. In V. T. Berry & C. L. Manning-Miller (Eds.), *Mediated messages and African American culture* (pp. 24–39). Thousand Oaks, CA: Sage.

Jones, J. (2007). Institutions that fail, narratives that succeed: Television's community realism versus cinema's neo-liberal hope. *Flow.* Retrieved from http://flowtv.org/2007/10/institutions-that-fail-narratives-that-succeed-television's-community-realism-versus-cinema's-neo-liberal-hope/

Lewis, A. E. (2004). "What group?" Studying Whites and whiteness in an era of "colorblindness." *Sociological Theory, 22* (4), 623-646. doi: 10.1111/j.0735-2751.2004.00237.x/abstract

Martin, J., Krizek, R., Nakayama, T., & Bradford, L. (1996). Exploring whiteness: A study of self labels for White Americans. *Communication Quarterly, 44*(2), 125–144. doi: 10.1080/01463379609370006

Mastro, D., & Greenberg, B. S. (2000). The portrayal of racial minorities on prime time television. *Journal of Broadcasting and Electronic Media, 44*(4), 690–703.

Mastro, D., Lapinski, M., Kopacz, M., & Behm-Morawitz, E. (2009). The influence of exposure to depictions of race and crime in TV news on viewers' social judgments. *Journal of Broadcasting & Electronic Media, 53*(4), 615–635. doi: 10.1080/08838150903310534

McIntosh, P. (1990). White privilege: Unpacking the invisible knapsack. *Independent School, 49*(2), 31–36.

Newitz, A., & Wray, M. (1997). Introduction. In A. Newitz, & M. Wray (Eds.), *White trash: Race and class in America* (pp. 1–11). New York: Routledge.

Oh, C., & Banjo, O. O. (2012). Outsourcing postracialism: Voicing neoliberal multiculturalism in *Outsourced. Communication Theory, 22*(4), 449–470. doi: 10.1111/j.1468-2885.2012.01414.x

Oliver, M. B., Jackson, R. L., Moses, N. N., & Dangerfield, C. L. (2004). The face of crime: Viewers' memory of race-related facial features of individuals pictured in the news. *Journal of Communication, 54*(1), 88–104. doi: 10.1111/j.1460-2466.2004.tb02615.x

Painter, N. I. (2010). *The history of White people*. New York: W. W. Norton.

Portwood-Stacer, L. (2007). *Consuming 'trash': Representations of poor Whites in U.S. popular culture*. Paper presented at the International Communication Association Convention, San Francisco.

Ramasubramanian, S. (2010). Television viewing, racial attitudes, and policy preferences: Exploring the role of social identity and intergroup emotions in influencing support for affirmative action. *Communication Monographs, 77*(1), 102–120. doi: 10.1080/03637750903514300

Reid, M. (2005). *Black Lenses, Black Voices: African American Film Now*. Lanham, MD: Rowman and Littlefield.

Rhines, J. A. (1996). *Black film, White Money*. New Brunswick, NJ: Rutgers University Press.

Roediger, D. (1991). *The wages of whiteness: Race and the making of the American working class*. New York: Verso.

Squires, C. (2009). *African Americans and the media*. Cambridge: Polity.

Tajfel, H., & Turner, J. C. (1979). An integrative theory of intergroup conflict. In W. G. Austin & S. Worchel (Eds.), *The social psychology of intergroup relations* (pp. 33–47). Monterey, CA: Brooks/Cole.

Tierney, S. (2006). Themes of whiteness in *Bulletproof Monk, Kill Bill* and *The Last Samurai*. *Journal of Communication, 56*(3), 607–624. doi: 10.1111/j.1460-2466.2006.00303.x

Toti, N. (2010). *Poor White trash: Contextualizing an American movie monster*. Kirksville, MO: Truman State University Press.

Vera, H., & Gordon, A. (2003). *Screen saviors: Hollywood fictions of whiteness*. Lanham, MD: Rowman & Littlefield.

Watts, E. K., & Orbe, M. (2002). The spectacular consumption of "true" African American culture: "Whassup" with the Budweiser guys? *Critical Studies in Media Communication, 19*(1), 1–20. doi: 10.1080/07393180216554

Wise, T. (2011). *White like me: Reflections on race from a privileged son*. Berkeley, CA: Soft Skull.

CHAPTER NINETEEN

Black Masculinity and Representation in Popular Culture: A Case Study of Quentin Tarantino's Film *Django Unchained*

TAMMIE JENKINS

INTRODUCTION

As the single mother of two Black males, whose ages at the time of the *Django Unchained* release in 2012 were 17 and 11, I wondered what affect, if any, the images of Jamie Foxx as Django would have on discourses about Black masculinity and representation in popular culture. Often objectified in larger societal discourses of otherness, Fanon (1952) argues that Blacks', particularly males, visual representations are usually framed at the various intersections of race, gender, class, sexuality, and geography.

To explore the internal and external narratives, I asked each of my sons: What are some of your concerns as a Black male living in the South? My older son thought being viewed as dangerous or a threat because of his skin color and his size was an issue, whereas my younger son was concerned with not having the latest fashion and being ridiculed by other kids. Even though neither of my sons blatantly said the words, I realized that each in his own way was caught in a dominant discourse fueling larger societal perceptions of Black masculinity and representation in the 21st century.

This chapter traces the origins of these larger societal discourses centered on Black males. It will examine the use of stereotypical depictions and other forms of imagery in *Django Unchained* as a case study of Black masculinity and representation in 21st-century popular culture. Using Stake's definition of case study as "the study of the particularity and complexity of a single case, coming to understand its activity within important circumstances" (1995, p. xi), I viewed the film *Django Unchained* with my sons. Afterward, we discussed the historical underpinnings in Tarantino's use of intertextuality to connect Sergio Corbucci's motion picture *Django* (1966) with American slavery, elements of Bass Reeves's life ([1838–1910]; one of the first Black Deputy U.S. Marshalls), components of blackface minstrelsy, stereotypes associated with Black males, and components of Blaxploitation films (Carpio, 2013; Gray, 1995).

According to Porter (1986), intertextuality involves "the bits and pieces of text which writers or speakers borrow and sew together to create new discourses" (p. 34). I extend this notion to include visual images of Black masculinity and representation, specifically in *Django Unchained*. These images exist at and often transgress the intersections of race, gender, class, and sexuality as socially constructed discourses ingrained with overlapping stereotypical archetypes disseminated through mass media outlets. Gray asserts that representations of Black masculinity and representation are part of much larger dialogues between the Black community and dominant society in which "contemporary images of black masculinity continue to challenge hegemonic constructions of whiteness even as they rewrite and reproduce forms of patriarchal authority" (p. 402). Gray argues that these discourses of blackness and Black culture are often points of contention. Carefully camouflaged as entertainment, *Django Unchained* revisits and reinterprets larger societal discourses of Black masculinity and representation in a 21st-century western parody blended with historical fact and fictions.

In this chapter, public pedagogy and performance studies are the conceptual frameworks used to explore the ways in which *Django Unchained* appropriates the use of space (physical and imagined) as embedded locations where multiple discourses occur simultaneously. Hence, enabling me to view the film as a series of interpretative texts in which signs, gestures, and vocal intonations serve as symbolic dialogues situating discourses of Black masculinity and representation in larger societal conversations of Black males as other (Freishtat & Sandlin, 2010; Giroux, 2000; Jenkins, 2013; Nunley, 2007; Sandlin & Milam, 2008). To understand the ways in which Jamie Foxx's portrayal of Django provides an alternative interpretation of the lived experiences and social realities of Black males past and present, performance studies is used to examine the visual, written, and auditory texts Tarantino uses as part of his "creative practice." Through performance studies the film can be read as storied text investigating the use of physical spaces, oral delivery of the scripted dialogues, and the bodily articulations of each character as related to Black masculinity and representation.

In this chapter the following questions are assessed:

1. In the context of Black masculinity and representation, what does it mean to be "unchained"?
2. What are the problematics of portrayals of Black masculinity and representation in the film *Django Unchained* when non-Black individuals are the directors, producers, and writers?
3. What are the hidden transcripts that emerge from Jamie Foxx's portrayal of Django?
4. How is *Django Unchained* used as pedagogy addressing discourses of Black masculinity and representation in popular culture?

I use narrative inquiry and narrative analysis as my experience-centered qualitative research methodologies to enable me to analyze, interpret, and articulate the data from multiple points of view simultaneously. This analysis of Tarantino's cinematic narrative will situate larger societal conversations of Black masculinity and representation in the present-day context by tracing its roots to past discourses anchored in stereotypical depictions, Blackface minstrelsy, Blaxploitation films, and Bass Reeves's biographical information (Andrews, 2004; Cortazzi, 2001; Jenkins; Jones, 2004; Maynes, Pierce, & Laslett, 2008; Mishler, 1995; Mukai, 1992; Reissman, 2005, 2008; Sandelowski, 1991; Smith, 2000). First, the role of stereotypical depictions, Blackface minstrelsy, and Blaxploitation films in popular culture understandings of Black masculinity and representation as portrayed in *Django Unchained* are discussed. Next, a brief biographical overview of the life of Bass Reeves is provided in comparison and contrast to that of the character of Django. Last, the ways in which Quentin Tarantino uses *Django Unchained* and Jamie Foxx's portrayal of Django to explore discourses of Black masculinity and representation are explained.

BLACK MALE: FREE, BUT ENSLAVED BY THE FRAME

The use of stereotypes in the American public sphere to visually depict discourses of Black masculinity and representation is not a new phenomenon but has a long history dating back to the 1830s (Henry, 2004; Lott, 1992; Mahar, 1999; Rogin, 1996; Smith, 1997). Stereotypes regarding Black people began during the institution of slavery as a way for Whites to justify their enslavement and harsh treatment of persons of African descent. During the 19th century, blackface minstrelsy actors used stereotypical representations of Black males, such as Uncle Tom, Coon, and the Black brute, to resituate discourses of Black masculinity and representation in relation to the political climate of the United States, a place where enslavement versus freedom was a point of contention between citizens of the North and South (Bogle, 2002; Cockrell, 1997; Lott; Mahar, 1999).

Beginning in large northern cities of the United States, such as New York and Philadelphia, blackface minstrelsy performances reigned from the antebellum period through Reconstruction, Jim Crow, and the great northern migration of Blacks from the South. Featuring unrealistic, exaggerated portrayals of Black lived experiences and social realities, black-faced White actors used the vernacular of multiple ethnic groups to reinforce socially constructed stereotypes that provided visual images of White superiority and Black inferiority (Henry, 2004; Lott). This unique style of artistic expression was "created" by Thomas "T. D." Rice, who, in 1830, performed in blackface in Pennsylvania for the first time (Bogle, 2002; Cockrell, 1997; Leab, 1995; Lott; Rogin, 1996). Rice provided audiences with his interpretations of "Jim Crow," a trickster character that evolved into various visual representations such as "the slave," "the dandy," and a host of others that were commonly associated with Black people, specifically Black males, in the 19th and 20th centuries (Bogle; Cockrell; Rogin). Performed in public spaces, usually in three acts, blackface minstrelsy served as a way to show the larger society the otherness of Black people as blackface actors danced, told jokes, enacted skits, and sung songs (Bogle; Cockrell; Mahar, 1999; Rogin).

The birth of motion pictures in the late 1800s witnessed the demise of blackface minstrelsy, serving as a more engaging form of entertainment. Visual parodies of Black masculinity and representation moved from the stage to movie theaters. One of these early films is D. W. Griffith's *The Birth of a Nation* (1915), in which White actors in blackface depicted Black characters and associated racial stereotypes (Bogle; Cockrell; Guerro, 1993; Lawrence, 2008; Rogin) in ways that "reinforced prevalent racist attitudes" (Lawrence, p. 1). The developing motion picture industry used enhanced and revamped versions of traditional stereotypical depiction of Black masculinity and representation situating them in a present-day context. This is evidenced by the introduction of the Black buck archetype appearing in movies as a violent, abusive, and usually nameless Black male character (Bogle; Charania, 2013; Cockrell; Leab, 1995; Lott, 1992; Rocchio, 2002; Rogin; Smith, 1997). He was seen as an "over-sexed savage" (Bogle, p. 14) with a propensity for revenge surpassed only by his "lust for white flesh" (Bogle, p. 14). It was a tradition that would resurface in 20th-century films beginning in the late 1960s.

Blaxploitation movies emerged as a popular genre from 1965 to 1976 (Bogle; Guerro; Lawrence; Leab; Lott; Smith, 1997; Vognar, 2013). A key element to the initial success of these films was the fact that they "centered on black narratives" (Guerro, p. 69) and provided Black audiences with representations of the Black race while making its dialogues suitable or palatable for White audiences (Guerro; Lawrence). During the Blaxploitation era, the Superspade archetype was characterized as "indestructible, flippant, romantic, and triumphant in Hollywood's best private-eye tradition" (Leab, p. 4). The character of Shaft, in the movie *Shaft* (1971) is a primary example of the Superspade in the post–civil rights era (Bogle; Guerro; Iton, 2008; Lawrence; Leab; Lott; Vognar). Presenting "[a] Black hero or heroine who is both socially and politically conscious" (Lawrence, p. 18), Blaxploitation films included the use of stereotypical portrayals of blackness and Black culture (Gray, 1995; Henry, 2004; hooks, 1992; Iton; Rocchio; Smith, 1997) through the creation of "black urban spaces" (Lawrence, p. 19) as part of larger societal discourses, thus showing the resilience of Black people through characters who "possessed the ability to survive in and navigate the establishment while maintaining their blackness" (Lawrence, p. 18). Relying on stereotypical archetypes to reinforce social constructions of otherness, Smith (1997) contends that notions of blackness and Black culture have been tainted by ideas of a shared history and commonalities among the lived experiences and social realities of Black people as a race and an ethnic group. Prevailing discourses anchored in stereotypical portrayals of Black masculinity and representation were key in Blaxploitation films set in the South. They were typically parodies, westerns, or comedies situated during the antebellum period or the years following emancipation, such as *Skin Game* (1971), *The Legend of Nigger Charley* (1972), *Blazing Saddles* (1974), *Boss Nigger* (1975), *Mandingo* (1975), *Posse* (1993), and *Wild Wild West* (1999). Although the films *Posse* and *Wild Wild West* were made after the Blaxploitation era ended, both, like *Django Unchained*, contain elements of Blaxploitation and continued to use stereotypes to present depictions of Black masculinity and representation.

Django Unchained combines elements of blackface minstrelsy and Blaxploitation to create dichotomies between Django and other characters in the film such as Dr. King Schultz (Christoph Waltz), Calvin Candie (Leonardo DiCaprio), Broomhilda (Kerry Washington), and Stephen (Samuel L. Jackson). Through his relationship with Dr. Schultz, Django is able to extract his vengeance upon White men without the threat of reprisal and make money in the process. Black masculinity and representation in Django's actions are heightened by the inclusion of music both on the screen and the soundtrack, in much the same way as Blaxploitation films and blackface minstrelsy used songs to situate the protagonist's narrative and motivation in the context of the overall narrative plot, thus blending "the Superspade [archetype] and the old-black-as-threat-to-White-society image" (Leab, 1995, p. 225). Conversely, in *Django Unchained*, Tarantino adapts characteristics found in Blaxploitation "heroes" such as Shaft, transplanting them to the character of Django in the antebellum South. Employing imagination, antebellum Black colloquial speech and vernacular, as well as stereotypical depictions of the Black male body derived from blackface minstrelsy and Blaxploitation films and the narratives of Bass Reeves's lived experiences, Tarantino redefines a contemporary Black masculinity and representation through the character of Django.

BASS REEVES: WERE YOU THE INSPIRATION
FOR *DJANGO UNCHAINED*?

The story that surrounds the character of Django on film struck a chord with me as I remembered watching the History Channel's segment on the life of Bass Reeves. *Django Unchained* opens with a scene, somewhere in 1858 Texas, with six enslaved men shackled together by the ankle, walking accompanied by two White men with rifles on horseback. The music of a traditional western plays as the singer narrates the events preceding the moment we, as the audience, catch a glimpse of Django. As the film continues, the audience learns that Django is a slave who had been purchased in Greenville, Mississippi. He had a wife named Broomhilda who was sold as punishment for running away. Upon viewing *Django Unchained* for the third time, I noticed similarities between Reeves's lived experiences and those Tarantino included in his cinematic construction of the character of Django. Born a slave in the Arkansas Territory in 1838, Bass Reeves, a towering man six feet two inches tall and weighing 180 pounds, grew up in Texas (Brady, 2005; Burton, 2008; Littlefield & Underhill, 1971).

During the Civil War, Reeves escaped his enslavement by finding refuge in the Indian Territory among the Cherokee, Choctaw, Chickasaw, Creek, and Seminole tribes (Brady; Burton; Littlefield & Underhill). As a result, Reeves knew the Indian Territory well and spoke several Native American dialects. While residing in the Indian Territory, Reeves learned tracking and how to shoot a gun and rifle very well, skills that became essential to his success as a lawman. Bass Reeves, who had been working as a farmer, guide, and occasional bounty hunter, was deputized by James F. Fagan, a White U.S. Marshal, who sought Reeves for his tracking skills, knowledge of the Indian Territory, and his ability to communicate with the Native American tribes in the region (Brady; Burton; Littlefield & Underhill). In 1875, Reeves was commissioned into the U.S. Marshal Service and assigned to the Indian Territory where he began his 32-year career (Brady; Burton; Littlefield & Underhill). This also made Reeves one of the first Black bounty hunters and U.S. Marshals in the country, but it did not prevent him from experiencing discrimination and racism with regard to being Black, male, and a former slave with a badge (Brady; Burton; Littlefield & Underhill). Over the course of his career, Reeves became a well-known and feared lawman, who arrested more than 3,000 fugitives and killed 14 criminals in self-defense.

Embodying similar physical attributes of Bass Reeves, Jamie Foxx, as Django, in some ways became a visual manifestation of Reeves. Like Reeves, Foxx is approximately six feet tall and weighs about 185 pounds. Reeves, in the same manner as Django, had been a slave, and was offered a job as a lawman by a White man, which was a nontraditional occupation for Black men in the United States during the late 19th and early 20th centuries. Prior to becoming a marshal, Reeves resided in Texas and, in the film, Django was traveling through Texas when he encountered Dr. King Schultz. Reeves escaped to freedom while Django was set free by Schultz, who purchased him for $125; each became an employee of the U.S. government after being recruited by a White male. In the beginning sequences of the film, Django meets and agrees to work with Dr. King Schultz as a bounty collector. This evolves into a partnership that enables Django to later become "unchained."

DJANGO "UNCHAINED": UNBRIDLED REVOLUTIONS... TRANSLATING THE OTHER

In the dominant discourses of Black masculinity and representation, the notion of being unchained exists on many interconnected planes enveloped in larger societal discourse of Black males as other. Returning to the beginning of the movie, Django is physically chained to five other Black males. Each is barefooted, shirtless, and wearing tattered pants. Once the group encounters Schultz, Django becomes verbally unchained as he responds to the question posed by Schultz. Stating that he is interested in a particular slave, Schultz approaches Django and continues to ask him questions. Satisfied with Django's responses, Schultz purchases Django's freedom and uses the key he obtains from one of the Speck brothers—who work for the slaves' new owner—to release Django from his shackles and his physical connection to the other slaves. Newly freed, Django steps out from the group, dramatically removes his blanket from his body revealing the marks of his enslavement written across his back, after which he secures a coat and a pair of boots, before proudly mounting a horse. This opens the door toward a new perception of Black masculinity and representation. It is no longer rooted in blackface minstrelsy, stereotypical depictions, and Blaxploitation cinema, in which Black males are rewritten as desexualized, hyper-masculine, violent, and aggressive. This makes the concept of being unchained in the film more complicated by Django's physical, mental, emotional, and individual journey toward freedom (Fanon, 1952; Gray, 1995; Henry, 2004; Rocchio, 2002; Rogin, 1996; Smith, 1997).

The problematics of being unchained, as depicted in the film *Django Unchained*, were ultimately developed by Tarantino, who wrote, directed, and appeared in the film. His reliance on intertextuality, parody, satire, and the White imagination in the re-creation of discourses of Black masculinity and representation, in the mid-19th-century antebellum South offers traditional symbolic images (Charania, 2013; Gates, 2013; Gray; Henry; hooks, 1992; Lott). Ignoring political aesthetics and other cultural contexts, Tarantino's watered-down inclusion of marginalized discourses of Black masculinity and representation are exasperated by the symbolic images he used to write and visualize the Black male body (Gray; Henry; Hammad, 2011; hooks; Johnson, 2013; Rogin). For example, his approach initially hindered the character of Django's ability to be mentally and emotionally unchained, but enabled him to reconstruct larger societal discourses that underpin Foxx's portrayal of Django's actions, behaviors, and mannerisms. The film is a "marriage" between Tarantino's desire to direct a western and to re-create the slave South in American history. But, without having the cinematic narrative historically based, Tarantino used *Django Unchained* to acknowledge various Blaxploitation movies like *Skin Game*, *Blazing Saddles*, and *Mandingo*, as well more recent releases like *Posse* and *Wild Wild West* (Francis, 2013; Gates, 2013).

Drawing on plot themes made popular during blackface minstrelsy and in Blaxploitation films, Schultz explains to Django that they will have to role-play as they travel to collect bounties. For the first time probably in Django's life, he is allowed to choose his own clothes, and he chooses the attire worn by blackface minstrelsy actors to portray the character of Zip Coon, a stereotype of Black masculinity and representation made popular by George Dixon in 1834 (Bogle; Leab; Mahar, 1995). One scene is particularly striking because it shows Django riding a horse slightly ahead of Schultz's carriage and shows the reactions of the slaves on Bennett's plantation as he passes. Although Django was "permitted" to participate in his narrative in public spaces, it was still a series of guided interactions orchestrated by Schultz. In *Django Unchained* the silencing of the Black male's voice and the removal of his agency is a prevailing underpinning Tarantino brings to his cinematic offering. The character of Django remains silent and allows Schultz to explain on his behalf until Django is reunited with his wife, Broomhilda, and Schultz is murdered (Carpio, 2013; Gates, 2013; Johnson, 2013). After the death of Schultz, Django embarks on a path toward Black masculinity and representation that transgresses the socially reconstructed discourses to become a violent and abusive archetype.

Rewriting the dichotomy of otherness versus blackness, Foxx uses his performance to open discursive sites of resistance, especially when the character of Django goes rogue before the movie reaches its climax (Freishtat & Sandlin, 2010; Giroux, 2000; Gray; Hammad, 2011; Jenkins; Nunley; Lott; Sandlin & Milam, 2008). As a product of popular culture, Black masculinity and representation in *Django Unchained* enables the male body to be rewritten (Hammad, 2011) as a "site of imagined freedom" (Johnson, 2013, p. 19). Foxx's portrayal of Django illustrates elements of Black masculinity and representation including empowerment, the exercise of freedom, violence as a solution and necessity, the power of surrender, and self-definition. Each manifests throughout Foxx's performance from the beginning of the film when he is freed by Schultz from his physical chains to its conclusion where he extracts his revenge breaking the mental chains from Stephen and Calvin Candie in absentia. Using his physical actions, facial expressions, intonations, and clothing choices, Foxx provides unique visual depictions of Black masculinity and representation that are unchained despite the problematics embedded in the film's overall discourses. Francis (2013) suggests that "Jamie Foxx's African American body signifies African American history, and so lends authenticity to the film" (p. 34). Anchored in the legacy of slavery, along with larger societal conversations surrounding Black masculinity and representation, Tarantino employs elements of blackface minstrelsy, stereotypical depictions, and Blaxploitation films to redefine discourses of Black masculinity and representation in his present-day context as pedagogy in popular culture (Gray; hooks; Wright, 1993).

Driven, initially, by his desire to rescue and to free his wife, Broomhilda, Django engages in several acts of revenge, such as killing the Brittle brothers, before embarking on his "hero journey." The death of Schultz demonstrates that manhood requires both communal support and individual effort (Carpio, 2013; Gates; Johnson, 2013; Vognar, 2013). Chronicling Django's transition from slave to freeman to bounty hunter to hero, Wright's notion of pedagogy emerges as "empowerment [that] comes from acting on one's own behalf" (p. 26). *Django Unchained* is about Django's journey toward freedom as evidenced by his desire to overcome his history of enslavement through action (partnering with Dr. Schultz means revenge, violence, and certain public behaviors and mannerisms). *Django Unchained* is more about Django's "freedom" as a Black man within dominant discourses of Black masculinity and representation, than avenging and revenge. Johnson (2013) maintains that "freedom to Django, doesn't mean being 'free to go.' It means being free to stay, and to punish at will those White people who have wronged him in the past, to make his own history in the South rather than in exile" (p. 18). Using fictions or stories to engage others in Django's narrative, Tarantino places a "blackness of the tongue" (Gates, 1988, p. ixx) around his film, in an effort to situate knowledge of slavery, history, and freedom as part of the larger societal discourses concerning Black masculinity and representation (Bonilla, 2013; Catteral, 2005; Dyson, 2005). Connecting cultural and historical artifacts of slavery in *Django Unchained* intertextually strung together through Foxx's depiction of Django's pattern of behaviors, clothing, and language are attributes of Black masculinity and representation (Carpio, 2013; Gray, 1995; Henry; hooks; Porter, 1986). Yet, focusing primarily on Django's physical appearance, his body bore the scars and visual reminders of the ways in which Black masculinity and representation have been marked by the legacy of slavery (hooks).

Essentially, *Django Unchained* is a cinematic and theatrical version of neo-slave narratives and speculative fiction, in which Tarantino uses the character of Django to retell the life of Bass Reeves. He anchors these problematic narratives in blackface minstrelsy, stereotypical depictions, and Blaxploitation films of the 1960s and 1970s, all situated within Hollywood's spaghetti western tradition (Carpio;

Francis, 2013; Gates, 2013; Johnson, 2013; Vognar, 2013). Tarantino's interconnected dichotomies and power dynamics of slavery versus freedom and "realism" versus "fiction" is a powerful part of his cinematic narrative. By telling "the story of a slave named Django" (Carpio, p. 1) and providing audiences with a unique visual portrayal of a Black slave narrative, Tarantino moves stereotypical depictions made popular in blackface minstrelsy and reestablished during the Blaxploitation era into 21st-century discourses of Black masculinity and representation.

CONCLUSION

This chapter traces the theatrical and cinematic depictions in *Django Unchained* using blackface minstrelsy as a point of departure and extending this exploration to Blaxploitation films, specifically slave movies, comedies, and westerns. The film's portrayal of Black masculinity and representation was contextualized as a case study examining the meaning of being "unchained." The exploration of various problematics concerning White depictions of Black masculinity and representation reveals hidden transcripts embedded in Foxx's portrayal of Django, particularly the ways in which pedagogy develops and emerges throughout the film. The role of stereotypical depictions of Black males in the development and dissemination of social narratives often used to situate accepted discourses of Black masculinity and representation in larger societal conversations is revised through the life of Bass Reeves. His narrative is connected to the character of Django, and the film is used to describe Reeves's life, behaviors, and motivations through Django.

Scholars wishing to advance research in this area may also consider including slave narratives, neo-slave narratives, and Black diasporic films in their investigation. A final suggestion for future inquiry in this area is for scholars to study the role of American slavery in the development of larger societal discourse of Black masculinity and representation.

BIBLIOGRAPHY

Andrews, M. (2004). Counter-narratives and the power to oppose. In M. Bamberg & M. Andrews (Eds.), *Considering counter-narratives: Narrating, resisting, sense-making* (pp. 1–6). Philadelphia: John Benjamin.

Arnold, J. (Producer & Director). (1974). *Boss nigger* [Motion picture]. United States: Dimension Pictures.

Bogle, D. (2002). *Toms, coons, mulattoes, mammies, and bucks: An interpretive history of Blacks in American films* (4th ed.). New York: Bloomsbury Academic.

Bonilla, Y. (2013). History unchained. *Transition, 112,* 68–77.

Brady, P. L. (2005). *The Black badge: Deputy U.S. Marshal Bass Reeves from slave to heroic lawman*. Los Angeles: Milligan.

Burton, A. T. (2008). *Black gun, silver star: The life and legend of frontier Marshal Bass Reeves*. Lincoln: University of Nebraska/Bison.

Carpio, G. R. (2013). "I like the way you die, boy": Fantasy's role in *Django Unchained*. *Transition, 112*, iv–12.

Catteral, B. (2005). Is it all coming together? Further thoughts on urban studies and the present crisis: (4) space-time(s), meanings, trapped situations, and mediations. *City*, 9(1), 150-158.

Charania, M. (2013). Django unchained, voyeurism unleashed. *Contexts, 12*(3), 58–60.

Cockrell, D. (1997). *Demons of disorder: Early blackface minstrels and their world*. Cambridge: Cambridge University Press.

Corbucci, S. (Director & Producer). (1968). *Django* [Motion picture]. Italy: B.R.C. Produzione S.r.l. Tecisa.

Cortazzi, M. (2001). Narrative analysis in ethnography. In A. P. Atkinson, A. J. Coffey, S. D. Delamont, J. Lofland, & L. Lofland (Eds.), *Handbook of ethnography* (pp. 384–394). Thousand Oaks, CA: Sage.

De Laurentis, D. (Producer), & Fleishcher, R. (Director). (1975). *Mandingo* [Motion picture]. United States: Paramount Pictures.

Dixon, T. F. (1905). *The clansman: An historical romance of the Ku Klux Klan*. New York: Doubleday.

Dyson, A. H. (2005). Crafting "the humble prose of living:" Rethinking oral/written relations in the echoes of spoken word. *English Education*, 37(2), 149–164.

Fanon, F. (1952). *Black skin, White masks*. New York: Grove.

Francis, T. (2013). Looking sharp: Performance, genre, and questioning history in *Django Unchained*. *Transition, 112*, 32–45.

Freishtat, R. L., & Sandlin, J. A. (2010). Shaping youth discourses about technology: Technological colonization, manifest destiny, and the frontier myth in Facebook's public pedagogy. *Educational Studies, 46*(5), 503–523.

Gates, H. L. (1988). *The signifying monkey: A theory of African-American literary criticism*. New York: Oxford University Press.

Gates, H. L. (2013). "An unfathomable place": A conversation with Quentin Tarantino about *Django Unchained*. *Transition, 112*, 47–66.

Giroux, H. A. (2000). Public pedagogy as cultural politics: Stuart Hall and the "crisis" of culture. *Cultural Studies, 14*(2), 341–360.

Gray, H. (1995). Black masculinity and visual culture. *Callaloo, 18*(2), 401–405.

Griffith, D. W. (Producer & Director). (1915). *Birth of a nation* [Motion picture]. United States: Epoch Producing.

Guerro, E. (1993). *Framing blackness: The African American image in film*. Philadelphia: Temple University.

Hammad, L. K. (2011). Black feminist discourses of power in *For colored girls who have considered suicide when the rainbow is enuf. Journal of Interdisciplinary Studies in Humanities, 3*(2), 258–264.

Henry, M. (2004). He is a "bad mother *$%@!#": Shaft and contemporary Black masculinity. *African American Review, 38*(1), 119–126.

Hertzberg, M. (Producer), & Brooks, M. (Director). (1974). *Blazing saddles* [Motion picture]. United States: Warner Brothers.

Holmes, P. (Producer), Steele, J. (Producer), & Van Peebles, M. (Director). (1993). *Posse* [Motion picture]. United States: Gramercy.

hooks, b. (1992). *Black looks: Race and representation.* Boston: South End.

Iton, R. (2008). *In search of the black fantastic: Politics and popular culture in post-civil rights era.* New York: Oxford University.

Jenkins, T. (2013). *A case study of Tracie Morris's Project Princess.* Doctoral Dissertation. Louisiana State University, Baton Rouge.

Johnson, W. (2013). Allegories of empire. *Transition, 112,* 13–21.

Jones, R. L. (2004). "That's very rude, I shouldn't be telling you that": Older women talking about sex. In M. Bamberg & M. Andrews (Eds.), *Considering counter-narratives: Narrating, resisting, sense-making* (pp. 1–6). Philadelphia: John Benjamin.

Keller, H. (Producer), Bogart, P. (Director), & Douglas, G. (Director). (1971). *Skin game* [Motion picture]. United States: Warner Brothers.

Lawrence, N. (2008). *Blaxploitation films of the 1970s: Blackness and genre.* New York: Routledge.

Leab, D. J. (1995). *From Sambo to Superspade: The Black experience in motion pictures.* Boston: Houghton Mifflin.

Littlefield, D. F., & Underhill, L. E. (1971). Negro marshals in the Indian Territory. *The Journal of Negro History, 56*(2), 77–87.

Lott, E. (1992, Summer). Love and theft: The racial unconscious of blackface minstrelsy. *Representations, 39,* 23–50.

Mahar, W. J. (1999). *Behind the burnt cork mask: Early blackface minstrelsy and antebellum American popular culture.* Urbana-Champaign: University of Illinois Press.

Maynes, M. J., Pierce, J. L., & Laslett, B. (2008). *Telling stories: The use of personal narratives in the social sciences and history.* Ithaca, New York: Cornell University Press.

Mishler, E. G. (1995). Models of narrative analysis: A typology. *Journal of Narrative and Life History, 5*(2), 87–123.

Mukai, T. (1992). Learning from women's biography. In T. Iles (Ed.), *All sides of the subject: Women and biography* (pp. 152–161). New York: Teachers College Press.

Nunley, V. L. (2007). "Crash": Rhetorically wrecking discourses of race, tolerance, and White privilege. *College English, 69*(4), 335–346.

Parks, G. (Director). (1971). *Shaft* [Motion picture]. United States: MGM.

Peters, J. (Producer), & Sonnenfield, B. (Producer & Director). (1999). *Wild wild west* [Motion picture]. United States: Warner Brothers.

Porter, J. E. (1986). Intertextuality and the discourse community. *Rhetoric Review, 5*(1), 34–47.

Reissman, C. K. (2005). *Narrative, memory, and everyday life.* Huddersfield, UK: University of Huddersfield Press.

Reissman, C. K. (2008). *Narrative methods for the human sciences.* Los Angeles: Sage.

Rocchio, V. F. (2002). *Reel racism: Confronting Hollywood's construction of Afro-American culture.* Boulder, CO: Westview.

Rogin, M. (1996). *Blackface, white noise: Jewish immigrants in the Hollywood melting pot.* London: University of California Press.

Sandelowski, M. (1991). Telling stories: Narrative approaches in qualitative research. *Journal of Nursing Scholarship, 23*(3), 161–166.

Sandlin, J. A., & Milam, J. L. (2008). "Mixing pop (culture) and politics": Cultural resistance, cultural jamming, and anti-consumption activism as critical public pedagogy. *Cultural Inquiry, 38*(3), 323–350.

Sher, S., Hudlin, R., & Savone, P. (Producers), & Tarantino, Q. (Director). (2012). *Django unchained* [Motion picture]. United States: Weinstein.

Smith, C. P. (2000). Content analysis and narrative analysis. In R. T. Reiss & C. M. Judd (Eds.), *Handbook of research methods in social and personality psychology* (pp. 313–335). New York: Cambridge University Press.

Smith, D. L. (1997). What is Black culture? In W. Lubiano (Ed.), *The house that race built: Original essays by Toni Morrison, Angela Y. Davis, Cornel West, and others on Black Americans and politics in America today*. New York: Vintage.

Smith, V. (Ed.). (1997). *Representing blackness: Issue in film and video*. New Brunswick, NJ: Rutgers University Press.

Spangler, L. (Producer), & Goldman, M. (Director). (1972). *The legend of Nigger Charley* [Motion picture]. United States: Paramount Pictures.

Stake, R. E. (1995). *The art of case study research*. Thousand Oaks, CA: Sage.

Vognar, C. (2013). He can't say that, can he? Black, White, and shades of gray in the films of Tarantino. *Transition, 112*, 23–31.

Wright, J. (1993). Lesbian teacher comes out: The personal is pedagogy. *Feminist Teacher, 7*(2), 26–33.

CHAPTER TWENTY

Bridging the Digital Divide: The Case of Black Twitter as a 21st-Century Platform for Cultural Expression

GEORGE L. DANIELS, THEADORIS MORRIS, AND ELLISA BRAY

When the *Journal of Broadcasting & Electronic Media* published the article "Twitter as Cultural Conversation" (Brock, 2012), it was the first time the phenomenon of Black Twitter was given attention in scholarly literature. Since then, another scholar has examined the microblogging service in an analysis of the Black American cultural tradition of "signifyin" to perform racial identity online (Florini, 2013). Both of these scholarly treatments, though, predate what some might call the coming of age of Black Twitter with a series of controversies that put the phenomenon on the national radar in 2013.

This chapter will explore the relevance and importance of social networking sites in today's society—with a focus on Twitter—probing the Black Twitter phenomenon. Rather than the result of a single research project, what is provided here is an overview of the phenomenon and an examination of its significance for the broader society's understanding of Black culture and what is on the minds of Black people.

Twitter connects more than 200 million users and took three years, two months, and one day to generate its first billion tweets (Rousseau, 2012). One report on Twitter Inc.'s performance of 2014 noted that, like another highly successful social media platform Facebook, Twitter is reaping the benefits of consumers' shift to mobile—and the advertising dollars that follow (Koh, 2014). Compared to Facebook, Twitter still has a way to go in terms of number of users. Facebook added about 40 million users in the first quarter of 2014, five times more than Twitter

(Koh). Twitter's success can be measured in strategies such as its special efforts to organize information for users during the 2014 World Cup or the proliferation of hashtags as social markers and advertising campaigns (Phillips, 2014).

Approximately 1 billion tweets are sent over the platform every week (Rousseau, 2012, p. 1). When the legendary King of Pop, Michael Jackson, died in June 2009, Twitter users set a new record at the time of 456 tweets per second (TPS), and by March 2011, the TPS record was 6,939 (@twitter, 2011a). In August of that same year, news of singer Beyoncé's pregnancy at the MTV Awards set a new TPS record of 8,868, with the execution of Troy Davis in September of that year being the second highest with 7,671 TPS (@twitter, 2011b). On New Year's Eve 2011, Japanese tweeters set a new record of 16,197 TPS and crashed the site as a result (Hastings & Fisher, 2012).

Multiple studies have shown that Blacks are overrepresented among those using Twitter (Duggan & Smith, 2013; Smith, 2011; Smith, 2014), so this platform might be the answer to bridging the so-called digital divide. It certainly adds a new dimension to the conversation about representations of race in the digital media.

A RACIAL PARADOX?

Even though White males make up most of the employees at Twitter (Huddleston, 2014), according to the Pew Center's Internet and American Life Project, African American Internet users make up the largest subgroup of users compared to other races. This racial paradox makes having a discussion about Black Twitter even more timely and relevant.

Just two days before the end of 2013, the Pew Research Center released its *Social Media Update 2013* (Duggan & Smith, 2013) report, revealing that African Americans are still in the lead with 29%, Whites are 16%, and Hispanics are 16% among online adults (Duggan & Smith). Days later, a second Pew Study on African Americans and Technology (Smith, 2014) offered a demographic portrait. It was released January 6, 2014, the first in a series of demographic snapshots of technology use and adoption among different groups of adults in the United States. The study revealed that African Americans have higher levels of Twitter use than Whites (22% of online Blacks are Twitter users, compared with 16% of online Whites). Younger African Americans have especially high rates of Twitter usage—a full 40% of African American Internet users ages 18–29 say that they use Twitter, compared with 28% of Whites of the same age (Smith).

Ironically, even though racial minorities outpaced other groups in using its social media platform, Twitter Inc. readily admits, like other companies in Silicon

Valley, it is lacking in diversity. In its first report detailing the demographic makeup of its workers, Twitter acknowledged that 59% of the company's employees are White and only 12% identify as something other than White or Asian (Huddleston, 2014). In a post on the company's blog, Twitter's Vice President for Diversity and Inclusion Janet Van Huysse announced in July 2014, "We are joining some peer companies by sharing our ethnic and gender diversity data. Like our peers, we have a lot of work to do." She went on to list things the microblogging company is doing to improve its "diversity standing," including recruiting from historically Black colleges and universities (HBCUs) and supporting initiatives such as Girls Who Code (Van Huysse, 2014).

WHAT IS BLACK TWITTER?

Black Twitter has been defined many ways. In some circles, it is known by the Twitter tool that ties similar 140-character tweets together, the hashtag (using the # symbol). When one sees #BlackTwitter, he or she knows it's part of Black Twitter. The term "Black Twitter" can be viewed in a larger sociopolitical context as a collective of active, primarily African American Twitter users who have created a virtual community that participates in continuous real-time conversations (Jones, 2013). Others see Black Twitter as a social construct created by a self-selecting community of users to describe aspects of Black American society through their use of the Twitter platform (Williams & Domoszlai, 2013).

In his groundbreaking article, "From the Blackhand Side: Twitter as a Cultural Conversation," Dr. Andre Brock explains, "Black Twitter came to online prominence through creative use of Twitter's hashtag function and subsequent domination of Twitter's 'trending topics'" (2012, p. 529). Two years later, after further development of Twitter data and the exploration of how Twitter is used demographically, Brock clarified how hashtags and trending topics differ regarding Black Twitter in an online interview.

> Trending topics differ from hashtags in that they are generated algorithmically based on some mysterious alchemy of topicality, timeliness, uptake, reach, and interest; this means that topics that suddenly explode across networks of followers tend to "trend" as opposed to the constant outpourings of the "Beliebers" or the "Beygency." I have speculated that trending topics have been tweaked to actually diminish the frequency of Black Twitter hashtags reaching "trending" status, because African Americans never lack for anything to "go off on" or signify about in ways, which are either funny or cathartic (or both) and thus reach viral status quite quickly. Given these realities, it may be in Twitter's financial (and technocultural) interest to promote topics of interest to its most affluent (as opposed to active) users, in order to continue gaining funding and advertising dollars. (personal communication, May 5, 2014)

Historically, Black Twitter's public element revolves around the hashtag. Black Internet usage has become increasingly visible because of the integrations of social media into everyday communication habits (Brock, 2012). The hashtag (#+topic) was initially implemented to filter and organize multiple tweets on a particular topic (Messina, 2007). The discovery of "Black Twitter" is also the discovery that Black usage of the popular social networking site at times has dominated the Twitter microblog. This went against popular perceptions of White-dominated Internet use (Brock, 2012).

Castells (2004) notes that societies are cultural constructs and if culture is understood as the set of values and beliefs that inform and motivate people's behavior, it creates a specific society; therefore, we should be able to identify the culture of the network society—in this case Black Twitter—as its historical marker.

REDEFINING THE DIGITAL DIVIDE?

The digital divide has traditionally been used as a term to describe the gap between the "information haves and have-nots" or those Americans who use or have access to telecommunication and information technologies and those who do not (Kruger & Gilroy, 2013). This discussion, often among policymakers, was especially prevalent in the 1990s when personal computers made their way into households and the World Wide Web was growing. At the time, studies showed women, minorities, the elderly, the poor, and the less educated were using computers less often (Strover, 2014). Lately, while some say the proliferation and popularity of mobile phones have given virtually everyone access to the Internet, there are reasons to question what mobile Internet might mean for the digital divide (p. 119).

Since research shows that Blacks and other minorities utilize Twitter in greater numbers than other racial groups, does this mean the microblogging service can bridge the gap between these particular minority groups and Whites? A more sophisticated understanding comes with the analysis of online content creation (OCC) as Brake (2014) has done in his work. Brake notes that it remains very unclear what proportion of the minority groups who use Twitter at a greater rate than Whites were using it for OCC as opposed to social monitoring, gathering news, or entertainment consumption (Brake).

TWITTER AS A TOOL FOR PROTEST

Instead of resorting to violence or riots as African Americans have done in the past, the Twitter platform has become a 140-character global megaphone. Brock believes that not only Black Twitter, but also any platform that broadcasts the unfiltered voices of Black people, is effectively used as a megaphone to the world. "We have been silenced in so many ways across American history. Unfortunately, as Derrick Bell writes, the problems of the Black middle class have been cast as the problems of the entire Black community, which isn't fair OR true. Thus, Twitter's facility at reporting the mundanity of everyday life often obscures more 'important' issues" (personal communication, May 5, 2014).

Hilton (2013) talked about the "secret power of Black Twitter" when she reviewed a number of recent controversies where Black Twitter was in full effect. Hilton found that Twitter served as a visual community for viewers of popular television shows such as *Scandal* while also serving as a rallying point for those reacting to a scandal involving Southern celebrity chef Paula Deen. According to Hilton's research, as Twitter has grown and become more central to daily conversation, the influence of its active groups has also grown exponentially. Today, Black Twitter is no longer something you can only find if you know where to look. It's permeating timelines, even if people are not paying attention (Hilton).

For example, the trial of George Zimmerman, the man accused in the February 2012 death of unarmed teenager Trayvon Martin in Sanford, Florida, placed Black Twitter on the national stage. Along with tweets during the trial, Twitter activity was heightened after the accused gunman, Zimmerman, was acquitted. Also, one of the jurors in the case was set to have a book deal to reveal her experience. As one of six jurors in a popular, controversial, racially divided U.S. case it would have undoubtedly been successful. But an outcry engineered, in part, through Black Twitter, resulted in the agent cancelling the book deal.

Another example involves a small sample of tweets, 57, posted on a single day after President Obama commented on the trial and acquittal of George Zimmerman in Sanford, Florida. Among the 57 tweets that were captured, there were 15 tweets from news outlets and 6 tweets with hashtags. The analysis of the tweets from July 20, 2013, revealed that most of those who were sending tweets had negative opinions of the president's untimely and not-so-aggressive remarks. The connection that President Obama made to the slain Florida teenager was appreciated but viewed by many as coming too late, almost a week after the verdict was rendered. For those who included links in their tweets, the links were to images of rallies held across the country following the Zimmerman verdict. Much of the Twitter activity on July 20, however, was also focused on various celebrities who publicly threw their support behind the family of Trayvon Martin in much the same way as the president did in his remarks.

Within the network society theory the power in networks correlates with Twitter and the Black Twitter phenomena. Castells, in his research, asked who has power in the dominant networks. The response was that it depends on how power is defined (2004). Castells lists two answers: First, "Power is the structural capacity to impose one's will over another's will. There can be bargaining, but in the last resort, power is exercised when, regardless of the will of someone (a person, a social group, a category of people, an organization, a country, and the like) that actor must submit to the will of the power-holder—or else be exposed to violence of different forms" (p. 31). Second, "Each network defines its own power system depending on its programmed goals." This explanation of power can be viewed as an example of what roles the Twitter platform and Black Twitter play. For example, in the Zimmerman trial Black Twitter had no control over what the judge's ruling was in that case, but Black Twitter did virtually band together and exercise its power of digital assembly by stopping one of the jurors from receiving a book deal to make money from the event.

Black Twitter has also conveyed its power by promoting the firing of several public figures, such as Paula Deen for using the N-word and displaying other racist behavior, and New York PR Executive Justine Sacco for her racist tweet regarding a trip to Africa and not being able to catch AIDS because she is White. Both women experienced the power of Black Twitter participants banning together and creating an internationally built blow to their careers.

Feminist Miriam Sweeney mentions that she does not think Twitter ever replaces certain tactics (marches and riots), but she believes it is certainly a new communication channel for people to share information and organize.

> Groups have used Twitter for organizing and activism—I am thinking about the Arab Spring and rainbow revolutions, as well as feminist discussions like #solidarityisforwhite-women. Twitter, like all social media, is a bit Janus-faced. On the one hand a "free" channel for mass communication, on the other a surveillance platform for the military-industrial complex that relies on the exploitation of people of color and other minorities groups. As Facebook would say, "it's complicated." (Sweeney, 2014)

This complication is echoed by Castells when he discusses how social media movements that first spread in the Arab world were confronted with murderous violence by Arab dictatorships. They experienced diverse fates, from victory to concessions to repeated massacres to civil war (2012, p. 3).

TWITTER AS A TOOL FOR REACHING BLACK FOLKS

"While SNSs (social networking sites) are designed to be widely accessible," boyd and Ellison (2008) note, "many attract homogeneous populations initially, so it is not uncommon to find groups using sites to segregate themselves by nationality, age, educational level, or other factors that typically segment society, even if that was not the intention of the designers" (p. 214). A number of cases reflect less on what African Americans are doing and more on how others (outside the African

American community) use a hashtag to link up with and join the conversation. In other words, it has become a 21st century way of "tapping into the Black community." Two links occurred based on governmental and political issues, two others were on high-profile entertainment and sporting events, like the Academy Awards and the 2014 Sochi Winter Olympics.

In the spring of 2013, we examined the contents of a total of 190 tweets sent during two events that had a high relationship to the African American community: the presence of Black Twitter during the February 27, 2013, unveiling of Rosa Parks' statue at the U.S. Capitol and the March 3, 2013, reenactment of the voting rights marches in Selma, Alabama. The hashtags #RosaParks and #Rosa were typed into the Twitter search box and all tweets that mentioned her name and used the specific hashtag on the day of the event were copied and documented (114 tweets total). Also, all tweets that mentioned and used the hashtags #VotingRightsAct and #VotingRights were copied and documented on the day of the reenactment event (28 tweets total).

These two national, historically Black events were chosen specifically to capture the Twitter presence of all races. Since the two events gained worldwide attention and were controversial and race affiliated—specifically focused on Blacks—those two events were chosen to capture the presence of different racial groups and to also explore the significance of Black twitter. From February 24, 2013, to March 10, 2013, approximately two weeks, tweets under the hashtag #BlackTwitter were copied and analyzed for their content (48 tweets total). In this study retweets were also considered and each tweet was categorized and calculated by race.

Later, in the summer of 2013, we analyzed tweets that were sent in connection with the 50th anniversary of Martin Luther King's acclaimed I Have a Dream speech delivered during the March on Washington on August 28, 1963. Events surrounding the 50th anniversary of the March began well in advance of the August 28th anniversary when President Obama and former presidents Jimmy Carter and Bill Clinton participated in a commemorative event at the Lincoln Memorial.

Findings under the #RosaParks and #Rosa hashtags showed that out of 114 tweets, 25 of those tweets contained the specific hashtags and the majority were from Black twitter subscribers. There were 10 tweets by Black participants with Hashtags; 8 tweets by Whites with Hashtags; 1 tweet by Another Race (non-Hispanic); and 6 tweets with Race Undetectable. Under the #VotingRightsAct and #VotingRights hashtags, it was found that out of 28 tweets, 0 of those tweets contained the specific hashtags. There were 0 tweets by Blacks with Hashtag; 0 tweets by Whites with Hashtag; 0 tweets by Other Races (non-Hispanic); and 0 Race Undetectable tweets. Under the #BlackTwitter hashtag it was found that out of 48 tweets surrounding the topic, 16 total tweets actually contain the specific Black Twitter hashtag with the majority of them being from Black subscribers. There were 14 tweets by Blacks with Hashtag; 1 tweet by Whites with Hashtag; 1 tweets by Other Races (non-Hispanic) with Hashtag; and 0 Race Undetectable tweets.

So, initial findings indicate that most of the hashtags used during the two events and the hashtags studied were from African Americans, but the gap between tweets with hashtags posted by Blacks and tweets with hashtags posted by Whites was not significantly different. For the March on Washington that took place at the end of August 2013, there were several hashtags utilized for this events; #MarchonWashington, #MOW50, #MLKDream50, and the #MarchonWashington had the most tweets. One major finding revealed the significant extent to which the mainstream media relied on Twitter to promote and sell its diverse coverage of the commemorative events in Washington, DC.

The most far-reaching effects of the Black Twitter movement and the most dynamic responses are connected with entertainment. The 2014 Academy Awards showed that Twitter coverage was clearly split down racial lines, with emphasis being placed on actor Leonardo DiCaprio and host Ellen DeGeneres on one end, and the film *12 Years a Slave* and actress Lupita Nyong'o on the other. Throughout the awards ceremony, many surprises kept Twitter buzzing, especially DeGeneres' famous selfie (which shut her Twitter page down momentarily). But the real surprise was the announcement of Nyong'o as Best Supporting Actress and *12 Years a Slave* as Best Picture. The coverage from Black Twitter, with major hashtags #12YearsASlave and #Lupita, immediately bled into the Twitter mainstream, forcing the media to notice and promote it as well. The reception of this coverage crossover had positive effects for multiple industries; Lupita Nyong'o was named an ambassadress for Lancôme Paris, which increased their sales tremendously among African Americans. Black Twitter used this announcement to their advantage, forcing mainstream institutions to recognize the validity and power of Black-made movies and the impact they could have on other industries.

In one final case, we looked at the 2014 Winter Olympics, held in Sochi, Russia. In stark contrast to coverage of the 2012 Summer Olympics in London, which was headed by the success of Gabby Douglas and the U.S. National Gymnastics team, Sochi was rarely mentioned within the Black Twitter community, except to note the unsurprising lack of African Americans competing in the Olympics. Popular hashtags regarding Sochi weren't relevant to the competition but noted the many blunders that occurred like #SochiProblems as the most used. In cases like this, Black Twitter refocuses on other, more relevant, incidents. Because of the lack of participation from African Americans, Black Twitter had no interest in the event, even though it was trending worldwide.

UP NEXT: BLACK TWITTER AS PLACE FOR BLACK LEADERS?

The definition of a Black leader may be shifting a bit in the online world of Twitter. He or she who leads often does so by sending a seemingly endless stream of 140-character missives at all hours of the day and night from everywhere. Some 280,000 followers can view TV One's Roland Martin's missives on Twitter. Meanwhile, with more than 260,000 followers PBS's Tavis Smiley uses the hashtags #Entrepreneur and #advocate to describe himself on Twitter. Both of these men have managed to garner larger followings than CNN anchor Don Lemon, who has 241,000 followers. Do these three Black men have an audience on Twitter because of their audiences on TV? That's a question to be further explored. But their role as opinion leaders is clearly bolstered by the high level of activity on the Twitter social media platform. Future research might examine to what degree this compares with the Twitter activity of Black elected officials or Black culture icons such as musicians or athletes on Twitter.

For the most part, Black Twitter is proving to be more than a collection of hashtags and conversation lines, becoming an accurate microcosm of African American culture in America's social media age. It is used as a tool to share relevant news, as well as a protest platform and a trigger for growing movements. This is important to note because of the implications on identity and culture when considered racially and socially. Black Twitter also has the potential to be used as an effective marketing and advertising tool when the proper demographics are taken into account.

The most important thing to take away from this chapter is that the voices of African Americans do matter. They are approximately a tenth of the U.S. population, an overwhelming majority of social media. Black Twitter is an important step in understanding the potential of social media platforms as a catalyst for the future of media and African American culture as a whole.

BIBLIOGRAPHY

boyd, d. m., & Ellison, N. B. (2008). Social network sites: Definition, history, and scholarship. *Journal of Computer-Mediated Communication, 13*(1), 210–230.

Brake, D. R. (2014). Are we all online content creators now? Web 2.0 and digital divides. *Journal of Computer-Mediated Communication, 19*(3), 591–609.

Brock, A. (2012). From the blackhand side: Twitter as a cultural conversation. *Journal of Broadcasting & Electronic Media, 56*(4), 529–549.

Castells, M. (2004). *The network society: A cross-culture perspective.* Cheltenham, UK; Northampton, MA: Edward Elgar.

Castells, M. (2012). *Networks of outrage and hope: Social movements in the internet age.* Cambridge; Malden, MA: Polity.

Duggan, M., & Smith, A. (2013). *Social media update 2013*. Pew Research Internet Project. Retrieved from http://www.pewinternet.org/2013/12/30/social-media-update-2013/twitter-users/

Florini, S. (2013, March 7). Tweets, tweeps and signifyin': Communication and cultural performance on "Black Twitter." *Television & New Media*. Retrieved August 31, 2013, http://tvn.sagepub.com/content/early/2013/03/07/1527476413480247

Goodman, J. D., & Baker, A. (2014, December 3). Wave of protests after grand jury doesn't indict office in Eric Garner chokehold case. *New York Times*. Retrieved from http://www.nytimes.com/2014/12/04/nyregion/grand-jury-said-to-bring-no-charges-in-staten-island-chokehold-death-of-eric-garner.html?_r=0

Gottfried, M. (2014, July 30). Twitter's soaring ambition. *The Wall Street Journal*, p. C12.

Hastings, C., & Fisher, D. (2012, January 1). Twitter crashes after 16,000 New Year tweets a SECOND lead to meltdown. *The Daily Mail*. Retrieved November 21, 2013, from http://www.dailymail.co.uk/sciencetech/article-2080814/twitter-outage-16k-happy-new-year-tweets-second-lead-mealtdown.html

Hilton, S. O. (2013, July 16). The secret power of Black Twitter. BuzzFeedNews. Retrieved August 31, 2013, from http://www.buzzfeed.com/shani/the-secret-power-of-black-twitter

Huddleston, T. (2014, July 23). Twitter workers mostly White, mostly male *Fortune Magazine*. [Electronic version]. Retrieved from http://fortune.com/2014/07/23/twitter-diversity-statistics/

Jones, F. (2013, July 17). Is Twitter the underground railroad of activism? *Salon*. Retrieved August 31, 2013, from http://www.salon.com/2013/07/17/how_twitter_fuels_black_activism/singleton/

Koh, Y. (2014, July 30). Twitter silences its naysayers as users surge. *The Wall Street Journal*, p. A1.

Kruger, L. G., & Gilroy, A. A. (2013). Broadband internet access and the digital divide: Federal assistance programs. *Journal of Current Issues in Media & Telecommunications, 5*(4), 303–329.

Lee, J. H., & Kim, J. (2014). Socio-demographic gaps in mobile use, causes, and consequences: A multi-group analysis of the mobile divide model. *Information, Communication & Society, 17*(8), 917–936.

Messina, C. (2007, August 25). "Groups for Twitter; or a proposal for twitter tag channels." Factoryjoe.com. Retrieved from http://factoryjoe.com/blog/2007/08/25/groups-for-twitter-or-a-proposal-for-twitter-tag-channels

Phillips, E. E. (2014, July 30). Blinded by the blizzard of hashtags. *The Wall Street Journal*, pp. D1, D3.

Rousseau, S. (2012). *Food and social media you are what you tweet*. Lanham, MD: Altamira/Rowman & Littlefield.

Smith, A. (2011). *Twitter update 2011*. Pew Internet and American Life Project. Retrieved from http://pewinternet.org/Reports/2011/Twitter-Update-2011.aspx

Smith, A. (2014). *Detailed demographic tables. Internet use and broadband adoption*. Retrieved from http://www.pewinternet.org/2014/01/06/detailed-demographic-tables/

Strover, S. (2014). The US digital divide: A call for a new philosophy. *Critical Studies in Media Communication, 31*(2), 114–122.

Sweeney, M. (2014, January 25). Black Twitter. Interview by Theadoris Morris, University of Alabama. Retrieved from http://miriamsweeney.net/2014/01/25/black-twitter-interview/

Van Huysse, J. (2014). Building a Twitter we can be proud of [Blog]. Retrieved August 3, 2014, from https://blog.twitter.com/2014/building-a-twitter-we-can-be-proud-of

Williams, A., & Domoszlai, D. (2013, August 6). #BlackTwitter: A networked cultural identity. The Ripple Effect. Retrieved August 31, 2013, http://harmony-institute.org/therippleeffect/2013/08/06/blacktwitter-a-networked-cultural-identity/

About the Contributors

Donnetrice C. Allison, PhD, currently serves as an associate professor of both Communication Studies and Africana Studies at Stockton University. Dr. Allison has published articles on the challenges faced by Black professors who teach at predominantly White colleges and universities, the impact of hip hop culture on the identity development of African American teens, and the crisis communication of former New Orleans mayor Ray Nagin and former New York mayor Rudolph Giuliani. She is currently working on a manuscript examining the portrayals of African American women on reality television.

Tamara A. Baker, PhD, is an associate professor in the Department of Psychology at the University of Kansas. She received her PhD in Biobehavioral Health from Pennsylvania State University, and completed her postdoctoral training at the University of Michigan's School of Public Health. Dr. Baker is a Gerontological Society of America Fellow, editor of the *Handbook of Minority Aging*, editor of the journal *Gerontology and Geriatric Medicine*, and serves on the advisory board for the Resource Center for Minority Aging Research and the executive board for Senior Service America.

Omotayo O. Banjo, PhD, (Penn State University, 2009) is an assistant professor in the Department of Communication and an affiliate of African Studies and Women's, Gender, and Sexuality Studies. Her research focuses on representation and audience responses to racial and cultural media. Dr. Banjo also examines the impact of media messages on individuals' perceptions of self and others.

Jean Berry is an artist living in Coralville, Iowa. She works with corrugated cardboard collage, charcoal, pastels and figure drawings. Her art training includes the Kansas City Art Institute and a B.A. degree from Drake University in art. Her work is featured in international galleries such as the Gencor-Gallery at the Rand Afrikanns University in Johannesburg, South Africa, along with galleries like the African American Historical Museum and Cultural Center in Cedar Rapids, the Waterloo Art Museum and many private collections.

Venise T. Berry is an associate professor of African American Studies and Journalism and Mass Communication at the University of Iowa in Iowa City. She is the author of three national bestselling novels: *So Good, An African American Love Story* (1996), *All of Me, A Voluptuous Tale* (2000), and *Colored Sugar Water* (2002). She is also the coauthor of two nonfiction resource books, *The Historical Dictionary of African American Cinema* (2007 and 2015) and *The 50 Most Influential Black Films* (2001). She is currently working on her memoir, *Driven*. To learn more visit: www.veniseberry.com.

Staja "Star" Booker, RN, MS, is a doctoral student in College of Nursing at the University of Iowa. Star received her bachelor of science in Nursing (BSN) from Grambling State University and Master of Science (MS) in Gerontological/ Adult Health Nursing from Pennsylvania State University. She is a current 2013– 2015 National Hartford Center for Gerontological Nursing Excellence Patricia G. Archbold scholar, a 2013–2015 Mayday pain scholar, and was a 2014 Michigan Center for Urban Aging African American Research (MCUAAAR) fellow.

LaToya T. Brackett is currently adjunct faculty at Whitworth University in the History Department. She is also a quarterly faculty member at Eastern Washington University in the Race and Culture Studies program. Dr. Brackett received her doctorate degree in African American and African Studies from Michigan State University in 2011. In 2012, Dr. Brackett worked on a campaign to inform people, especially young people, about Social Security and this sparked her interest in the economic situations of African Americans. Dr. Brackett works to highlight micro-aggressions on all levels in an effort to assist in creating active and forward-moving discussions. Her focus expands beyond the realm of race; it broadens to encompass gender, sexual orientation, disability, economic status and religion. Dr. Brackett strives to make a difference in all communities.

Ellisa M. Bray is an undergraduate student at the University of Alabama, majoring in Journalism and International Studies. As a first-year student, Bray was selected for the University of Alabama Emerging Scholars Program. Her award-winning research on Black Twitter was recognized at the 2014 Undergraduate Research Conference. The Houston, Texas, native also works as a writer for *The Crimson White*, the award-winning student daily at the University of Alabama.

Derrick R. Brooms, PhD, is an assistant professor of Sociology at the University of Louisville. He is a taskforce member to the African American Male Initiative Program and a faculty affiliate to the Student African American Brotherhood. Dr. Brooms' research investigates representations of African American identity and culture within the media. Brooms holds a bachelor's degree in African and African American Studies from the University of Chicago and a doctorate in Sociology from Loyola University Chicago.

Tabbye M. Chavous, PhD, is a professor at the University of Michigan in the Combined Program in Education and Psychology (CPEP) and in the Personality and Social Contexts area in the Department of Psychology. Her research focuses on racial and gender identity development and schooling in secondary and post-secondary settings. She is also a principal investigator and co-director of the university's Center for the Study of Black Youth in Context, funded by the National Science Foundation (NSF) for research, professional training, and community engagement supporting positive development among Black youth and families.

Stephana I. Colbert has served as an attorney for several colleges and universities, the government, and private industry. She has also taught in law and undergraduate programs for more than 30 years. Stephana is a published author of legal articles, fiction and nonfiction, and founder of Jewell-Jordan Publishing. A graduate of Brown University and Boalt Hall School of Law, Stephana is a native of Oklahoma City, where she currently resides. The author gratefully acknowledges the assistance of Dr. Wynell M. Neece for her review and comments on several drafts of this article.

George L. Daniels is Assistant Dean of the College of Communication and Information Sciences at the University of Alabama where he is an associate professor of Journalism. A native of Richmond, Virginia, Daniels is a cum laude graduate of Howard University and received both his master's degree and PhD in mass communication from the Grady College of Journalism and Mass Communication at the University of Georgia. He's an eight-year veteran of local television news at stations in Richmond, Virginia, Cincinnati, Ohio, and Atlanta, Georgia. His research involves diversity in the media workplace, plus change and new technology in the television newsroom.

E-K. Daufin is an educator, social activist, performance artist, fine artist, feminist minister, writer, and a professor of communication at Alabama State University in Montgomery, Alabama. Founder of the Love Your Body; Love Yourself workshops, her research and writing specialty explores weight stigma in the media and its effects, along with race, gender, and class in the media. Dr. Daufin is a HAES expert, a columnist for the *Health and Size Diversity Journal*, a Spoken Word poet, EFT practitioner and consultant. To learn more visit: http://home. earthlink.net/~ekdaufin and Daufi-nation "where all the definitions are daufini-tions" http://daufination.blogspot.com.

ayo dayo has worked at Prince William Public Library System in Prince William, Virginia, for more than 25 years. She is currently the manager of Cataloguing, Inter-library Loan, and Physical Processing Services. She is also a member of the Amer-ican Library Association, the Black Caucus of the American Library Association, and the Public Library Association. Her master of library science degree is from the University of Texas at Austin (1984), she has a master of arts from the University of Iowa (1981), and a bachelor of fine arts from Pacific Lutheran University.

Anita Fleming-Rife, PhD, a retired professor, is a diversity consultant. She has taught at the University of Northern Colorado (UNC), Penn State, Clark Atlanta, and other universities before returning to her alma mater, UNC, in 2008, as the inaugural Special Assistant to the President for Equity and Diversity. Her research in international communications, minority representations in the media, framing analysis of public policy, and politics has been published in academic journals, and she has a book chapter in *Brown and Black Communication: Latino and African American Conflict and Convergence in Mass Media and Cross-Cultural Context*.

John A. Fortunato, PhD, is a professor at Fordham University in the School of Business, Communication and Media Management area. He is the author of four books, including *Commissioner: The Legacy of Pete Rozelle*, *Making Media Content*, and *Sports Sponsorship: Principles & Practices*. Dr. Fortunato previously taught at the University of Texas at Austin in the Department of Advertising and Public Relations, and he received his PhD from Rutgers University in the School of Communication, Information, and Library Science.

Kristina Graaff is an assistant professor at Humboldt University of Berlin in the Department of English and American Studies. She holds a PhD from the same department and an MA in Comparative Literature and Media Studies from Free University of Berlin, Germany. She has been a fellow at the Transatlantic Grad-uate Research Program Berlin–New York and a visiting scholar at Fordham Uni-versity's African American Studies Department and the Bronx African American History Project. Her research includes several areas: Black popular culture, the U.S. criminal justice system, Critical Race Theory, and law in literature.

Vanessa Irvin has 30+ years' experience serving in academic, special, school, and public libraries. Her research interests include librarian professional development, social literacy practices in the public sphere, and reader response to "transgressive texts." Dr. Irvin's teaching areas are reference services, public libraries, youth services, and technology. She is the author of the award-winning book, *The Readers Advisory Guide to Street Literature* (2011) and the award-conferring blog site, StreetLiterature.com. Dr. Irvin is an expert on the genre of urban literature, librarian professional practices, and diversity. Her next book, *Reading While We Work: Public Librarians, Leisure Reading, and Professional Development*, is forthcoming.

Tammie Jenkins is an independent scholar who holds a PhD in Curriculum and Instruction from Louisiana State University. She currently lives in Baton Rouge, Louisiana, with her two sons, where she works in a local school system as a special education teacher.

Seanna Leath received dual Bachelor of Arts degrees in Psychology and Africana Studies at Pomona College. Currently, she is a doctoral student in the Combined Program in Education and Psychology at the University of Michigan and a Graduate Fellow in the university's Center for the Study of Black Youth in Context (CSBYC). Leath is a 2014 Ford Foundation Pre-doctoral Fellow for her work examining young African American mothers' resilience in achieving academic success in higher education, and has research interests in how Black women's racial and gender identity, as well as their status as mothers, informs their experiences in school.

Theadoris M. Morris is a native of Birmingham, Alabama. She earned her BA in Journalism and a minor in Dance from Auburn University. Her MA is in Telecommunication and Film with a concentration in Broadcast Journalism from the University of Alabama. Before pursuing her master's degree, she worked as a general assignment reporter for the *Clanton (Ala.) Advertiser* newspaper, where she was awarded 2nd Place Best Sports Feature Story in the 2012 Alabama Press Association Better Newspaper Contest. Ms. Morris currently resides in Tampa, Florida, where she is currently a freelance multimedia journalist.

Nikita Murry is a licensed professional counselor, educator, and group facilitator. Currently, she is the clinical services coordinator for a dual services violence prevention agency located in the Midwest. Ms. Murry earned a doctorate in Counselor Education and Supervision from Western Michigan University, with special emphasis on counselor preparation, social justice issues, and human sexuality. She has a master of arts in Professional Counseling and conducts a variety of workshops for community agencies and schools.

William Oliver is an associate professor in the Department of Criminal Justice at Indiana University. He served on the Steering Committee of the Institute on Domestic Violence in the African American Community at the University of Minnesota from 1996 to 2008. He is the author of *The Violent Social World of Black Men* (1998) and his paper "Black Males and Social Problems-Prevention through Afrocentric Socialization" (1989) is among the 20 most frequently cited papers in the *Journal of Black Studies*. Oliver received his BS in political science from Tuskegee University and his masters and PhD in criminal justice from the School of Criminal Justice at the State University of New York at Albany.

Armon R. Perry, PhD, MSW, is an associate professor at the University of Louisville's Kent School of Social Work where he teaches Introduction to Social Work and Social Work Practice. Armon's research interests include fathers' involvement in the lives of their children, particularly the role of African American men in family functioning. In addition to his research, Armon has professional experience in the areas of parent education and child protective services.

Sonja Peterson-Lewis, PhD, is an associate professor in the Department of African American Studies at Temple University in Philadelphia. She earned her PhD in Social Psychology at the University of Florida, Gainesville. Her teaching interests center on social research methods, for which she has created two skills-based games. Her research interests include examining the nature of popular culture produced for different communities, along with exploring social-psychological factors from academics to violence in communities of color. She is currently researching the quest for formal education among African Americans in a Northeast Florida community, 1865–1965.

Asher Pimpleton is a counselor educator and assistant professor at Arkansas State University in the Department of Psychology and Counseling. She also serves as the coordinator for the Clinical Mental Health program. She earned her Masters of Arts in Professional Counseling from Central Michigan University and completed her doctoral degree in Educational Psychology, with an emphasis in Counselor Education and Clinical Mental Health, from Southern Illinois University, Carbondale. Her research interests include topics such as sexual health and decision making, cultural competence, and social justice.

De Anna J. Reese, PhD, is an associate professor in the Department of History and the Africana Studies Program at California State University, Fresno. She is also the program coordinator of the Africana Studies Program. Reese earned both an MA and PhD in U.S. History from the University of Missouri-Columbia. Her research explores the relationship between Black beauty culture, Black female entrepreneurship, and the career of beauty pioneer and philanthropist Annie

Turnbo Malone. Reese also examines the intersection of race, gender, class, culture, and identity for Black women both historically and within popular culture.

Bridget L. Richardson is a doctoral candidate in the Personality and Social Contexts area of Psychology at the University of Michigan. Bridget graduated magna cum laude with her Bachelor of Science degree in Psychology from Bowling Green State University in 2010. Bridget continues to focus her scholarship on the perceptions and lived experiences relating to race and racial identity development among African American youth as a Graduate Fellow in the university's Center for the Study of Black Youth in Context (CSBYC). Her PhD will be completed in 2015.

Ilia Rodríguez is an associate professor of Journalism and Media Studies at the University of New Mexico in Albuquerque. Her research focuses on the history of journalism, news discourse, ethnic minorities and media, and media representation of race and ethnicity. She received her PhD in Journalism and Mass Communication from the University of Minnesota. She has an extensive professional background in print journalism.

Malik Simba received his PhD in history from the University of Minnesota. He has held professorships in the Departments of History at Binghamton University in New York and Clarion University in Pennsylvania. Presently, he is professor emeritus and past coordinator of Africana Studies at California State University-Fresno. Publications include his book *Black Marxism and American Constitutionalism: From the Colonial Period to the Ascendancy of Barack Obama*; essays "The Obama Campaign 2008" published in *Western Journal of Black Studies* and "Gong Lum v. Rice: The Convergence of Law, Race, and Ethnicity" published in *American Mosaic*.

Siobhan E. Smith, PhD, became an assistant professor in the Department of Communication at the University of Louisville in August 2010. She has produced critical analyses of race and gender portrayals in television texts such as *I Love New York, College Hill*, and *T. I. and Tiny: The Family Hustle*. She is also part of a team of interdisciplinary scholars who explore sources of food knowledge and access to healthy foods in Louisville and Hopkinsville, Kentucky. Smith is a proud graduate of Xavier University of Louisiana (Bachelor of Arts, Mass Communication), Louisiana State University (Master of Mass Communication), and the University of Missouri (Doctor of Philosophy, Communication).

Danielle M. Wallace, PhD, is an assistant professor of Africana-World Studies at William Paterson University in Wayne, New Jersey. She earned her PhD in African American Studies at Temple University in Philadelphia. Her teaching and research interests include the Black family, gender and sexual politics in the

Black community, and the gender socialization of Black men and women. Her current research focuses on Black male-female relationships, especially the dating, marriage, and ideal mate selection of Black men and women.

Kayla Renée Wheeler is a PhD student in the Department of Religious Studies and a Dean's Graduate Research Fellow at the University of Iowa. Her research interests include Black religion, gender, and media representations of Islam. Her dissertation explores how Black American Muslim women use social media to transmit religion and culture and the implications that it has for constructing and reconstructing authority.

Ernest L. Wiggins is an associate professor in the School of Journalism and Mass Communications at the University of South Carolina. A former reporter and urban affairs editor at *The State* (Columbia, S.C.), Wiggins holds an MA in mass communications and has done postgraduate study in social theory and social structures. His teaching and research interests include reporting and editing, media literacy and criticism, and the intersection of journalism and social justice. His recent publications include "Walking a Tightrope: Obama's Duality as Framed by Selected African American Columnists" (2014) in *Journalism Practice*, coauthored with Kenneth Campbell.

Jerome D. Williams is a Distinguished Professor and the Prudential Chair in Business in the Marketing Department at the Rutgers Business School-Newark and New Brunswick (RBS). He was a member of the Institute of Medicine Committee on Food Marketing and Diets of Children and Youth. He is coeditor of two books, *Advances in Communication Research to Reduce Childhood Obesity* and *Diversity in Advertising: Broadening the Scope of Research Directions*, and coauthor of the forthcoming book, *Consumer Equality: Race and the American Marketplace*. He currently serves as an associate editor of *Journal of Public Policy & Marketing*.

ROCHELLE BROCK,
RICHARD GREGGORY JOHNSON III,
& CYNTHIA DILLARD,
Executive Editors

Black Studies and Critical Thinking is an interdisciplinary series which examines the intellectual traditions of and cultural contributions made by people of African descent throughout the world. Whether it is in literature, art, music, science, or academics, these contributions are vast and far-reaching. As we work to stretch the boundaries of knowledge and understanding of issues critical to the Black experience, this series offers a unique opportunity to study the social, economic, and political forces that have shaped the historic experience of Black America, and that continue to determine our future. Black Studies and Critical Thinking is positioned at the forefront of research on the Black experience, and is the source for dynamic, innovative, and creative exploration of the most vital issues facing African Americans. The series invites contributions from all disciplines but is specially suited for cultural studies, anthropology, history, sociology, literature, art, and music.

Subjects of interest include (but are not limited to):

- EDUCATION
- SOCIOLOGY
- HISTORY
- MEDIA/COMMUNICATION
- RELIGION/THEOLOGY
- WOMEN'S STUDIES

- POLICY STUDIES
- ADVERTISING
- AFRICAN AMERICAN STUDIES
- POLITICAL SCIENCE
- LGBT STUDIES

For additional information about this series or for the submission of manuscripts, please contact Dr. Brock (Indiana University Northwest) at brock2@iun.edu; Dr. Johnson (University of San Francisco) at rgjohnsoniii@usfca.edu; or Dr. Dillard (University of Georgia) at cdillard@uga.com.

To order other books in this series, please contact our Customer Service Department:

(800) 770-LANG (within the U.S.)
(212) 647-7706 (outside the U.S.)
(212) 647-7707 FAX

Or browse online by series at www.peterlang.com.